SHAKESPEARE'S NATURE

Shakespeare's Nature

From Cultivation to Culture

CHARLOTTE SCOTT

OXFORD

UNIVERSITY PRESS

OXFORD

UNIVERSITY PRESS

Great Clarendon Street, Oxford, OX2 6DP,
United Kingdom

Oxford University Press is a department of the University of Oxford.
It furthers the University's objective of excellence in research, scholarship,
and education by publishing worldwide. Oxford is a registered trade mark of
Oxford University Press in the UK and in certain other countries

© Charlotte Scott 2014

The moral rights of the author have been asserted

First Edition published in 2014

Impression: 2

Published in the United States of America by Oxford University Press
198 Madison Avenue, New York, NY 10016, United States of America

British Library Cataloguing in Publication Data

Data available

ISBN 978–0–19–968508–0

As printed and bound by
CPI Group (UK) Ltd, Croydon, CR0 4YY

Links to third party websites are provided by Oxford in good faith and
for information only. Oxford disclaims any responsibility for the materials
contained in any third party website referenced in this work.

To my family

Acknowledgements

Everything I have ever thought or written about Shakespeare has been provoked or supported by an extraordinary body of scholars and their work. Without Joan Thirsk's defining contribution to the social history of agriculture, and all of those who have developed on her work, this book could not have been written. There are six people, however, whose intellect, generosity, insight, and judgement have shaped and defined the development of this book, and without whom this book would have been a vestige of its current form: Jerry Brotton, Patrick Cheney, William C. Carroll, Russ McDonald, Subha Mukerji, and Robert Watson have given me the rare gift of both their time and their intellect. Having read parts or, indeed, all of this book they have questioned, cautioned and encouraged me at various and vital stages on this journey. Without them I would feel very differently about the process as well as the subject, and I am indebted to all of them. Andrew McRae and Garrett Sullivan have been perceptive and shrewd readers and their vast knowledge of the land has been central to the shaping of this monograph. Keith Thomas reminded me of the importance of thinking behind the sixteenth century as well as beyond it; Ruth Morse never let me stop thinking at all, and in sharing her essay on 'landskips' early on encouraged my understanding of precisely the concepts that came to shape this book. Michael Leslie and Timothy Raylor's work supported the on-going development of this subject, as did their commitment to the field. The support of both Peter Holland and Lukas Erne has been fundamental to me.

In the development and writing of this book I have been lucky enough to discover Jacqueline Baker as both an editor and a friend: she has proved herself exceptional in both capacities. Jackie Pritchard and Rachel Platt were meticulous and tenacious aids at OUP. I am also extremely grateful to the anonymous readers at OUP whose perspicacity and judgement redefined the perimeters of the project.

The writing of this book could not have been done without the generous support of the Arts and Humanities Research Council. As funders of a research fellowship the AHRC provided a fundamental role in the development of this book, for which I am profoundly grateful. My own institution, Goldsmiths College, also supported me with research leave, and the students I have taught and teach there go on stimulating me and reminding me of why we think about Shakespeare in the first place.

To them I am always grateful. Russ McDonald has been a great support to me: I deeply admire him as a teacher and as a scholar and I am also lucky enough to call him a friend as well as a colleague. His time, care and attention have made this a better book.

My mother wakes up every day and farms the land I grew up on—her understanding of nature has been a constant companion in the shaping of my moral and aesthetic life. She taught me that 'nature never did betray the heart that loved her'—and, to her, my services are bound.

My friends and family go on making everything I do occasionally impossible but always worthwhile. Everything I do is devoted to them— and this book is dedicated to Jerry and my children, who, like Shakespeare, are my reasons to get up in the morning.

Contents

1

Introduction

'Nature being *known,* it may be *master'd, managed,* and *used* in the Services of humane Life.' (Joseph Glanvill)[1]

'Shakespeare was a farmer. Why not?', begins an article in the journal of *Agricultural History.* The wry tone of its opening points to a tendency in literary criticism to obfuscate the role of agronomy in the development of the aesthetic arts. As the authors of this piece point out, however, Shakespeare

demonstrated substantial knowledge of the subject. On the same basis, many scholars have claimed for him experience in the law, in the military, in humanistic studies and so on. His credentials in agriculture, however, are rather better than in many other alleged competences.[2]

The authors can make this claim not only on the basis of the occupations of Shakespeare's father and grandfather but also on the extent, precision and depth of the agrarian images within the plays and poems. Through a brief analysis of agrarian figures, this article reveals a dominant investment in the figurative range of Shakespeare's husbandry.[3] The agrarian landscape to which Shakespeare belonged defined both the social and economic values of Elizabethan England. The agrarian discourses to which the poet-playwright attends are capacious, transitional, and instructive,

---

[1] *Plus Ultra* (London, 1668), 87.

[2] Robert F. G. Spier and Donald K. Anderson, Jr, 'Shakespeare and Farming: The Bard and Tusser', *Agricultural History,* 59/3 (July 1985), 448. It is also well known that Shakespeare's father and grandfather were husbandmen. This, as I have suggested, is highly usual given the extent of England's agrarian economy but it also refers us to the presence of husbandry in the shaping of Shakespeare's domestic values.

[3] Examining the number and extent of agrarian images in the plays, the authors reveal that Shakespeare was primarily interested in their figurative range of meanings. Within these terms, the playwright appears to have employed agrarian images in short figures, 'broad in scope', short figures, 'narrower in scope and more vivid', and, finally, long figures, 'three or more lines that present extended and detailed comparisons'. Spier and Anderson, 'Shakespeare and Farming', 459.

engaging in one of the central dialogues of his age: namely, the value of nature and the nature of value.

Such values, this book will suggest, are predicated on the terms and practices of husbandry. To 'husband nature's riches from expense', as sonnet 94 declares, is to become the 'lord and owner' of yourself.[4] To take possession of oneself through the terms of cultivation is to engage in a form of self-mastery that belongs to a moral discourse of control, production, and posterity. It is this moral discourse that this book will pursue. I will return to the complexities of sonnet 94 in Chapter 2, but here a brief rehearsal of the term 'husbandry' serves to suggest the complex value system that such a practice implies. Sustained by an agrarian economy, Shakespeare's England was driven by a system of intervention in the natural world in which profit—moral and economic, social and political—was determined by both action and affect. Husbandry—'the tillage or cultivation of the soil'—records the multiple ways in which communities have not only survived but developed.[5] These practices of development belong to a long tradition of value in which human groups have marked and interpreted their world. We are perhaps most familiar with these terms through the work of New Historicism, in which ideas of cultivation emerge as statements of self-fashioning, in which the subject is defined according to a process of self-mastery, control, and strategic representation.[6] In Stephen Greenblatt's essay 'The Cultivation of Anxiety: *King Lear* and his Heirs'[7] the term refers to a form of human, psychological production, in which the subject is only partially aware, yet fully capable, of intervening in the realities of those around him. A morally ambiguous concept, cultivation is a form of both power and expression through which the individual may impose itself upon the lives of others. As sonnet 94 suggests, however, to cultivate is to exercise a control that can separate as much as integrate: and to exercise control is to fulfil human potential, as well as suppress it. The history of these terms—husband, till, reap, sow, yield, harvest (terms we

---

[4] In *Bodies and Selves in Early Modern England: Physiology and Inwardness in Spenser, Shakespeare, Herbert, and Milton* (Cambridge: Cambridge University Press, 1999), Michael Schoenfeldt discusses the dialogue between desire and restraint that this poem suggests. Often troubling to contemporary criticism, the sonnet's apparent promotion of the 'cold' and 'unmoved' sits uneasily alongside an image of passion under restraint. Schoenfeldt shows, however, that the sonnet partakes of a Christian and classical dialogue in which self-control is a form of development rather than repression.

[5] The *OED* defines the now obsolete use of the term as 'household management' (*c.*1290), followed by the current uses as 'the business or occupation of a farmer, husbandman' and the 'tillage or cultivation of the soil (including also the rearing of livestock or poultry)' (*c.*1380).

[6] Stephen Greenblatt, *Learning to Curse: Essays in Early Modern Culture* (London: Routledge, 1990).

[7] *Raritan*, 2 (1982), 92–124.

have imported fluently into everyday conversation)—are predicated on a complex legacy of both Christian morality and urgent economic imperatives. Understanding these imperatives, this book will argue, is fundamental to the exploration of Shakespeare's husbandry and the rich landscape of human relations that it invokes.

In 1.3 of *Othello*, Iago meets a distracted Roderigo, who is suffering the pangs of unrequited love. Irritated, bitter, and dismissive of his friend's self-pity, Iago confronts him with an image of autonomy drawn from the language of cultivation:

> Virtue a fig! 'tis in ourselves that we are thus, or thus. Our bodies are our gardens, to which our wills are gardeners. So that if we plant nettles or sow lettuce, set hyssop and weed up thyme, supply it with one gender of herbs or distract it with many, either to have it sterile with idleness or manured with industry—why, the power and corrigible authority of this lies in our wills. (1.3.320–7)

Rejecting Roderigo's attempt to absolve himself of any capacity to change, Iago denies an immutable sense of 'virtue' within human nature.[8] Celebrating subjective determination above a preconditioned body, Iago sermonizes on his companion's weakness. Iago's horticultural images support a lucid language of individualism, in which he can chastise his friend's defeatism as a form of irresponsibility.[9] Human life, Iago suggests, is what you make it.

Even within the context of the play, and Iago's machinations, this speech is surprisingly sinister. Despite the putatively Christian language of the sermon, Iago is directing his companion to follow his own 'will' and exercise the 'power and corrigible authority' of his own desires.[10] The

---

[8] In *Humouring the Body: Emotions and the Shakespearean Stage* (Chicago: University of Chicago Press, 2004), Gail Kern Paster discusses virtue within the context of 'the meteorology of passions', in which the weather supports an image of virtue and sin as a confluence of qualities, in need of management, containment, and a degree of vigilance so that, according to Thomas Wright, 'they serve onley to drive forward, but not to drowne Vertue', 65. For Wright, weather provides the analogy by which the human must control his body; for Iago it is cultivation. In *Roman Shakespeare: Warriors, Wounds and Women*, Coppélia Khan discusses the idea of 'virtue' in Renaissance texts. Examining the etymology of the term—its derivations from the Latin for both 'man' and 'power'—she identifies the ways in which the concept of virtue operated as an exemplar for both moral and historical authority (London: Routledge, 1997), see 11–15. Specifically she ties the term to classical codes of civility and strength, exposing the ways in which the idea of virtue operates within a collective consciousness as something that represents a common good.

[9] Intriguingly, the name Iago comes from 'Jacob', meaning to supplant, since legend has it that he was born holding his twin brother's heel.

[10] As Lois Potter observes 'will' was a densely inflected word: ' "Will" is a crucial word in Christian doctrine, since the extent to which human beings had free will was one of the main Reformation controversies. "Will" was also a slang term for the penis, the physical means by which men commit sexual sin,' *The Life of William Shakespeare: A Critical*

garden, for Iago, supports the language of private authority precisely because it registers the effects of human intervention. Such intervention, we discover as the play develops, has the capacity to destroy as well as create; to manufacture as well as deracinate.

As Iago explains, to reap what you sow exposes a vital dynamic between action and effect. Yet what Iago does not explain, however, is the Christian morality that conventionally accompanies this image.[11] Within the Christian tradition, this horticultural metaphor is used to invoke human accountability, through which only the righteous profit from their cultivation. Emptied of the accompanying morality of a Christian authority, Iago points to the natural world as the province of a radical individualism. For him, horticulture endorses an image of human will precisely because it manifests the processes of intervention and reward; a process which he recasts as personal, rather than collective. From Roderigo's denial of any intrinsic 'virtue' to Iago's celebration of individual determinism, the exchange between these two men divests these conventionally biblical images of their moral registers. Iago does not call on this analogy for the comfort of spiritual wisdom but for a release from the social bonds that threaten personal ambition. For Iago, 'reason' steps into the breach between the human and its nature: 'If the balance of our lives had not one scale of reason to poise another of sensuality, the blood and baseness of our natures would conduct us to the most preposterous conclusions' (1.3.326–9). Opposing sensuality, Iago identifies reason as an individualized impulse to both control and succeed.[12]

Cultivation, as *Othello* suggests, is a form of reason precisely because it imposes human patterns of control on an otherwise non-human world. These forms of control also manifest as means to production: fertility, subjugation, intervention, order, and investment record the ways in which humans rationalize the natural world. Sexing the garden, Iago locates his attitude to successful manipulation through the ability to control production. Whether it is 'sterile with idleness or manured with industry' is not the point; it is the 'will' that denotes the 'balance of our lives'. Iago's

---

Biography (Oxford: Wiley-Blackwell, 2012), 5–6. See also Stephen Booth's fulsome note on the word in his edition of the *Sonnets* (New Haven: Yale University Press, 2000), 466–7.

[11] See 2 Cor. 9: 6: 'The person who sows sparingly will also reap sparingly, and the person who sows generously will also reap generously'; Gal. 6: 8: 'because the person who sows to his own flesh will reap corruption from the flesh, but the one who sows to the Spirit will reap eternal life from the Spirit'.

[12] As Michael Schoenfeldt explains in regard to sonnet 94: 'Far from indicating an inhuman dispassion, the coldness the sonnet counsels represents the victory of unruffled reason over insurrectionary desire,' *Bodies and Selves*, 88. Reason is celebrated as a form of human cultivation—an intervention in the natural, wild even, body of the human.

metaphor reveals the extent to which he determines individual agency, but it also appeals to a powerful set of semantic relationships by which he understands the 'power' of the human agent beyond the language of consensual morality.

Shakespeare's dramatic gardens are compelling places: Old Hamlet is apparently murdered in one, Richard II's gardeners define corruption in one, Richard, Duke of Gloucester, sends Ely to fetch some strawberries from a garden in Holborn, so that he can plot the death of Hastings, Suffolk retires to the garden to ruin Humphrey of Gloucester; and the worlds of Jack Cade and Alexander Iden collide in one.[13] In the comedies, on the other hand, the garden lends itself to those in search of amorous intrigue, or to manipulate affections.[14] For many of Shakespeare's characters the garden becomes a space of relative privacy in which plots of desire or death can be orchestrated, and fears and hopes expressed.[15] The metaphorical garden, however, is often more complex.[16] As Iago's analogy

---

[13] The garden in *Richard II* features most prominently in critical studies. In '(Re)fracted Art and Ordered Nature: Italian Renaissance Aesthetics in Shakespeare's Richard II', in Michael Marrapodi (ed.), *Shakespeare and Renaissance Literary Theories: Anglo-Italian Transactions* (Farnham: Ashgate, 2001), Susan Payne explores what she calls a '"horticultural aesthetic" as a containing, controlling inward paradigm', 222. See also Thomas Cartelli, 'Jack Cade in the Garden: Class Consciousness and Class Conflict in *2 Henry VI*', in Richard Burt and John Michael Archer (eds.), *Enclosure Acts: Sexuality, Property and Culture in Early Modern England* (Ithaca, NY: Cornell University Press, 1994), 48–67.

[14] The word orchard was often used to mean garden. As the *OED* explains, 'Originally: a garden (freq. enclosed), esp. for herbs and fruit trees' (1). In *Twelfth Night*, Olivia discloses her love for Cesario in the garden in 3.1. In *Much Ado About Nothing*, the orchard provides the space in which the women can trick Beatrice into thinking she is loved by Benedict, and in *Love's Labour's Lost*, Navarre reads Costard's letter to Jaquenetta, which he wrote from 'the west corner of thy curious knotted garden' (1.1). Janette Dillon writes that gardens 'represent a locus for what is best in human beings, a setting in which even fallen men came come closer to the good life, free from envy, ambition and greed, and finding peace and contentment in quiet contemplation and willing hospitality; and they are also regularly used to represent the state or the commonwealth, in order to measure how far it achieves or fails to achieve the ideal harmony and order that the garden recalls', *Shakespeare and the Staging of English History* (Oxford: Oxford University Press, 2012), 14.

[15] In Martin Brükner and Kirstin Poole's 'The Plot Thickens: Surveying Manuals, Drama and the Materiality of Narrative Form in Early Modern England', *English Literary History* (2002), 617–48, the authors discuss the linguistic relationship between the plot of land and the plot of the play, including the multiple variations on the word. See also Margreta de Grazia's *Hamlet without Hamlet* (Cambridge: Cambridge University Press, 2007), esp. 37–43.

[16] Recent work on material and metaphoric gardens includes John Dixon Hunt, *Greater Perfections: The Practice of Garden Theory* (Philadelphia: University of Pennsylvania Press, 2000), Rebecca Bushnell, *Green Desire: Imagining Early Modern English Gardens* (Ithaca, NY: Cornell University Press, 2003), Patricia Seed, *Ceremonies of Possession in Europe's Conquest of the New World, 1492–1640* (Cambridge: Cambridge University Press, 1995), Robert Pogue Harrison, *Gardens: An Essay on the Human Condition* (Chicago: University of Chicago Press, 2008).

suggests, images of cultivation can reveal individual narratives within an apparently common language of appreciation.

Understanding landscape in this way explains why, as Denis Cosgrove has argued, it 'represents a way in which certain classes of people have signified themselves and their world through their imagined relationship with nature, and through which they have underlined and communicated their own social role and that of others with respect to external nature'.[17] Communicating through the landscape allows the individual to underline their own social role within the context and language of a shared external nature. For Iago, nature becomes a place of communication precisely because it supports the intercession of the individual within a putatively socialized, and predominantly Christian, context. For Iago, however, the Christian legacy of moral husbandry is redundant in his personal narrative of autonomy; yet for Hamlet, such structures of virtue are vital for the revelation of iniquity. Discoursing on his mother's 'hasty' marriage, Hamlet turns to cultivation as a form of moral action:

> Fie on't! ah fie! 'tis an unweeded garden,
> That grows to seed; things rank and gross in nature
> Possess it merely. (1.2.135–7)

For Hamlet, the garden mutates from the physical space in which his father was murdered to a figurative image of wholesale iniquity. The 'unweeded garden' emerges as a form of neglect in which inaction allows 'things rank and gross' not only to rise to the surface but to take root.[18] The garden analogy allows husbandry to manifest as a practice of moral intervention, in which action, or weeding, is an inherently sociable practice of moral cleansing. In *Henry V*, Burgundy's 'best garden of the world' (5.2.36) refers to a condition of social and economic sustainability in which the 'lovely visage' of peace functions as an image of ethical security. Like Burgundy, Hamlet draws the infected garden into view as a vivid symbol of moral failure. Central to Hamlet's indictment is a qualitative assessment of value in which the human is responsible for the cultivation of the good and the deracination of the bad.

Focusing on the role of human agency in the construction of a natural world, Shakespeare's plays and poems situate husbandry at the forefront of their social and moral economies. As Timon says, cursing the earth as the

---

[17] Denis Cosgrove, *Social Formation and Symbolic Landscape* (London: Croom Helm, 1984), 15.

[18] In *Hamlet without Hamlet*, Margreta de Grazia explores the multiple ways in which the land manifests within the play: from earth, space, stage, dust, and grave. See especially 23–44.

womb that engenders human iniquity: 'Dry up the marrows, vines and plough-torn leas | Whereof ungrateful man with liquorish draughts, | And morsels unctuous, greases his pure mind, | That from it all consideration slips' (4.3.194–7). Condemning the processes by which 'ungrateful man' has served himself, Timon strikes, quite literally, at the root of human development, from which 'all consideration slips'. Destroying the processes by which ungrateful man may live provides Timon with a fantasy of human cleansing: ridding the earth of humans and leaving it to nature's 'new monsters'. The moral discourses that inhere in these images belong to a landscape in which the human is both instrumental and accountable.

As this book will demonstrate, cultivation is more than tillage; it is a social discourse—and, by implication, an ideology—through which both human action and intention can be judged as well as expressed. For the Elizabethans, however, the word cultivation had yet to emerge as distinct from the term culture. Variously described as tillage, husbandry, or culture, processes of agrarian and horticultural intervention entered into the English language as moral as well as practical examples of human agency.[19] Writing of Virgil's 'observations of husbandry' in what he calls the 'Georgickes of the mind', Francis Bacon explains that:

the maine & primitiue diuision of *Morall* knowledge seemeth to be into the EXEMPLAR or PLATFORME of GOOD, and the REGIMENT or CVLTVRE OF THE MIND; The one describing the nature of Good the other prescribing rules how to subdue, apply and accomodate the will of man therevnto.[20]

For Bacon 'heroicall actions' provide a 'platforme of good' and culture, or cultivation, allows the human to act upon them. In this way, cultivation emerges as a set of prescribed 'rules', which mediate between the moral and material worlds, subduing, applying, and accommodating the will of the human. In Bacon's observations we can find traces of both Hamlet's and Iago's 'gardens': morally accountable yet cognitively flexible. For Bacon, cultivation is comprehensive, capable of imposing upon, and yet also accommodating, the personal will.

Appropriating the language of cultivation, Shakespeare's characters take part in a discourse of human action, in which such terms as harvest, till, plough, reap, and sow, for example, denote an affective relationship between the individual and their social world. Through representations

---

[19] The *OED* defines *culture* as 'The cultivation of land, and derived senses' (1a) from 1450. As the *OED* observes, the more modern meaning of culture as 'the development of the mind, manners etc.; improvement by education' (c.1510) stems from sense 1a.

[20] *The Two Books of Francis Bacon, Of the proficience and aduancement of learning, diuine and humane To the King* (London, 1605), book two, 69.

of both the garden and the landscape we perceive what James Turner has called 'an instrument of thought. A useful analogue for personal and social values.'[21] Equally important, however, is Cosgrove's reminder that 'landscape is a social product, the consequence of a collective human transformation of nature'.[22] Represented through the husbandry manuals of the sixteenth and seventeenth centuries, collective human transformations materialized as practices of cultivation, in which the human could both inhabit, and profit from, the natural world. As an 'instrument of thought', however, the landscape also mediated between the human and the divine to allow profit to take multiple forms of ethical and economic intention, promoting human agency in accordance with a providential structure of divine will.[23] When Banquo, after the murder of Duncan, observes 'There's husbandry in heaven, | Their candles are all out', night's prudence—the management of the sky—registers a cosmic response to human iniquity. Night's husbandry imitates moral action in a non-human environment.

'And husband nature's riches from expense (sonnet 94)'

Observing the proliferation of images of husbandry in early modern English colonial practices, Patricia Seed writes: 'Why gardening and agricultural metaphors appealed so strongly to the English (and to them alone) is worthy of consideration.'[24] As the primary site of England's economy, agrarian and animal husbandry dictated the conditions by which people lived.[25] As a practice fundamental to representations of a sustainable commonwealth, husbandry also supported the terms through

---

[21] *The Politics of Landscape* (Cambridge, Mass.: Harvard University Press, 1979), 36.

[22] Cosgrove, *Social Formation and Symbolic Landscape*, 14.

[23] Alexandra Walsham's *The Reformation of the Landscape* (Oxford: Oxford University Press, 2011) explores the highly complex relationship between religion and the natural world, through both intervention and interpretation. Walsham particularly focuses on spaces of worship as they are both constructed on and mediated through the natural world. See also Lorraine Datson and Katherine Park, *Wonders and the Order of Nature, 1150–1750* (New York: Zone, 2001).

[24] *Ceremonies of Possession*, 27.

[25] There is a great deal of work which deals with the relationship between the human and the non-human through the animal. Although my work is necessarily informed by the critical and theoretical models that support these investigations my primary interest is in cultivation and the ways in which the land supported the socio-economic values of those living under Elizabeth I and James I. For an exploration, however, of anthropocentrism see Bruce Boehrer's *Shakespeare Among the Animals: Nature and Society in the Drama of Early Modern England* (Basingstoke: Palgrave, 2002); Erica Fudge, *Perceiving Animals: Humans and Beasts in Early Modern English Culture* (New York: St Martin's Press, 1999) for an interrogation of what she calls 'the border figure'; and Andreas Höfele's *Stage, Stake and Scaffold* (Oxford: Oxford University Press, 2011) for a highly informed exploration of the ways in which the theatre developed alongside institutions of both cruelty and entertainment.

which Elizabethans structured their social and economic lives. Simultaneously moral, economic, civic, and industrious, husbandry came to reflect the practical and social codes of daily life.

The term husbandry develops from the word 'husband' to mean the ordering and management of the house.[26] Importing the conditions of male administration, husbandry comes to translate the mastery of a household unit into the wider concerns of animal and agrarian management.[27] Through cultivation the relatively contained practices of household management are transformed into something more discursive in the texts of the husbandry manuals.[28] Lorna Hutson observes this transition as spatial, whereby the interior household becomes the province of 'wife training' and the outdoors an exclusively male space in which husbandry and warfare are defined as civic duties. Within humanist terms 'the notion of husbandry as necessary toil [was replaced] with the notion of husbandry as an art of existence which is the sign and essence of the most fortunate, the rulers of the commonweal'.[29] Hutson's attention to humanism marks a fundamental aspect in the reproduction of husbandry manuals.[30] According to Michael Leslie and Timothy Raylor, sixteenth-century husbandry manuals allow us access to 'a time when new conceptions of the

---

[26] Wendy Wall, in her essay 'Unhusbanding Desires in Windsor', in Richard Dutton and Jean E. Howard (eds.), *A Companion to Shakespeare's Works: The Comedies* (Oxford: Blackwell, 2008), esp. 381. Shakespeare uses the term within the more parochial context of household management in *The Merchant of Venice*, when Portia 'commits' into Lorenzo's 'hands' 'The husbandry and manage of my house' (3.4.25).

[27] Douglas Bruster, in *Drama and the Market in the Age of Shakespeare* (Cambridge: Cambridge University Press, 1992) examines the term 'husband' within the context of both labour and cuckoldry, explicitly drawing a link between the cuckold and the practitioner of husbandry, 51–4.

[28] Recent criticism has tended to read the husbandry manuals as an extension of the domestic unit, rather than a development of it. While Wall claims that 'These guides made domestic oeconomia a touchstone for marking the "proper" definitions of social groups', Joyce Appleby claims that we cannot make the interpretative move from the household to husbandry so easily, since, within the context of Xenophon, the household functions as a specific unit not as an economic model of development, see *Economic Thought and Ideology in Seventeenth-Century England* (Princeton: Princeton University Press, 1978), 24.

[29] *The Usurer's Daughter: Male Friendship and the Fictions of Women in Sixteenth Century England* (London: Routledge, 1994), 35, 38.

[30] See also Jennifer Richards, *Rhetoric and Courtliness in Early Modern Literature* (Cambridge: Cambridge University Press, 2003), where she discusses 'conversational courtesy . . . [as] the rule of good economic conduct', 100. Jenny C. Mann, in her exploration of the development of English rhetoric, identifies the significance of spatial logic in the creation of English style: 'When they ground their translations in the territory of "England," these manuals localize spatial metaphors already available within the rhetorical tradition,' *Outlaw Rhetoric: Figuring Vernacular Eloquence in Shakespeare's England* (Ithaca, NY: Cornell University Press, 2012), 31.

natural world were actively and consciously created'.[31] Partly dependent, however, upon a classical tradition for both their authority and their ideologies, these manuals, as Hutson suggests, presented cultivation as a form of civilization through a specific representation of both civic duty and social approbation. Examining the relationship between *Oeconomicus* and rhetoric, Jennifer Richards writes: 'husbandry is a public good because it provides a forum for the development of skills required for paternalistic government, namely an ability to order one's resources'.[32] Most obviously expressed through deference to writers like Columella, Virgil, Cato, and Varro, husbandry manuals often established the strength of their material through long paratexts attending to the multiple authorities through which their information moved.

Conrad Heresbach's *Foure Bookes of Husbandrie*, translated from the Latin by Barnabe Googe in 1577, begins with a long section devoted to 'The names of such Authores and Husbands whose Authorities and Observations are used in this book.'[33] Immensely popular, this manual takes the form of a classical dialogue between the relative values of the court and the country.[34] Following classical precedents, Heresbach constructs his representations of husbandry through a specific value system in which the husbandman represents the 'true and perfect lyfe'.[35] Within this discourse, husbandry comes to reflect a set of moral standards by which human relations are both developed and judged. Echoing Socrates and drawing on Cicero, Heresbach claims that:

Cicero calleth it the mistresse of iustice, diligens, and thriftinesse: some others call it the Mother and Nurs of al other artes. For wheras we may liue without the other, without this we are not able to sustayne our life: besides, the gayne that hereof aryseth, is most godly, and least subiect to enuie, for it hath to deale with the Earth, that restoreth with gayne such thinges as is committed vnto her, specially y [if] it be furthered with the blessing of GOD. The only gentlemanly way of encreasing the house, is the trade of husbandry.[36]

---

[31] Michael Leslie and Timothy Raylor (eds.), *Culture and Cultivation in Early Modern England: Writing and the Land* (Leicester: University of Leicester Press, 1992), 1.

[32] *Rhetoric and Courtliness*, 97.

[33] Sig. 5. Thomas Hill's *The gardeners labyrinthe, containing a discourse of the gardeners life* (1577) includes a similar paratext, under the heading 'Authores from whom this worke is selected'.

[34] Heresbach's book went through seven editions between 1577 and 1631. See Andrew McRae, *God Speed the Plough: The Representation of Agrarian England, 1500–1660* (Cambridge: Cambridge University Press, 1996), 138–42.

[35] Conrad Heresbach, *Foure Bookes of Husbandrie*, trans. Barnabe Googe (London, 1577), 2ʳ. All further references are to this text.

[36] *Foure Bookes of Husbandrie*, 7ʳ. Joan Thirsk attributes this observation to Socrates, 'Making a Fresh Start', in Leslie and Raylor (eds.), *Culture and Cultivation*, 21.

In this justification of husbandry, spoken by the Christian advocate Cono, we can read the extent to which agrarian cultivation is allied with conventions of good living.[37] Importing terms of justice, diligence, and thrift, as well as survival, godliness, and civility, the practice of husbandry records the complex networks of our social, economic, and spiritual lives. As a comprehensive term for good living, husbandry supported a doctrine of social and civic duty. When, in *Coriolanus*, Volumnia urges Virgilia to rejoice in her husband's absence as a mark of his commitment to Rome, she envisages him in war and harvest:

> Methinks I see him stamp thus, and call thus:
> 'Come on, you cowards, you were got in fear
> Though you were born in Rome!' His bloody brow
> With his mailed hand then wiping forth he goes
> Like to a harvest-man that's tasked to mow
> Or all or lose his hire. (1.3.29–34)

Importing the 'harvest-man' into the soldier's armour, Volumnia borrows the agrarian figure as an image of both duty and commitment. Bound by an imperative to survive as well as serve, the harvest-man supports a wider discourse of labour and duty which Volumnia values. In this speech, the presiding emotion is one of pride predicated on hardship, civic responsibility, and result. For Volumnia, the harvest-man—like the ploughman—is a figure of duty in which personal needs are sacrificed to a commonwealth. Briefly—and ironically—collapsing the social distinctions upon which Coriolanus' power depends, Volumnia impresses upon her daughter-in-law that his duty is not to her but to the city: 'If my son were my husband, I should freelier rejoice in that absence wherein he won honour than in the embracements of his bed where he would show most love' (1.3.1–4). Good husbanding lies beyond the bed and in the journey from 'man-child' to 'man'. As Coriolanus will later testify:

> Let the Volsces
> Plough Rome and harrow Italy! I'll never
> Be such a gosling to obey instinct, but stand
> As if a man were author of himself
> And knew no other kin. (5.3.33–7)

Redefining cultivation as an act of aggression—destruction even— Coriolanus separates himself from images of collective action as a force

[37] McRae understands this assertion as drawing the 'active landlord' 'into the centre of a vital and essentially natural social order of life and productivity', 'Husbandry Manuals and the Language of Agrarian Improvement', in Leslie and Raylor (eds.), *Culture and Cultivation*, 41.

against nature. Defying the socialized codes of husbandry to which his
mother had appealed, Coriolanus dissociates himself from the social landscape in order to 'know no other kin'. This kind of aggressive isolation
compromises the socio-economic ideals of cultivation, in which the plough,
according to Elizabeth I's statutes, 'upheld' 'the kingdom'.[38]

The gendering of these virtues enabled husbandry to become a highly
visible language of social commentary within the Tudor landscape.
According to Joan Thirsk, 'In the past, great men in government were
summoned from the plough to deliver the state . . . . This wisdom, so often
repeated by the classical writers, was to become an axiom in Elizabeth's
reign.'[39] The physical toil of husbandry, as Volumnia indicates, endowed
'great men' with a bodily strength, while the utilitarian values it represented supported the transition from plough to state. Augmented by a
proliferation of books on the subject, the language of husbandry emerged
in texts on religion, conduct, pedagogy, cultivation, and politics as it
supported an apparently transparent relationship between the moral and
social lives of the Elizabethans.[40] Anthony Low makes this explicit when
he writes that 'new practices in agriculture in turn influenced and reinforced people's thinking about life, generally, their sense of themselves,
and even their most intimate relationships'.[41] 'Recognizing that land is
crucial to the moral economy of the period' helps us to understand the
roles that husbandry manuals played in the re-presentation of social
relationships, as well as their rehearsal through economic practices.[42]

Central to these relationships is 'the idea of community' upon which
cultivation depended. As Mark Overton explains, however, the term
'community' is a complex one; 'In the early sixteenth century, belonging

---

[38] 39 & 40 Eliz. Cap. II.

[39] 'Making a Fresh Start', in Leslie and Raylor (eds.), *Culture and Cultivation*, 21.

[40] Mike Rodman Jones, in *Radical Pastoral, 1381–1594* (Farnham: Ashgate, 2010),
identifies the 'arresting and complex symbol of the plough' in the medieval period, and
'well before we reach Tyndale's and Erasmus's rhetoric', 86. Erasmus' invocation of the
plough, however, in the preface to his *Novum Testamentum* (1516) is a powerful example of
the social and emotional range that such an image of cultivation could support: 'I would . . .
that the farmer sing some part of them at the plow.' See also McRae, *God Speed the Plough*,
23–57. Rebecca Bushnell, in *A Culture of Teaching: Early Modern Humanism in Theory and
Practice* (New York: Cornell University Press, 1996), explores some of the ways in which
metaphors of cultivation were appropriated by pedagogic humanist writers like Ascham and
Elyot; see particularly 73–116. Equally relevant is Bushnell's *Green Desire: Imagining Early
Modern English Gardens* (Ithaca, NY: Cornell University Press, 2003), which explores the
role of gardening manuals in the reconstruction of early modern conceptions of both
pleasure and profit, 84–107.

[41] 'Agricultural Reform and the Love Poems of Thomas Carew; with an Instance from
Lovelace', in Leslie and Raylor (eds.), *Culture and Cultivation*, 63.

[42] Garrett A. Sullivan, Jr, *The Drama of Landscape: Land, Property and Social Relations on
the Early Modern Stage* (Stanford, Calif.: Stanford University Press, 1998), 7.

meant being a participant in the life of a community and sharing not only institutions, but, in commonfield villages, work as well'. In a country where 80 per cent of its economic output was agrarian, the majority of these relationships were those of the land.[43] Cultivation formed the major axis upon which community turned, and, to that extent, these texts record the contests over 'the very meaning of rural England'.[44] Henry V's rousing call to his yeomen to become soldiers—to defend the land upon which their living depends—not only supports an image of territorial identity but it also recognizes a set of moral codes apparently inherent in their pasture, in which growth governs futurity, posterity, and success:

> And you, good yeomen,
> Whose limbs were made in England, show us here
> The mettle of your pasture; let us swear
> That you are worth your breeding; which I doubt not. (*Henry V*, 3.1)

Henry's rhetoric of war depends upon the suggestive relationships between 'good', 'yeomen', 'England', 'worth', and 'breeding'. These terms belong to a discourse of action in which the human subject is both dependent on and responsible for the land upon which he (or she) lives. The yeoman, Elizabeth's 'good and able subject' and 'the ancient glory of England', belongs to the landscape in a social and moral discourse 'worthy of analysis'.[45]

As the rural landscape supported the representation of belonging so too did belonging inform the representation of cultivation.[46] Mediated through the printed text, the husbandry manual produced a shared practice of a shared ambition. While Elizabeth's Act against the decaying of houses of husbandry (1597–8) could represent this ambition as the 'great estate and flourishing of this kingdom', books on husbandry recorded profit, thrift,

---

[43] Overton, *Agricultural Revolution in England: The Transformation of the Agrarian Economy 1500–1850* (Cambridge: Cambridge University Press, 2011), 45. Overton provides this statistic.

[44] McRae, *God Speed the Plough*, 2. As McRae points out, however, 'Although early modern England was unquestionably fractured by regional interests and identities, generations of writers formed vital new forms of nationhood' through the representation of the land, 6. Richard Helgerson's *Forms of Nationhood: The Elizabethan Writing of England* (Chicago: University of Chicago Press, 1992, 1994) explores this subject in greater detail.

[45] 39 & 40 Elizabeth Cap. I; Frances Trigge, *A Humble Petition of the Church and Commonwealth* (London, 1604), D4ᵛ; and McRae, talking of the 'immense cultural authority accrued in the name of Christian morality', *God Speed the Plough*, 17.

[46] As Wendy Wall asserts: 'From the epic grandeur of Spenser's *Faerie Queene* to the more mundane tracts on husbandry and farming flooding the book market in the late sixteenth and early seventeenth centuries, we find writers meditating upon and documenting relationships between these terms,' 'Renaissance National Husbandry: Gervase Markham and the Publication of England', *Sixteenth Century Journal*, 27/3 (Autumn 1996), 767.

and management as collective goals of the individual farmer, tenant, or landlord.[47]

According to Wendy Wall, husbandry manuals, and particularly the works of Gervase Markham, were fundamental to a sense of Englishness, or what she calls 'englishing the soil'. As one of the most prolific English writers on the subject, as well as playwright and poet, Gervase Markham has become a central figure in the exploration of the subject of cultivation as well as the book trade.[48] Markham's extraordinary capacity to reproduce numerous works on much the same material evinces the English appetite for this subject but it also discloses the ways in which the landscape is a text, to be simultaneously marked and read: 'Echoing the well-known metaphor of the pen as plow, Markham insists upon the shared nature of the tasks of writing and farming.'[49] Endlessly reiterating the formidable role of the husbandman, Markham imbues the figure with its own mythic status:

A Husbandman is the Maister of the earth, turning sterrillitie and barrainenesse, into fruitfulnesse and increase, whereby all common wealths are maintained and vpheld, it is his labour which giueth bread to all men and maketh vs forsake the societie of beasts drinking vpon the water springs, féeding vs with a much more nourishing liquor. The labour of the Husbandman giueth liberty to all vocations, Arts, misteries and trades, to follow their seuerall functions, with peace and industry, for the filling and emptying of his barnes is the increase and prosperitie of all their labours. To conclude, what can we say in this world is profitable where Husbandry is wanting, it being the great Nerue and Sinew which houldeth together all the ioynts of a Monarchie?[50]

The quasi-magical status that Markham affords the husbandman allows him to become master of the earth by virtue of his capacity to transform sterility into fruitfulness.[51] Such abilities, I suggest, are discernible in Prospero. Incapable of cultivating the island, Prospero reproduces the work of the husbandman in illusion. Fabricating such transformations

---

[47] 39 & 40 Elizabeth Cap. I.

[48] Michael Best's introduction to a modern edition of *The English Housewife* humorously observes that Markham was so productive that he was required, in 1617, to sign a memorandum by the Stationers, in which he promised 'hereafter never to write any more book or books to be printed of the diseases or cures of any cattle, as horse, ox, cow, sheep, swine, goats etc.', *The English Housewife*, ed. Michael Best (London: McGill-Queen's University Press, 1986), xiv. Markham had, at this point, produced five books on the health of horses!

[49] Wall, 'Renaissance National Husbandry', 784.

[50] Gervase Markham, *The English Husbandman* (London 1613), A3ʳ. All subsequent references, unless otherwise stated, are to this edition.

[51] This sense of mastery is reiterated throughout the text, as the ploughman becomes 'master of such a soile', H3ᵛ.

in the masque, Prospero, as Markham allows, turns sterility and barrenness into fruitfulness and increase: or, in Ceres' words, 'foison and plenty'.
The capacity for production and reproduction situates human agency at
the forefront of fantasies about the future, as well as a recuperation of the
past.

The transformative abilities of the husbandman support his role within
the English social economy, in which he is also custodian of such civic virtues
as 'liberty', 'prosperitie', and 'peace'. Markham is a central figure in the
reproduction and translation of husbandry manuals, and it is through his
1616 translation of Charles Estienne's *The Countrey Farme* that Wall identifies the ideological relationships between national identity and cultivation, in
which Markham offers his project as 'both recuperative and innovative'.[52]
The dynamic between the past and the future—recovery and discovery—
becomes a productive alliance in which husbandry represents a collective
ideal in the creation of a distinct, and 'flourishing', England.

Like Heresbach's *Foure Bookes of Husbandrie*, Estienne's was a popular
text and endeavoured to present the gentleman farmer as a central figure in
the transmission of knowledge and the development of economic liberty.
Like Heresbach, Estienne identifies his work as part of a historic continuum in which:

we may see our late kinde of Husbandrie to attaine and bring with it the like issue
and effects which that of the Auncients did, which is nothing else, but to liue of
the encrease of the Earth, well husbanded and tilled by vs.[53]

Estienne's 'us' celebrates a shared vision of the earth and the means by
which human endeavour has learned to profit from it. This comprehensive
view of a universal human enterprise recognizes the extent to which
cultivation has come to represent a set of values as well as practices: 'because
no other thing bringeth more gaine vnto the master thereof than the earth, if
it be well husbanded and reasonably maintained'.[54] Reproducing his own
language of mastery, Markham's translation supports Estienne's vision
through a common discourse of reward, as well as expectation.[55]

---

[52] In this way, Markham's texts appear to 'recover a lost native England (the authentic
"difference of our customs" that have gone by the wayside because of published foreign
information and revising agrarian practices so as to increase profit, as any good Englishman
desires (those formulas "fittest" for the husbandman's "use and commodity")', Wall, 'Renaissance National Husbandry', 777–8. Estienne's *The Countrey Farme*, written in 1577, translated from Latin to French by Richard Surflet in 1600 and from French to English by Gervase
Markham in 1616.

[53] Estienne, *The Countrey Farme*, trans. Gervase Markham (London, 1616), 2.

[54] Estienne, *The Countrey Farme*, 3.

[55] In her book *Rhetoric and Courtliness*, Jennifer Richards identifies the process of
translation as fundamental in the shaping and reproducing of certain humanist values, see
especially 110–12.

Although we may find traces of this discourse in almost all forms of literary texts, reconstructing specific groups of readers, defined by social and economic status, is problematic.[56] As a translator and writer, however, Gervase Markham re-presents much of this material in his own vast body of works on husbandry. Markham's own works, however, and those of his predecessor, Thomas Tusser, were not only more affordable but offered a comprehensive image of the duties and demands of a seventeenth-century yeoman as well as gentleman.[57] The most popular of all such texts, however, was Thomas Tusser's *Five Hundred Points of Good Husbandry*, originally expanded from his *A Hundreth Good Points of Husbandrie* (1557), which went through twenty-three editions between 1557 and 1638. While Markham's work has been described as having been 'read to pieces', Tusser's work 'led the market', and was 'a Tudor best-seller'.[58] Written in verse, and as a kind of *vade mecum* for the lower classes, the manual covers the agricultural year with a vivacity not present in the more elitist manuals: including recipes, prayers, marital advice, and medicinal remedies, Tusser represents husbandry as a founding virtue of human life. Beginning with his own etymology—'of husband, doth husbandrie challenge that name, | of husbandrie, husband doth likewise the same'—he moves on to establish the practice as life giving: 'what hath any life, but I helpe to preserve'.[59] While many of the more classically inflected texts bury the stark necessity of agrarian production for human survival, Tusser's bald assertion recognizes one of the most important elements of these manuals: namely that without cultivation the Elizabethan economy could

---

[56] As Andrew McRae observes, while the Latin works 'are necessarily directed toward an educated elite... the size of the contemporary texts (... *Foure Bookes of Husbandry* covers 54 sheets and *The Countrie Farme* 140) would have made them unaffordable to most farmers of lower than gentry status'. Estienne's *The Countrey Farme* observes that his text is not for the 'ordinarie husbandmen, the fonde and ignorant sort... but of renowned men which have loved and caused to flourish the life and exercises of the countrie house' (sig. B5b). McRae, *God Speed the Plough*, 139.

[57] Markham's catalogue included 'four books on horses; six on husbandry, including two editions of works by other writers; four on military discipline; four on various country sports and recreations, including one edition of an earlier one; and one on housewifery. Two collections of his works, one of those on husbandry and one on military affairs, were issued in his lifetime; and there were also four abridgements of his popular works, two issued during his life, two issued after his death,' *The Good Housewife*, ed. Best, xv–xvi. To this formidable list we might add the extent to which the *Oxford English Dictionary* draws on Markham's work.

[58] F. N. L. Poynter, *A Bibliography of Gervase Markham, 1568?–1637* (Oxford: Bibliographical Society, ns XI, 1962), introduction. See McRae, *God Speed the Plough*, 146; Thomas Tusser, *Five Hundred Points of Good Husbandry*, ed. Geoffrey Grigson (Oxford: Oxford University Press, 1984), xviii.

[59] Tusser, *Five Hundred Points of Good Husbandry*, 12, 11. For ease of readership I use Grigson's facsimile edition, which retains some original orthography but omits the most alienating spellings for a modern audience.

not survive and neither could its subjects. The country's dependence on grain for bread, barley for malt, and animal husbandry for meat and material does not distinguish it from any one country or any other epoch. What does distinguish this period, however, is the representation of that production in ways that not only sought to valorize expectations of profit but also came to reflect and define a moral discourse of social relations. If, as Tusser suggests, personifying husbandry, 'I seeme but a drudge, yet I passe any King | To such as can use me, great wealth do I bring', then we need to understand the ways in which such images of authority, success, and mastery manifested as human interpretations of the natural world.

This is not to suggest, however, that such 'wealth' was always righteous: on the contrary, the sheer necessity of human agency in processes of husbandry meant that it became a powerful place for the initiation of individual will. As Iago understood the will as the province of 'power and corrigible authority' in his bodily garden, York, in *2 Henry VI*, on the other hand, will reap the rewards of others' harvests. Articulating his moves to the throne, he declares:

> Why then from Ireland come I with my strength
> And reap the harvest which that coistrel sowed.
> For Humphrey being dead, as he shall be,
> And Henry put apart the next for me. (3.2.380–3)[60]

Far from establishing a moral right to reward, the semantics of husbandry present a discourse in which the human agent is consistently under scrutiny, and images of mastery (or kingship) are in contention. Aggressive and effective, the sword and the plough belong to a language of strength.

'One touch of nature makes the whole world kin (*Troilus and Cressida*)'

For most people living in Elizabethan England, and until the nineteenth century, the natural world was a text, 'God's folio', through which they could interpret the Scripture of the Christian faith. As Alexandra Walsham explains, even within denominational conflicts, people 'shared the conviction that nature was a vehicle by which God communicated, as it were, telegraphically, with human beings'.[61] Husbandry became a way of

---

[60] Earlier on in the play, York declares that he will make Henry 'yield the crown' (1.1.257). For York the terms of his assault on Henry's kingship are in the form of juxtapositions, in which Henry is 'bookish' and he, York, is active. The language of cultivation endorses this self-image, in which he is affective and interventionist in ways that benefit him alone.

[61] *The Reformation of the Landscape* (Oxford: Oxford University Press, 2011), 353. Even through the development of scientific rationalism, Walsham observes that 'it was not until the era of Darwin that the principles which underpinned it met with drastic challenge to

demonstrating human commitment to God through reclamation of the earth after the fall. Within these terms, fortuitous climates, successful harvests, and fertile ground could be read as signs of God's approval as well as the human capacity to intervene in its fallen condition. John Fitzherbert, whose *Boke of Husbandry* (1523) appears as the first comprehensive husbandry manual in print, declares:[62]

He that laboureth nat | sholde nat eat | & he ought to labour & do goddes warke y^t wyll ete of his goodes or gyftes | the whiche is an harde text after ye lytterall sence.[63]

Fitzherbert equates survival with godliness: conflating spiritual and physical labour with the rewards of heaven and earth, the text and the land (legibility and survival) become markers of human worth.[64]

'That ancient adjudication that sentenced Adam to eat bread by the sweat of his brow' is translated in the Tudor complaint into a social doctrine for improvement.[65] Hugh Latimer's 'sermon of the Plough', delivered at St Paul's Cross in 1548, exposes the profundity of the image in the early modern imagination:

And now I shal tel you, who be the plowers, for Gods worde is a seede to be sowen in Goddes fielde, that is the faythful congregacion, & the preacher is the sower. And it is in the gospell … He that soweth, the husbanman, the plowghman wente furth to sowe his seede, so that a preacher is resebled to a ploughman.[66]

Presenting the congregation as the field in which the preacher ploughs the seeds of God's word appropriates the image of the ploughman for reformist purposes. Defending his analogy, Latimer goes on to explain that

their underlying validity. Scripture was still the ultimate prism through which the majority viewed the natural environment,' 392.

[62] Walter de Henley's *Boke of Husbandry* is published by Wynken de Worde in 1508. It is a short book which gives basic advice and is much less discursive than Fitzherbert's.

[63] 'A new tract or treatise most profitable for husbandman' (London, 1530), A2^r.

[64] During the sixteenth century this relationship is wholly transparent. While John Fitzherbert's *Boke of Husbandry* (1523) is structured according to the Christian calendar, Heresbach's list of authors and observations, for example, begins with the Bible.

[65] Bartlett Jere Whiting, *Early American Proverbs and Proverbial Phrases* (Stanford, Calif.: Harvard University Press, 1977), 426. Robert Pogue Harrison, in *Gardens: An Essay on the Human Condition* (Chicago: University of Chicago Press, 2008), identifies 'the inglorious toil by which we secure our biological survival. … What distinguishes us in out humanity is the fact that we inhabit relatively permanent worlds that precede our birth and outlast our death, binding the generations together in a historical continuum,' 9.

[66] Hugh Latimer, *A notable sermon* … xviii January 1548, third sermon (London: John Day, 1562), fo. 12^v. Cf. McRae, *God Speed the Plough*, for a discussion of this passage, 30.

For as the ploughman first setteth futth his plough, and then tilleth hys lande, and breaketh it in furroughes, and sometyme ridgeth it vp agayne. And at an other tyme harroweth it, & clotteth it, & somtyme doungeth it, & hedgeth it, diggeth it, and weedeth it, pourgeth and maketh it cleane: So the prelate, the preacher hath many diuers offices to do.[67]

Revealing labour as a form of both preparation and investment, Latimer exposes the active processes by which the word and the seed may grow. Speaking through a recognizable image of toil, Latimer draws on a much longer history of Christianity in which the landscape is God's book and cultivation the human labour towards atonement and gratitude.[68] Conversely, John Gerard's *The herbal, or general history of plants* (1597) extends Adam's paradise beyond the fall as an example of the 'harmeless' 'treasure' of the earth:

'Harmelesse I call [it], because they were such delights as man in the perfectest state of his innocencie did erst inioy: and treasure I may well [call] them, seeing both Kings and Princes haue esteemed them as Iewels . . . Methinks it should be a pleasure to you, when you come weary out of the fields from plow, or any other labour, to sit down in the evening, and read that chapter which concerns that particulars business, & *refresh* your *Souls* even from that which hath *wearied* your *bodies*. Were your hearts but heavenly, & more time allowed for spiritual husbandry your inward comforts, would be much more, & your out ward gains not a jot less; for it the success of all your civil labours and imployments depend upon the pleasure & will of God; (as all that are not Atheists do acknowledge) then certainly, your business can succeed never the worse, for your endeavours to please him, upon whose pleasure it so intirely depends.[69]

Apparently building on Fitzherbert's claim, Gerard represents reading and husbandry as comparative exercises of labour for the Christian man, through which cultivation simultaneously acknowledges and enhances the spiritual soul. 'Success', he claims, depends upon labour and 'spiritual husbandry' and is enabled by the 'pleasure & will of God'. The readability of husbandry supports its prolific use in Christian literature. Thomas Tuke's *The picture of a true protestant, or God's house of husbandry* (1609), as the title suggests, takes cultivation as its central analogy. The spiritual person, Tuke writes, labours:

---

[67] Latimer, fourth sermon, unpaginated.

[68] Walsham, in *The Reformation of the Landscape*, discusses the understanding of nature as God's text. A conception, she identifies, that persisted well into the period we associate with the kind of scientific rationalism that defined nature as secular, see 327–56.

[69] John Gerard, *The Herball* (London, 1597), The Epistle to the reader.

for God, and vnder God, in the tilling and husbanding of his *Ground,* in the planting and dressing of his *vineyard,* and in the building & repairing of his *House* or *Temple.*[70]

Images of labour are mediated through discernible forms of human industry: the field, the vineyard, and the house. In this way we are encouraged to understand faithfulness as a form of cultivation in which toil and investment invite the rewards of God's grace. Similarly, in William Jackson's *The Celestial Husbandrie, or the tillage of the Soul* (1616) he establishes his metaphor in the following terms:

This earth is a diuine, spirituall and immortall nature, called the fallow ground, by a metaphor. This ground is incapable of suffering terrene fragillity. This is Gods ground, and that in an high and mysticall sence yet proper enough. *The earth is the Lords.* Yet he hath not such respect to this ground, as he hath to man, for whome he made it: but chiefely to the soule of man, which is this fallow ground.[71]

In Jackson's arcane description both the earth and the soul become 'fallow ground' supporting spiritual tillage and heavenly harvests. Yet even outside explicitly Christian literature the metaphor of husbandry provided a rich language for the idea of human development. Thommaso Buoni in *Problems of Beautie and all Humane Affections*, trans. S.L. (1606), writes of human potential:

and therefore man hauing receaued from the selfe same nature, that two-fold desire, of knowledge, and of good, as two spurres, accompanied (besides) with an inclination, both of witte accommodated to speculation, and of hands the fittest instruments of all others to act any thing, and being moreouer inuited, by the perfection of so many Beautifull works of nature, which make rich the *Theater* of this world, hee would with a sweete kinde of Culture, and tillage of his vnderstanding powers, habituate, and accustome himselfe to vertuous actions.[72]

Cultivation, 'a sweete kind of Culture', brings the human to an understanding of the 'rich Theater of this world' and his or her place within it. Cultivation harnesses the human to its metaphysical world, reflecting and defining its capacity for growth. In this way, the cultivated landscape becomes a figurative hinterland between the physical and metaphysical worlds.

---

[70] Tuke, *The picture of a true protestant: or, Gods house and husbandry wherein is declared the duty and dignitie of all Gods children, both minister and people* (London, 1609), B2ʳ.
[71] *The Celestial Husbandrie,* 8.
[72] *Problems of Beautie and all Humane Affections,* 196–7.

This sense of habitation assumes a sympathetic relationship between the human and non-human worlds. Disrupted husbandry is a powerful indication of human discord. Discoursing on Oberon's 'forgeries of jealousies' in *A Midsummer Night's Dream*, Titania invites the audience to imagine elemental distraction in thwarted human husbandry:

> The ox hath therefore stretched his yoke in vain,
> The ploughman lost his sweat, and the green corn
> Hath rotted ere his youth attained a beard.
> The fold stands empty in the drownéd field,
> And crows are fatted with the murrain flock. (2.1.93–7)

'We are their parents and original,' Titania claims, suggesting the creational responsibility that she and Oberon bear towards the human and its husbandry. Titania's picture of a broken order focuses on husbandry— arable and animal—and the means by which humans regulate, enjoy, and sustain their lives. Oberon's 'brawls' corrupt a set of conditions which are translated by the fairy queen into something like abnegation. Thwarted husbandry signifies a corruption of both duty and responsibility.

'Great creating nature (*The Winter's Tale*)'

Within these terms scholars have often read nature as part of a grand philosophical and cosmological narrative, in which certain intrinsic 'laws' can be identified as organizing impulses.[73] In Shakespeare studies, such doctrines have been fundamental to a gradual move towards historicizing the texts and attempting to situate the plays within the wider discursive contexts in which they were written. John F. Danby's *Shakespeare's Doctrine of Nature: A Study of King Lear* and E. M. Tillyard's *The Elizabethan World Picture* both sought in different and defining ways to understand Shakespeare's work within the Christian intellectual traditions of the late sixteenth and early seventeenth centuries.[74] Similarly, notions

---

[73] The grand epistemologies of nature that come to define thinkers such as Galileo, Bacon, Kepler, and Telesio in the sixteenth and seventeenth centuries are defined by a need to reposition nature as a knowable substance, and one that became subject to scientific and mathematical principles. In the classic study *The Idea of Nature* (Oxford: Clarendon Press, 1945), R. G. Collingwood rehearses the intellectual trajectory from Aristotle to Galileo, tracing the various stages of comprehension through which Nature moved, from a sensory experience, to a godly machine, to a set of independent, though necessarily connected, causes, 1–106.

[74] Danby's discussion of *King Lear* remains unparalleled but he focuses on a high tradition of intellectualism through the works of Hooker, Bacon, and Hobbes, *Shakespeare's Doctrine of Nature: A Study of King Lear* (London: Faber and Faber, 1949). Tillyard's claim for a universal nature is now unfashionable but he nevertheless draws attention to the cosmological traditions through which Elizabethans made sense of their world, *The Elizabethan World Picture* (New York: Vintage, 1959).

of the georgic and the pastoral have been identified in Shakespeare's representation of nature through intertexts and the formative role of Virgil's *Eclogues* and *Georgics* in the grammar school curriculum.[75] While the pastoral and georgic emerge as 'literary' modes of interpretation, imposing specific ideological codes on the representation of the grazed or tilled landscape, I would like to deviate from those belletristic models and reposition Shakespeare's landscapes within a far more urgent conception of agrarian production. This is not to suggest, however, that the pastoral or georgic models are absent from Shakespeare but rather to recognize that the overarching narratives of cultivation are perhaps more informed by the imperatives of daily life than the 'public shorthand' of their classical referents.[76] Within all these conceptions of nature, the natural world has emerged as an intellectual pattern through which the human makes sense of its life. The codes by which that sense is determined radically differ according to providential, classical, or mechanistic perceptions of the world, but they remain consistent as networks of interpretation. This book builds on this body of work. By offering husbandry as a seminal network through which providence morphed into prudence and ethics into equity we can examine the multiple ways in which the human turned its cultivation into its culture.

The rationalization of the landscape through the production of surplus, the loosening of feudal and tenurial obligations, and the creation of waged

---

[75] See Annabel Patterson, *Pastoral and Ideology: From Virgil to Valéry* (Berkeley and Los Angeles: University of California Press, 1987), Margaret Tudeau-Clayton, *Jonson, Shakespeare, and Early Modern Virgil* (Cambridge: Cambridge University Press, 1998), Anthony Low, *The Georgic Revolution* (Princeton: Princeton University Press, 1985), which does not deal with Shakespeare. On the pastoral see Rosalie Colie, *The Oaten Flute: Essays on Pastoral Poetry and the Pastoral Tradition* (Cambridge, Mass.: Harvard University Press, 1975) and Paul Alpers, *What is Pastoral?* (Chicago: University of Chicago Press, 1996).

[76] It is within this context that I do not address the plays more traditionally allied with the pastoral vision. A great deal of important work has been done on *As You Like It*, *The Merry Wives of Windsor*, and *A Midsummer Night's Dream*. The anonymous *Mucedorus* is a further example of literary interest in the pastoral, although the play seems more committed to the forest space as one of licentious fantasy, as suggested by C. L. Barber's classic study, than to any specific allegiances to Thessalonian shepherds. Even within this context, critical enquiry has tended to divide itself into various forms of approach, including feminist, ecocritical, formalism, anthropocentrism, and historicism. In that order, see Jeanne Addison Robert's *The Shakespearean Wild: Geography, Genus, and Gender* (London: University of Nebraska Press, 1991); Karen Raber, 'Recent Ecocritical Studies of English Renaissance Literature', *English Literary Renaissance*, 37/1 (2007); Robert N. Watson, *Back to Nature: The Green and the Real in the Late Renaissance* (Philadelphia: University of Pennsylvania Press, 2006, 2008); C. L. Barber, *Shakespeare's Festive Comedy* (Princeton: Princeton University Press, 1959); Bruce Boehrer, *Shakespeare Among the Animals: Nature and Society in the Drama of Early Modern England* (Basingstoke: Palgrave, 2002); Richard Marienstras, *New Perspectives on the Shakespearean World* (Cambridge: Cambridge University Press, 1985).

labour supported a re-evaluation of the ways in which agronomy defined social values.[77] As Robert Brenner asserts, 'commercial activities... [are] social and political, as well as economic processes', and as Tudor commerce is defined by husbandry, it is an essential part of the social and political context through which individual lives moved.[78] Brenner's work focuses on social reorganization as the agent of economic change, in which he explores the fundamental role class relations have played in the development of the agricultural economy. Revealing the complex ways in which peasants (serfs or villeins) were bound by customary systems of control (financial, laboured, or legal) Brenner demonstrates how these class relations prevented mobility or capital productivity.[79] When these forms of control began to give way, due to demographic changes or changes in land use, serfdom began to decline making way for social mobility as well as developing property rights.[80] In Estienne's advice on the positioning of the country farm he exposes the ways in which mobility, financial gain, and land or property acquisition allowed husbandry to emerge as a form of self-development or advancement: 'to the end that victuals may with the lesse cost be transported thence to other places for your better commoditie sake: as also neere some great good Towne, that so

---

[77] In Robert Brenner's 'The Agrarian Roots of European Capitalism', *Past and Present*, 97 (November 1982) he argues that 'The system-wide consequence of this structure of reproduction [feudalism]—especially given the tendency to long-term demographic increase—was a built in secular trend towards declining productivity of labour and ultimately to large-scale socio-economic crisis,' 17. See also Nicola Whyte, *Inhabiting the Landscape: Place, Custom and Memory, 1500–1700* (New York: Windgather Press, 2009).

[78] Brenner, 'The Social Basis of English Commercial Expansion, 1550–1650', *Journal of Economic History*, 32/1 (March 1972), 362.

[79] Brenner's analysis is largely indebted to Marx's account of primitive accumulation. In *The Poetics of Primitive Accumulation: English Renaissance Culture and the Genealogy of Capital* (Ithaca, NY: Cornell University Press, 1991), Richard Halpern elegantly explores Marx's thesis within this context. Rejecting Adam Smith's representation of 'ethical merits' in industry and thrift, Halpern examines Marx's contention that 'The legend of theological original sin tells us concretely how man came to be condemned to eat his bread in the sweat of his brow; but the history of economic original sin reveals to us that there are people to whom this is by no means essential,' 65. Joyce Appleby, however, maintains that Smith's interpretation of a mercantile economy as dependent upon state intervention is 'as old as the first social organization of human beings'. 'The minute details of economic activity had always been controlled by society through custom and law. It is the differentiation of things economic from their social context that truly distinguishes the writings of the so-called mercantilist period,' *Economic Thought and Ideology*, 26. See also Jean Howard and Scott Cutler Shershow (eds.), *Marxist Shakespeare* (London: Routledge, 2001), particularly the essays by Walter Cohen, 'The Undiscovered Country Shakespeare', 128–58 and Dympna Callaghan, 'Looking Well to Linens', 53–81.

[80] 'Simply stated, it will be our contention that the breakthrough from "traditional economy" to relatively self-sustaining economic development was predicated upon the emergence of a specific set of class relations in the countryside, that is capitalist class relations,' Brenner, *The Poetics of Primitive Accumulation*, 47.

the things of readiest sale may be sold for the best aduancement and making of the most of the reuenues of the same'.[81] Focusing on trade and profit, Estienne suggests that economic considerations instruct the positioning of a 'perfect and exquisite' country house. Yet within the imaginative reconstruction of the commonwealth, husbandry was a determining factor for collective industry and social gain. Within these terms, any threats to the cultivation of the commonwealth could manifest as parasitic or cankerous. In *Richard II*, a play which is deeply invested in the rhetoric of land, Bolingbroke identifies Bushy and Bagot as 'caterpillars of the commonwealth', which he swears to 'weed and pluck away' (*Richard II*, 2.3.165). Representing Bolingbroke as a good husbandman ascertains his moral integrity, particularly in contrast to Richard who has 'leased' England 'Like to a tenement or pelting farm' (2.1.60). The 'shame' which Gaunt locates in 'this dear, dear land' is that of Richard's failed husbandry. Imprudence, debt, and bad management ransom the landscape—as well as its inhabitants—to an insecure future.

Although Estienne focuses on a personal reader, the formal 'you', the ideologies at stake in these manuals tend to refer to a collective for 'the commoditie and benefite of others'.[82] Towards the end of the sixteenth century, however, conflicts between private and public gain began to manifest in the language of the projector. In 1585, a large-scale employer of labour for the production of woad, Robert Payne, writes:

> If we are generally inclined to profit the commonweal as each man is to increase his own private gain, we might well keep continually winter and summer all our poor peoples on work to their great relief and comfort, whereby not only they might be sustained but also their poor young children trained up in some good and honest exercise, and not still to continue to idleness, the nurse of all vices, leading not only unto many mishaps but also to the utter ruin and destruction of themselves and many others.[83]

Articulating an image of an industrious commonwealth, productive, coherent, and utilitarian, Payne absorbs the language of Christian morality into the developing terms of capitalism. Idleness and vice are reduced through labour, which in turn produces relief and comfort. Alerting us to the presence of a new workforce, women and children, Payne's comment points to an emerging class of labour in which production preserved people from 'utter ruin and destruction'. Exploring the development of

---

[81] *The Countrey Farme* (1616), 5.
[82] Googe's preface to Heresbach's *Foure Bookes of Husbandrie*, 2.
[83] As quoted in Joan Thirsk, *Economic Policy and Projects: The Development of a Consumer Society in Early Modern England* (Oxford: Clarendon Press, 1978), 19.

the agrarian economy in this period allows us to reassess the values through which social virtue was developed.[84]

In Shakespeare's works, the language of cultivation and economic endeavour supports a discursive ethical fabric through which questions of subjectivity, responsibility, and obligation move. Central to these images is the relationship between morality and selfhood, in which the subject is fashioned according to his or her status within a common discourse of socially acceptable goals.[85] According to Charles Taylor's exploration of 'selfhood', discipline emerges as one of the key factors in the formation of the human subject, or 'The...ideal of a human agent who is able to remake himself by methodical and disciplined action.'[86] Husbandry is one such form of discipline: mediated through classical, biblical, and humanist texts the labour of the earth becomes the formative expression not only of human dominion over nature but also of its transformation. For Heresbach, husbandry is a method of training—from the child to the 'master's prize':

wherin a man must from his very Chyldehood be brought vp: and surely it is meete that ye husband, or Bayliffe, haue ben brought vp, or trayned in all these trades, and to come by degrees to his maisters pryze.[87]

Elaborating on his image, Heresbach explains:

And most true it proueth in this that commeth to passe in all other gouernmentes, that such are best able to take charge of gouernment, that passing by degrees and offices, haue from being vnder gouernment, come to gouerne them selues.

Authority is determined by a history of service, of experience, and of exposure to the very systems of control through which the self emerges as

---

[84] This is a notorious issue within the context of Marxism and the reproduction of certain values within the terms of accumulation and capital. My project here, however, is not to intercede in this debate but to attend to the ways in which these values emerged and why certain ethical credence was given to investment and thrift within the context of England's social and moral economy. For recent discussion of this debate within the context of Shakespeare, see de Grazia, *Hamlet without Hamlet* and Halpern, *The Poetics of Primitive Accumulation*, Gabriel Egan, *Shakespeare and Marx* (Oxford: Oxford University Press, 2004), Jean E. Howard and Marion F. O'Connor (eds.), *Shakespeare Reproduced* (London: Methuen, 1987), Jean E. Howard and Scott Cutler Shershow, *Marxist Shakespeare* (London: Routledge, 2001).

[85] Joyce Oldham Appleby observes the construction of these goals as central to the economic developments that took place in the seventeenth century: 'only if the pursuit of unlimited profit becomes a socially acceptable goal can the market exercise the pervasive influence attributed to it. Once properly tuned to a new social ethic, however, the market can become a powerful instrument for change,' *Economic Thought and Ideology*, 16.

[86] *Sources of the Self: The Making of Modern Identity* (Cambridge: Cambridge University Press, 1989), 159.

[87] 153^r.

autonomous. As Iago suggested, the government of oneself requires careful cultivation.

As this introduction has established, husbandry manuals wrote way beyond the boundaries of agronomy and into the very codes and values of human life. Through their Christian legacy, these texts imported a comprehensive image of social welfare in which morality was distinctly bound to labour, productivity, and reward.[88] The production of cereal crops, malt, wool, and meat charted the survival not only of the individual but also of the visible communities through which they had formed codes of belonging. Explaining why, for the Tudors, food production was a social endeavour rather than an exclusively economic one, Joyce Appleby writes:

> Grain was not seen as a commodity to be moved through the countryside in search of the best price, nor was it ever absolutely possessed by the producer. The farmer who grew it—be he tenant or landlord—did not really own the corn; he attended it during its passage from the field to the market.[89]

Within these terms we can begin to see how production and reproduction become ethical transactions between the land, the individual, and the communities through which the product passes.[90] Withholding, storing, or engrating (hoarding grain to sell it at a higher price during periods of scarcity) are forms of sin: they register greed and disenfranchisement as well as a profound hiatus in the productive relationships of human beings. The acute state interest in the restitution of tillage after intense periods of dearth and famine exposes Elizabeth's reactionary investment in the land as a site of social welfare.[91] The controversial 'Act against the decaying of houses of husbandry' and 'An Act for the Maintenance of Husbandry and Tillage' (1597–8) explicitly identified the future and security of the

---

[88] In *The Ends of Life: Roads to Fulfilment in Early Modern England* (Oxford: Oxford University Press, 2009), Keith Thomas discusses the shifting representations of work in this period and the ways in which labour came to be re-appropriated as a force for development rather than as an image of service. Cf. Tom Rutter, *Work and Play on the Shakespearean Stage* (Cambridge: Cambridge University Press, 2008).

[89] Appleby, *Economic Thought and Ideology*, 28.

[90] As both anthropologists and historical geographers have observed, land provides the fundamental space through which the human builds and develops his or her community. Habitation, drainage, and agricultural land are the three main factors in the development of both human life and its civilization, which, as Cosgrove explains, 'involve fundamental reorganisation of society's relationship with the environment and resources', *Social Formation and Symbolic Landscape*, 5. See particularly H. C. Darby, 'The Changing Historical Landscape', *Geographical Journal*, 117 (1951), 377–98; and Cosgrove, *Social Formation and Symbolic Landscape*.

[91] As Appleby explains: 'There was no truly economic Tudor legislation, for statesmen did not then distinguish the grain trade from the social cycle of harvesting, marketing, and feeding,' *Economic Thought and Ideology*, 30.

kingdom as dependent upon cultivation: 'the said husbandry and tillage is a cause that the realm doth more stand upon itself'.[92]

As this book will explore, however, the social imperatives of Tudor policy gave way to a relatively more economic model of analysis under James I. England moved from the periphery of a Mediterranean-based trade route to the centre of an Atlantic trade route, in which the nobility were extremely instrumental in the reshaping of the economy.[93] To this end, the social policies of the sixteenth century were 'badly shaken' and the new market economy emerged as a 'complicated, new social organization, which could not be understood without attention being paid to its particularities.... Unlike the great public institutions of church and state it had not been shaped by central authority but rather through informal initiative.'[94] Attitudes to cultivation expose the shaping of cultural identities: partly through their reconstruction of the land itself and partly through their mobile discourses which range through common tradition, morality, and social welfare to individual initiatives and private industry. The 'plurality of images' through which the land is represented requires our attention.[95]

Husbandry supports a network of such images and, as this book will argue, a fundamental aspect of Elizabethan and Jacobean culture (and cultivation).

'where my land and living lies (*The Winter's Tale*)'

As I hope to have suggested, husbandry was fundamental to Elizabethan life: a practical method of production, a social record of community values and economic welfare, and a moral discourse of righteousness, images of husbandry permeated all forms of literature, as well as government debates. Perhaps more than any other playwright of his cohort, Shakespeare attends to cultivation as a discourse of value.[96] As an indication of injustice,

---

[92] 39 & 40 Elizabeth Cap. II.

[93] I am paraphrasing Appleby, *Economic Thought and Ideology*, 31.

[94] Appleby, *Economic Thought and Ideology*, 34–5. Christopher Dyer, however, in *The Age of Transition* (Oxford: Clarendon Press, 2005), argues that many elements of this new economy had been in place since the fourteenth century. Citing examples of peasant consumption, regional mobility, profit, and surplus, Dyer identifies the existence of a nascent capital economy well before most historians concede it. Exploring Dyer's data, however, these instances remain relatively sporadic and parochial. Without the forms of rationalization enabled by print, foreign trade, and the breakdown of feudal ties, any such developments are necessarily fragmented.

[95] As McRae writes: 'The representation of the land in the early modern period requires interpretation. Confronted by the rich plurality of images and arguments, one must attend to "the processes by which meaning is constructed" in earlier periods,' *God Speed the Plough*, 3. Here McRae is quoting Roger Chartier.

[96] A number of biographers have understood Shakespeare as a 'rural' figure, somebody who 'was our first great literary commuter' (Stanley Wells, *Shakespeare for All Time*

a vision of peace, an image of futurity, or a record of failure, husbandry persistently emerges as a lucid language for the representation and interpretation of the relationships between nature and culture; the individual and the social. Precisely occupying the space between these opaque terms, husbandry is the point at which art becomes nature and nature becomes art. Tracing this relationship allows us a unique glimpse into the beginnings of a system that would redefine English conceptions of improvement, civility, and worth: 'For where is she so fair whose unear'd womb | Disdains the tillage of thy husbandry' (sonnet 3, lines 5–6).

Beginning with Shakespeare's Sonnets, I explore the poetic range of images of husbandry from tillage, harvest, store, reap, yield, and reproduction. Exploring the ways in which these terms propose figures of worth, I read a selection of the sonnets through the conditions of value upon which such images depend. Moving through the social expectations of reproduction to the values of futurity, I suggest that the language of husbandry presents a complex network of social approbation in which the subject is required to take part in a set of collective values upon which the future of the poetic voice depends. Chapter 2 follows the development of these images within the poetic imagination. Attending to the ways in which they emerge as moral markers of both creativity and futurity, this chapter establishes the ways in which the Christian humanist tradition of investment and duty fed into a quotidian language of production and reward. Central to this chapter is a decentring of the idea of a unique beloved through the poet-speaker's application to shared convictions of worth.

Following a chronological structure, in order to reflect on the cultural relationship between cultivation and social politics, Chapter 3 focuses on

(London: Macmillan, 2002), 37) between London and Stratford, and as rooted in a specific way of life, 'deep in the shires' (Jonathan Bate, 'The Humanist Tempest', in *Shakespeare La Tempête: Études critiques, Acts du colloque de Besançon* (1993), 35). Graham Holderness's *Nine Lives of William Shakespeare* (London: Continuum, 2011), however, wittily exposes the biographer's subjective involvement in such portraits, tracing their own lives onto the scanty documentary evidence of Shakespeare's life, 2–32. As is commonly known, Ben Jonson tends to pursue social discourses through the language of mercantilism; Christopher Marlowe more usually invokes the pastoral; and John Fletcher, Thomas Middleton, and Thomas Dekker employ a synthesis of the two. Perhaps the most curious figure is Thomas Nashe, whose *Summer's Last Will and Testament* dramatizes the agricultural year as a contest of duty, failure, and legacy. As Summer stands in the middle of the year, dying, she puts the rest of the seasons on trial to see who is fittest to be her successor. Strangely punitive and cynical, Summer calls forms of husbandry to account in her trial of both the seasons and their import: 'Harvest, hear what complaints are brought to me. | Thou art accused by the public voice,' *The Unfortunate Traveller and Other Works*, ed. J. B. Steane (Harmondsworth: Penguin, 1972), 172. Particularly curious, however, is Summer's valediction which directly mirrors the structure and language of Richard II's self-deposition.

Shakespeare's *Henry V*. Frequently discussed through the historical perspectives of both war and nationhood, *Henry V* has often been read as part of Shakespeare's theatrical investment in 'a feeling of national awareness, even of national identity, among Englishmen at a time when their nation was emerging as a great power'.[97]

The land, as both Richard Helgerson and Garrett Sullivan has shown, forms a fundamental part of this discourse.[98] Yet while most scholars turn their attention to the politics of Henry's war, this chapter focuses on the politics of his peace: a peace which the Duke of Burgundy defines as cultivation itself: 'Dear nurse of arts, plenties and joyful births.' Echoing the classical justifications of husbandry, Burgundy establishes the necessity of good husbandry to the future of France, invoking a highly politicized language of security, morality, and sustainability. Possibly excised from the first printed quarto (1600) and put into the mouth of the opponent, these scenes offer us a vivid discourse on the nature of good government, and the politics of improvement.

The first section of the book may be loosely themed under the heading of selfhood, concerned as it is with the role of cultivation in the evaluation and expression of a socialized—not individualized—subjectivity. Drawing the individual—be it Henry or the poetic subject of the Sonnets—into a discourse of responsibility, husbandry provides an extended discourse on the nature (quite literally) of investment and reward, ethics and obligation.

The fourth chapter marks a shift towards the problems of cultivation as culture—its complex adhesion to competing interpretations of nature and the challenges we face in trying to distinguish between the two. Focusing on *Macbeth*, this chapter approaches the subject of culture through the play's representations of the boundaries between the human and non-human worlds. Understanding cultivation as a form of human intervention, Chapter 4 examines the role of human interference in a putatively natural world. Tracing the implications that such intervention has for the existence of moral binaries, this chapter highlights an idea of essentialized nature in the creation of social codes. Invoking nature as a form of oppression the Macbeths seek to explode a set of apparently fixed conditions as the key to both their ambitions and their liberation. Drawing on nature as a biological determinant, a military strategy, and a providential sign, human intervention appears as both the salvation and destruction of

---

[97] Philip Edwards, *Threshold of a Nation: A Study in English and Irish Drama* (Cambridge: Cambridge University Press, 1979), 113.

[98] Garrett Sullivan Jr, *The Drama of Landscape: Land, Property and Social Relations on the Early Modern Stage* (Stanford, Calif.: Stanford University Press, 1998). Helgerson, *Forms of Nationhood*, 25–39.

the play's moral vision. Having established the apparently essential bonds between social morality and the cultivation of land, Macbeth seeks to explode them in order to 'stop up the access and passage to remorse' and break free of the bonds that have simultaneously created and bounded our human world.

The last section of the book focuses on two of Shakespeare's late plays within the context of the changing conditions of the seventeenth-century rural economy. Bringing *The Winter's Tale* into dialogue with Jacobean trade initiatives, this chapter attempts to reread the action of Bohemia within the context of its vibrant engagement with the *cost* of truth. In a play that fetishizes truth, the cost, emotional, ethical, and economic, is always under discussion. Focusing on the role of Autolycus within the putatively 'pastoral scene' of the sheep-shearing feast, Chapter 5 identifies the role of consumerism in the construction of fantasy. In this chapter, I suggest, economic mobility supports a new discourse of illusion in which everything—even truth—is commoditized. Ending with Shakespeare's last single-authored play, *The Tempest*, Chapter 6 reads the most insistently 'colonialist' of Shakespeare's plays within the context of its lack of cultivation. Examining the play's illusory landscapes, those of the masque and Gonzalo's plantation, this chapter analyses the role of cultivation in the construction of both ceremony and institution. Showing how husbandry forms the interface between nature and culture, this chapter exposes cultivation as the highest form of human art: the point at which the art itself is nature and nature itself is natural. As the husbandman is the 'master of the earth' and Prospero the 'master of a full poor cell', this last chapter looks at the relationship between the primal magic of 'collective human transformation' as it is mediated through illusion.

Conditioning the human subject to accept his or her dominion over the natural world as simultaneously unique and innate has supported a gradual development of social values. In these values, culture has emerged as the dominant, superlative force in which human singularity has found a model of both approval and ambition within the natural world. If culture is belonging then that sense of belonging has been constructed through an image of nature in which the human is both sympathetic and alienated. Within these terms, to be under-developed, or even developing, is to be without the mechanisms and structure for economic progression and social stability.[99] Central to narratives of progress is the suppression of those communities 'that inconvenience or disturb the implied trajectory of

---

[99] In *The Ethics of Development*, Des Gasper explores how the term 'development' has becomes so enmeshed in the politics of vindication and motivation that the value terms we adopt in its use have become hidden (Edinburgh: Edinburgh University Press, 2005), 24–7.

unified national ascent'.[100] Such narratives of national ascent underpin the history of cultivation as they emerge through logics of progression and improvement. It is my contention in this book that the sixteenth century marked a decisive point in the shift from nature to culture and that this shift was dependent upon an increasingly articulate investment in the language of cultivation.[101]

This is not to suggest, however, that all discourses of cultivation are presented as progressive: on the contrary, as improvement, enclosures, and projects intervened between the human and their moral landscapes, husbandry became a provocative discourse for the betrayal of commonality.[102] Preaching a sermon at Faversham, Tuke refers to the 'corrupt and vicious times', in which 'Couetousnesse is counted good husbandrie.'[103] Identifying the mutation of thrift into accumulation, Tuke refers to the ways in which we continue to read this image of virtue despite its change of status.[104]

Until recently, however, discussions of early modern perceptions of nature have remained relatively free of the concepts of environmentalism. Viewed as inherently progressive, enlightened, and rational, narratives of cultivation appeared to take little account of questions of sustainability, renewable resources, and the fragile balance of the ecosystem.[105] Recent ecocriticism, however, has drawn attention to the existence of such concerns in the early modern period and provided a critical methodology which crosses 'the boundaries of literary and cultural studies, to draw in politics, philosophy and ecology'.[106] While we can trace contemporary

---

[100] Rob Nixon, *Slow Violence and the Environmentalism of the Poor* (Cambridge, Mass.: Harvard University Press, 2011), 150.

[101] As Kate Soper warns, however, looking at the history of these semantics we must necessarily 'assume that we are talking of the relations of Western humanity to nature, rather than humanity in general', *What is Nature? Culture, Politics and the Non-human* (Oxford: Blackwell, 1995), 61.

[102] Paul Warde explains, however, the term was not exclusive to agronomy but emerged as 'a metaphor for betterment in all walks of life', 'The Idea of Improvement, *c*.1520–1700', in Richard W. Hoyle (ed.), *Custom, Improvement and the Landscape in Early Modern Britain* (Farnham: Ashgate, 2011), 128.

[103] Thomas Tuke, *The True Trial and turning of a sinner* (1607), C2ʳ.

[104] The relationship between covetousness and husbandry, however, was not uncontentious. Frequently allied with enclosures, improvement, and fundamentalist religious discourses, covetousness could masquerade as good husbandry, particularly under the guise of development. McRae is especially eloquent on this subject in *God Speed the Plough*, see 23–57, 71–2, 75–6, 169–70.

[105] Arthur Standish's *The Commons Complaint* (1611) is unique in this regard as it addresses the depletion of natural resources, especially those of wood. I discuss this text in the Conclusion.

[106] Gabriel Egan, *Green Shakespeare: From Ecopolitics to Ecocriticism* (London: Routledge, 2006), i. See also Lynne Bruckner and Dan Brayton (eds.), *Ecocritical Shakespeare* (Farnham: Ashgate, 2011).

anxieties on the status of woodlands, mineral resources, and land use they do not, as yet, emerge as fully formed environmental debates.[107] Shakespeare's lifetime, however, witnessed an extraordinary growth in the discourses of cultivation: moving from the relatively reactionary social policies of Elizabeth's government to the development of economic models of analysis under James I, discourses of husbandry extended way beyond the boundaries of social status and into questions of economic growth, scientific development, and national stability.

'His land's put to their books (*Timon of Athens*)'

Finally, we need to ask what is the direct relationship, if any, between Shakespeare and the husbandry manuals discussed in this book. The question as to what Shakespeare did or did not read is perennially fascinating to scholars since it might provide a glimpse into the methods of the writer and the resources he valued. Stanley Wells, for example, imagined Shakespeare in New Place, which, he speculated, 'contained a comfortable, book-lined study situated in the quietest part of the house'.[108] I might also speculate that Thomas Tusser, Gervase Markham, and John Fitzherbert appeared in that book-lined study—but I have no idea. What I hope to show, however, is that whether read directly, imbibed in sermons, absorbed into humanist writings, or put together from the ballads of London pedlars, the ideologies of the husbandry manual were suffused into Elizabethan culture. Alongside the role of these images in the imaginative reconstruction of Elizabethan values, however, there are brief fragments and allusions that appear to offer us a direct relationship between the manual and playwright.

In Tusser's *Five Hundred Points of Good Husbandry*, he provides the reader with certain precepts as a 'Ladder to Thrift':

> To answer stranger civilie,
> But shew him not thy secresie.
> To use no friend deceitfully,
> To offer no man villeny.
> To learne how foe to pacifie,
> But trust him not too trustilie
> To keepe thy touch substanciallie,
> And in thy word use constancie.

[107] Standish, *The Commons Complaint*, Paul Warde, *Energy Consumption in England and Wales, 1560–2000* (Rome: Instituto di Studio sulle Società del Mediterraneo, 2007), and Paul Slack, *From Reformation to Improvement: Public Welfare in Early Modern England* (Oxford: Clarendon Press, 1997). I explore this further in the Conclusion.
[108] Wells, *Shakespeare for All Time*, 37.

To make thy bandes advisedly,
&Com not bound through surety.[109]

Tusser's precepts to good living are reflected with startling similarity by Polonius in his advice to Laertes before he leaves for France:

Those friends thou hast, and their adoption tried,
Grapple them to thy soul with hoops of steel;
But do not dull thy palm with entertainment
Of each new-hatch'd, unfledged comrade. Beware
Of entrance to a quarrel, but being in,
Bear't that the opposed may beware of thee.
Give every man thy ear, but few thy voice;
Take each man's censure, but reserve thy judgment.
Costly thy habit as thy purse can buy,
But not express'd in fancy; rich, not gaudy;
For the apparel oft proclaims the man,
And they in France of the best rank and station
Are of a most select and generous chief in that.
Neither a borrower nor a lender be;
For loan oft loses both itself and friend,
And borrowing dulls the edge of husbandry. (*Hamlet*, 1.3.62–77)[110]

Polonius' 'husbandry' appears to emerge from the pages of Tusser, fully formed into an extraordinarily perceptive language of human behaviour. It is to this language of human behaviour that the book attends. These semantic relationships are governed by a narrative of cultivation, in which human intervention in the natural world changes the terms of social living. From a paradigmatically Christian heritage of the earth as 'God's book', to an economic imperative towards exploitation and industry, human attitudes to cultivation bespeak a far wider discourse of social relations. How we live by, exploit, manage, create, and sustain the natural world becomes the foremost doctrine of our social selves.

---

[109] Chapter 9, 13.
[110] Steven Doloff observed the similarities, in 'Polonius's Precepts and Thomas Tusser's Five Hundred Points of Good Husbandrie', *Review of English Studies*, 42/146 (May 1991), 227–8.

2

The Sonnets, Early Modern Husbandry Manuals, and the Cultivation of Value

Shakespeare's sonnet 116 is probably the most quoted sonnet of the collection. Used in anthologies of love, marriage services, valentine's cards, and romantic missives everywhere, 'Let me not to the marriage of true minds' expresses a love that is enduring, unconditional, and unbreakable, and, at least in the popular imagination, encapsulates a particular perception of the Sonnets as romantic. Central to this image is the statement that

> Love's not Time's fool, though rosy lips and cheeks
> Within his bending sickle's compass come;
> Love alters not with his brief hours and weeks
> But bears it out even to the edge of doom. (116, ll. 9–12)

Invoking the traditional image of Time, armed with a sickle or scythe, ready to cut down human life, the sonnet suggests a love that can outlast this process of mortal cultivation: a love that can outlast life—even Time itself.[1] The image of the sickle, however, belongs to another discourse within the Sonnets: a discourse of husbandry that seeks to explore the expectations of love as they are harvested, stored, destroyed, or wasted. In a literary climate fascinated by the nature of metamorphosis and mutability, husbandry provides a discourse for both the study and expression of change. What makes this more powerful, however, is the status of the human as the agent of change. As the interactive body between the social and natural worlds the human supports and creates the terms and values under which such metamorphoses become productive. The Sonnets, concerned with forms of production in creativity and creation, imagine the speaker in various positions, whether in fantasy or anticipation, of intervention. Much of the language of change is predicated on the terms

---

[1] As Michael Schoenfeldt writes, this sonnet, and the equally familiar sonnet 18, are 'among the most famous descriptions of the tenderness and authenticity which love is capable of producing', *A Companion to Shakespeare's Sonnets* (Oxford: Blackwell, 2007), 4.

through which agrarian husbandry describes forms of production and the ethical and economic imperatives they invoke.

In sonnet 116, however, the human body is the matter of cultivation, as Time, the constant gardener, represents the irrepressible cycle of production and decay. While rosy lips and cheeks will fall under Time's sickle, love, the unquantifiable narrative of the Sonnets, will remain; perfect, whole, and entirely exempt from the processes of birth and decay that govern human life. Juxtaposing the contingent and the eternal, the speaker invokes Time's harvesting as a form of alteration from which love is exempt: 'Love alters not with his brief hours and weeks, | But bears it out even to the edge of doom.' Beyond the cultivation of human life, devotion remains contained in the lines that describe it. The prolific life of this sonnet through the imaginations of generations of lovers testifies to the poet's truth. Set against the arch-cultivator, Time, love stands as the fantasy of perfect form and human remains: or as Philip Larkin put it in the twentieth century: 'What will survive of us is love.'[2] The discourse of cultivation to which Time belongs touches on the endless cycles of production to which the human is bound. While in sonnet 116, however, those processes control the speaker, in many of the sonnets the speaker controls them.

Throughout the collection, I shall suggest, Shakespeare draws on the culture of cultivation as a means of expressing the very terms of love and creativity he seeks to interrogate. In search of human remains—child, poem, or transcendental love—discourses of husbandry provide an extensive language for the exploration of that which can be stored, invested, or produced. Deeply embedded in a culture in which 'good husbandry' represented an economic as well as an ethical ideal, the language of cultivation belongs to a valuable discourse of social expectation. In the Sonnets, Shakespeare draws on this discourse for the exposition of legacy and the value—sometimes quite literally—of human investment.

The fascination with Shakespeare's Sonnets is partly informed by their range of human emotion, anxiety about sexual orientations, and the opacity of the speaker's subjectivity, as well as the object's identity.[3] Since

---

[2] 'An Arundel Tomb'.

[3] Criticism of Shakespeare's Sonnets is a vast subject and the best criticism, including editorial discussions, includes Stephen Booth, *Shakespeare's Sonnets* (New Haven: Yale University Press, 2000), Dympna Callaghan, *Shakespeare's Sonnets* (Oxford: Blackwell, 2007), Patrick Cheney, *The Cambridge Companion to Shakespeare's Poetry* (Cambridge: Cambridge University Press, 2007), Joel Fineman, *Shakespeare's Perjured Eye: The Invention of Poetic Subjectivity in the Sonnets* (Berkeley and Los Angeles: University of California Press, 1986), Joseph Pequigney, *Such is my Love: A Study of Shakespeare's Sonnets* (Chicago: University of Chicago Press, 1985), John Crowe Ransom, 'Shakespeare at Sonnets', *Southern Review*, 3 (1937–8), 531–53, J. M. Robertson, *The Problems of the Shakespeare Sonnets* (London: George Routledge, 1926), Adena Rosmarin, 'Hermeneutics versus

the language of husbandry is critically informed by images of production, submission, and intervention it is a provocative place to explore both erotic and social relations.[4] Critical work has identified the importance of images of husbandry within the first eighteen sonnets. Thomas Greene's influential essay 'Pitiful Thrivers' argues that husbandry is the 'semantic node' through which Shakespeare's Sonnets explore complex questions of value, creativity, and posterity. Throughout the collection of the Sonnets, he observes the 'poet's obsessive concern with metaphorical wealth, profit, worth, value, expense, "store," [and] "content"'.[5] Examining clusters of such images the essay demonstrates how the language of husbandry provides a dense network of quantitative terms through which the poet confronts his friend, self, dark lady, or patron with anxieties of dearth and fulfilment, recompense and futurity. For Greene, the semantics of husbandry import an economic value system through which the poet can measure his love, success, legacy, and failures in which 'thriving' is the desired objective: 'To compose poetry is expensive, just as loving is expensive, and the unformulated implication of the work as a whole seems to be that expense is never truly recuperated.'[6] Within these terms husbandry provides access to an emotional economy through which terms of profit or loss can be generated: powerfully determined

Erotics: Shakespeare Sonnets and Interpretive History', *PMLA* 100 (1985), 20–37, Eve Kosofsky Sedgwick, *Between Men: English Literature and Male Homosocial Desire* (New York: Columbia University Press, 1985), James Schiffer, *Shakespeare's Sonnets: Critical Essays* (London: Routledge, 1999), Michael Schoenfeldt, *The Cambridge Introduction to Shakespeare's Poetry* (Cambridge: Cambridge University Press, 2010), Michael Schoenfeldt, *A Companion to Shakespeare's Sonnets* (Oxford: Blackwell, 2010), Helen Vendler, *The Art of Shakespeare's Sonnets* (Cambridge, Mass.: Harvard University Press, 1997), Stanley Wells and Paul Edmonson, *Shakespeare's Sonnets* (Oxford: Oxford University Press, 2004), George T. Wright, *Shakespeare's Metrical Art* (Berkeley and Los Angeles: University of California Press, 1988).

[4] On this point see particularly, Heather Dubrow, *English Petrarchanism and Its Counter-discourses* (Ithaca, NY: Cornell University Press, 1995), Bruce Smith, *Homosexual Desire in Shakespeare's England: A Cultural Poetics* (Chicago: University of Chicago Press, 1991), Margreta de Grazia, 'The Scandal of Shakespeare's Sonnets', *Shakespeare Survey*, 46 (1994), 35–49. The relationship between the domestic economy and women has been explored by Wendy Wall, *Staging Domesticity* (Cambridge: Cambridge University Press, 2002), Natasha Korda, *Shakespeare's Domestic Economies* (Philadelphia: University of Pennsylvania Press, 2002), and Laura Gowing, *Domestic Dangers* (Oxford: Oxford University Press, 1996). Within the context of the husbandry manuals, however, although almost all manuals included a section for 'huswifes', including Fitzherbert, Tusser, and Markham, it is Gervase Markham who makes a defined space for women as he not only demarcates their roles as specific and valuable but he also gives them traditionally male roles, suggesting a certain, albeit relative, equality within the household. I explore this issue fully in my chapter on *Macbeth*.

[5] Thomas Greene, ' "Pitiful Thrivers": Failed Husbandry in the Sonnets', in Patricia Parker and Geoffrey Hartman (eds.), *Shakespeare and the Question of Theory* (New York: Methuen, 1985), 231.

[6] Greene, ' "Pitiful Thrivers" ', 241.

by Christian morality, human intervention, food production, and the manifest realities of the creative world, sixteenth- and seventeenth-century discourses of husbandry extended way beyond the terms of rural cultivation.[7] This is a language that seeks to evaluate even as it describes; that anticipates a product even as it invests; and that accords significance to the dynamic between the human and its habitable worlds. In Shakespeare's Sonnets we encounter the terms of husbandry through an insistent narrative of production. Fretted through images of love, desire, creativity, or reproduction the poet employs the language of cultivation as a discursive shorthand for the exposition of value.

By bringing the Sonnets into a clearer dialogue with the husbandry manuals of the sixteenth century, however, this chapter will suggest that the terms through which Shakespeare mediates his language of desire disclose a vital discourse of both ambition and appreciation. The complex terms of production through which the Elizabethans had come to recognize moral and material value rest on a vast network of human action. In this way the child, the future, the poem, or the self all come to reside in images of legacy: and it is to these images that the poet-speaker defers as markers of value. By invoking cultivation as a model of human interference the poems repeatedly question the means by which humans make sense of themselves in relation to others.[8] Fraught with abstract images of value—economic, moral, personal, and social—the pragmatic terms of husbandry collide with the affective landscapes of emotion to produce an ongoing dialogue between the speaker and the subject in which the putative objectives of action—child, poem, consummation, or recognition—are always in a process of definition.[9] How, the Sonnets appear to ask, does the self become both fulfilled by and assimilated into a collective discourse of worth? In this way, I am deviating from recent criticism, which reads the Sonnets as explorations in an emergent subjectivity. Such questions of worth, however, belong steadfastly to images of the collective

---

[7] George T. Wright, one of the most enduring writers on Shakespeare's poetic metre, uses cultivation and the landscape as a metaphor for the writer's art: the 'text changes metrical modes (or shifts to prose) as a landscape changes, not whimsically but in response to pressures', 'Troubles of a Professional Meter Reader', in Russ McDonald (ed.), *Shakespeare Reread: The Texts in New Contexts* (Ithaca, NY: Cornell University Press, 1994), 75.

[8] In *Shakespeare, Rhetoric and Cognition* (Cambridge: Cambridge University Press, 2011), Raphael Lyne observes the heuristic nature of the Sonnets and the 'conjunctions between speech and thought'. Lyne's interpretative model is very helpful within the context of this chapter as he seeks to explore the 'metaphorical texture' of the poems through heightened attention to the ways in which image networks support or disclose patterns of thought, 198–225.

[9] See David Schalkwyk, 'Is Love an Emotion: Shakespeare's *Twelfth Night* and *Antony and Cleopatra*', *Symplokē*, 18 (2010), 99–130.

and are deeply rooted in a dialogue between value and cost, investment and productivity. For the Elizabethans, husbandry provided a model through which they could affect as well as interpret their world.

Beginning with a selection of the early sonnets, the so-called procreation sonnets—and the ways in which the logic of cultivation determines the speaker's attitude to (re)production and profit—I will examine the use of agrarian metaphors. Focusing on these sonnets' construction of value, and the terms of social appreciation and moral censure through which they move, I will situate their concern with reproduction within the context of Elizabethan attitudes to both productivity and a commonwealth. Arguing against W. H. Auden's 'single person . . . of infinite sacred importance', I will suggest that the Sonnets' images of value are dependent on a coherent structure of consensual duty to which the beloved is bound, both morally and economically.[10]

While the first eighteen sonnets are explicit in their emphasis on models of production and the value of the reproducibility of the young man, the rest of the sequence reinvents terms of cultivation through a persistent enquiry into the nature—both human and metaphysical—of creativity. Reading the modulation of the language of husbandry in the Sonnets leads me to identify the sequence as the product of some kind of structural logic, based on how the language of husbandry develops and disperses across the poems. There is a certain figurative narrative to the development of the images of increase or productivity within the early sonnets: throughout the rest of the sequence, however, these images return in more diffuse, playful, or speculative ways that appear to coincide with an unhingeing of these terms from their specifically, or rigidly, Christian heritage.[11] Increasingly concerned with questions of value—social, economic, sexual, or

<hr>

[10] In *Reading Sixteenth Century Poetry* (Oxford: Wiley-Blackwell, 2011), Patrick Cheney discusses the 'mystical revelation about the emotion of desire as an eternizing experience, which Auden distinguishes from our ordinary desire for a particular sexual being within a social setting', 272. In *Bodies and Selves in Early Modern England*, Michael Schoenfeldt suggests that this vocabulary of psychological inwardness', (Cambridge: Cambridge University Press, 1999), 75. For Schoenfeldt, this vocabulary is dependent upon a contained self—or 'care of the self'—in which the subject responds to forms of self-discipline inherently regarded as social.

[11] Although there is still some debate as to Shakespeare's role in the ordering of the 1609 quarto's sonnet sequence, there is no doubt that there is some structural logic here, authorial or not. Katherine Duncan-Jones, *Shakespeare's Sonnets* (London: Thomas Nelson, 1997) and John Kerrigan, *The Sonnets and A Lover's Complaint* (Harmondsworth: Penguin, 1986); both support the sonnet sequence as authorial, Stephen Booth, however, suggests that 'we have no strong reason to assume the 1609 order to be the order of their writing or the order in which Shakespeare would have wanted them read', 545. Colin Burrow, on the other hand, suggests that the dark lady sonnets were written before the sonnets to the young man, *The Complete Poems and Sonnets of Shakespeare* (Oxford: Oxford University Press, 2004), 134.

creative—the Sonnets expose the multiple ways in which husbandry directs and informs Shakespeare's poetics of worth.

Dependent on processes of investment, intervention, productivity, and utility, ideas of cultivation inform almost every aspect of our human lives. Although husbandry is rooted in the representation of the landscape, animal and crop management, as well as horticulture, it defines a set of human and non-human relationships prescribed by the conditions in which organic life has both survived and developed. As James Turner writes: 'Landscape is an instrument of thought', and, as such, the ways in which humans intervene in that landscape reveal an act of interpretation, as well as cognition.[12] In this context, husbandry articulates an apparently universal language of profit and management in which certain values—economic and social—underpin, as well as express, human relations.

The sheer ubiquity of the language of cultivation reveals the extent to which agrarian economics not only supported an interpretation of human welfare but the political and social ideals through which images of welfare could move. Unlike many of his contemporaries, Shakespeare does not create landscapes, or even landskips, within the Sonnets: he does not use rural images as a way of constructing independent spaces of alterity.[13] Nor does he, like Marlowe or Jonson, invoke the countryside as an ideological antithesis to the court.[14] Although Shakespeare's drama uses the natural world as a theatrical space, in the Sonnets the natural images tend to adhere to figurative structures predominantly associated with Time, and its incumbent relationship to mortality. The language of husbandry, however, occupies an apparently different space within the imaginative

---

[12] *The Politics of Landscape*, 36. Garrett Sullivan, in *The Drama of Landscape*, similarly discusses the ways in which the land facilitates social identity. Within the field of cultural geography, Denis Cosgrove has written extensively on the subject: see particularly *Social Formation and Symbolic Landscape* and Cosgrove and Stephen Daniels (eds.), *The Iconography of Landscape* (Cambridge: Cambridge University Press, 1988).

[13] On the distinction between landscape and landskip, as well as the, as yet, unformed notion of landscape in early modern interpretations of the countryside see Walsham, *The Reformation of the Landscape*, 6–7. Sullivan, *The Drama of Landscape*, 2–7.

[14] The court/country relationship is, of course, invoked within the drama, most notably *As You Like It* and *The Merry Wives of Windsor*. Jonson's 'To Penshurst' is an exemplary instance of the ways in which the rural landscape was used ideologically by early modern poets, as is Marvell's 'Upon Appleton House'; Marlowe's 'Passionate Shepherd to his Love', on the other hand, imagines pastoral life as an idealized refuge for desire as well as devotion. The nature of the country in Renaissance poetry has been explored by many illustrious scholars, not least of all William Empson, *Some Versions of Pastoral* (New York: New Directions, 1974), Raymond Williams, *The Country and the City* (Oxford: Oxford University Press, 1973, 1975), James Turner, *The Politics of Landscape* (Cambridge, Mass.: Harvard University Press, 1979), Low, *The Georgic Revolution*, and Watson, *Back to Nature*.

reconstruction of nature.[15] While images of the natural world are fundamental to the poet's art—Sidney's Golden world as opposed to Nature's 'brazen' one—the language of the agrarian economy reflects a different nature: laboured, economic, productive, and essential to human survival.[16]

While Jonson may suppress the methods of production and their socio-economic implications in 'To Penshurst', for example, Shakespeare imports these terms into his Sonnets to expose a conflict at the heart of the poet's project: the values—economic, emotional, and ethical—of love, creativity, and posterity.[17] At the centre of many of the sonnets is the question of profit: what is it? Sex, love, marriage, children, or poetry itself come to occupy the potential spaces of productivity, and the values they confer upon the speaker or subject are always in contention.

In order to highlight some of the ways in which the language of husbandry develops through Christian to secular writing, agrarian manuals to lyric verse, or even humanist writings to popular ballads, we need to initially look at the wider discourses of the agrarian economy.[18]

---

[15] Thomas Nashe is an interesting figure here since his writing appears to occupy the hinterland between pastoral poetics and agrarian industry, the interlude and the masque. *Summer's Last Will and Testament* (1600) personifies the seasons in an exploration of the way in which Nature, here an allegorized image of social structure, supports an endless cycle of generation and destruction.

[16] The literary relationship between the georgic and the pastoral is central to the ways in which the landscape is constructed and interpreted in early modern literature. Patterson, in *Pastoral and Ideology*, discusses the ways in which both modes developed simultaneously in Virgil's work and their impact on later writers. Patterson observes the ways in which Virgil's work was appropriated in humanist education and used ideologically in such a way as to elide its original context in support of a more contemporary one. Anthony Low, however, argues that the genres remained distinct in their appropriation by writers who understood their values of labour or pleasure as constituent with certain political and social agendas. In Shakespeare's work I argue that husbandry—its terms and discourse—supports an alternative context for the pastoral. This context is not literary in its elision of labour but local, civic, pedagogic, and socio-economic.

[17] Although, as has been lucidly shown in the criticism of Raymond Williams and James Turner, this type of natural world was often elided in Renaissance poetics, which tended to focus on the creative potential of 'enamelled' nature rather than the urgent demands of food production. Helen Wilcox, in her essay 'Lanyer and the Poetry of Land and Devotion', in Patrick Cheney (ed.), *Early Modern English Poetry* (Oxford: Oxford University Press, 2007), 246, credits Aemilia Lanyer with writing the first 'country house poem' in English literature, 'The Description of Cooke-ham'.

[18] Even within these shifts, however, the language of husbandry retains traces of its Christian heritage: indeed, as the book demonstrates, the moral fabric of cultivation is dependent upon a network of Christian images through which constructions of physical and spiritual profit move. In *Shakespeare, National Poet-Playwright* (Cambridge: Cambridge University Press, 2004), Patrick Cheney observes the persistence of scriptural images within the Sonnets: 'to present the particular instance or thing of love so that it partakes of the eternal essence, thereby freeing it from the dust of death—in effect, to write verse that allows the young man to prepare for (or participate in) Christian immortality', 228.

Driven by the tangible imperatives of food production, the Elizabethan economy was dependent upon an idea of subsistence in which supply had to meet demand. Poor harvests, dearth, plague, increased population, and rural migration radically affected the day-to-day lives of the Elizabethan populace. As Joyce Appleby claims: 'In the law economic relationships appeared enmeshed in a social context where duties and rights were closely tied to the needs of security and survival. As long as the principal elements in the economic structure remained visible and tangible, the understanding of the system was the possession of the whole society.'[19] Agrarian cultivation was a fundamental part of that tangible and visible structure: terms of production, profit, growth, and renewal thereby informed a coherent language of social relations. Wherever we look we can find traces of this visible economy; harvesting kisses (128), 'increasing store' (64), profiting from production (127), or thriving in beauty (14) cultivation reflects a particular language of value deeply embedded in Elizabethan socio-economics:

> Then, if he thrive and I be cast away,
> The worst was this: my love was my decay. (80)

Juxtaposing images of thrift and decay, the speaker perverts terms of success. Love, conventionally a creative force, is here a destructive one, and thrift, traditionally allied to ethical values of improvement, is associated with careless individualism. Similarly, creativity and creation can reside in an image of growth which is outside the speaker's control, determined by a force other than himself:

> Love is a babe; then might I not say so,
> To give full growth to that which still doth grow? (115)

The terms through which the human understands the landscape were in transition. And such a transition makes it a powerful resource for the exploration of the social lives of those living under the reigns of Elizabeth I and James I. Anthony Low makes this point succinctly when he declares that 'new practices in agriculture in turn influenced and reinforced people's thinking about life generally, their sense of themselves, and even their most intimate relationships'.[20] For Low, changing agricultural practices made way for a new social mobility that supported utility, endeavour, and reciprocity in such a way as to value profit and reward as an individual act of improvement or investment. As the nature of obligation came under scrutiny from a developing system of economic

---

[19] *Economic Thought and Ideology*, 25.   [20] Low, 'Agricultural Reform', 63.

individualism, so medieval manorial relations began to give way to a more pragmatic attitude to patronage as well as exchange.[21] The economic emphasis on increase, profit, and thrift exposes a re-evaluation of the conservative ideals of an immutable hierarchy, so that, as McRae observes, 'the ideal of manorial self-sufficiency is transformed through the engagement with the market into an unending process of accumulation'.[22] As new processes of accumulation emerge so too do new expectations of value. Whilst Greene has noticed Shakespeare's 'obsessive concern' with the semantics of husbandry, so Low has identified that Thomas Carew's 'redefinition of love and patronage relates to economic exchange'.[23] Despite the thirty or so years that separate the publications of Shakespeare and Carew, their language of worth reveals a radical new diction in the exploration of human relationships. As a transcription of social relations the landscape has always been a register for human endeavour, customs, and beliefs.[24] As those practices come to shape human relations, as well as reflect them, the metaphors of cultivation become more mobile. Whether loving, creative, economic, or self-reflexive, the semantics of worth developing through the agrarian economy begin to inform almost every aspect of social identification; in Shakespeare's Sonnets such semantics disclose an urgent reinterpretation of the expectations of productivity and the values of worth.

> For where is she so fair whose unear'd womb
> Disdains the tillage of thy husbandry.

It is now a commonplace of Shakespeare studies to characterize the first eighteen sonnets as concerned with procreation.[25] The speaker's insistent

---

[21] Low characterizes Carew in these terms when he writes: 'A destructive confrontation with father, family, and culture forced him to find other forms of patronage and love, no longer feudal in principle . . . . He was enabled to find those new forms aided by the example of agricultural reform, which offered him a new model of service,' 69. Similarly, Ian Donaldson, in his biography of Ben Jonson, describes how the playwright, despite a few scrapes with the authorities, advances with an assiduous practicality up the social ladder to James's court, *Ben Jonson: A Life* (Oxford: Oxford University Press, 2011), esp. 202–5. Such social mobility is made possible through a change in attitudes to feudal obligations which begins with agricultural reform.

[22] Andrew McRae, 'Husbandry Manuals and the Language of Agrarian Improvement', in Leslie and Raylor (eds.), *Culture and Cultivation*, 42.

[23] Low, 'Agricultural Reform', 75.

[24] See Alexandra Walsham's formidable exploration of the ways in which belief (religious, pagan, mythological, and customary) shaped the early modern landscape, *The Reformation of the Landscape*; Keith Thomas, *Man and the Natural World* (London: Allen Lane, 1983) explores the relationship between humans and their landscape through various motifs, including animals, forests, etc.

[25] For recent criticism on the nature of these sonnets, as well as their language of economy, see Schoenfeldt (ed.), *A Companion to Shakespeare's Sonnets*, particularly Garrett

attitude to reproduction frequently focuses on the subject's beauty and the putative irresponsibility that he shows in not replicating that beauty through a child. The poet's investment in this image uses reproduction as a sexualized compliment that seeks recompense not in the form of desire itself but in the production of profit. The imagined and idealized offspring becomes a fantasy of profit through which the 'lovely boy' can be judged. The complex interrelations evinced through these imaginary relations provide Shakespeare with a powerful network of bodies through which he can examine notions of reward and recompense, production and value.[26] Central to this exploration is the language of husbandry and the economic conflict between individual gain and collective duty.

Sonnet 1 opens with a general observation that 'from fairest creatures we desire increase | That thereby beauty's rose might never die' (ll. 1–2). The abstraction that human desire will always want to reproduce what is beautiful is carried through an image of 'increase' that is simultaneously quantitative and emotional. Peter Herman, in his essay 'What's the Use?', explores 'the reduction of human subjects to the status of things or commodities', a reduction which Don Wayne understands 'when the circulation of social energy is expressed as the circulation of money'.[27] The language of 'increase' for the representation of desire, procreation, and profit runs throughout the early sonnets and comes to reflect the multiple ways in which husbandry manuals accommodate their developing social economy. Where sonnet 1 invokes states of 'famine' or 'abundance' to suggest the speaker's tension between personal desire and social duty, sonnet 2 takes the image of the land as its defining metaphor:[28]

> When forty winters shall besiege thy brow
> And dig deep trenches in thy beauty's field,

Sullivan's 'Voicing the Young Man: Memory, Forgetting and Subjectivity', 331–42, and Schiffer (ed.), *Shakespeare's Sonnets: Critical Essays*, particularly those by Peter C. Herman, Thomas Greene, and Lars Engle.

[26] In *Intimacy and Sexuality in the Age of Shakespeare*, James M. Bromley argues that Shakespeare's poetry does not represent the privileging of 'normative' or heterosexual coupling whereby certain institutions of marriage and family are endorsed but a 'multiplicity' of 'affective relations', including homosocial, polyamorous, and non-penetrative sexual relations (Cambridge: Cambridge University Press, 2012).

[27] Peter C. Herman, 'What's the Use? Or, The Problematic of Economy in Shakespeare's Procreation Sonnets', in Schiffer (ed.), *Shakespeare's Sonnets: Critical Essays*, 264.

[28] According to Arthur Marotti and Laura Estill's examination of the circulation of the *Sonnets* in manuscript, 'By far the most transcribed poem is Sonnet 2, found in 13 manuscripts. Presented as an anonymous piece and made to embody conventional belief that it is good to marry and have children,' Arthur Kinney (ed.), *The Oxford Handbook of Shakespeare* (Oxford: Oxford University Press, 2012), 59. The implication is that such conventionality made it popular, endorsing a belief in the happy appropriation of institutionalized attitudes to marriage and procreation.

Thy youth's proud livery, so gazed on now,
Will be a tottered weed of small worth held

The figurative field establishes an image which is vulnerable to both neglect and decay. The landscape supports an image of hypothetical ageing since, like the seasonal imperatives of the farmer's duties, it records the passage of time. Conflating the meanings of weed, as both clothing and valueless plant, the idea of ageing resides in images of destruction or neglect. The deep trenches dug by time are not those of arable husbandry but those dug for drainage or to lay hedges to enclose fields.[29] Yet, as the sonnet is concerned with memory—the potential memory of the young man's youth—so the landscape becomes a marker of our history, a vestige of our past.[30] The desired treasure, construed as produce or productivity, anticipates a childless life as dissolute and valueless. The forty winters of gradual decay—imagined as the natural assaults of seasonal patterns— establish old age as the dominant threat to production. Pitching a battle between the human and natural worlds, the sonnet imagines procreation as a form of intervention in our mortality:

Then being asked where thy beauty lies—
Where all the treasure of thy lusty days—
To say within thine own deep-sunken eyes
Were an all-eating shame and thriftless praise.

If the 'lovely boy' does not reproduce, the speaker will accuse him of a shameful waste of his 'treasure'.[31] Invested in putative questions of worth, the sonnet establishes the landscape as a sympathetic image of human endeavour wherein the body can potentially reclaim its past in the value of its offspring/production. Cultivation thereby becomes a process in which humans mark their landscape, their personal history, and their future in a thrifty attitude to (pro)creation. Such acts of intervention and manage-ment disclose the land/body as a focus for moral responsibility in which both the self and the community are assembled. Drawing on the emotive registers of shame and thriftlessness, the poet-speaker invites the young man to consider his isolation and decay:

---

[29] Fitzherbert, Tusser, and Heresbach all discuss trenches within the context of hedge-laying.

[30] Simon Schama's *Landscape and Memory* (London: Harper Perennial, 2004) explores the ways in which cultures mark, make, and interpret their landscapes, particularly in relation to myth, religion, and paganism. More specifically early modern, however, is Philip Schwyzer's *Literature, Nationalism and Memory in Early Modern England* (Cambridge: Cambridge University Press, 2004), Nicola Whyte's *Inhabiting the Landscape*, and Alexan-dra Walsham's *The Reformation of the Landscape*.

[31] As has often been noted, the allusions to masturbation represent semen as a resource to be used productively in conception rather than 'wasted'.

> If thou could answer, 'This fair child of mine
> Shall sum my count, and make my old excuse,'
> Proving his beauty by succession thine.
> This were to be new made when thou art old,
> And see thy blood warm when thou feelst cold. (ll. 10–14)

Counting the child as a commodity and a justification for expenditure, the sonnet draws the young man into a bleak, hypothetical future in order to *give* him a future in the form of succession. Alongside the language of accounting is the language of passion, where warmth and cold become prosthetic social values. Anxieties of shame or waste often accompany the language of cultivation since they impose a vivid set of expectations upon the reader, which are rooted in ideas of charity as well as atonement.[32]

In his introduction to chapter I of Markham's *Farewell to Husbandry*, the author sets out our common duty to the earth:

But the Barren and Sterrill Earth, to make it full of increase and plentie, is *Gratum opus Agricolis,* and such a generall benefit to all good men, that the concealement can be no lesse an offence then theft, robbing a mans Country of that treasure (by negligence) which no other industry, in him, can after restore. (4)

The import of Markham's sentiment is clear: supression or neglect of the earth's resources is considered an offence to the extent that no other industry can restore its treasure except husbandry. The density of the social implications is suggested by the multiple ways in which Markham creates anxiety: the earth is a vast resource available to all; to neglect it is to commit a crime (against both God and each other); such is the significance of husbandry that it cannot be replaced by another 'industry'.

Shakespeare's speaker adopts a similar attitude in reprimanding his subject with images of 'all-eating shame'. Part of this shame is in the kind of solipsism that invests only in the present and neglects the future. Succession here is also investment, in recognition of the value of futurity: 'If thou could answer, "This fair child of mine | Shall sum my count and make my old excuse"— | Proving his beauty by succession thine.' The pecuniary terms used to describe the child rest on images of production in which the male child is both his legacy and surety. The emphasis that these first sonnets place upon future indemnity is largely articulated through the

---

[32] In sonnet 129, Schoenfeldt observes the paradox of waste and production when he writes: 'The often-noticed pun on "waste" and "waist" (buttressed by "shame", the English for pudendum, the Latin word for the genitals, meaning the "shameful parts") demonstrates the unproductive economy of the self that the poem finds essential to the act of sex,' *Bodies and Selves*, 83.

land as an exercise in profit and production as a form of human sustain-ability. Good husbandry comes to reflect the type of careful management which produces both profit and yield; and in turn profit and yield come to represent futurity and sustainability. The suggestive ways in which the speaker seduces the subject with a desire for his 'increase' invokes the pleasure/treasure conceit employed by Markham. Similarly, Thomas Tusser's introductory panegyric to husbandry draws on this dynamic: 'So many as loue me, & vse me aright, | with treasure & pleasure, I ritchly acquite.' Whilst Tusser's pleasure in treasure may be financial and Shakespeare's sexual, much of the language of husbandry collapses the boundaries between different types of pleasure, for the 'generall benefit to all good men'.[33]

Common to all images of benefit is the idea of carefulness or thrift. As waste, carelessness, and loss invoke shame and provoke censure, prudence and posterity become defining images of success. In sonnet 4 we can see the profound ways in which social value is determined by production:

> Unthrifty loveliness, why dost thou spend
> Upon thyself thy beauty's legacy
> Nature's bequest gives nothing but doth lend
> And being frank she lends to those are free.

The speaker's accusation that the subject wastes his beauty on himself is supported by the legal language of ownership. To hold things in 'frank' or 'free' refers to a type of tenancy, as John Rastell's *Terms of the Lawes of this Realm* (1579) explains. Frank tenure means:

To hold in free hold is to hold for terme of his owne lyfe, or for terme of an other mans life. And in this case the fee & the right remaineth in the person of him, of whome he holdeth.[34]

Playing on the legal terms of *free* and *frank*, Nature gives the subject tenure for the term of his life. Since the 'fee & right remaineth in the person of him', he has a duty, so the speaker tells him, not to waste Nature's bequest. The complex terms of legal endowment associated with the land show Nature as the creational landlord and the lovely boy as her life tenant who must invest his legacy rather than spend it. These terms of

---

[33] In *The Origins of Sex*, Faramerez Dabhoiwala cites a bawd who in the early seventeenth century encouraged a young relative to view sex as both pleasurable and useful, telling her 'that she had a good cunt and bid her make use thereto for if she did not she would do herself wrong, for if ground were not tilled and manured it would be overgrown with thorns and briars' (London: Allen Lane, 2011), 18.

[34] John Rastell, *An exposition of certaine difficult and obscure words, and termes of the lawes of this realme* (London, 1579), 201ʳ.

obligation and endowment are compressed through a series of images in which the lovely boy becomes increasingly bound to a legal Nature. The speaker's anxiety over the future of the subject's loveliness is further defined by the language of expenditure:

> Then beauteous niggard why dost thou abuse
> The bounteous largess given thee to give?

The poet sets up a series of paradoxes in order to expose the perversity of the subject's behaviour: the 'profitless usurer' who uses 'so great a sum of sums yet canst not live?'[35] Condemning his subject to a kind of ethical poverty he imagines him as destitute and bankrupt. The density of these financial images leads us back to the tenant subject: 'when nature calls thee to be gone, | What acceptable audit canst thou leave?' The consistent emphasis on the future as a marker of one's achievements situates the young man at the centre of an emotional conflict which rests on the economic terms of expenditure and investment. Unlike the more opaque service relations of feudalism in which gift and reward service a customary system of obligation, the financial equations here are directly responsive to investment and return. Since nature has given the subject freehold for the duration of his lifetime, what remains undeveloped at death is condemned rather than bequeathed:

> Thy unused beauty must be tombed with thee,
> Which usèd lives th' executor to be.

The emphasis on the executor, or the manager, of the 'usèd beauty' returns us to the sonnet's overarching investment in beauty's bequest. The cycle of regeneration that procreation promotes is articulated through the legal language of land ownership in which rights of possession and tenancy reflect opportunity, ownership, and use. The complex value system which requires 'use' as a fulfilment of potential is grounded in Christian images of labour as well as a developing awareness of the relationship between equity and integrity.[36] Tusser, for example, makes this observation:

> Once placed for profit, looke neuer for ease
> except ye beware of, suche mychers as thease.

---

[35] Herman's essay addresses images of usury within these sonnets. The concept of husbandry as usury supports an ideological ambivalence within many of these texts: while in agrarian literature usury tends to reflect the earth's treasury for the benefit of mankind, in many of the invectives against city corruption husbandry becomes usury in the corruption of apparently rural values to mercantile profit.

[36] The developing models of economic analysis emerging in the seventeenth century, particularly the work of Gerald Malynes, will rely heavily on the putatively ethical relationship between equality and equity: see my chapter on *The Winter's Tale*.

vnthriftnes, slouthfulnes, careles & rashe,
that thrusteth thee hedlong, to runne in the lashe. (fo. 8ᵛ)

The note in the margin here reads '4 beggars', warning of the dangers of 'unthriftnes, slouthfulness, careless & rashe'. Bad management can swiftly slide into sin through the image of slothfulness, and the spectre of ruin is always lurking for the unthrifty or careless. In Shakespeare's early sonnets, nature supports a social system of reciprocity in which the goddess gives and so the lovely boy must give back: or, as the seventeenth-century writer Ralph Austen explains, husbandry is the 'art' of 'lawful usury'.³⁷ The land is a place of profit, in which investment determines reward. Austen's remark deems such usury lawful because it belongs to a Christian tradition of investment and expectation. This notion of reciprocity is haunted by an acute awareness of 'devouring time' and the irrepressible pace of our human life. Appropriate use of the seasons is necessarily crucial to the agricultural year, and Shakespeare's use of temporal metaphors reveals his interest in the traffic of human life. But within the context of the husbandry manual, the seasons take on a further power simultaneously expressing our legacy and our livelihood. Tusser is equally explicit in his apprehension of time:

> In spring time we reare, we do sowe & we plant,
> in Sommer get vittels, least after we want.
> In haruest, we cary in corne & the fruite:
> in Winter, to spend, as we neede of eche suite.

> The yeare I compare, as I finde for a trueth,
> the spring, vnto childhode, the Summer to youth.
> The haruest to manhode, the winter to age,
> all quickly forgot, as a Play on a stage.

> Time past is forgotten, ere men be aware,
> time present is thought on, with wonderful care.
> Time comming is feared, & therefore we saue:
> yet oft ere it come, we be gon to the graue. (fo. 27ʳ)

Tusser's synthesis of a man's life into an agricultural year as well as a stage play is obviously resonant within the context of Shakespeare's works, but what remains central to both these metaphors is the irrepressible passage of time: a life, a year, a play.

For Tusser and Shakespeare, time stands in relation to an urgent present and a hypothetical future in which progress and reproduction become measures of success. Within these time frames, the past is always receding, demanding a present that is always in motion, creating and sustaining an imaginary future. In the first sonnets of Shakespeare's sequence, the

³⁷ Austen, as cited by McRae, *God Speed the Plough*, 161.

speaker urges the lovely boy away from the kind of solipsism that has
no concept of legacy or sustainability. Central to the speaker's argument is
a notion of thrift which governs personal reason and civic duty. In
sonnet 11, no longer dependent on the rhetoric of beauty alone, the speaker
turns to images of the unique in berating the subject's refusal to reproduce:

> If all were minded so, the times should cease,
> And threescore year would make the world away.
> Let those whom nature hath not made for store,
> Harsh, featureless, and rude, barrenly perish.

Nature's 'store' must be replenished only by the beautiful and the rest left
to perish. This kind of selective storage suggests that only beauty is worth
investing in and those condemned to 'barrenly perish' are of no value to
either nature or the speaker. The speaker's representation of nature is, of
course, unsettlingly eugenic and reflects a quasi-platonic view of beauty
inflected by contemporary interests in market value. For the poet-speaker,
value is determined by an aesthetics that governs its reproducibility: the
subject is a commodity that must be made available in reproduction but
equally, as in modern notions of consumerism, the unique nature of that
commodity makes it more valuable. The economic model which demands
that value is both unique and reproducible recognizes a crucial paradox at
the centre of capitalist structures of commerce. Value is accorded to that
which we desire; and desire is promoted through unavailability. Inviting
images of possession, withholding, desire, and acquisition, the sonnet
draws the subject into a contemporary discourse on the nature of the
commodity itself. For the Elizabethans, however, the term commodity
almost always meant 'use' or utility, so that the idea of production
necessarily meant useful, and useful usually meant beautiful, too.[38]
Googe's translation of Heresbach's *Foure Bookes of Husbandrie* blends
these meanings in his dedication when he commends the text:

> which you may vse (yf it please you) for your recreation: and afterwards (if so you
> thinke it meete publish under your protection, to the commoditie and benefite of
> others.

---

[38] Keith Thomas makes the point that use and beauty were considered inseparable in the
Tudor imagination, since human intervention, even on its most quotidian scale, enhanced a
primary natural product, landscape, or garden: 'But such men did not normally put utility
above beauty. To them a tamed, inhabited and productive landscape was beautiful. Theirs
was the ancient classical ideal which associated beauty with fertility,' *Man and the Natural
World*, 255. Rebecca Bushnell, however, understands the seventeenth-century gardening
manuals as instrumental in the creation of a relationship between aesthetics and labour,
pleasure, and beauty, *Green Desire*, 93–5. The *OED* defines the earliest uses of the term
commodity as 'The quality of being commodious'.

In sonnet 11, the speaker distinguishes between two types of bodies—those to be reproduced and those that are expendable. The rather bald economic message reflects an Elizabethan interest in changing conceptions of value which can be traced to an evolving investment in surplus. The sonnet's emphasis on 'use' and quality reflects what Joan Thirsk has described as 'a deep prejudice...against goods that held value only by virtue of the labour applied to them'.[39] The development of consumerism supported a growing desire for luxuries or 'fripperies' so that beauty, elegance, or fashion informed people's spending rather than need: 'Now it was becoming possible to indulge in a few luxuries to delight the eye.'[40]

The eye's delight seems to be the driving logic of the procreation sonnets and looks to a world where, to bowdlerize Keats, beauty is use and use beauty. Yet such an economy is justified through a selective appropriation of Platonic Ideas of beauty as well as a contemporary legacy of Christianized nature, wherein the natural world represents a resource for which we bear the moral responsibility of cultivation. Synthesizing the moral and the economic allows the regenerative images that accompany both husbandry and the body to emerge as qualitative forces: 'For where is she so fair whose uneared womb | Disdains the tillage of thy husbandry?' (3, ll. 5–6). The construction of Shakespeare's images supplies us with an implied value system in which nature self-selects through a complex mix of creation and destruction.[41]

The dense metaphorical pressures that such images place upon the subject put him at the centre of a regenerative system in which he bears full responsibility for its successful continuance. The idea that nature leases the subject his body for the duration of his life amplifies the pressure to profit from that body before he dies. In sonnet 13, the leased body is also the home for which the subject must make careful provision before 'your self's decease':

> O that you were yourself, but love you are
> No longer yours than you yourself here live.
> Against this coming end you should prepare,
> And your sweet semblance to some other give.
> So should that beauty which you hold in lease

---

[39] *Economic Policy and Projects: The Development of a Consumer Society in Early Modern England* (Oxford: Clarendon Press, 1978), 15.

[40] *Economic Policy and Projects*, 15.

[41] The Darwinian relationship between natural and sexual selection has been recently explored by David Rothenberg, in *Survival of the Beautiful: Art, Science and Evolution* (London: Bloomsbury, 2012). Here Rothenberg tries to make sense of the reproduction of beauty beyond Darwin's theories of natural selection, interrogating the survival of aesthetics in both humans and artefacts.

> Find no determination—then you were
> Yourself again after your self's decease,
> When your sweet issue your sweet form should bear.

To be oneself is to take part in an endless cycle of beginning and ending, borrowing and giving, in which the conclusion ('determination') of nature's lease gives birth to another cycle of habitation through the 'sweet issue'. Here, the formation and management of the self emerge as a vital part of its reproduction. In this way, the single self reaches its fullest potential in perpetuating a cycle of sociability in which the body both contains and enables life. In order to appeal to the subject's sense of responsibility, the poet-speaker invokes the 'house' as a site of social prudence:

> Who lets so fair a house fall to decay,
> Which husbandry in honour might uphold
> Against the stormy gusts of winter's day
> And barren rage of death's eternal cold?
> O none but unthrifts, dear my love you know,
> You had a father, let your son say so.

The language of husbandry supports a powerful value system in which the subject is duty bound to take care of his body as he would maintain a house in perpetuity. The 'honour' of such maintenance belongs to a social network of responsibilities in which the 'house' is the spiritual body, a familial legacy, a domestic structure, and a representation of social order.[42] This honourable husbandry no longer exclusively belongs to nature but to the human world, in which we must make provisions against the ravages of winter and the inevitability of death. The architecture of human habitation denotes a material structure through which the human imposes his dwelling on the landscape, simultaneously possessing and marking it. That the house can outlast the bodies who dwell in it allows the space to occupy a place in the human imagination in which the future is contained as well as provided for. Invoking honour in this context allies the images of house and husbandry to their Christian heritage by recalling the duty that we owe to God for our resources and our genesis:

What woorkeman is there in the world, that is able to frame or counterfeyte suche heauenly woorkes? Who could of a slender grasse make Wheate or Bread, and of a tender twigge bring foorth so noble a licour as Wine? but only that mightie Lorde

---

[42] Elizabeth Fowler, in *Literary Character: The Human Figure in Early English Writing* (Ithaca, NY: Cornell University Press, 2003), explores the 'social person', and its attendant habitus, through The Pardoner's Tale, in which she identifies the 'shaping of the body that comes from practices and social environment', 67.

that hath created all thinges visible and inuisible. With these sightes doo I recreate my mind, and geue thankes vnto GOD, the creator and conseruer of all thinges, for his great and exceeding goodnesse, I sing the song, to thee O Lorde...beseeching GOD to blesse the giftes that he hath geuen vs through his bounteous liberalitie, to enriche the Feeldes, and to prosper the Corne and the Grasse, and that he wyll crowne the yeere with his plenteousnesse, that we may enioy the fruites of the Earth with thankesgeuing, to the honour of him, and the profite of our neighbour. (3ᵛ)

Here, Heresbach puts husbandry at the centre of our spiritual, social, and material worlds, suggesting the 'bounteous liberalitie' of God's resources as well as the 'honour' of husbandry and the 'profite of our neighbour'. The comprehensive role that Heresbach gives nature supports a network of ideological terms in which cultivation serves to represent authority (crowne), magnanimity (bounteous liberalitie), and profit (prosper). Within these terms the husbandman becomes a key figure between heaven and earth: working with God's material for the benefit of mankind. The dominant images, however, remain economic as the language of 'plenteousnesse' directs us to the prevailing call for 'profite'. The rhetoric of success situates husbandry at the centre of the ideological relations between the human and landscape. Investing these terms with a God-given design registers the moral expectations involved in production as well as pleasure. To profit is to enjoy; to reap is to be grateful; and to prosper is to be celebrated by both the 'visible and invisible' worlds.

The 'obsessive concern' with metaphorical wealth, profit, worth, value, expense, 'store', 'content' that the Sonnets expose reveals the extent to which these ideological relations are being reshaped in Elizabethan socio-economics.[43] Armed with a semantic storehouse of effective images, the poet can lay siege to the subject's sense of self through direct engagement with his sense of duty. The gendering of many of these images makes duty itself a powerful discourse, since it not only reflects domestic, spiritual, and economic imperatives, but sexual too. Despite their emphasis on engendering or production it is the male body that becomes the focus of the early sonnets, celebrating a version of masculinity in which the male ploughs, sows, or tills the female body.[44] Whilst the poet insists on this masculine language of intervention and reproduction, he reiterates the

---

[43] Greene, 'Pitiful Thrivers', 231. For Greene, this language is ultimately driven by the poet's overarching need to fill a void that is simultaneously sexual, personal, and 'cosmic' in which 'husbandry emerges as a universal, existential concern that transcends the addressee's marital status', 232.

[44] Greene discusses this in relation to creativity in which poetry becomes the regenerative process and the author the woman who gestates the verse through the penetration of the male subject. See especially 232–41.

socialized nature of the husbandry manuals in which the 'profite of thy neighbour' underscores manorial relations:

> For having traffic with thyself alone,
> Thou of thyself thy sweet self dost deceive.
> Then when nature calls thee to be gone,
> What ácceptable audit canst thou leave? (4)

The human bonds that can support a system of growth, regeneration, and renewal find their most persuasive language in cultivation. Thomas Tuke, in his *Picture of a true protestant* (1609), uses husbandry as an extended metaphor in his definitions of faith, gratitude, knowledge, grace, and social duty:

we are his *Fleld,* his *Vineyard* and *Garden* of delight; our duty therefore is to cleanse & adorne our harts to be faire and fruitfull, pleasing and not offensiue. The *Sunne* of righteousnesse hath shone long amongst vs with exceeding brightnesse (in the *Gospell*) and with his heat hath moulten the *Cloudes* aboue vs, which haue emptied themselues like *bottles* vpon vs; and therefore to testify our pleasantnesse and fertility for the remo[n]stratio[n] of our gratitude, we should abound in grace, increase in knowledge, and perfume the aire about vs with our fragrant sauors, and not poison it with filthy fumes, like stinking dunghils. (dedicatory epistle)[45]

Recognizing fertility as a form of gratitude, and grace as a path to knowledge, Tuke formulates his evangelical rhetoric on the basis of an emotive relationship between the body and the landscape. Unlike the neglected wild, human intervention celebrates a progressive logic—'When I perceive that men as plants increase' (15)—so that the poet-lover can express devotion through a profitable synthesis with the subject: 'And all in war with time for love of you | As he takes from you, I engraft you new' (15). Increase becomes a mutual process of growth, profit, and renewal which can, albeit briefly, simulate a war with Time, which capitalizes on progression but defeats mortality. The speaker performs his own intervention not only in the irrepressible passage of human life but also in the patterns of nature—engrafting as a process of renewal rather than hybridization. The grafting of sonnet 15 reflects a process of regeneration. In sonnet 37, however, that process of attachment is more conflicted, reproducing a set of hierarchical relations rather than a mutual investment in profit:

> Take all my comfort of thy worth and truth.
> For whether beauty, birth, or wealth, or wit,

----

[45] *The picture of a true protestant* (1609).

> Or any of these all, or all, or more,
> Entitled in thy parts do crowned sit,
> I make my love engrafted to this store. (37)

Grafting himself to a store of worth, the poet-speaker exposes the confusion of such terms—'Or any of these all, or all, or more'—as he hopes to extend and so become them: 'So then I am not lame, poor, nor despised.' The process of grafting exposes the powerful way in which such terms support a range of figurative possibilities in which the lover can benefit (briefly or permanently) from his object of devotion. Drawing on a contemporary language of grafting, the speaker uses it to express his dependence on the subject's superiority, rather than a belief in the value of experimentation or expansion. In this way, grafting reproduces hierarchical structures of worth, in which there is an enhanced object of reproduction.[46] Transposing ideas of value onto the natural world, the speaker determines his own self-image through practices of husbandry. In both cases, however, the enemy is Time, threatening—in the very passages of growth that the Sonnets depend on—to compromise the full proficiency of the speaker or his subject. Representing human intervention and production as the valuable course of action, the Sonnets draw on the language of cultivation as a method of synthesizing ethical and economic relations. The value of these relations lies in the speaker's ability to define the progressive logic of production: the physicality of this making—books, children, youth, and beauty—determines a set of aspirations that are socially desirable.

Instructing the 'lovely boy' to reproduce before he dies, sonnet 13 asks: 'Who lets so fair a house fall to decay, | Which husbandry in honour might uphold.' The house of the boy's body becomes an image of care and preservation, which the subject has a duty to 'honour'. The emotive use of the term honour calls the subject to account in such a way as to suggest a far wider breach of moral values than reluctance to procreate initially implies. For honouring is a dynamic act, requiring both a subject to and an object of devotion. Replete with Christian imperatives of duty, the term invokes a heady mix of social, personal, and religious expectations as it registers the individual's responsibility to a wider world. In his prefatory dedication to *Venus and Adonis*, Shakespeare had put himself within this position of accountability when he wrote:

---

[46] Markham's translation of Estienne's *Countrey Farme*, however, notes that trees may self-graft if they are planted next to each other: a process he refers to as a 'jumble', and without profit: 'Hereof are sufficient vvitnesses, I know not how many sorts of Apples, Peares, and Cherries, this iumbled together by offering force vnto nature without judgement or reason: and but that they become somewhat admirable vnto the eye, they yeeld no profit vnto the bodie of any man,' 239.

Only, if your Honour seem but pleased, I account my self highly praised, and vow
to take advantage of all idle hours, til I have honoured you with some graver
labour.

Playing on the grammatical variants of honour, Shakespeare sets himself
within the context of accountability, worth, and labour. The dedication
goes on to elaborate on these sentiments through images of agrarian
industry which supports the complex interrelations between moral, financial, personal, and social reward. Honour, however, as an object of choice
as well as a personal duty, reflects Shakespeare's interest in the terms of
responsibility. Translating these terms into an area of conflict, sonnet
13 forces the reader to engage with the moral implications of personal
choice. Using the boy's body as the central form through which concepts
of honour must move, Shakespeare uses a conventional image for the
exploration of transcendence. The body/house metaphor has a long
history in Christianity, supporting the division between the material and
spiritual worlds of the body and the soul. George Abbot, a prolific
seventeenth-century preacher, invokes St Augustine's use of the house in
a metaphor for mortality: 'Hee alludeth to an old house, whereof when the
walles doe moulder and fitter away, the roofe is vncouered, the timber is
disiointed, it is an euident argument, that it will not be long before this
house fall. Such tokens of the mortalitie of our bodies, are those decaies
and imperfections.'[47]

     Within a Christian tradition the body houses the soul: subject to decay
and on a fixed-term lease, the body-house represents only one stage in the
human's journey to God: 'The old house must to the ground, that so the
tenant of it, may ascend vnto God by a kinde of remooue, till the building
be new repaired.'[48] The houses of our bodies are merely lent to us for the
durations of our lives, at the end of which we return our souls to God.[49]
The journey between habitation and desertion is developed through a
further metaphor of construction and decay in the image of cultivation:

In the next place, our flesh is compared to the grasse. Grasse, than which nothing
is more common; nothing more vile. Which groweth, and in an instant is cut
downe, and then withereth, & is either deuoured as fodder, or if it be of a bigger

[47] George Abbot, *A Sermon Preached at Westminster* (London: William Aspley, 1608),
26 May 1608, 4.
[48] See also Matthew 13: 44–9: 'Again the kingdom of heaven is like unto a treasure hid in
the field, which when a man hath found, he hideth it, & for joye therof departheth and
selleth all he hathe, and byeth that field.' See Booth, *Sonnets*, 505.
[49] James Turner explores this metaphor in the poetry of George Wither where the
destroyed house, like enclosures or engrating, is a symptom of economic oppression, *The
Politics of Landscape*, 121–3.

size, is burned in the ouen, as Christ himself speaketh. The daies of man are as grasse: as a flower of the field, so flourisheth he.[50]

Abbot focuses on the material world as merely one stage in our human journey to God. By invoking the temporality of material things—the passage from growth to decay, habitation to desertion—he isolates our tangible realities as frail and subject to corrosion. Pursuing such resonant metaphors determines the power of cultivation in the imaginative reconstruction of Elizabethan values. Here the body forms a vital image in the naturalized networks of growth and decay, fodder and sustenance: human and humus. This image of human life within a grand system of loss and regeneration is central to a Christian narrative of transcendence. By isolating the processes of growth and decay in material images he subjects their significance to doubt and their endurance to scrutiny. But where, for Abbot, meaning resides in our metaphysical relationship to God, for the speaker of sonnet 13 meaning resides not in the spiritual life but in the physical life of production and progression. In sonnet 13's appeal to the subject's honourable husbandry, the poet asks him to make provision for decay and to respect his own beauty in the reproduction of a child: 'O none but unthrifts, dear my love you know, | You had a father, let your son say so.' The sonnet urges the subject into a position of responsibility through terms of reproduction, authority, and prosperity, reflecting the patriarchal discourses of thrift that were so embedded in European husbandry manuals.[51] Thomas Tusser, the most demotic writer on husbandry, records a similar sentiment when he writes: 'The father an unthrift, what hope to the sonne? | The ruler unskilful, how quickly undone?'[52] The language of authority encoded in terms of the father is reflected in the play on God, the father, and Adam, the first son, duty bound to labour: 'In the sweate of thy face, thou shalt eate thy bread' (Gen. 3: 19).

Similarly, the biblical injunction to 'multiply and replenish the earth, and subdue it' (Gen. 1: 28) supported a wide range of doctrines in which cultivation and production reiterated God's commandment to Adam. As such injunctions were taken up in approaches to colonizing in the New World so they also came to reflect attitudes to possession and reclamation.[53] Drawing on both the language of Genesis and the Elizabethan

---

[50] Abbot, *Sermon*, 8.
[51] Heresbach states 'that the best doung for the feelde is the maisters foote', *Foure Bookes of Husbandrie*, 4ᵛ; a saying which is still in use today.
[52] Tusser, *Five Hundred Points of Good Husbandry*, 11.
[53] Patricia Seed, in *Ceremonies of Possession*, explores the ways in which Genesis informed English colonization, 31–9.

Book of Common Prayer, the Anglican Richard Eburne exposes the relationship between cultivation and possession:

It was God's express commandment to Adam Gen[esis] 1: 28 that he should fill the earth and subdue it. By virtue of which charter he and his have ever since had the privilege to spread themselves from place to place and to have, hold, occupy and enjoy any region or country whatsoever which they should find either not preoccupied.[54]

Echoing marriage sermons, to 'have, hold, occupy and enjoy' registers the multiple ways in which profit, pleasure, and production could move through the Elizabethan imagination.[55] Fundamental to images of cultivation, however, was a sense of futurity which made provision for both ownership and enhancement. Written deep into the language of husbandry is a complex discourse of duty in which care, production, and management reflect a righteous attitude to your neighbour, yourself, the earth, the future, and God. In this way, husbandry becomes a mobile metaphor for the exploration of a social self, dependent on sustainable networks of labour and profit, intervention and exchange, rather than unique notions of individualism. The language of husbandry provides us with a vast discourse on the semantics of social duty; as Gervase Markham's *Farewell to Husbandry* establishes: 'but the truth is, that there is nothing more needfull and necessary then this knowledge for all sorts of people, as well the poore as rich.'[56] This 'knowledge' not only enables the sustainability of an agrarian economy but it also teaches the necessity of exchange in the perpetuity of the commonwealth.[57] The future of the

---

[54] As quoted by Seed, *Ceremonies of Possession*, 32–3. The semantics of profit and possession are reflected in Petruchio's intention 'Happly to wive and thrive as best I may' in *The Taming of the Shrew* (1.2).

[55] Philip Reynolds, in *To Have and to Hold: Marriage and its Documentation in Western Christendom* (Cambridge: Cambridge University Press, 2007), identifies the first use of these terms in the twelfth century, 28. Valerie Wayne, however, observes that The Book of Common Prayer (1559) excised certain ideas of marriage that included friendship and focused more on the production of children and as 'a remedy against sin, and to avoid fornication', 35 n. 67, *The Flower of Friendship: A Renaissance Dialogue Contesting Marriage* (Ithaca, NY: Cornell University Press, 1992). Elizabeth Fowler discusses the ways in which the female is absorbed into the male through marriage and her subsequent lack of agency, or identity, *Literary Character: The Human Figure in Early English Writing* (Ithaca, NY: Cornell University Press, 2003), 107. William Blackstone's explanation of unity in marriage states: 'By marriage, the husband and wife are one person in law: that is, the very being or legal existence of the woman is suspended during the marriage,' *Commentaries on the Laws of England: A Facsimile of the First Edition 1765–1769* (Chicago: University of Chicago Press, 1979), I: 430.

[56] Gervase Markham, *Farewell to Husbandry* (London, 1620), 106.

[57] As McRae observes in his essay 'Agrarian Improvement' and develops in his book *God Speed the Plough*, the rise of projects in the early seventeenth century created an intense

country and the future of oneself became intricately bound up in the language of possession as well as production.

Anxieties of withholding or hoarding occupy the centre of Shakespeare's 'procreation sonnets', since it is to the subject's social duty that the speaker appeals. This duty, he claims, is to beauty, the future, and, more complexly, an ideology of care in which use, thrift, management, profit, and store become the prevailing metaphors of a love that is putatively civic, but predominantly idealistic.[58] The flexibility of these metaphors to move between secular and Christian literature meant that the value of that production was always in contention. William Jackson, a seventeenth-century lecturer at Whittington College, and author of *The Celestial Husbandrie, or Tillage of the Soul* (1616), rigorously pursues the metaphor of husbandry through the land as an image of righteousness:

There is a third fallow ground: namely, the field of oppression: A very bad ground, and dangerous to the commonwealth; such is the sinne of Engrossery, that hoard vp commodities of all sorts, and so make a dearth, without a scarcity. These are worse then the deuill; for he had some charity in him, labouring to make a plenty, where there was a scarcity; when hee would haue had Christ, to *turne stones into bread:* But these cormorants cause a scarcitie in the midst of plenty, in turning bread into stones. (C3ᵛ)

Despite his proselytizing tone, Jackson is drawing on one of the realities of Elizabethan life: engrating or engrossing was a genuine threat to the lives of the poor and an indication of the way in which the social imperatives of Tudor policies would become more mercantile under the Stuarts. In the sixteenth century corn was not a commodity but a means of survival; to that extent it could not be hoarded up, transported, or sold at a later date. It was food and food meant life. In the seventeenth century, however, commercial conditions changed to enable producers to use their food product as a means of profit.[59] Jackson traces the emotion of a tangible anxiety through the conditions of food production: conflating deprivation and sin, he exposes a landscape that is simultaneously social and political. Withholding or storing is traced through a set of imaginary relations in which such acts are revealed as immoral. Jackson's language belongs to a receding climate of social politics in which welfare takes precedent over

---

anxiety as to who was the beneficiary of agrarian improvement, the commonwealth or the improver. See also Thirsk, *Economic Policy and Projects*, 133–58.

[58] See also Greene's essay ' "The expense of Spirit" and Social Class', Harold Bloom (ed.), *Shakespeare's Poems and Sonnets* (Broomall: Chelsea House, 1999), in which he observes a 'constant concern with husbandry', 69.

[59] See Appleby, *Economic Thought and Ideology*, 25–7.

profit, but these perceptions were in transition in the seventeenth century and storing was one of the first steps from subsistence to surplus.

The recurrent emphasis on the Sonnets' subjects filling a void is suggestive of a changing investment in the creative process in which social relations imitate productivity. The economy, however, that drives the language of the Sonnets charts 'powerful and painful forms of cost and expense'.[60] The Sonnets' ceaseless search for productivity and recompense can be read within the terms of love, creativity, sexuality, or economy: husbandry is a point of reference where all these concerns meet, importing as it does an elaborate network of values predicated on investment and reward, intervention and control. In Shakespeare's poetry husbandry supports a mobile language of love, whether it is maternal, narcissistic, sexual, improvised, or social; the ties that bind a social economy of thrift and labour necessarily expose an anxiety of possession and reward.

Yet central to Shakespeare's exploration of reward is a sensitivity to the changing expectations of previously defined relationships. The apparently immutable roles of gender, class, and financial status are gradually shown to be more adaptable according to economic movement.[61] The conservative ideologies of the early husbandry manuals begin to be replaced by an emphasis on productivity, which in turn gives way to a new moral discourse of appreciation and social mobility. One of the most significant changes that took place through agricultural practice was the movement from feudalism to manorial self-sufficiency which not only created a new class of industry, but changed the ways in which obligation and duty were perceived.[62] Changing conceptions of cosmology as well as the capacities of humans to exploit their landscape unhinged Nature from its previously fixed position in the Elizabethan cultural imagination.[63] The human ability to affect the surrounding world opened up vast new possibilities

---

[60] Greene, 'Pitiful Thrivers'.

[61] Robert Brenner, in his influential article 'The Agrarian Roots of European Capitalism', *Past and Present*, 97 (November 1982), shows how England, unlike France or Germany, for example, broke free of its feudal class relations: 'In particular, the rise of the landlord/ capitalist tenant/wage-labourer system provided the basis for the transformation of agriculture and, in turn, the breakthrough to the ongoing economic development which took place in early modern England,' 18.

[62] On this point see Joan Thirsk, 'Plough and Pen: Agricultural Writers in the Seventeenth Century', in T. H. Aston et al. (eds.), *Social Relations and Ideas: Essays in Honour of R. H. Hilton* (Cambridge: Cambridge University Press, 1983), and *Economic Policy and Projects: The Development of a Consumer Society in Early Modern England* (Oxford: Oxford University Press, 1978); McRae, 'Husbandry Manuals and the Language of Agrarian Improvement', and Low, *The Georgic Revolution*.

[63] On this point, see Collingwood, *The Idea of Nature* and, for a more modern and penetrating study, see Soper, *What is Nature?*, and Stephen Horigan, *Nature and Culture in Western Discourses* (London: Routledge, 1988).

for the construction of socially acceptable ideals. In Shakespeare's poetry, duty occurs again and again as a requisite of passion and an anxiety of love: endlessly fraught by conflicts of obligation, the semantics of husbandry provide the poet with an urgent discourse on the ethics of expectation and the politics of reward. Obligation to oneself, God, or another became a subject under scrutiny as changing economic structures made room for greater independence and economic mobility. Within the context of these changing structures certain terms emerged as central to the social economy, particularly those of thrift, improvement, and profit.[64]

As previously discussed sonnet 4 begins with a confrontation between the natural and social worlds, the bodily and the economic in which the poet-speaker imports particular terms of value in order to exercise his subject with images of shame, neglect, or waste. For Helen Vendler, the poet-speaker uses the 'contaminated' language that the young man understands: 'the language of social, not natural exchange'.[65] Such an interpretation, however, retains a polarization of nature and society that is inappropriate within the context of these terms. There is no 'natural exchange' within the evolution of these terms: models of thrift, tenancy, and legacy are governed by an image of human intervention which is productive, managed, and democratic.[66] Translated as a virtue through classical texts on husbandry, thrift entered into the language of social relations as a form of human justice. According to Heresbach's reading of Cicero, for example, husbandry is 'the mistresse of justice, diligens, and thirftinesse' whereas in Tusser's 'The Ladder to Thrift', the term registers a comprehensive mode of living in which civility, trust, profit, and knowledge coexist.[67] When Shakespeare was writing his Sonnets, the term 'thrift' was in transition: developing from a generalized meaning of prosperity in the sixteenth century, the word accrues an economic precision in its relationship to frugality and saving (*OED* 3a). As a result, as McRae observes: 'In these senses "thrift" emerges as an ideal which legitimises and

---

[64] Aaron Kitch's *Political Economy and the States of Literature in Early Modern England* (Farnham: Ashgate, 2009) observes 'Shakespeare's concern with thrift' in this sonnet, 65, as well as the performative relationships between civic virtues of 'thrift and honesty' and the classical virtues of magnificence and liberality in the court masque and public progress, 160–1. See also Quentin Skinner, *The Cambridge History of Renaissance Philosophy* (Cambridge: Cambridge University Press, 1988), 342–3.

[65] *The Art of Shakespeare's Sonnets*, 62.

[66] According to Loys le Roy translation of *Aristotles politiques, or Discourses of gouernment* (1598): 'For the best sort of people are the Husbandmen, so that a Democracie may bee established, where they liue by Husbandrie or pasture,' 342.

[67] Heresbach, *Foure Bookes of Husbandrie*, 142. Tusser, *Five Hundred Points of Good Husbandry*, 13.

celebrates the economic aspirations and achievements of individuals.'[68] An index of the significance of this term can be found in the last reprinting of Fitzherbert's *Boke of Husbandrye* (1598) in the sixteenth century, in which the printer, James Roberts, introduced the term 'thrift' into the text as part of its modernization and its urgent reflection of 'the manner of a newer—and distinctly English—style of husbandry manual'.[69] The language of thrift belongs less to a 'contaminated' discourse of 'natural exchange' than to a rapidly developing landscape of values in which social success is determined by economic relations.

The network of terms that the poet-speaker introduces to pressurize the young man supports an idea of social relationships predicated on individual responsibility to a commonwealth. Nature here is no bountiful goddess but a landlady, setting the terms of her lease against the span of one man's life. The young man is set within a context of relationships determined by both the speaker's need as well as the socio-economic expectations placed upon him through the terms of thrift. In this way, the language of husbandry introduces us to a set of expectations that are developing even as Shakespeare writes. Central to this development, however, is a conflict between duty and desire, between personal advancement and social responsibility. Such a conflict, of course, is nowhere more powerfully expressed nor politically motivated than in the language of the national economy.[70]

The complex languages of creation, nurture, investment, and productivity find multiple expressions in doctrines of dominance and order. Whilst the husbandry manual reproduces an image of the land as a human resource, it also carefully constructs versions of mastery through manorial relations, domestic power structures, and a creative order in which 'man' works for God and is repaid by Nature. These notions of dominance and subservience are constantly being rehearsed at the level of animal and arable husbandry as well as in the domestic sphere.[71] Within

---

[68] *God Speed the Plough*, 144.

[69] See McRae on this point, *God Speed the Plough*, 143–5.

[70] Wendy Wall, in her essay 'Renaissance National Husbandry: Gervase Markham and the Publication of England', *Sixteenth Century Journal*, 27/3 (Autumn 1996), 767–85, explores the relationship between print and nationhood within the context of Markham's work. For Wall, Markham 'nationalises' English husbandry, simultaneously defining and creating a unique set of values associated with the English landscape. Equally resonant today, the rhetoric of the national economy informs an apparently collective understanding of human welfare. In a recent BBC news article, David Cameron is quoted as saying that '"popular capitalism" should allow "everyone to share in the success of the market"', BBC News Politics, 19 January. It is not clear, however, what 'popular capitalism' means in terms of social ethics.

[71] David Schalkwyk, *Shakespeare, Love and Service* (Cambridge: Cambridge University Press, 2008) explores the relationship between dominance and subservience in the Sonnets

these multiple power relations the child becomes an ideal subject for images of cultivation, since it discloses the importance of nurture and intervention in the creation of recompense. What forms such repayment takes are the subject of many humanist doctrines on education as well as marriage. Erasmus, for example, frequently employed the metaphor of the plough to invoke an image of labour that could produce profit, spiritual or civic. From his preface to *The New Testament* to *The Education of a Christian Prince*, the image of the plough sustained a humanist discourse of education and investment.[72] As Rebecca Bushnell discusses, however, in her exploration of early modern teaching, Erasmus 'warned parents . . . [that] "nature surrenders to you a newly plowed field (*natura tibi tradit in manus nuale, vacuum quidem, sed soli felicis*); if neglected it will bear thorns and brambles, which you will root out later only with great labour (*tu per incurium sinis hoc vepribus ac spinis occupari, vix vlla industria in posterum euellendis*)"'.[73] As the child is the fertile soil, so the parent/teacher is the husbandman, responsible for the growth and recompense of the young person. Within these grand doctrines of social duty and responsible pedagogy, the idea of fertile soil becomes a powerful metaphor for potential. In turn, potential then becomes a complex site of reward, profit, or expectation. Thomas Wilson's *The Arte of Rhetorique* (1553), for example, pursues the metaphor of the plough through a dense network of suggestions relating to the body, sex, procreation. and duty:

If that man be punished who little heedeth the maintenance of his tillage (the which although it be never so well manured, yet it yeildeth nothing else but wheat, barely, beans, and peasen), what punishment is he worthy to suffer that refuses to plough that land which being tilled yieldeth children? And for ploughing land, it is nothing else but painful toiling from time to time, but in getting children there is pleasure which, being ordained as a ready reward for painstaking, asketh a short travail for all the tillage.[74]

---

through the model of service in which the word 'friend' 'tolls with an insistent ambiguity throughout these poems, simultaneously direct, suggestive, and opaque as it shadows the early modern connotations of "companion", "lover", and "servant"', p. 115.

[72] Rebecca Bushnell's *A Culture of Teaching* discusses Erasmus, as well as a number of other prominent European humanists, within the context of these metaphors, esp. 73–116. She focuses particularly on the discursive analogies between gardener and teacher, which she follows up in her most recent book, *Green Desire*.

[73] *A Culture of Teaching*, 99. From Erasmus' *De pueris*, 75, translation is Bushnell's own.

[74] Thomas Wilson, *The Arte of Rhetorique* (London, 1553), fo. 29ᵛ. Herman, in 'What's the Use?', draws attention to this passage in the context of Shakespeare's procreation sonnets and points out that Wilson is almost entirely indebted to Erasmus for his observations on marriage in 'Epistle to Persuade a Young Gentleman to Marriage', 267.

Wilson moves from the figure of the neglectful husbandman to the man who will not reproduce by virtue of the image of cultivation. For Wilson, producing profitable crops and children is part of the same semantic landscape in which labour is a necessary part of pleasure and reward.[75] Wilson's dense metaphor is predicated on a certain value system which recognizes children as 'a ready reward' for 'painful toiling', whilst simultaneously identifying sex as a pleasurable part of that process. In order to make the leap from fieldwork to fatherhood, however, Wilson exposes the seriousness of human responsibility, both to the landscape and to reproduction. Paradoxically, however, it is in an image of bad husbandry that Wilson finds his most powerful social register:

> if a man had lande that wer very fatte and fertile, and suffered the same for lacke of maneryng, for euer to waxe barren, should he not, or wer he not worthy to be punished by the lawes, consideryng it is for the common weales behoue, that euery man should wel and truly husbande his awne.[76]

The interplay between the language of one's 'awne' and the commonwealth reveals the significance of the semantics of cultivation, since they are constantly seeking to articulate an active duty that is simultaneously civic and personal, urgent and universal. The temporal and social dynamic identified by these terms makes them lucid signs in the exploration of love. The constant demand for recompense or the persistent registers of labour make cultivation a powerful language in the expressions of love since such terms are always representing action, expectation, or desire. For Wilson, the play on 'husband' here recognizes marriage and children as to the benefit of the commonwealth.[77] The land and the body are both sites of duty in which yield and fertility represent a moral turnover. As the child becomes a representative image of social values as well as a metaphor for value itself, the semantic relationships between culture and cultivation become ever more complex.

Central to the mechanistic structure of social relations was an idea of sufficiency in which both the individual's and the community's needs were met. In his preface to the reader, Tusser explains:

---

[75] McRae examines the dialogue between pleasure and profit that informed much of the ideology of sixteenth-century husbandry manuals. As he notes, as a direct translation from the Latin 'utilitas', the word profit 'bears almost no financial connotations': through the works of agrarian writers, and Thomas Tusser in particular, 'the classical "profit and pleasure" neatly translates into "treasure and pleasure"', 'Husbandry Manuals', 49.

[76] Wilson, *The Arte of Rhetorique*, fo. 29ᵛ.

[77] Sonnet 8, for example, through an extended metaphor of musical notes, uses the figure of the 'husband' to invoke a necessary part of a harmonious whole, consisting of both a mother and a child.

> I have been praid
> To shew mine aid,
> In taking pain
> Not for the gaine
> But for good will,
> To shew such skill
> As shew I could:
> That husbandrie
> With huswiferie
> As cock and hen,
> To countrie men,
> All strangenes gone,
> Might joine in one,
> As lovers should. (7)

Tusser presents himself as the beneficent, but self-effacing, giver of knowledge for a community bound, in the image of husband and wife, cock and hen, in mutual benefit. The analogy of lovers exposes the emotive way in which Tusser presents his project as simultaneously ideological and ideal. Embedded in these terms, however, are specific models of behaviour which seek to expose as well as interrupt social relations. By extracting the child, the husband, or wife from their familial unit Shakespeare disturbs the household model in order to isolate the emotive potential of individual production. In sonnet 8, however, the poet-speaker likens these roles to musical chords in which harmony can only be produced in unison:

> Mark how one string, sweet husband to another,
> Strikes each in each by mutual ordering,
> Resembling sire and child and happy mother
> Who all in one, one pleasing note do sing:
> Whose speechless song, being many, seeming one,
> Sings this to thee: 'thou single wilt prove none'.

The 'husband' of 'mutual ordering' invokes the familial model as productive whilst those who are single 'prove none'. The emphasis here on concord and production supports a vision of the husband that was fundamental to the development of the values—social and personal—of husbandry.[78] In the Sonnets, good husbandry extends to the production

---

[78] Wendy Wall, in an essay on *The Merry Wives of Windsor*, explores the etymology of husbandry through the root husband: to be 'husbanded' is to be controlled, managed, herded by the male householder. For Wall, *Merry Wives* 'is saturated in the language of domestic management, as it investigates what might be called an affective husbandry'; in this way 'the uneasy relationship of desires to early modern discourses about husbandry thus leads us to reconsider the social norms that the play endorses'. Wall, '*The Merry Wives of Windsor*: Unhusbanding Desires in Windsor', in Richard Dutton and Jean E. Howard (eds.),

of a household that includes children as both a commodity and a profit. The home as an economic model of production becomes a powerful space for the exploration of the politics of love.[79]

Whilst the husband may provide the focus for the 'pleasing note' of social harmony, the wife occupies a more oblique role in the representation of domestic stability. Imagining a grieving world as a 'makeless wife', condemned to mourning by the young man's failure to reproduce, sonnet 9 articulates the 'single life' in terms that directly expose the subject to moral contempt:

> Look, what an unthrift in the world doth spend
> Shifts but his place, for still the world enjoys it;
> But beauty's waste hath in the world an end,
> And kept unused, the user so destroys it. (ll. 9–12)

Employing the language of unthrift and waste, the poet-speaker accuses the 'issueless' man of destroying both the order and the moral economy of reproduction. The word 'waste' was particularly emotive within the context of socio-economics. In pro-enclosure literature, for example, the term 'waste' was frequently invoked to represent common-land as a form of failure. In such tracts, reason was appealed to as a version of moral rationality:

The 'wild vacant waste lands, scattered up and down this nation...(like a deformed chaos) to our discredit and disprofit', put to shame 'an ingenious and industrious people', claims an Interregnum pamphleteer. Through enclosures, the land will be 'cleansed and purged of [its] former deformities'.[80]

In general use in the sixteenth century, the term 'waste' specifically applied to uncultivated land; in legal terminology, however, it refers to an unauthorized act of tenancy which infringes upon, or destroys, inheritance (*OED* 7). In sonnet 9, the young man is accused in both senses— destroying his own inheritance and leaving his beauty uncultivated. For the Elizabethans, beauty was cultivation because it represented order in an otherwise chaotic or waste landscape. Such beauty took the form of symmetry or visual harmony, as planted trees, furrowed land, strip farming, or growing harvests registered at every level the intervention of

---

A Companion to Shakespeare's Works, iii (Oxford: Blackwell, 2003), 379. See also Wall's *Staging Domesticity*, esp. 18–58, and Korda, *Shakespeare's Domestic Economies*, 15–51.

[79] In *Thinking with Shakespeare: Essays on Politics and Life* (Chicago: University of Chicago Press, 2011), Julia Reinhard Lupton explores *The Taming of the Shrew* within the context of the domestic economy, and, in particular, the domestic politics of housewifery, 25–7.

[80] McRae, *God Speed the Plough*, 162.

the human.[81] The image of the 'makeless wife', however, defines the subject's isolation in terms that impose upon society as a whole. Married to the 'world', the young man leaves it grief stricken and empty without the 'form of thee' 'behind'. As neither husband nor father, the 'single life' imagines a lovelessness akin to murder, or suicide:

> No love toward others in that bosom sits
> That on himself such murderous shame commits. (ll. 13–14)

Through the language of cultivation moral attitudes can be trafficked between the values of both production and expenditure, the individual and the 'world'.[82] But the domestic economy is not always an image of social sustainability.

The first eighteen sonnets rely on an idea of procreation to support an ethical code of production and profit, and the figure of the child continues to appear throughout the collection as an image of creativity that determines posterity. In sonnet 127, for example, the child emerges as a production of the mind:

> Look, what thy memory can not contain
> Commit to these waste blanks, and thou shalt find
> Those children nursed, deliver'd from thy brain,
> To take a new acquaintance of thy mind.
> These offices, so oft as thou wilt look,
> Shall profit thee and much enrich thy book.

Through the physical image of a child, thoughts and memories come alive—'deliver'd from thy brain'—in order to expose an image of creation that is simultaneously beneficial and productive. Part of the creative project is its futurity and images of profit come to rest on the material results of invention as production. The procreation sonnets work hard to establish these semantics of profit and the child becomes a valuable vehicle for the journey between the present and the future, investment and reward. As treatises on both education and housewifery testify, the language of profit and cultivation provided a powerful discourse for the representation of social value in line with economic production. Sir Arthur

---

[81] Keith Thomas, in *Man and the Natural World*, describes the ways in which the Tudors and Stuarts understood human intervention as aesthetic precisely because it recorded the imposition or order on an otherwise 'wild' landscape, 254.

[82] David Wootton's biography of *Galileo: Watcher of the Skies* (New Haven: Yale University Press, 2010) identifies the shift in the seventeenth century in which the term world could be understood to mean a global terrestrial space. In Galileo's destruction of 'the distinction between terrestrial and celestial affairs, the earth became part of the heavens and the heavenly bodies took on the appearance and followed the laws of the earth's surface'.

Capel, for example, in 1611 wrote a letter to his sister, concerning his daughter, in which he explains her qualities as well as her potential:

> She is young and inexperienced in housewifery which I hold one of the best qualities . . . stir her up to industry and diligence that idleness, one of the enemies of mankind, may be banished from her. Thus through God's blessing she may be a means to build and maintain the house where she is now planted.[83]

Employing Ciceronian terms of husbandry—diligence and industry— Capel endorses the ways in which the child supports a model of sustainability; 'planted' in a structure of housewifery that replicates both social and economic values. Within the domestic economy women's roles were clearly defined and replicated a patriarchal structure of relations that underpinned the agrarian industry. In the procreation sonnets, however, the child emerges as a figure of increase and legacy, playing on issues of legitimacy, posterity, and reward. Driven by more transparently economic registers, the early sonnets reveal a unique investment in the language of cultivation.

Beyond the role of husband or wife, Shakespeare uses the image of the mother to examine a version of love not predicated on production or unity, but on devotion and duty. Conventionally a figure of beneficence, bounty, and creation, the idea of the mother tends to accompany images of cultivation through growth. When Heresbach justifies his husbandry, he refers to it as 'the Mother and Nurse of all arts', conflating two often distinct roles.[84] While the mother may engender, the nurse nurtures; both provide the necessary factors for the growth and production of the human world.[85] Husbandry is both the earth and the mother, allowing the human to become the creator as well as the cultivator of life.

The role of the mother is written extensively throughout early modern husbandry manuals, partly as a reflection of Nature herself, partly as a

---

[83] As quoted by Anthony Fletcher, *Growing Up in England: The Experience of Childhood 1600–1914* (New Haven: Yale University Press, 2008), 260. See also Bushnell, *A Culture of Teaching*.

[84] Joan Thirsk attributes this thinking to Socrates: see *Culture and Cultivation*, 21. I discuss the resonance of this figure in further detail in *Henry V* and the biologically constructed ideas of the mother in *Macbeth*.

[85] In *The Winter's Tale*, Leontes distinguishes these roles in his vituperative attack on Hermione: 'Give me the boy: I am glad you did not nurse him; | Though he does bear some signs of me, yet you | Have too much blood in him' (1.2). The circulation of fluid—blood and milk—suggests the ways in which the image of mother and nurse endorses cultivation as a sympathetic relationship between the human and non-human worlds. Lynn Enterline observes, however, that 'in the Galenic tradition, a woman's blood and milk were interchangeable', *Shakespeare's Schoolroom: Rhetoric, Discipline and Emotion* (Philadelphia: University of Pennsylvania Press, 2012), 144.

model of nourishment upon which all forms of life depend, and partly as an exercise in housewifery. Sonnet 143's use of a maternal metaphor recognizes the multiple forms maternity plays in expressions of intimacy, kinship, growth, sex, and prudence.[86] The sonnet begins by introducing the domestic economy as both thrifty and emotional:

> Lo, as a careful housewife runs to catch
> One of her feathered creatures broke away,
> Sets down her babe, and makes all swift dispatch
> In pùrsuit of the thing she would have stay—
> Whilst her neglected child holds her in chase,
> Cries to catch her whose busy care is bent
> To follow that which flies before her face,
> Not prizing her poor infant's discontent:[87]

The sonnet introduces the image of the 'careful housewife' in order to explore the misplaced priority of quotidian responsibility over profound love. The tenor of the domestic metaphor is dependent upon an image of the housewife as caught in an urgent struggle between economic thrift and maternal duty.[88] The conflict of needs expressed by the moment in which the housewife is drawn two ways—one to rescue her escaped chicken, and two to comfort her crying baby—is used to identify the frailty of human judgement. The value of this metaphor for the poet-speaker is to expose the subject's judgement to scrutiny. Condemning her choice to follow the chicken, the poet-speaker constructs himself as the neglected child. Revealing the tensions within her value system, the poet composes the lovers as images of duty as well as production. The sophisticated emotional landscape that Shakespeare creates through the image of the housewife/ mother is supported by a range of values implicit in their roles, as it is also

---

[86] Naomi J. Miller explains that 'mothers in particular emerged as figures who combined their sexuality required for procreation with considerable authority over their offspring, male as well as female', 'Playing "the mother's part": Shakespeare's Sonnets and Early Modern Codes of Maternity', in James Schiffer (ed.), *Shakespeare's Sonnets: Critical Essays* (Oxford: Routledge, 1999), 347. Janet Adelman's *Suffocating Mothers: Fantasies of Maternal Origins in Shakespeare's Plays* (London: Routledge, 1992) remains the pre-eminent book on this subject.

[87] The accompanying sonnets, 142 and 144, explore these 'two loves' in a more metaphysical register and certainly in a more bitter way. The 'chains of desire', as Vendler terms them, record the speaker's love as thwarted, obstructed, or 'alienated'. See *The Art of Shakespeare's Sonnets*, 598–9.

[88] In *Literary Character*, Elizabeth Fowler explores the relationship between women and economy in *Piers Ploughman*. In this text, she argues, Langland 'describes a circulation of vicious surplus value.... The uncontrollable nature of this surplus circulation of payment is portrayed as feminine, and through this portrayal, the text claims that the economy must be morally analyzed and socialized by strict controls, just as marriage controls women and sexuality,' 119.

amplified by the presence of 'featured creatures'. In her dismissal of 'this preposterous analogy' Vendler neglects the powerful role of such feathered creatures within the Elizabethan cultural imagination.[89] Conrad Heresbach's *Foure Bookes of Husbandrie*, for example, discusses the benefits of poultry in the following terms:

In this Byrd there are three poyntes of naturall affection cheefely to be woondred at. The first, the great carefulnesse that they haue during the time of theyr sitting, wherin for the desire of hatching theyr young, they seeme to be carlesse of eyther meate or drinke. Secondly, that they beare such loue to them, as they sticke not to hazard theyr owne liues in the defence of them. And thirdly, that in the storme, great cold, or sicknesse, they preserue and nourish them vnder theyr winges, not making for the whyle any account of theyr owne selues. There is hereof a most sweete comparison in the Gospel, wherin our Sauiour *CHRIST* compareth him self to the Henne that gathereth her Chickins vnder her winges.[90]

Heresbach's chapter is dedicated to the profitability and uses of poultry, yet even within this utilitarian context the bird emerges as an identification of idealized social relations. The hen herself represents a version of the love that sonnet 143 tries to express: unconditional, prudent, and faithful. Heresbach extends our understanding of this love through the image of Christ and the ways in which these multiple images infuse notions of care and protection with a divine heroism. The heroic devotion of the hen is represented as the kind of love that is akin to sacrifice, without 'any account of thyr owne selues'. Many of Shakespeare's Sonnets, including 143, rehearse forms of love which are dependent on wider networks of care and not the individual needs of a single soul. The woman of sonnet 143 who is caught between her infant and her hens articulates a version of love in its competing forms—the love that transcends self-interest and the love that anticipates repayment. The sonnet proposes a set of images through which different loves can be explored: the needs of an infant, the duties of the housewife, the care of a mother, and the demands of a lover. If we read the maternal within the context of Heresbach's hens then

---

[89] Helen Vendler, however, calls it a 'preposterous little allegory', which 'offers no real analogy to sexual infidelity', *The Art of Shakespeare's Sonnets*, 601. It seems to me that Vendler fails to account for either the role of the mother or the bird in the Elizabethan imagination. This sonnet is not about infidelity but object choice: there is no indication that the woman is having a relationship with both object choices but chooses one over the other. Keith Thomas, *Man and the Natural World*, explores the role of the bird as a pet. James I, apparently, loved robins and had a pet kingfisher, 111–15. Bruce Boehrer, *Animal Characters: Nonhuman Beings in Early Modern Literature* (University Park, Pa.: University of Pennsylvania Press, 2010), examines the role of the parrot in the sixteenth- and seventeenth-century imagination.

[90] Heresbach, *Foure Bookes of Husbandrie*, 158^r.

we find the ultimate love of Christ, a love which is characterized as protective and unconditional. The sonnet registers these forms of love in the figure of the housewife, who is an image of both devotion and duty: yet, the domestic economy through which the sonnet moves works to desexualize the love under scrutiny whilst simultaneously recognizing the multiple ways in which obligation constructs emotion. Complicating these figures of devotion and duty is the poet-speaker, however, who, in comparing himself to the neglected child, suggests the figure of the hen as competition. Yet rather than see the analogy as competing lovers we might see it as competing loves: instant gratification as opposed to an unconditional commitment.[91]

Like social status, the reconstruction of gender through agricultural practice allowed for some degree of mutability in the representation of women. Whilst most husbandry manuals included a section for or about women, there were a number of manuals directed exclusively at women. Among these manuals, Gervase Markham writes the most comprehensive since he covers what he considers the necessary 'duties' of the 'complete woman', which include her 'inward' and 'outward' virtues as well as recipes, medicinal preparations, culinary advice, and kitchen gardening. In *Countrey Contentments* (1616; 1623), Markham begins with a summation of what constitutes a good housewife:

To conclude, our English Hus-wife must bee of chast thought, stout courage, patient, vntyred, watchfull, diligent, witty, pleasant, constant in friendship, full of good neghbour-hood, wise in discourse, but not frequent therein, sharpe and quicke of speech, but not bitter or talkatiue, secret in her affaires, comfortable in her counsels, and generally skilfull in the worthy knowledges which doe belong to her vocation. (4)[92]

The expectations of the housewife are high, and it is anticipated that she will fulfil these demands both within and outside of the domestic sphere.[93] Sonnet 143's glimpse into the conflicted duties of domestic demands and private devotion appear to recognize this conflict as running deep in human behaviour. The diction plays upon ideas of 'care' and neglect that begin through images of female domesticity but shift into sexual desire. The speaker of the sonnet moves himself into the position of the infant, apparently neglected, and chasing after the object of his devotion.

---

[91] The divided self of sonnet 144 can also be traced here in the figure of the housewife, through which the speaker projects his needs.

[92] Markham had published a version of this text in *The English Housewife* in 1615.

[93] Lorna Hutson, *The Usurer's Daughter: Male Friendship and Fictions of Women in Sixteenth Century England* (London: Routledge, 1994), explores the formation of cultural female identities through domestic space, esp. 47–50.

As the mother becomes the lover, the domestic images metamorphose into abstract ideas: the feathered bird becomes the subject's consuming hope; the distressed infant becomes the rejected lover:

> So run'st thou after that which flies from thee
> Whilst I, thy babe, chase thee afar behind;
> But if thou catch thy hope, turn back to me,
> And play the mother's part, kiss me, be kind.
> So will I pray that thou mayst have thy will,
> If thou turn back and my loud crying still.

Returning to the idea of the 'careful housewife', the speaker invokes that most sociable of emotions, kindness, only to transform it back into sexual desire through the pun on 'will'. The synthesis here between sexual desire, maternity, and domestic duty is not peculiar to Shakespeare's Sonnets. The housewife as a sexual object as well as a maternal presence is constantly articulated in husbandry manuals and conduct books through an absolute acceptance of her body as procreative as well as domestically responsible. There are numerous recipes for female infertility, mastitis, lactation, premature labour, inducing labour, the 'mother', and other conditions associated with women, as well as advice on conception and labour in which the female body is assimilated into abstractions on cultivation. One of the most fascinating registers of the female body is its representation in agrarian practice: women are so profoundly embedded in images of labour and productivity that they are absorbed into forms of male intervention. Charles Estienne's *Countrey Farme* devotes a good deal of text to female bodies and in his section on medicinal herbs he advocates the multiple properties of Bishops-weed (now more commonly known as Herb William), which:

craueth such ground and such tillage as Annise, which being once sowne, doth lightly grow there euerie yeare by the seed falling from it: it groweth chiefely in rested grounds. The seed is excellent good against Wringings and Gripes, to prouoke Womens termes, and Vrine, if it be drunke with Wine, so that it be vsed but seldome, for otherwise it causeth a pale colour. The perfume doth mundifie and cleanse the Matrix, and maketh barren women fruitfull, if together with this suffumigation the barren woman doe take euerie second morning the weight of a dramme of the powder of this seed, three houres before shee eat anie thing, continuing it for foure of fiue times: but in the meane time, the husband must lye with his wife vpon such daies as shee shall vse this powder: a thing proued diuers times. (249)

Making the barren fruitful ('Be fruitful and multiply' (Gen. 29: 31)) is central to the work of the good husbandman, and by isolating the womb as a site to be cleansed, filled, and reaped, the female body becomes a place of cultivation. Advising on growth, prescribing the herb followed by a directive to intercourse, Heresbach reiterates the role of the husbandman as the source of both production and authority. In this way, cultivating, curing, and procreating are seamlessly integrated into a chapter on 'Sweet smelling herbes', whilst the 'matrix' dominates the representation of the woman, her 'termes' and 'barren[ess]', suggesting a 'fruitful[ness]' associated with both the body and the land that supports her. The comprehensive way in which cultivating, sex, and procreation are accommodated into the language of husbandry manuals suggests the ways in which women were vital—figuratively and literally—to domestic production.

Isolating the image of the wife, mother, housewife, the speaker of sonnet 143 prompts the reader to engage with the woman as a figure of expectation as well as fulfilment, censure as well as admiration.[94] The kindness that sonnet 143 begs for is, within the context of 'the mother's part', informed by both compassion and duty and reflects the complex networks of expectations placed upon 'the careful housewife' that Markham reiterates. The ideas of labour that determine both sexes within the Tudor social economy are clearly defined: whilst the husbandman labours the earth for profit and improvement, the housewife nurtures the home in labour and productivity. Both discourses of labour imply a yield that can surface as infant or investment. Where the early sonnets, however, placed the child at the centre of a social economy, dependent on Christianized forms of duty, here sonnet 143 turns the lover into the child exposing love itself as form of investment and profit. The insistent anxieties about reciprocity that the Sonnets raise become increasingly defined by the tangible conditions of reward, asking the question: what is the return on my investment? As numerous humanist manuals on pedagogy show, the child is an exemplary figure in this context since the more you invest the greater your remuneration. Transposing this image onto the multiple networks of love allows the poet-speaker to interrogate competing forms of expectation—the unconditional love of a parent, the duties of obligation, and the rewards of investment. The ties that bind become increasingly defined by images of production and return.

---

[94] In the seventeenth century, however, women will become labourers and wage earners in the development of the domestic industry. Joyce Appleby discusses the role of women workers in the evolution of a capitalist economy and the rise of the dual domestic industry where husbandman and housewife could produce wool, spin, and weave as a cottage industry. Such entrepreneurialism, however, could not last as the gathering pace of the capitalist structure of the alienation of land and labour forced workers into longer hours. See *Economic Thought and Ideology* and Joan Thirsk, *Economic Policy and Projects: The Development of a Consumer Society in Early Modern England* (Oxford: Clarendon Press, 1978).

Practices of cultivation are one of the ways in which the human has
tried to intervene in, and capitalize on, nature's temporal patterns and it is
hardly surprising, therefore, that images of husbandry support an articulate language of ageing.[95] In a series of divine meditations entitled *The
Muses* (1612) which explore how the sinner faces death through a final
examination of the soul, John Davies draws on images of the land as a
vantage point between life and death, in which the flawed self must face
the consequences of its temporal actions.[96] As Davies confronts the ageing
body he turns to the metaphor of husbandry:

> I long haue cultur'd this but *flinty-field*,
> which yeelds but Crops of *Cares*, *Woes*, *wrongs*, and *spight*;
> Yeelding the more *annoy* the *more* they yeeld;
> whose very *Ioyes* are *Tares* that pine the *Spright*!
>
> Then, it is time to change (by heauenly *Arte*)
> the thriftlesse *course* of so course *Husbandry*;
> And with *Remorse* to furrow vp my Heart,
> melting the *Clods* with *teares*, that are too dry.
>
> And so to sow *Loues* seedes that faire encrease,
> to fat the *Soule* in vertue, till shee melt
> In flames of *Charitie* (till *Faith* doth cease)
> to giue more *taste* of *heauenly* pleasures *selt*.
>
> And sith my *Spring* is spent, my *Summer* past,
> and to the *Fall of leafe* my *Tyme* arriues: (84)

Here the action of one man's life is compared to methods of cultivation.
While the quality of that life may be flinty, the individual is still required
to labour and invest, furrow and sow. Yet here condemned to barren
resources his harvests emerge less as achievements and more as afflictions.
The image tells us that despite his labour, the soil was poor and the output
excoriating. Davies understands his life within the terms of predestination
in which he has little control over his final destination. By drawing on
images of cultivation, however, he obscures the emergent tradition to
which such images belong. Husbandry presupposes the affective role of
the human within his or her life. For Davies such actions are redundant,

---

[95] The Sonnets' most obviously natural images tend to cluster around concepts of Time,
in which seasonal patterns record the passages of human life. Perhaps the most potent
exception to this is sonnet 20, in which Nature is a goddess of human emotion: sexualized,
fallible, and faintly mischievous. The hand with which nature paints 'the master mistress' of
the speaker's passion is imbued with a caprice that seems distinctly mortal.

[96] Like Cicero's Dream of Scipio, the image of one's life or duties on earth is shown as
only one part of a vast structure in which we have no part and only partial perspective.
Davies's poem 'Orchestra' picks up on the Pythagorean elements of Cicero's Dream in
which the music of the spheres are imbued with a geometric harmony.

evincing only a 'thriftless course' of earthly failure. That 'heavenly arte' should take up the project of life's failed husbandry reproduces the values of cultivation in spiritual terms. Facing death, the fields of his life seem to have yielded nothing but heartache, but as he furrows his heart with the spirit of remorse, the poet turns to divine meditation for the 'arte' of heaven. In Davies's poem, spiritual cultivation exposes faith as the affective landscape in which the love of God is the only yield upon which the poet can rely.

The interrelations between Christianity and cultivation are always in evidence through the ways in which terms of husbandry appeal to both the moral and economic conditions of human life. Nowhere is this perhaps more marked that in sonnet 146.[97] Often read within the terms of medieval dialogues between the body and the soul, the images within this sonnet belong to traditions of Neoplatonism as well as Christianity. Drawing on the language of poverty, dearth, tenancy, store, and earth, however, the sonnet brings questions of investment into dialogue with those of mortality:

> Poor soul, the center of my sinful earth,
> ... these rebel pow'rs that thee array,
> Why dost thou pine within and suffer dearth,
> Painting thy outward walls so costly gay?

The impoverished soul, which, as has been frequently pointed out, appears to initially refer to a beloved and then to the subjective poetic voice, is positioned within the centre of the earth. As Stephen Booth comments, however, the centre functions as 'an indication of relative value' but what that 'center' is remains oblique. Conventionally understood as an image of hell, the centre of the earth emerges as an image of torment or self-loathing. For John Gerard, however, the centre of the earth was a relative indication of the earth's worth—not through allegorical terms of suffering—but through efficient practices of cultivation. For Gerard, mining is entering into the 'bowels of the earth':

Were your hearts but heavenly, & more time allowed for spiritual husbandry your inward comforts, would be much more, & your out ward gains not a jot less; for it the success of all your civil labours and imployments depend upon the pleasure &

---

[97] There is a great deal of excellent scholarship on the subject of this immensely complex sonnet. Stephen Booth outlines some of the problems with both the enjoyment and interpretation of this sonnet when he writes, 'that it is satisfying to read, unsatisfying to think about, and likely to evoke critical analyses that satisfy only by *making* the poem satisfying to think about', *Sonnets*, 507. Booth lists some of the recent contributions to this critical debate, including B. C. Southam and Charles Huttar. I would add Michael Schoenfeldt, Patrick Cheney, and James Schiffer.

will of God; (as all that are not Atheists do acknowledge) then certainly, your business can succeed never the worse, for your endeavours to please him, upon whose pleasure it so intirely depends.

Gerard makes the distinction between the earth's centre and the 'treasure' of its fields, flora, and fauna, through an idea of husbandry which is both spiritual and practical—godly and civic. In this way, the heart can be understood as a centre of toil that radiates outward rather than inwards, towards 'civil labours' rather than personal vanity. The sonnet's terms of self-loathing through which the speaker projects his condition manifest as economic. 'Dearth', a very real description of famine in the 1590s, is a condition of the unproductive, 'sinful earth', in which the speaker's body emerges as corrupt, wasteful even:

> Why so large cost, having so short a lease,
> Dost thou upon thy fading mansion spend?
> Shall worms, inheritors of this excess,
> Eat up thy charge? Is this thy body's end?

Returning to the idea of nature's lease, the ageing body is cast as a structure which requires no further investment. There is no sense of futurity here; no mechanisms of perpetuity through which the fading mansion can be either preserved or recovered. Unlike the potential off-spring of the young man, there are no 'inheritors' here except the worms that return the body to the site of its historic genesis:

> And let that pine to aggravate thy store:
> Buy terms divine in selling hours of dross;

The central paradox of waste or negative investment comes to rest in the final couplet. The subject's body is mediated through terms of economic failure in which the body is burdened by a store of 'dross', from which only the soul can extract itself. The pining soul continues to weigh down the body in an image which not only suggests a Cartesian dualism but also figures the soul as in judgement upon the body which it inhabits. The imprudent economy of the body is putatively redressed by the soul's exchange of temporal dross for 'terms divine'. Castigating the body as a sinful earth, which imposes dearth upon the poor soul, the poet-speaker establishes the moral implications of his bodily economy. In spite of the soul's apparently successful exchange of dross for divine, the earthly body remains the central image of loss and failure. The reader is not convinced that the soul redresses the body's bad investments and the 'terms divine' appear more interrogative than consolatory.

Throughout the Sonnets the poet-speaker relies on the invocation of a dense value system in which certain images and ideas, and their internal networks of reference, import a powerful logic of social or personal reward. Husbandry is central to the representation of this value system since it has come to anticipate something economically and ethically good. Beyond the immediate impact of investment and labour, however, the language of husbandry records a set of relationships dependent upon both action and service: the servant body of sonnet 146, for example, or the 'lord and owner' of personal riches in sonnet 94.

In one of Shakespeare's most quoted sonnets, husbandry manifests as a reward for self-control, here construed as something that requires both labour and management:

> They that have the pow'r to hurt, and do none,
> That do not do the thing they most do show,
> Who moving others are themselves as stone,
> Unmovèd, cold, and to temptation slow—
> They rightly do inherit heaven's graces,
> And husband nature's riches from expense; (94)

Conventional readings of this sonnet have tended to interpret 'Unmovèd, cold, and to temptation slow' as something inherently negative, particularly when contrasted with the earlier sonnet's celebration of action. Michael Schoenfeldt, however, considers such readings 'anachronistic'. Situating the sonnet within the context of humanist models of self-management, Schoenfeldt identifies that the 'modes of constraint we construe as unhealthy repression are coveted as acts of self-government necessary for the maintenance of self and the protection of others'.[98] I would add to Schoenfeldt's argument the proposition that the terms of husbandry to which the sonnet appeals precisely belong to this humanist tradition of both self-mastery and potential.

Returning to the ethical implications of waste (expense), the speaker of sonnet 94 endows the subject with the reward of heaven's graces: the suggestion is that this store of grace can only be harvested by those who have the capacity to cultivate: here understood as a form of self-management. Composure—imagined in the form of the implacable stone—represents a version of patience, labour, and integrity associated with the values of husbandry. As Tusser and others observe: 'The stone that is rowelling can gather no Mosse, | For Master and Servant oft changing is losse.'[99] Stasis or stillness is a requisite of gain. In this way, the husband-man, or Markham's 'master of the earth', invokes the necessary qualities for success: controlled (and controlling), cautious, and thrifty. Identifying the subject as capable of husbanding 'nature's riches from expense', the

---

[98] *Bodies and Selves*, 84.   [99] *Five Hundred Pointes of Good Husbandrie*, fo. 70ᵛ.

poet-speaker celebrates the roles of knowledge and prudence in preventing waste. The ethical and moral integrity associated with the language of husbandry is almost always appropriated by humanists as a form of self-governance. As I discussed in relation to the procreation sonnets, Elyot's *Boke Named The Governor* or Erasmus' preface to *The New Testament* reflect education (whether of others or the self) as a form of both mastery and cultivation. The repressed tension suggested by those who *can* but do *not* hurt is indicative of the integrity afforded to those who have learned the value of control and its necessary role in production.

Moving from the abstract to the particular, the contest between an essential and controlled nature is manifest in the image of the lily versus the weed. Contesting any notion of essentialized perfection the lily represents a form of equivocal beauty; capable of putrefaction so significant in its departure from the ideal form that it is morally reprehensible. The sonnet presents the flower as governed by a larger network of conditions, here construed as summer, in which order and belonging denote the expectations of the individual. The 'summer's flower' is 'to the summer sweet' precisely because it belongs to a system of growth and replenishment in which the summer is the governing figure of value.[100] The sweetness of the summer's flower, whether to others or the summer—is determined by the ways in which it takes part in the season's expectations of growth and decay. Part of the celebration of this summer's flower is its ability to belong to a set of expectations other than its own.

As Schoenfeldt says, 'it has proven particularly difficult for modern readers to see how being unmoved can be imagined as an avenue to heaven'.[101] Within the context of the husbandry, however, we can begin to see how values of control, management, and prudence emerge as conditions of social and natural mastery. Drawing on the terms of management central to the conditions of self-governance, the poet-speaker asserts:

> They are the lords and owners of their faces,
> Others but stewards of their excellence.

---

[100] In *Summer's Last Will and Testament*, Thomas Nashe dramatizes the seasons through a mock trial in which a dying Summer must hand over her legacy to one of the other seasons. The play consistently draws on the language of husbandry as an example of the ways in which the seasons do or do not demonstrate their worth. Like Shakespeare's sonnet, Summer stands as the governing social image of both prosperity and integrity. As C. L. Barber writes, however, 'All except Harvest are found wanting and condemned to suffer the pains appropriate to their particular kind of excess,' *Shakespeare's Festive Comedy: A Study of Dramatic Form and its Relation to Social Custom* (Princeton: Princeton University Press, 1959), 60.

[101] *Bodies and Selves*, 84.

The images of reward suggested by 'nature's riches' and 'heaven's graces' exposes the subject of the sonnet as intricately tied to a manorial system in which 'they' own their body (or face) and the emotionally imperfect left behind are duty bound to support them. Through the language of husbandry, terms like 'inherit' 'steward', 'owner[ship]', and 'expense' reflect a manorial system in which those capable of governance (self and others) can reap the rewards, whilst those in the middle, the stewards, remain in service. As Iago suggests, husbandry is a form of control through which the 'will' (directed or repressed) emerges as reason, capable of cultivating and authorizing the self.

The language of the sestet shifts the focus from the social to the natural worlds by way of the floral images. Celebrating a form of both expectation and decorum in the image of the summer's flower, the poet-speaker re-engages with the terms of integrity through a sense of containment or self-possession in the ability to resist 'base infection'. Nobility, 'grace', or even beauty are not essential qualities but emerge in action or reaction. 'They that have the power to hurt and do none' are those people who are capable of exhibiting control. This control, so the sonnet suggests, is a form of cultivation in which the subject refrains from contamination through a supreme act of self-mastery:[102]

> The summer's flower is to the summer sweet,
> Though to itself it only live and die;
> But if that flow'r with base infection meet,
> The basest weed outbraves his dignity.
> For sweetest things turn sourest by their deeds;
> Lilies that fester smell far worse than weeds.

The value lies, as Iago would say, in the 'power and corrigible authority' of 'our will'. The festering lily, however, belongs to both proverbial and Christian wisdom, in which all human life is required to fulfil its potential, whether through salvation or damnation.[103] In an allegorical context the lily tended to represent a generic term for large, flamboyant flowers, whilst in a strictly horticultural context in England it referred to the delicate flowers of lily-of-the-valley. Although its rather exotic image may support

---

[102] Thomas Elyot, in *The Blanket of Sapience* (1564), describes a 'Good Man' as involved in this kind of balanced control: 'We maie call that man gratious, to hom nothinge is good or ylle, but a good mynde or an yll, whiche is a louer of honestie, contented onely with vertue, whom no fortune extolleth or oppresseth, nor knoweth any thing to be better, then that he may geue to him selfe, to whom veray pleasure is, to set lyttle by pleasure,' 24ᵛ.

[103] See M. P. Tilley, *A Dictionary of the Proverbs in England in the Sixteenth and Seventeenth Centuries* (Ann Arbor: University of Michigan Press, 1950), Posse et nolle, nobile, 'to be able to do [harm] and unwilling to do it is noble' (H170).

the exceptional beauty of the subject, its capacity to obscure sin is also resonant within the context of seventeenth-century symbolism. Thomas Adams's collection of sermons, entitled *A Divine Herbal* (1616), uses the flower as a curious image of both humility and corruption in his sermon on pride and covetousness:

> I could willingly steppe out a little to chide those, that neglecting Gods *Earth,* the Soule; fall to trimming with a curious superstition the *Earths* earth, clay and lome: a body of corruption painted, til it shine like a Lilly (like it in whitenesse, not in humility, the candor of beautie; for the lilly growes lowe; *Lilium conuallium,* a flower of the vallies and bottomes) a little slime done ouer with a past-boord; rottennesse hidde vnder golden leaues; stench lapp'd vp in a bundle of silkes: and by reason of poison suck'd from sinne and hell, worthy of no better attribute then glorious damnation.[104]

Adams initially invokes the flower, here lily-of-the-valley, as an example of glorified deception ('corruption painted') whilst simultaneously acknowledging its 'humility'. He then goes on, however, to vividly describe the coexistence of beauty and putrefaction, where rottenness hides under golden leaves, 'stench lapp'd up in a bundle of silks', to arrive at his condemnation (equally paradoxical): 'glorious damnation'. Like Claudius' 'painted word' or Lady Macbeth's serpent infested 'innocent flower', the image is one of duplicity or duality, where harm and good can coexist. Translating the acerbic tone of the initial praise into something altogether more accusatory, the image of the lily vividly invokes the potential corruption of beauty. Unlike the earlier sonnets in which beauty was a stable concept of Neoplatonic virtue, to be aspired to and reproduced, here beauty is truly skin-deep: and, uniquely for Elizabethan aesthetics, about behaviour as well as appearance. The lily does not conceal sin, like cosmetics or rhetorical flourishes, but can become sin itself. But unlike traditional figures of deception (Spenser's Duessa, for example) the lily's whiteness, fragility, and quintessential 'humility' appears to exonerate it from any charges of temptation. Conventionally, however, the festering lily is unusual since the flower is more typically a stable image of purity that may be *threatened* by 'thorns' or sin but is not capable of sin itself. Erasmus is conventional, for example, in his associating the lily with Christ:

> He was the lylie of the Ualleis amonge the thorny and vntylled gentiles, to whom it is perswaded, that he became man, and was borne of the Uirgin Marie without spotte of synne. Surely he was the euangelicall lilie, that god the father so clothed, as neuer Salomon was arrayed in al his great glory. For why, neither Salomon, nor

---

[104] Thomas Adams, *A divine herball together with a forrest of thornes* (London, 1616), 5.

yet none other, was euer borne of a pure virgin, defyled with no spotte of the fyrst parent. Who so euer couple them selfe by feyth to this lilie, bycause they are made one fleshe and one spirite with hym, they are pourged from fylthy synnes, they receyue the fayre white garment of innocency, and be also made Lylies.[105]

Within the context of Erasmus' and Adams's lilies, sonnet 94 exposes its subject's moral duty to questions of righteousness. Whether he is godly, elect, or perhaps an image of perfection within the speaker's eyes is not clear: what is clear, however, is that the image is radically more ambivalent than its Christian heritage would suggest. Sonnet 94 brings the social images of restraint and stasis to rest in the idea of a flower that has the capacity to putrefy: this is the language of self-management, social responsibility, and duty that became increasingly removed from its Christian prehistory and more and more defined by the politics of self-interest.

[105] Desiderius Erasmus, *The comparation of a vyrgin and a martyr* (London, 1537), 6ᵛ–7ʳ.

3

Henry V

Humanity and Husbandry

In 1597–8 Elizabeth's parliament passed 'An Act against the decaying of townes and houses of husbandry'. Controversial in its scope, this Act legislated for the restitution of tillage through the conversion of pasture to arable land and the reconstruction of any dwelling that had been destroyed or deserted as a result of enclosures.[1] Focusing on the moral and economic effects of the decaying of husbandry, the statute establishes the imperatives of this act:

Where a good part of the strength of this realm consisteth in the number of good and able subjects and whereas the decays of townes and habitations have by the ancient laws of this realm esteemed a high offence, and where in late years more than times past there have been sundry townes, parishes, and houses of husbandry been destroyed and become desolate, by means whereof a great number of poor people have become wanderers, idle, and loose, which is the cause of infinite inconveniences.[2]

The yeoman, the labourer, and the peasant—good and able subjects— represent the 'strength of this realm' in their ability to both supply and defend the country's interests. Through the loss of husbandry, those subjects

---

[1] Parliament debates between 1598 and 1601 continue to record the controversy of this Act. Notoriously divisive, the subject of enclosures dominated social attitudes to economic development. There was a certain hostility, expressed particularly by Raleigh, to having land use legislated: 'I do not like the constraining of them to use their grounds at our wills but rather let every man use his ground to that which it is most fit for, and therein use his own Discretion', H. T. Townsend, *Historical Collections* (1680), 188. As cited by Maurice Beresford, who explores some of the debates around toleration and agrarian specialization that continued to emerge throughout these years, *Essays in the Economic and Social History of Tudor and Stuart England*, ed. F. J. Fisher (Cambridge: Cambridge University Press, 1961), 40–69. While many saw Elizabeth's Act as regressive, others welcomed parliament's investment in the social effects of depopulation. The Act, however, did make concessions to regions which landscapes were ill suited to arable farming: Shropshire was allowed to remain largely pasture due to its soil composition as the 'Dayrie house to the whole Realme'.

[2] 39 & 40 Elizabeth Cap. I. Dramatized through the characters of Bardolph and Nim, the play presents such 'idle' and 'loose' figures as images of pity rather than censure.

have become poor, idle, and 'loose', devoid of the networks of labour and production upon which their lives depend. The transition from good subject to idle wanderer articulates a major anxiety in Elizabethan politics.[3] The Act makes its radical provisions for the restoring of the English landscape on the basis of the security of the commonwealth. Following on from this, 'An Act for the maintenance of husbandry and tillage' (1598) declares:

Whereas the strength and flourishing estate of this kingdom . . . is greatly upheld and advanced by the maintenance of the plough and tillage being the occasion of the increase and multiplying of people both for service in the wars and in times of peace, being also a principle mean that people are set on work and thereby withdrawn from idleness, drunkenness, unlawful games and all other lewd practices . . . and whereas by the same means . . . the greater part of the subjects are preserved from extreme poverty and the wealth of the realm is kept dispersed and distributed in many hands where it is more ready to answer necessary charges for the service of the realm; and whereas the said husbandry and tillage is a cause that the realm does more stand upon itself, without depending on foreign countries . . . [4]

Husbandry, according to the directives of both these Acts, provides a vital industry in the creation and maintenance of the country's strength.[5] Supporting labour, production, self-sufficiency, and service, agrarian cultivation upholds the country's moral and economic vision: 'the strength and flourishing estate of this kingdom'. The ethical attitudes written deep into this legislative framework can be traced through the persistent anxieties about idleness, disorder, foreign involvement, and private industry.[6] Husbandry supports, through the statutory representation of social and economic welfare, the future of Elizabeth's kingdom. Beyond the immediate impacts of food production, however, tillage also represents 'the occasion of the increase and multiplying of people both for service in the wars and in times of peace'. Husbandry, as this chapter will suggest, is central to the terms of both war and peace: managing borders, providing able subjects, sustaining economic advantage, and promoting regional security, attitudes to agrarian industry recorded deeply held convictions

---

[3] In An Act for the Relief of the Poor (1568), Elizabeth I licensed parish Justices to dispense relief to the poor; should, however, any of the 'said poor folks so licensed shall transgress the limits to them appointed . . . the party so transgressing shall be taken for a valiant beggar and punished according to the Statute', 5 Elizabeth, Cap. III, x.

[4] 39 & 40 Elizabeth Cap. II.

[5] In a commons debate in 1621, John Pym records that 'the husbandman beareth the greatest burthen of the commonwealth', Joan Thirsk and J. P. Cooper (eds.), *Seventeenth Century Economic Documents* (Oxford: Clarendon Press, 1972), 5.

[6] Patricia Fumerton, in *Unsettled: The Culture of Mobility and the Working Poor in Early Modern England* (Chicago: University of Chicago Press, 2006), explores vagrancy and migration, particularly in relation to population growth and rural depopulation, 3–32.

about the moral stability of England. Alongside 'the multiplying of people for service', agrarian cultivation supports an ethical vision, in which people are 'withdrawn' from sin and bound to local networks of state production: 'the greater part of the subjects are preserved from extreme poverty and the wealth of the realm is kept dispersed and distributed in many hands'.[7] Through the terms and practices of cultivation we begin to see how the politics of social welfare are intimately tied to an agrarian order, which promises—and promotes—stability and security.

Dramatizing a discernible past through forms of regional and national conflict makes the history plays a suggestive place for the exploration of ideas of cultivation.[8] From Richard II's 'sea-walled garden', to Hotspur's repeated call for the 'best of all my land' (3.1.96) the focus on fertility registers the land as an economic investment as well as a profitable possession.[9] Equally, the moral complexities of good government and the history of Tudor rule make the ethical representation of the landscape provocative.[10] As the history plays engage directly with monarchical authority so they also become touchstones for the critical exploration of England's historical past. But, as Richard Dutton observes, 'The great majority of chronicle history plays are in fact "generic hybrids" . . . blended with romance material—fantasies of love, of exile, of transformation, of the mingling of kings and commoners.'[11] As 'generic hybrids', however, the history plays' interrogation of good government often resonates

[7] In *An Age of Transition*, Christopher Dyer discusses the way in which England could function as a state, compared to the more segregated, regional politics of other European countries. In this way, state legislation supported little substantive local variation in England so that most inhabitants operated under unified polices, see esp. 111–14.

[8] Garrett Sullivan's *The Drama of Landscape* makes particularly fascinating use of Arden of Faversham in his interrogation of the 'cultural conflict between the imperatives of landscapes of stewardship, custom and absolute property', 32. Central to Sullivan's argument is 'a reconceptualization of the land, an emergent view of land not as social space but as commodity, as salable, manipulable lot,' 37–8.

[9] There is a formidable body of work that stands behind concepts of nationalism and nationhood, in this context, the most pertinent of which is Helgerson, *Forms of Nationhood*; Sullivan, *The Drama of Landscape*, esp. 57–91; Wall, 'Renaissance National Husbandry'; and Benedict Anderson's *Imagined Communities: Reflections on the Origin and Spread of Nationalism* (London: Verso, 1993), esp. 9–46.

[10] David Bevington, in Arthur Kinney (ed.), *The Oxford Handbook of Shakespeare* (Oxford: Oxford University Press, 2012), explores the critical history of interpreting these plays as propaganda, or as a representation of Tudor mythology, 307–15. Throughout the three plays of *Henry VI*, the 'strength and safety of our country' (*3 Henry VI*, 3.3) is in contention. Dramatized through a combination of weak leadership, divisive factions, and an economic depression, these plays expose the structure of the commonwealth to be unstable. The young king's cry for 'God's glory and my country's common weal' resounds throughout these plays as a tragic, and failed, vision. (*1 Henry VI*, 5.1).

[11] Dutton, 'The Dating and Contexts of Henry V', in Paulina Kewes (ed.), *The Uses of History in Early Modern England* (San Marino, Calif.: Henry Huntingdon, 2006), 171.

outwards from the monarch as the centre of power to the wider questions of civility, duty, and responsibility. The second tetralogy has often been interpreted within the framework of a discourse of leadership and the ways in which these plays complicate and expose notions of 'right rule'. In *Shakespeare and the Popular Voice*, Annabel Patterson interprets *Henry V* within the context of the political conflict between Elizabeth I and the Earl of Essex in which the terms of 'popularity' and 'obedience' come to represent the divergent contexts of the quarto and folio texts. For Patterson, *Henry V* evinces a hiatus in contemporary politics which was moving towards 'a new political environment, new definitions of the nation and the nature of monarchy'.[12] Much of the scholarly interest in *Henry V* has focused on the play as demonstrating a developing idea of nationhood and the eponymous hero as a figure of political significance, especially in relation to strategies of power.[13]

While in modern politics such strategies of power tend to emerge in commitment to war, Elizabeth I's agrarian policies identified the role of peace in the defence of a nation. Under Elizabethan statute, peace was England's greatest asset for 'the strength and flourishing' of the kingdom, and nowhere was peace more visible than in the cultivation of the landscape. Attending to the ways in which good husbandry could legislate against invasion, idleness, and poverty we become aware of the role of cultivation in the representation of the social security of the commonwealth.

Suggesting that *Henry V* 'looks forward to the restoration of husbandry and humanity', Joel Altman, in his critically defining essay 'Vile

---

[12] Reading the play as an attempt to mediate between the ambitions of Essex and the insecurities of the aged queen, Patterson points to the value of these processes in literature 'by reinstating within it a common-sense relation between events and human agents'. Patterson, *Shakespeare and the Popular Voice* (Oxford: Basil Blackwell, 1989), 92, 87.

[13] Almost all scholarship, in this context, finds Henry ambiguous: Hazlitt's 'amiable monster'; part schemer, part hero; both manipulative and charismatic. Some of the most articulate scholarship on this subject includes Stephen Greenblatt, *Shakespearean Negotiations: The Circulation of Social Energy in Renaissance England* (Berkeley and Los Angeles: University of California Press, 1988), Norman Rabkin, 'Either/Or: Responding to Henry V', in *Shakespeare and the Problem of Meaning* (Chicago: University of Chicago Press, 1981), Patricia Parker, *Shakespeare from the Margins: Language, Culture and Context* (Chicago: University of Chicago Press, 1996), Andrew Hadfield, 'Henry V', in Richard Dutton and Jean E. Howard (eds.), *A Companion to Shakespeare's Works: The Histories* (London: Blackwell, 2003), Graham Holderness, *Shakespeare: The Histories* (New York: St Martin's Press, 2000), Anne Barton, 'The King Disguised: The Two Bodies of Henry V', in Joseph G. Price (ed.), *The Triple Bond: Plays, Mainly Shakespearean, in Performance* (University Park, Pa.: Pennsylvania State University Press, 1975), A. P. Rossiter, *Angel with Horns: And Other Shakespeare Lectures* (London: Longmans,1961), Peter C. Herman, 'O 'tis a gallant king: Shakespeare's Henry V and the Crisis of the 1590s', in Dale Hoak (ed.), *Tudor Political Culture* (Cambridge: Cambridge University Press, 1995).

Participation', concludes 'that the fifth act, which so often appears as the obligatory coda to a rousing national epic, is performing a much richer historical function than we are normally in a position to appreciate'.[14] In what follows I would like to focus on the rich historical function of both husbandry and humanity to which Altman refers. In Shakespeare's *Henry V* these terms come to dominate the last section of the play. While a great deal of the scholarly interest in this play has focused on the politics of Henry's war, little attention has been paid to the politics of his peace. This peace, according to the Duke of Burgundy, is dependent upon the terms of husbandry, the 'Dear nurse of arts, plenties and joyful births.' Establishing the necessity of good husbandry to the future of France, Burgundy invokes a highly politicized language of security, morality, and sustainability. Possibly excised from the first printed quarto (1600), and articulated by the opponent, these scenes offer us a vivid discourse on the nature of good government.[15] Simultaneously social and economic, Burgundy's vision of his decaying country represents one of the most persistent debates in Elizabethan politics. As Richard Dutton asserts: 'Burgundy's long speech on the effects of war on "this best garden of the world" (5.2.36), France, ties in with the folio's altogether more complex and questioning approach to Henry's achievements than we find in the quarto: here it is the implication that warfare may ruin what it seeks to conquer.'[16] Focusing on the latter sections of the play, this chapter will explore how the terms of husbandry become central not only to the 'questioning' of 'Henry's achievements' but also to the representation of 'the strength and flourishing estate of this kingdom'.

Exploring Elizabeth's commitment to the agricultural economy and the terms through which that commitment shaped human relations, we begin

---

[14] Altman, ' "Vile Participation": The Amplification of Violence in the Theater of Henry V', *Shakespeare Quarterly*, 42/1 (1991), 32.

[15] Annabel Patterson understands the discrepancies between the quarto and folio versions of this play as a result of some kind of censorship. Suggesting that Shakespeare writes the folio version of the text in 1599, she surmises that it is cut in the 1600 quarto because the allusions to Essex, popular uprising, and the Choruses are too inflammatory. The quarto therefore becomes a more simplified, patriotic play. Although Patterson cannot present any substantive evidence, her argument is attractive precisely because the inclusion of the Essex material in the folio seems irrelevant at this stage, *Shakespeare and the Popular Voice*. Lukas Erne, however, perceives the longer folio text as a more literary construction, as opposed to a shorter, possibly memorial, performance text, *Shakespeare as Literary Dramatist* (Cambridge: Cambridge University Press, 2003), esp. 220–44. Both positions are necessarily speculative, but given how pertinent and political Burgundy's speech is in the light of recent Elizabethan statutes, there is a compelling argument in suggesting that they were excised in the quarto precisely because the sentiments emerge from France rather than England.

[16] Kewes (ed.), *The Uses of History*, 199.

to observe the ways in which *Henry V* draws on the politics of cultivation in its representation of war. The landscape is not only the site of conflict, it also comes to represent the values of those who fight, live, and die by it. The earth as a soldier's tomb, a monarch's possession, a nation's future, or a yeoman's livelihood recognizes the power of the landscape in the shaping of human lives. Drawing on all these elements, *Henry V* puts husbandry at the centre of its political relations, seeking to rationalize the land it dramatizes through the replacement of social welfare with economic gain.

In the final act of *Henry V*, the King of England declares, 'Peace to this meeting, wherefor are we met' (5.2.1), addressing the King of France and various members of their nobilities, including the Earl of Warwick and the Duke of Burgundy. After the formal greetings between the kings have been made, riven as they are with false felicity, the Duke of Burgundy steps forward with 'duty', he claims, to them both with 'equal love', and

> ... all my wits, my pains, and strong endeavours,
> To bring your most imperial majesties
> Unto this bar and royal interview,
> Your mightiness on both parts best can witness. (5.2.25–8)

Conflating the language of the royal and legal courts to set the gravity of the scene, and the nature of the place ('bar and royal interview'), Burgundy goes on to make one of the most sustained moral arguments within the play. This argument is built exclusively on the language of husbandry—of management, cultivation, improvement, welfare, and profit. Burgundy presents a landscape, boundless in its location, yet specific in its chorography of hedges, flowers, weeds, and produce, that comes to reflect some of the major concerns of the play: status, possession, duty, order, and futurity. The ethics of war come into conversation in a landscape that should belong to Peace:[17]

> What rub or what impediment there is
> Why that the naked, poor, and mangled peace,
> Dear nurse of arts, plenties and joyful births,
> Should not in this best garden of the world,
> Our fertile France, put up her lovely visage? (5.2.33–7)[18]

---

[17] Sidney's *Arcadia* (1590) talks of husbandry as 'the child of peace', 7ᵛ; of 'converting husbandrie to soldiery' with 'pitchforks and rakes', 223ʳ.

[18] This speech appears in the folio (1623), rather than the quarto text (1600). The debates as to the status of these texts are numerous but as Richard Dutton points out, 'For this reason a true historical close reading of the play is impossible,' *The Use of History*, 198. There are, however, as Dutton also notes, many compelling reasons for privileging the folio text above that of the quarto, a text which Gary Taylor observes as having been 'adapted and debased to make it conform to the very expectations about Henry which previous plays

Here Burgundy conflates two traditions in the representation of the land: the Ciceronian and the Complaint. One of the most popular conceits for the writer on husbandry was the classical affiliation between husbandry and virtue. According to Googe's translation of Heresbach:

Cicero calleth it [husbandry] the mistresse of iustice, diligens, and thriftinesse: some others call it the Mother and Nurs of al other artes. For wheras we may liue without the other ['richness'], without this we are not able to sustayne our life: besides, the gayne that hereof aryseth, is most godly, and least subiect to enuie, for it hath to deale with the Earth, that restoreth with gayne such thinges as is committed vnto her, specially [if] it be furthered with the blessing of GOD. (7ʳ)

For Burgundy, Peace is the 'Dear nurse of arts', the conditions under which the 'best garden of the world' should thrive. Yet 'mangled' as she is by war, the landscape is suppressed, impeded, and eventually destroyed. In Googe's translation, the earth is a God-given resource that registers our right to life; if we neglect it 'we are not able to sustain our life'. Echoing the sentiments of Elizabeth's Act, the relationship between husbandry and human welfare is made absolutely explicit: 'the said husbandry and tillage is a cause that the realm does more stand upon itself'. The sense of national-sufficiency to which these terms appeal presents the cultivated landscape as a record of human life, simultaneously locating and representing social systems of worth. The complex domestic economy supported—and controlled—by the manorial system allowed the landscape to be a register of distress, abuse, oppression, and need just as much as 'justice, diligence and thriftiness'. Most forcefully articulated in the Tudor complaint, agrarian land represented the extent to which the poor, the peasantry, and the tenant farmer could expect to survive. The threat of poverty through depopulation, dearth, or dispossession can only be managed—even hypothetically—through the land as the primary source of social and material production. The relationship between war and husbandry is subtle but persistent: the yeoman conscripted as a soldier; the increased demand on resources; the vulnerability of borders emptied of their labouring force all register the interrelationships between the service

would have aroused', *Henry V*, ed. Gary Taylor (Oxford: Oxford University Press, 2008), 43. I use the folio text precisely because it complicates this reading of Henry under the social and economic conditions in which the play was originally conceived. Within this context I adopt Lukas Erne's argument that the variant texts of *Henry V*, along with *Hamlet* and *Romeo and Juliet*, expose a transitional moment between the 'theatrical and literary'. 'Even though printed within a few years of each other, the variant texts of these three plays record different stages on the trajectory from a predominantly oral to a heavily literate culture,' *Shakespeare as Literary Dramatist*, 220. See also Evelyn M. Albright, 'The Folio Version of *Henry V* in Relation to Shakespeare's Times', *PMLA* 43 (1928), 722–56.

class and the land they are required to both produce from as well as defend.[19] As Elizabeth's legislation suggests: in order for a country to survive—war, invasion, poverty, or economic insecurity—it must have a network of resources upon which to depend. In *The True Historie of Civil Warres of France* (1591), Antony Colynet described the King of Navarre's speech to a rebel force, in which he outlines the devastation of war:

> The commons hee advertiseth to think how they are eased by these tumults, where their goods are exposed to the pray of the vilest sort, their traffike interrupted, their husbandrie altogether turned into wast, and desolation.[20]

Exposing the impact on trade, subsistence, and morality Navarre articulates the unaccounted costs of 'these tumults' moving fluently between the social and the economic.[21] Desolation here speaks of a moral as well as an economic rupture; a rupture which Burgundy himself will call 'unnatural'.

As Burgundy tries to bring the kings together through a language of common duty he turns to images of disintegration, of failure, and of waste. Referring the kings back to peace, Burgundy declares:

> Alas, she hath from France too long been chased,
> And all her husbandry doth lie on heaps,
> Corrupting in its own fertility.
> Her vine, the merry cheerer of the heart,
> Unprunèd dies; her hedges even-plashed
> Like prisoners wildly overgrown with hair
> Put forth disordered twigs; her fallow leas
> The darnel, hemlock, and rank fumitory
> Doth root upon, while that the coulter rusts
> That should deracinate such savagery. (5.2.38–46)[22]

The rusting coulter represents the letting loose of Elizabeth's able subjects as well as presenting an image of decay that appears to go beyond the tools

---

[19] Similarly, a figurative relationship between the plough and the sword is often employed by Shakespeare to suggest an act of violence that goes beyond the purely physical and into something comprehensive, essential even. As when Aaron, in *Titus Andronicus*, defends his child with the claim, 'this sword shall plough thy bowels up' (4.2).

[20] 386.

[21] It is intriguing that Shakespeare puts the language of social morality into the mouth of the opposition but it is also clear that there is some historical precedent for this characterization.

[22] In the shorter, quarto text of 1600, the drama moves straight from Henry's call to 'buy that Peace' to his 'blunt' wooing of Katherine. Whilst all modern editions incorporate the folio's scene with Burgundy, I follow Lucas Erne's argument that the earlier version of the play is a 'dim' (219), although not necessarily memorial, reconstruction of a performance text and that the longer folio versions represent a 'literary logic' (23), *Shakespeare as Literary Dramatist*. Given the timing of the play there is a certain 'logic' to the inclusion of this speech in its earlier performances.

of industry and into the moral security of the country as a whole. Burgundy's speech carefully reunites the moral and the social, the economic and political. Moving between the precise practice ('hedges even plashed') and the figurative image (prisoners wildly overgrown), Burgundy invokes a language of cultivation, in which human intervention through forms of pruning, laying (plashing), ploughing (coulter), and uprooting (deracinating) articulates a moral and economic relationship between the human and its landscape. Asserting a comprehensive vision of control and reward through labour and production, cultivation plays out the social formation of a cultural landscape.

When Burgundy tells us that the 'coulter rusts | That should deracinate such savagery' he plays upon the resonant symbolism of the plough.[23] The powerful image of cutting and uprooting savagery suggests the moral necessity of human intervention: impressing upon his audience the need for order and governance, Burgundy makes an emotive plea for the resurrection of a morally sustainable human society. Where Elizabeth cites the poor and the 'loose' as the victims of failed husbandry, Burgundy cites the prisoner; threatening and brutal, he or she is a consummate image of the kind of wildness that demands suppression through intervention. As he invokes the weeds traditionally associated with cultivated land ('darnel', 'hemlock', and 'rank fumitory') we are reminded of the play's concern with order—social and ethical.[24] These weeds, like the rusting coulter or

---

[23] These are highly nuanced terms since the semantic relationship between culture and cultivation is still in development. The 'coulter', in Old English 'culter', means to cut, and 'to cultivate' develops from the old French, 'cultus', meaning to till, as well as the Latin 'cultīvāre', from which our more modern sense of 'culture' emerges in the late seventeenth century. The language of husbandry has a fascinating history in the development of its terms since the symbolic structure in which it emerged had to give way to a developing practical system of empirical and material observations. Yet, as Joyce Appleby reminds us, the relationship between the idea and the response is always in formation: 'Before these responses could be made, however, people had to perceive the changes and incorporate them into an intelligible account of their meaning. Before there could be new modes of behavior, there had to be ideas to explain them.' As she explains: 'To respond positively to the opportunities for further economic development meant to abandon customary ways of holding and working the land. It required endorsement of new values, the acknowledgment of new occupations and the reassessment of the obligations of the individual to society,' *Economic Thought and Ideology*, 4.
[24] Much has been written about the significance of 'rank' in terms of nationhood and 'social stratification' in *Henry V*. A great deal of this criticism belongs to an understanding of the play as an imperialist discourse on the rhetoric of power and the creation of loyalty through what Benedict Anderson, now famously, called the 'imagined community', *Imagined Communities*, 15. Referring to Henry's great speech for his 'happy few, we band of brothers', Peter Womack sums up a century's worth of critical appropriation: 'The conceit draws attention to the social stratification whose suspension it declares: this is the very transient egalitarian moment of a deeply hierarchical order. It is not an accident that these lines have entered, through Churchill's allusions and Olivier's film, into the British

the 'disordered' hedge, refer to a kind of wildness that is socially disruptive and economically disastrous. But France is not, of course, a predominantly 'wild' landscape, untouched by human hands, but one that has seen, been marked and contained by, the practices of husbandry. War destroys the order of the landscape, and in doing so threatens the very practices upon which social—and historical—structures depend. For the Elizabethans, the image of the rusting and neglected plough became a vibrant symbol of national failure.

Largely informed by Christianity, however, the relationship between the plough and morality established a set of principles that were easily transformed into more urgent economic imperatives. Demonstrating the moral value of the image, William Jackson's *The Celestial Husbandrie* defines the analogy in these terms:

There is no small resemblance betweene the plowing vp of this terrene ground, and the heart: obserue, and you shall find them agreeing in these things, 1. The plow it cuts and teares the earth, one piece from another, 2. It layes open the inward parts of the earth, discouering the rootes within the ground, 3. The turning vp of the earth, causeth the weedes to dye and perish, 4. It makes the mould more tender, and more apt to receiue the seede.[25]

The image of the plough works to expose the processes by which the body must be prepared for salvation. As Jackson suggests, the plough dissects and interrogates the spiritual body: cutting, replenishing, and restoring. As the earth receives the seed so the body receives God's word and the image of the plough resonates throughout Christian literature as a symbol of interrogation, as well as creation. Widening the discourse between the land and the body, however, Burgundy extends the image from the moral to the economic lives of the French people.

Despite the profound ways in which Burgundy speaks through a recognizable landscape of moral disorder, the fifth act of the play is often denuded of any significance on the grounds that the war is won and therefore it is 'a bit like the bottom of Horace's fishy lady: a wiggly romantic comedy tacked on to a noble (or ignoble) epic struggle'.[26] But the terms through which peace is discussed form more than 'a romantic comedy'; this is not empty political rhetoric but an articulation of the fundamental structure upon which national security is based. If Henry is

iconography of World War II, at once the 'people's war' and the last throw of a class-ridden Empire', 'Imagining Communities: Theatres and the English Nation in the Sixteenth Century', in David Aers (ed.), *Culture and History, 1350–1600* (Detroit: Wayne State University Press, 1992), 94.

[25] London, 1616, 58.   [26] Altman, 'Vile Participation', 31.

to provide a future for the Tudors he must recognize the ideological significance of the terms of Burgundy's debate. Confronted with this future through the image of a vanquished country, Burgundy asks Henry to recognize the implications of such devastation. The power of Burgundy's speech, however, lies in his reflection not of France but England and the potent images through which he reconstructs a crisis in the social and economic viability of the Elizabethan economy. By transferring the terms of anxiety onto the French, the King of England is forced to listen to the description of the landscape as a register of moral failure. Setting the dialogue in motion, Burgundy presents Henry with his new England, and the intervention it requires. Criticism of this play, and the histories more generally, has frequently observed the discourse of good government at the centre of the struggles for power—nowhere is this discourse more accessible, and more relevant, however, than in the language of husbandry.

In a record of one of the debates that preceded the Act Against the Decaying of Houses of Husbandry, a representative for the Bishop of Durham makes an impassioned plea, declaring: 'The decay of tillage and dispeopling of villages offends God by spoiling the Church, dishonours the prince, weakens the commonwealth', identifying that it is 'nowhere more dangerous that in these northern parts'. He goes on to elaborate on his community:

In the bishopric of Durham, 500 ploughs have decayed in a few years, and corn has to be fetched from Newcastle, whereby the plague is spread in the northern counties; thus the money goes, and the people can neither pay their landlords nor store their ground. By this decay, the Queen loses 500 horsemen, who were bound with their servants to be ready armed, at an hour's warning. Also those that remain have to bear the burden of the 500 decayed. Of 8,000 acres lately in tillage, now not eight score are tilled; those who sold corn have to buy, and colleges and cathedrals are impoverished, because tenants cannot pay their rents; then whole families are turned out, and poor borough towns are pestered with four or five families under one roof. I beg the setting of these ploughs again, and present this to you in the absence of the Bishop, who tenderly affects this cause.[27]

The impact of the decay of husbandry is profound: starving families are forced to migrate into plague-infested cities, the country's borders are vulnerable to invasion, and people are suffering from overcrowded living spaces, poverty, and destitution. The 'setting of the ploughs again'

---

[27] 14/15 January? Mary Anne Everett Green (ed.), 'Queen Elizabeth—Volume 262: January 1597', *Calendar of State Papers Domestic: Elizabeth, 1595–97* (1869), 342–55.

becomes an image of social and economic salvation and one that resonates throughout these records. Burgundy draws directly on this image of the plough, summoning husbandry as a vital means of restoration. Theatrically, Burgundy steps in the breach between the kings, invoking a dialogic landscape in which Henry is called to account. His imaginative reconstruction of a neglected landscape sharply defines the needs of his social community. Drawing the rural landscape into view, Burgundy reminds Henry that war devastates more than simply the lives of those who fight in it. Impressing upon the king the legacy of conflict, he reconstructs a vision of peace that is commensurate with good management.

The significance of this scene—and Burgundy's role within it—is partly established by the end of the preceding scene in which Pistol exits the stage, worn, cynical, and apparently lost to a future of begging and wandering. Exposing Pistol's apparent hostility towards the Welsh, Gower reprimands him, leaving the errant soldier to discover the death of Doll:

> Well, bawd I'll turn,
> And something lean to cutpurse of quick hand.
> To England will I steal, and there I'll steal,
> And patches will I get unto these cudgelled scars,
> And swear I got them in the Gallia wars. (5.1.78–83)

Pistol articulates a bitter grief in which the legacies of war reside in the mock heroics of his 'cudgelled scars'. The pun on stealing amplifies England's instability, and reveals the country to offer little opportunity for Falstaff's former companion. Reconstructing his rather ignominious wounds as marks of heroism, Pistol invokes England as a place of destitution in which he must make his own—however unethical—opportunities. Left with this taste of England in our mouths we turn from the vagabonds to the kings and nobles who talk of peace. Set against this image, Burgundy's speech is a brave, but vital, vision.

Burgundy seems sharply aware of the risk he takes in presenting himself to both countries as an ambassador for ethical responsibility. The theatrical dynamics of this scene are determined by the authoritative power of the figures on stage. When Isabel refers to Henry's eyes as having carried an image of 'The fatal balls of murdering basilisks' (5.2.17) she identifies the King of England as a warmonger. Henry's murdering eyes, now bending their light towards love not war, support the dramatic power of physical as well as verbal confrontations. Understanding the significance of his own presence in the performance of office, Burgundy declares his objective: 'That face to face and royal eye to eye | You have congreeted' (5.2.30–1). Representing the body politic that stands between those faces and eyes Burgundy declares, 'let it not disgrace me | If I demand' the duties of a social vision. The duke puts himself at the centre of a highly powerful dynamic, in which both Catherine and country are at stake. Tracing the relationship between human and humus, Margreta de Grazia writes: 'ambition for land is a form of self-aggrandizement. The body extends itself through the acquisition of territory.'[28] Extending both his body and his lands to Catherine, Henry makes his acquisition complete: 'For if you hide the crown | Even in our hearts, there will he rake for it' (2.4.97–8). For Burgundy, however, the princess appears secondary to the land. Where for Henry the future may lie in the child that can bear the blood of the two kingdoms, in Burgundy's vision conflict must be resolved beyond the desire of the monarch and into the lives of the subject.

The relationship between war and husbandry was far from tenuous: as the Bishop of Durham's anxieties reveal, depopulation left regions vulnerable to attack and the yeoman was also a ready soldier, as Henry emotively suggests. Similarly, good husbandry was also equated with the kind of prosperity that supported peace. Discussing the state of Scotland after the Armada, in June 1589, a parliament addenda makes the note: 'You do not find the people so changed as is given out, for last year's imminent danger made them think there was good cause to be at charge. Subsidies, loans, and levy of soldiers are but trifles to bear, in respect of former times; and long peace and husbandry have made them so rich, and they handle the distribution of payments so cunningly.'[29] Burgundy's speech echoes the sentiments expressed here: peace and husbandry maintain a kingdom's strength in a time of crisis. But for Burgundy, the landscape that occupies a simultaneously social and ethical space in his imagination transcends any parochial interests now it is the property of England. The imperatives of this speech are socio-economic and they represent a community in search of order, containment, value, and profit.[30] As Burgundy cites peace over possession, he urges a vision that looks less to a country's 'imperial throne'

---

[28] *Hamlet without Hamlet*, 34. Equally apposite within the context of this play, and Henry VI's subsequent loss of France, de Grazia writes: 'The desire of nations to expand themselves through territory yields no more than a burial ground for the army which fought for it, just as the desire of individuals to enlarge themselves through land in the end amounts to no more than a grave plot,' 37.

[29] Mary Anne Everett Green (ed.), 'Addenda, Queen Elizabeth—Volume 31: June 1589', *Calendar of State Papers Domestic: Elizabeth, Addenda 1580–1625* (1872), 270–5.

[30] Equally prescient is the anonymous text *God Speede the Plough*, published in 1601, which specifically draws attention to this period: 'I might prophecie that as the two precedent yeares ruined it [husbandry]: so the two succedent yeares will leave no memorie of it,' A2ᵛ.

and more to a local landscape.[31] What becomes essential to this vision is the translation of 'cultural myth' into agrarian improvement.[32] Burgundy's rhetoric belongs to a powerful tradition of communal values which can situate the landscape at the heart of sociable living. The plough represents a vast network of human needs that is written deep into Christian and secular literature: from feudalism and serfdom, through charity and donation to individual improvement, the idea of the plough could encompass an entire country's needs as well as its ethical responsibilities.[33] Emotively reconstructing these imperatives through the language of waste and decay, Burgundy offers Henry the responsibility of possession.

Burgundy's images of neglect reflect a landscape that is morally unstable but also ripe for improvement. The dramatic tension of this scene lies in its conflicted registers: while Burgundy may speak from a tradition of feudal values he invokes the consequences of mismanagement; and while he may search for the rhetoric of social responsibility he receives only the response of the improver. The power of Burgundy's speech lies not only in its contemporary registers but also in its ability to manifest the social ethics of a space that has been emptied of its inhabitants in the politics of war. Neither Henry, nor France for that matter, observes the land as places of living: it is a territory, a possession, and a map of their objectives as well as their acquisitions.

Although the glorious rhetoric of Henry's war imagines a common project for a cohesive society, that society almost entirely drops from view once the war is won. Burgundy's France, on the other hand, offers Henry a vision of contemporary England which demands the same commitment to peace that the king appears to have to war. The emotive strength of Henry's speech before Agincourt, its sheer virtuosity and rhetorical skill,

---

[31] Canterbury can call England an 'imperial throne' (1.2.35) because, after the Reformation, it owed no allegiance to any foreign superior: 'This realm of England is an empire' (Act 24 Hen. VIII, c. 12), see *Henry V*, ed. Taylor, 101.

[32] The celebration of an agricultural past in line with 'traditional' values of labour, community, honesty, and mutual care is one embedded in religious as well as classical and literary texts. See Christopher Hill, 'The Norman Yoke', in *Puritanism and Revolution: Studies in the Interpretation of the English Revolution and the Seventeenth Century* (London: Secker & Warburg, 1958), Low, *The Georgic Revolution*; McRae, *God Speed the Plough*, 23–79.

[33] McRae covers this very deftly in his first chapter. The turn of the century tract *God Speede the Plough* exposes at the outset that husbandry has been 'for many years neglected' and that the purpose of the text is to 'set an edge to good husbandrie', A2ʳ. This anonymous text begins with a history of husbandry through the lens of human civilization in which development, agrarian and human, begins with the 'wooden dagger', and ends, at least for now, with the plough. The progressive logic situates husbandry at the forefront of our human history.

supports an image of an apparently socialized king: one who speaks *with* the happy few but *for* the entire nation.[34] At the beginning of the seventeenth century, however, the happy few were starkly at odds with the band of brothers who held the sword or plough: and nowhere was the tension between individualism and community registered more powerfully than in the language of the landscape.

Observing the different attitudes to the landscape reveals the often conflicted ways in which 'profit' was presented. William Lawson, for example, in his *New Orchard and Garden*, offers a personal confession on the writing of his book: 'I must not denie now the publishing of it (which then I allotted to my priuate delight) for the publike profit of others,' whilst later on celebrating the private over the public in recommending that a good gardener is somebody who will 'not purloine your profit nor hinder your pleasures'.[35] Through print, Lawson identifies his project as for the common good while also making space for personal achievement. As a record of social welfare as well as a potential site of private development the landscape presented a conflicted register in the pursuit of common interests. Heresbach's text, on the other hand, appears genuinely confused by the imperatives of profit, moving as it does from the 'profite and reliefe of his poore distressed neighbour' to warning against untrained yeoman who may 'hinder the profite of their master'.[36] In order to accommodate the conflicting notions, or perhaps beneficiaries, of 'profit', a language of efficiency emerged in which value was accorded to production rather than intention.

Whilst Burgundy invokes apparently conventional values of a georgic vision, he also speaks of an agrarian industry upon which France's rural economy depends. The coulter and scythe emerge as the tools of labour upon which both 'beauty and utility' depend. The disorder and neglect that follow loss of labour and intervention record an economic as well as moral depression. Husbandry, as state proclamations and statutes reveal, denotes the survival of an increasingly 'nationalized' value system. Wendy Wall has provided a very helpful model for the interpretation of national values through the work of Gervase Markham. Focusing on a formative relationship between husbandry and nationalism through print, Wall

---

[34] Nowhere, of course, is this interpretation of the play more visible than in modern politics and the ways in which the film versions of the play (specifically Olivier's (1944) and Branagh's (1989)) exposed the conflicting ideological representations of war, specifically Second World War and post-Falklands. For a discussion of the play's recent stage history, see Peter Holland, *English Shakespeares: Shakespeare on the English Stage in the 1990s* (Cambridge: Cambridge University Press, 1997).

[35] William Lawson, *A New Orchard and Garden* (London, 1631), bk 3, p. 1.

[36] Heresbach, *Foure Bookes of Husbandrie*, Google's dedication, 14ʳ.

identifies 'Markham's nationalising of English husbandry' through what she calls the 'englishing of soil'.[37] For Wall, print plays a fundamental role in establishing difference as Markham fashions his texts and his readers as uniquely responsive to their English ground. Echoing Helgerson's argument about the role of surveys in the breakdown of dynastic affiliations, Wall writes:

> ... Markham posits a nation that coheres through a shared set of customs and practices based on geographical affiliation; it is a nation, in short, not identical to the state or sovereign, but one based essentially on the land.[38]

When Burgundy reconstructs France to Henry, however, he appears to resurrect the boundaries of both difference and dynasty that seem incompatible in the work of Markham. Although several English farmers had tried to grow vines, wine-making remained an industry strongly allied to the French. Burgundy's invocation of the vine, 'the merry cheerer of the heart', is the only referent that could define the landscape as part of France, and yet in appealing to Henry he asks that we take responsibility for that landscape universally not regionally. For Burgundy, national difference can be elided under common possession precisely because husbandry is a shared custom. Despite the imperative to agrarian production, Burgundy's landscape is predominantly social. As Garrett Sullivan explains, 'land formed the basis for a social world; to identify it first and foremost as a commodity was to expose the fragility of that world, or, at least, to dislocate land from the moral economy that was supposed to be inseparable from it'.[39] Between Henry's and Burgundy's France lies the debate between a social or commercial landscape. According to Henry, Burgundy's peace will come at a price and that price appears to empty the land of its moral registers:

> If, Duke of Burgundy, you would the peace
> Whose want gives growth to th'imperfections
> Which you have cited, you must buy that peace
> With full accord to all our just demands. (5.2.68–71)

Exposing France's fields as neglected, corrupted, and disordered reveals the extent to which cultivation sustains a social order of both welfare and industry. Burgundy dramatically reconstructs this landscape, as Altman suggests, through a dual image of husbandry and humanity in which one

---

[37] 'Renaissance National Husbandry', 767.
[38] Wall, 'Renaissance National Husbandry', 776. See also Richard Helgerson's *Forms of Nationhood*.
[39] Sullivan, *The Drama of Landscape*, 10.

appears to reinforce the other. The humanity that he attempts to appeal to in Henry is social responsibility—an enlightened commitment to both the cause and the effect. Fighting a war, he suggests, is also about securing peace beyond the legal contracts and into the lives of human individuals. Dressing his imaginative landscape with hedges construed as prisoners, disordered and unruly, provokes a vivid image of mismanagement. Synthesizing the social and agrarian in the image of the hedge-prisoner, this chaotic limit reflects both the failings and the expectations of human society.[40] Recasting these provocative figures as neglected boundaries supports an image of critical failure. For the English from Anglo-Saxon times, the hedge operated as a unique symbol of possession: 'their visible presence on the landscape physically indicated actual English occupation and communicated English rights'.[41] Burgundy appears to offer Henry a challenge to good husbandry through a vision of a dispossessed landscape.

Alongside Burgundy's image of unnaturalness in the neglected landscape of peace, Mountjoy's description of the aftermath of war represents an alternative image of unnaturalness which focuses on the human, rather than the non-human:

> I come to thee for charitable licence,
> That we may wander o'er this bloody field
> To book our dead and then to bury them,
> To sort our nobles from our common men—
> For many of our princes, woe the while,
> Lie drowned and soaked in mercenary blood.
> So do our vulgar drench their peasant limbs
> In blood of princes, and our wounded steeds
> Fret fetlock-deep in gore, and with wild rage
> Jerk out their armèd heels at their dead masters,
> Killing them twice. O give us leave, great King,
> To view the field in safety, and dispose
> Of their dead bodies. (4.7.65–78)

Mountjoy's request to 'sort our noble from our common men' exposes a similar fear of disorder. Attempting to intervene in death's ability to level all human bodies to dust, Mountjoy proposes to 'dispose | Of their dead bodies' in an act of social segregation. Speaking through the terms of unnaturalness, Mountjoy observes a chaos that extends to the perversion

---

[40] The period of wars with Ireland between 1560 and 1602 had a huge impact on English resources and came closest, according to Cyril Falls, to 'destroying the security of the Elizabethan state', *Elizabeth's Irish Wars* (London: Methuen, 1950). Equally punishing for the economic stability were the periods of dearth, poor harvests, and famine that characterized the end of the sixteenth century.

[41] Seed, *Ceremonies of Possession*, 23.

of service as the horses, frantic, 'Jerk out their arméd heels at their dead masters | Killing them twice'.[42] The French voices continually refer us back to the ways in which war corrupts the social fabric. Unlike Henry's valiant call to 'limbs made in England', the bodies of France are brutalized, chaotic, and 'soaked in mercenary blood'.

One of the most fascinating questions that arises at this point is why does Shakespeare put the language of social welfare, order, and management into the mouths of the opponents? Perhaps one answer to this might be that France provides a space of alterity: a hinterland between English and foreign occupation, it becomes, quite literally, a transitional ground for the exploration of the costs of war. Reflecting the politicized language of Elizabeth's Acts against Decay and for Tillage, the French characters expose the reactionary policies of a social economy.[43] As a new England, France becomes a projection of a possible future: a space for development, improvement, and a vibrant reminder of the need for social as well as economic stability.

The lost landscape of Burgundy's vision presents France as suffering from a major breach in the ethical economy. Crying out for human intervention, he presents Henry with a moral duty to redress the gross imbalance in their natural worlds:

> The even mead—that erst brought sweetly forth
> The freckled cowslip, burnet, and green clover—
> Wanting the scythe, withal uncorrected, rank,
> Conceives by idleness, and nothing teems
> But hateful docks, rough thistles, kecksies, burs,
> Losing both beauty and utility.
> And all our vineyards, fallows, meads, and hedges
> Defective in their natures, grow to wildness,
> Even so our houses and ourselves and children
> Have lost, or do not learn from want of time,
> The sciences that should become our country,
> But grow like savages—as soldiers will
> That nothing do but mediate on blood—
> To swearing and stern looks, diffused attire,
> And everything that seems unnatural. (5.2.48–62)

---

[42] For a discussion of this speech see James R. Siemon, 'Landlord not King: Agrarian Change and Interarticulation', in Burt and Archer (eds.), *Enclosure Acts*, 18–19.

[43] Joyce Oldham Appleby makes the point that up until the seventeenth century all economic policies were driven by social concerns. Devoid of any fiscal model of economic analysis, Elizabethan statutes reflected a reactionary drive to maintain a social security and a sustainable commonwealth.

'Wanting' intervention, management, and control we return to the anxiety that runs through the post-war landscapes of the play; the 'uncorrected' and 'rank' in which 'nothing teems'. Here the fear is loss, waste, and sterility, a fear that can simultaneously speak to a Christian duty of use and endeavour as well as a market economy of profit and 'utility'. The language of misuse, decay, and disorder which was associated with the unthrifty Hal of *1 Henry IV* returns spectre like to remind the now King of England of his duty. Burgundy's appeal strikes to the heart of an image of commonwealth in which social life represents moral and economic stability. Directly invoking the decay of houses of husbandry that informed so much of Elizabeth's late sixteenth-century policies, Burgundy extends his emotive images through education, industry, and security. The defects that Burgundy isolates are those of nature itself 'uncorrected' by human intervention and threatening to violate the human control of nature. Burgundy's stark picture articulates a fear of human neglect in which the natural is not celebrated but feared: a marker of incivility he ushers in examples of aberrance to remind Henry that the land—like its people— needs order and control. Returning to the image of savagery, Burgundy brings the soldier to the forefront of his moral economy. Defining the soldier's bestiality, Burgundy locates war as fundamental to the moral crisis he describes. Soldiers are brutal, he suggests, and a structure that relies on brutal men (instead of husbandman) will become brutalized— 'unnatural'.

When Burgundy speaks through the debris of war about a country that is 'Corrupting in its own fertility' he invokes a powerful semantic field in which the language of the land is also that of the social body. Invoking an image of negative mutation—as though without governance such fecundity will either mutate or breakdown—Burgundy secures the landscape as a moral rebuke as well as a warning. Employing the precise terms of both husbandry and humanism, the loss of France's 'beauty and utility' secures its severance from collective values. Within the context of the speech, utility speaks to the kind of profit—ethical, educational, social, and financial—through which many of the early modern husbandry manuals established their claim on the English imagination.[44]

From the play's outset, particular values—responsibility, community, management, and productivity—are expressed though the language of the land. Burgundy's vision of a landscape occupied in peace, productive,

[44] Imported from their classical precedents, in the work of Varo, Philo, and Columella, as well as humanist disquisitions on pedagogy, the terms *utilias* tended to accompany *voluptas*, or pleasure, and was widely reproduced in gardening and husbandry manuals. In *The English SchoolMaster* (1596), Edmund Coote glosses the term 'utility' as 'profit'.

socially responsible, and without the human defects of war (soldiers or prisoners), reflects the land as a form of ethical consciousness. The land's capacity to manifest human sin in the forms of corruption, neglect, and waste presents the physical landscape as a just marker of the sustainability of our social worlds. The Christian tradition in which the natural world could be 'read' as God's book points to the phenomenological world as a mirror of our moral worth. Within this tradition, however, the natural world tends to be interpreted through what we would now call natural disasters or occurrences (dearth, crop destruction, weather, and eclipses, for example). For the Elizabethans, however, they were only natural inasmuch as they manifested elementally but they were orchestrated by God: or, as Walsham explains, 'Nature stood alongside the Bible as a source of ethical and theological instruction.'[45] Despite Burgundy's interpretation of his landscape through a social and moral perspective, he reads his rural vision in strictly human, not divine, terms.[46] Henry may attribute his victory to God but his duty is to the people.

The distinction between the landscape as God's book and the land as the product of human intervention—the means by which the 'strength and flourishing of this kingdom' is 'upheld'—is an important one within the context of the play.[47] Despite Henry's interpretation of his victory as divine, Ely and Canterbury's providential readings of nature are represented as inherently suspect. Self-serving and corrupt, the bishops persuade Henry to war to avoid further taxation of the Church. Speaking retrospectively of the recuperation of Prince Hal in kingship, Canterbury declares:

> The courses of his youth promised it not.
> The breath no sooner left his father's body
> But that his wildness, mortified in him,
> Seemed to die too. Yea, at that very moment

---

[45] *The Reformation of the Landscape*, 328.

[46] In *1 Henry IV*, for example, we witness Hotspur, Mortimer, and Glendower define themselves, in relation to a map of England, Scotland, and Wales, as epic heroes, born of the earth and endowed with a strength that simultaneously transcends the land as well as represents it. Glendower, for example, tells his rebel companions: 'To tell you once again that at my birth | The front of heaven was full of fiery shapes, | The goats ran from the mountains, and the herds | Were strangely clamorous to the frighted fields' (3.1.38–41). Speaking on the benefits of sherry, however, Falstaff characterizes Hal in the terms of good husbandry: 'for the cold blood he did naturally inherit of his father, he hath, like lean, sterile and bare land, manured, husbanded and tilled with excellent endeavour of drinking good and good store of fertile sherris, that he is become very hot and valiant' (4.2.105–9).

[47] For a discussion of the ways in which nature continued to be interpreted as a manifestation of God's wrath (and, occasionally, approval), see Walsham, *The Reformation of the Landscape*, 327–94.

> Consideration like an angel came
> And whipped th'offending Adam out of him,
> Leaving his body a paradise. (1.1.24–31)

Suggesting a form of divine migration, in the passage of the king's soul from death to his son's rebirth, Canterbury imagines Hal as fallen body returning to paradise.[48] Canterbury's image of Henry positions the land as an edenic marker of his body, a metaphor which Ely immediately expands through the language of horticulture:

> The strawberry grows underneath the nettle,
> And wholesome berries thrive and ripen best
> Neighboured by fruit of baser quality;
> And so the Prince obscured his contemplation
> Under the veil of wildness—which, no doubt,
> Grew like the summer grass, fastest by night,
> Unseen, yet crescive in his faculty. (1.1.61–7)

In recent criticism, and through Greenblatt's model of subversion and containment, this speech has often been read as a 'revisionist account' of Hal as a 'calculating strategist'.[49] Yet in a horticultural context, Ely's metaphor expresses a conventional image of the coexistence of good and bad, of growth and contamination. Henry emerging from the 'wildness' resilient and productive focuses his values of righteousness on an inherent quality of potential thought to reside in Nature as a divine text.[50] Here, goodness written into the fabric of the king grows unseen and undetected—'under the veil of wildness'—as it is nurtured by the virtuous soul ('crescive in his faculty'). Although Ely and Canterbury veneer Henry

---

[48] The horse is a central figure in husbandry manuals, not only as an expression of status, humanism, and power but also a fundamental part of the language of control and management in the application of authority. Robert N. Watson's article 'Horsemanship in Shakespeare's Second Tetralogy', *English Literary Renaissance*, 13/3 (Autumn 1983), 274–300, remains a seminal piece of work in this regard. See Jerry Brotton and Lisa Jardine, *Global Interests: Renaissance Art between East and West* (London: Reaktion Books, 2000), esp. 132–86, Donna Landry, *Noble Brutes: How Eastern Horses Transformed English Culture* (Baltimore: The Johns Hopkins University Press, 2008). Bruce Boehrer has written extensively on the horse and, most recently, in his *Animal Characters: Nonhuman Beings in Early Modern Literature* (University Park, Pa.: University of Pennsylvania Press, 2010). The horse, horsemanship, horse breeding, and other equestrian concerns are prevalent images within the play that speak beyond the requisites of war. I shall return to the image of the horse later in the chapter.

[49] See Greenblatt, *Shakespearean Negotiations*, and Julie Crawford, 'Women's Secretaries', in Vin Nardizzi and Will Stockton (eds.), *Queer Renaissance Historiography* (Farnham: Ashgate, 2009) for a further discussion of this speech, 65.

[50] As Walsham explains: 'Interpreted through the lens of Scripture, the physical landscape provided the godly with unique insight into the mind of their Maker,' *Reformation of the Landscape*, 335.

with a retrospective gloss of divine ordination, in the second tetralogy it was not clear that the prince would grow into a king. Described as 'unthrifty' by Bollingbroke (*Richard II*, 5.3.1), and 'unyoked'(*1 Henry IV*, 1.2.196) by his father, the images of neglect are brought sharply into focus by Henry IV:

> Tell me else,
> Could such inordinate and low desires,
> Such poor, such bare, such lewd, such mean attempts,
> Such barren pleasures, rude society,
> As thou art match'd withal and grafted to,
> Accompany the greatness of thy blood,
> And hold their level with the princely heart? (*1 Henry IV*, 3.2.11–17)

The iniquity of the company Hal keeps is expressed in a series of adjectives that climax in barren pleasure and rude society. Henry IV's complaint, it seems, is not only the improper values that these people represent but a gross sense of waste—barren and rude, these men (and women) are of no worth, no profit; reminiscent of Elizabeth's disenfranchised subjects 'wanderers, idle, and loose'. Amplifying Hal's misjudgements, he accuses him of having 'grafted' his princely blood to a bad stock. The terms of Henry IV's invective specifically point to an abuse of nature, which is then apparently redressed through the Christianized language of the bishops. In the strawberry and the nettle, Ely and Canterbury allude to the primal struggle between good and evil—in Paradise, in Adam, in the individual—which Henry has apparently overcome.[51] The paradoxes that the bishops invoke in order to suggest the power of human destiny do not rely on the manifestation of individual will: Henry's 'offending Adam' was 'whipped' out of him by the angel 'Consideration'. Yet the starkly providential images mark the bishops as somewhat old-fashioned within the terms of the play: as Burgundy will powerfully explain, social welfare is not about destiny; it is about human intervention.

Throughout the play Henry identifies himself with action, partly as an amplification of his metamorphosis from wastrel prince into noble king, but also as a means of exposing the virtuosity of human will. Human agency—intervention and labour—was central to the assimilation of

---

[51] The image of the strawberry is particularly fascinating in the ways in which it is taken up by still life painters to register an allegorical image of the triumph of good over bad. Among plants, the strawberry was thought to have a unique capacity to grow alongside poisonous or aggressive plants (like, as here, the nettle) and so to thrive against its herbaceous opponents. Strawberries also have medicinal properties and are frequently used in herbals or books of secrets as cures for aches, agues, bruises, and dry hands! See especially, A.T., Practitioner in Physike, *A Riche store house or Treasury for the Diseased* (1596) STC (2nd edn.)/23606. See also Bushnell, *Green Desire*, 55–61.

cultivation into grander narratives of social improvement. In this regard, the land was a fertile space for mutual accommodation of competing discourses. In *The Countrey Farme*, for example, the dedicatory epistle uses a multitude of oppositions in order to invoke the magnitude of the role of husbandry:

Furthermore; of or from the earth, is ministred matter to defend or offend, [f]eed or famish, cherish or starue, make blind, or restore sight, to ouerturne, or build vp great towers, to giue, or take away light, to procure health or fickenese, foes or friends, peace or warre, pleasure or paine, sorrow or mirth, taste or distaste, sleepe or watchfulnesse, sores or soundnesse, barrennesse or fruitfulnesse, life or death: and what not? (A1ᵛ)

Here Estienne covers all of life itself, allowing the verbs to slip fluidly between the literal and the figurative (make blind, restore sight), the material and the Christian ('to overturne... or take away light'), the personal and the social ('to procure health or ficknenes, foes or friends'). The sheer capaciousness of our duty to the earth finds its natural expression in the rhetoric of oppositions, and the semantic tension that such conflicts provide pushes forward a rich language of representation. For Canterbury and Ely providential Nature provides a useful logic for the abrogation of human responsibility; for Burgundy, however, human action is central to the government of a successful socio-economic structure.

The rise in husbandry manuals gradually supported the intercession of the human in God's book of nature. Developing away from the more explicitly Christian structures of Fitzherbert, the later manuals presented human intervention as vital to the stability of the commonwealth. The idea of human intervention was extensive and often absorbed the language of nurturing as a model of improvement or cleansing, particularly at the level of teaching.[52] Ideas of 'growth' tended to belong to a value system, inherent to a humanist philosophy of education, in which learning and labour are synthesized for their representations of individual potential and public duty. In Thomas Elyot's *Book named The Governor*, for example:

I wyll vse the policie of a wyse and cunnynge gardener... he wyll fyrste serche throughout his gardeyne, where he can fynde the moste melowe and fertyle erth, and therin wyl he put the sede of the herbe to growe, and be norysshed, and in moste diligent wise attende, that no weede be suffred to growe or approche nyghe vnto it: and to the ende it maye thryue the faster, as scone as the fourme of an herbe ones appereth, he wyl set a vessel of water by it, in suche wyse, that it may contynually distyll on the rote swete dropes: and as it spryngeth in stalke, vnder ette it with some thinge, that it breake not, and alway kepe it clene from wedes.

---

52 Bushnell, *A Culture of Teaching*, see esp. 73–116.

Like ordre wyll I ensue, in the fourmynge the gentyll wyttes of noble mennes chyldren, who frome the wombes of theyr mother, shalbe made propise or apte to the gouernaunce of a publyke weale.[53]

For Elyot, the process of growth is not determined by providence but human control. As Rebecca Bushnell observes, Elyot's metaphor of the gardener is predicated on an image of mastery, yet it also assigns some kind of agency to the child: 'Through the gardening trope Elyot carefully balances the teacher's control over the student with the "noble" child's "natural" claim to superiority.'[54] Although Elyot belongs to a tradition of discriminating between inherent claims to superiority or wickedness, the value of his metaphor lies in the role of the gardener. As Bushnell comments, however, it is a fundametally conflicted model for Elyot since 'teachers and gardeners had a traditionally low status in the early modern household; both professions, however, took on new meaning in a culture that valued work, specialized knowledge, and "improvement" for the benefit of oneself and the commonwealth'.[55] The significance of the analogy is determined by a 'new' value system in which labour, intervention, or control represented an active development of potential (human or non-human).[56] In *Henry V*, Ely and Canterbury belong to a tradition that is already perceived as old-fashioned. Imagining Henry's body through a set of Christian referents, in which divine potential is represented as a predetermined force of nature, supports their representation of the war as righteous, or justifiable. Set against these arcane images, Burgundy's landscape of human neglect becomes a powerful register for the social consequences of war.

The political rhetoric of the commonwealth was readily absorbed into husbandry manuals: from prefatory dedications to chapters on bee-keeping, husbandry provided a model and a practice of socio-economic improvement.[57] It is perhaps no surprise that the history plays evince

---

[53] Thomas Elyot, *The Boke named The Governor* (London, 1537), 17.

[54] Bushnell, *A Culture of Teaching*, 82.

[55] Bushnell, *A Culture of Teaching*, 89.

[56] We might notice, in this context, the word 'nursery', which throughout the sixteenth and seventeenth centuries could simultaneously apply to 'a place where young plants or trees are grown (*OED*, 3a), 'a place where a quality or attribute is developed' (*OED*, 2a), and 'A room or area of a house set aside for babies and young children' (*OED*, 1a).

[57] Timothy Raylor's 'Samuel Hartlib and the Commonwealth of Bees', in Leslie and Raylor (eds.), *Culture and Cultivation*, 91–129, explores the pioneering work of Hartlib within the context of both social and horticultural reform. Although a little later than Shakespeare's play, the work of John Beale also exposes a fascinating cultural development in the reconstruction of social ideals through husbandry, see Michael Leslie, 'The Spiritual Husbandry of John Beale', in Leslie and Raylor (eds.), *Culture and Cultivation*, 151–72.

Shakespeare's most sustained engagement with the land, exploring as they do questions of social responsibility, political failure, national duty, and good government, but in *Richard II* Shakespeare rehearses a version of Burgundy's France in the king's garden.[58] To make the relationship between a happy commonwealth and an ordered garden explicit, Shakespeare stages a conversation between the king's gardeners at the point at which Richard is about to be deposed.[59] Carefully structured to amplify the resonance of its imagery at every point: the queen takes pains to introduce the scene, explaining that 'they will talk of state', and the gardeners immediately oblige with extended metaphors of control to establish what must be bound, pruned, or uprooted to ensure 'All must be even in our government' (3.4.27/36). Yet as soon as the head gardener has established the significance of the similitude, his assistant reinterprets the garden in stark terms of disillusionment:

> Why should we, in the compass of a pale,
> Keep law and form and due proportion,
> Showing as in a model our firm estate,
> When our sea-wallèd garden, the whole land,
> Is full of weeds, her fairest flowers choked up,
> Her fruit trees all unpruned, her hedges ruined,
> Her knots disordered, and her wholesome herbs
> Swarming with caterpillars. (3.4.40–7)

Exposing the gross hypocrisy of these competing images of England—the precious decorum of the king's garden, against the choked landscape of a neglected country—the first man points to the landscape as a marker of both oppression and inequality. Like Burgundy's description of France, the ethical issues emerge as forms of bad husbandry or neglect.

Specifically, however, the gardener draws our attention, like Burgundy, to areas of both containment (hedges) and control (pruning and weeding). The figure of the knot is central to the arrangement of images since it refers very particularly to a garden belonging to the aristocracy. In *The Countrey Farme* Estienne devotes a whole chapter to 'the garden of pleasure' in the 'second book of the country house'. Here Estienne explains that the knot is created by perfectly proportioned 'borders', to which certain rules apply

---

[58] The three parts of *Henry VI* as well as *King John* are all invested in the landscape as a language of social, and imperial, anxieties. See my Introduction as well as Chapter 4.

[59] Historically and theatrically Richard's relationship to the land is extremely fraught: as king he commissioned a number of 'surveys' in order to reveal large areas of unidentified land which he them 'reclaimed' as 'royal'. See Sullivan, *The Drama of Landscape*, 58–69. Dramatically, of course, Shakespeare amplifies this historical anxiety in terms of his treatment of the death of his uncle as well as his wars in Ireland. See also Siemon, 'Landlord Not King', 26–30.

depending on the shape, size, and composition of such borders, 'so the beautie and good proportion of the knot or quarter may bee seene or discerned more easily'(254). Once again we perceive human intervention as a mark of order, and order as an expression of beauty. Estienne also identifies that, popularly, these knots were created to represent heraldry, love-knots, or even faces, by crafting the size and shapes of the 'quarters', or individual sections: 'It is true, that within some round quarters, or squares of broken quarters, you may worke some small birds, men, or other such pourtraites made of Rose-marie, according to your pleasure, and inuention of your Gardener' (255). The knot was a horticultural signature of the lord of the manor, as well as the skill, or invention, of his gardener. The disorder that Richard's gardener laments suggests a profound hiatus in the king's government: corrupt in its inequality, the contrast between decorum and decay puts Richard's kingship at the centre of a moral indictment. According to Hannah Chapelle Wojciehowski, however, the knot was one of the complex images that emerged during this period to signify group identity. As an 'artful arrangement of figures in space', the knot represented a form of artistic intentionality that 'would entail a revolutionary rethinking of social combinations, according to which the collective was no longer defined by the usual categories of belonging'.[60] Outside of Richard's garden, however, the knot is an emblem of social disorder, the breakdown of an apparently once cohesive populace. The gardener's emphasis on a sense of ruin—that things once perfect or orderly have fallen into disrepair—evokes a powerful sense of the extent to which the country is fragmented. Against Estienne's image of private design, the figure becomes a vivid sign of the ways in which aesthetic arrangements could signify exclusion, self-interest, or individual improvement.

Taking up the discourse that lies at both the material and figurative level, the gardeners go on to explicate Richard's position. Developing their conversation through the language of cultivation they conclude: 'O, what pity is it | That he had not so trimmed and dressed his land | As we his garden' (55–7), at which point the queen breaks in on their knowingness with shrieks of sin:

> Thou, old Adam's likeness, set to dress this garden,
> How dares thy harsh rude tongue sound this unpleasing news?
> What Eve, what serpent hath suggested thee
> To make a second Fall of cursed man?
> Why dost thou say King Richard is deposed? (3.4.73–7)

---

[60] *Group Identity in the Renaissance World* (Cambridge: Cambridge University Press, 2011), 71.

Castigating the gardener, the queen reminds him of his service and his human condition, fallen, labouring, and sinful. Cursing the men who have simultaneously maintained and threatened Richard's self-delusion, she turns on the very terms of their indictment: 'Gardener, for telling me these news of woe, | Pray God the plants thou graftest may never grow' (100–1). Reasserting the power of cultivation to support social relations, the queen unwittingly predicts her husband's downfall. Momentarily oblivious to an emblematic relationship between the gardener and the king's garden, the queen proffers bad husbandry as a form of both punishment and exclusion. In both plays, cultivation provides a language of access to the political elite. Supporting the terms of moral and social commentary, characters normally excluded from or on the margins of political power are given a critical role through a discourse of husbandry.

The Tudor complaint was instrumental in supporting an articulate relationship between citizen and commonwealth. According to Lawrence Manley, the language of the complaint 'was deployed by Tudor writers . . . to portray the ills of England as a social and economic anomaly, as transgressions and violations against a just and ancient order'.[61] Infused with a sense of protest, the mid-Tudor complaint frequently used the landscape as a marker of transgression 'dramatizing in the collapse of an ancient and well-defined order the disruptive influences of forces as yet too obscure to be named'.[62] The sense of disruption expressed by Burgundy and Richard's gardener belongs to this tradition of protest, in which the land is both an image and an expression of social collapse. But as Jennifer Richards has shown, the moral interpretations of good husbandry extend beyond the economic conditions of social welfare and into the more opaque discourses of courtesy: 'where honesty is produced through physical and intellectual husbandry'.[63] In this way, the discourses of land management could develop into moral prompts in multiple ways. Perhaps nowhere more pervasively, however, than in the form of prayer: *The Book of Private Prayer* (1553), a primer under Edward IV, includes a tenant's prayer to his landlord:

We heartily pray thee to send thy holy spirit into the hearts of them that possess the grounds, pastures, and dwelling-places of the earth, that they, remembering themselves to be thy [i.e. God's] tenants, may not rack and stretch out the rents of their houses and lands . . . after the manner of covetous worldlings . . . but so

---

[61] Lawrence Manley, in *Literature and Culture in Early Modern England* (Cambridge: Cambridge University Press, 1995), discusses the rise of the complaint through both print and Protestantism, 73.

[62] Manley, *Literature and Culture*, 74.

[63] *Rhetoric and Courtliness*, 111. See also 87–112.

behave themselves in letting out their tenements, lands, and pastures, that after this life they may be received into everlasting dwelling places.[64]

The language makes explicit the relationship between heaven and earth in a particularly emotive way, since the prayer recognizes our 'dwelling place' as a moral responsibility as well as a God-given entitlement. Intriguingly, the prayer also invokes social conscience over economic individualism, not only recording the growing difference between them but the vulnerability of the tenant. The detail of the prayer as it registers the precise terms of income, land-holding, and future security reproduces an atmosphere of obligation in which cultivation, land use, and holding rights represent a discourse of heavenly reward. Praying that those who 'possess the grounds, pastures and dwelling places of the earth' remember that they too are (God's) tenants registers a profound awareness of the language of social welfare. As the land does not belong to the people neither does the future. Confronting Henry with the future, however, prompts him to demand remuneration: France 'must buy that peace'.

Peace, like war, has a price and, for Henry, that price is now in contention. According to Sir Thomas Smith, however, in *The Common-wealth of England* (1589): 'The prince . . . hath absolutely in his power the authority of war and peace', in which he may use martial law 'without process of law or form of judgement'.[65] Without recourse to systems of justice, the monarch may pursue the conditions of war or peace with 'absolute power'. The absolutist authority that Smith describes takes no account of the social structures that Burgundy has tried to invoke. More than any other history play, *Henry V*, and its prelude in *Henry IV*, parts 1 and 2, is defined by the dynamic between kingship and community. As Henry moves further and further away from the Hal of the tavern, the rupture between economic gain and social stability becomes ever more pronounced. Mocking Burgundy's language of cultivation, Henry repositions his image of growth within a qualitative context of 'imperfection'. Henry can perfect France, he suggests, but he will need to own it first. Despite Henry's paeans to the community of war, the brotherhood of bloodshed, and the power of a consensual vision, the territory he acquires is part of a commercial enterprise. Fashioning himself as an improver, Henry makes his claim within an imperial context of ownership in which possession determines profit. The landscapes that Burgundy evokes and Henry interprets are very different places and speak of the play's competing discourses of socio-economic values. For Burgundy the French

---

[64] As cited by Sullivan, *The Drama of Landscape*, 34.   [65] Bk II, chapter 4.

landscape is a map of human endeavour, of social relations and political imperatives; for Henry it is territory, emptied out of individual lives, historical markers, and national forms. The meeting that takes place between the opposing dignitaries supports a complex dynamic between emotional and economic concerns. Burgundy's self-positioning between the two kings as a voice of cohesion demands that the monarchs take notice. Insisting that peace is a human right, the duke confronts Henry with the legacy of war beyond its immediate ratification of territorial acquisition.

At a local level, however, Henry's attitude reflects a growing investment in individual property rights. To purchase peace was, essentially, to own private property and to be in a position to defend it. Charles Estienne's *Maison rustique, or The Countrey Farme* understands the intrinsic relationship between peace and possession as one of private ownership. Writing on 'the building or enclosing of our countrie farme' he begins: 'Peace being purchased, then build thine house, saith the wise and prudent householder'; a few chapters later, however, he moves from the understanding of peace as a commodity of ownership to the cultivation of personal relationships for the avoidance of unrest. Advising on the treatment of one's neighbours, he urges tolerance and forbearance and 'to seeme to be at one with them, as if h[e]d never understood anything to move him to the contrarie. And thus he may purchase peace and rest.'[66] Estienne's mode of living represents a version of Henry's attitude to his country—you buy what you can, fortify your assets, and then fool your neighbours into thinking they are your friends.

Amid the violations of war, Burgundy presents a potential image of growth: carefully constructed through images of neglect, the landscape of peace supports order and productivity as a return to something that once existed. This is not about novelty or redevelopment, but about returning to the plough that lies rusting in the field, pruning the withered vine, and plashing the disordered hedges. The dormant and decaying landscape offers the potential for change through the very terms on which it already exists. Cultivation is a moral duty, as well as an economic necessity, and offers Henry the opportunity to invest in the dynamic codes of both 'husbandry and humanity'.

The question of good government haunts the history plays. Often read as an attempt to construct a 'Tudor mythology', the history plays represent chronological crises in which monarchical authority is continually

---

[66] Charles Estienne, *Maison rustique, or the Countrey Farme* (London, 1616), 13, 21.

under scrutiny. Whilst Burgundy confronts Henry with the most lucid articulation of the ethics of management, the subject of social order emerges at other points in the play. During Henry's discussion with Exeter and Canterbury, as they persuade him to go to war, Canterbury describes the order of things as 'heaven divides | The state of man in divers functions, | Setting endeavour in continual motion; | To which is fixed, as our aim or butt',

> Obedience. For so work the honey bees,
> Creatures that by a rule in nature teach
> The act of order to a peopled kingdom. (1.2.187–9)

Canterbury goes on to explore 'obedience'—a doctrinal virtue for the Elizabethan—through the extended metaphor of the bee colony.[67] From the outset, Canterbury applies to 'a rule in nature' in which he discerns, by way of his metaphor, a fixed and 'peopled kingdom'. This 'rule of nature' is explored through the image of the king, his 'officers of sorts', magistrates, merchants, soldiers, and citizens. Peopling his image, Canterbury draws on a long history of the bee which is almost always glossed through its religious significance. The bee, however, was a vital emblem in the expression of an efficient commonwealth importing, as Canterbury suggests, a Protestant ideology of labour, industry, and profit.[68] Almost all books on husbandry have a section on bees and bee-keeping, as the apparently orderly construction of the colony made it a valuable image for social decorum. The bee simulated in her (or his, according to the Elizabethan) hive a system of rule that recognized, indeed was dependent

---

[67] In his essay, 'Shakespeare and the Best State of the Commonwealth', in David Armitage, Conal Condren, and Andrew Fitzmaurice (eds.), *Shakespeare and Early Modern Political Thought* (Cambridge: Cambridge University Press, 2009), 256, Eric Nelson explains that 'the political writers who furnished the intellectual background of Shakespeare's age were in fundamental agreement that there was a best regime for any given community, and that it was a matter of moral urgency to identify and institute'.

[68] The emblem of the bee has a longer history than its appropriation into Protestant ethics of work. Virgil uses the bee in the fourth book of the Georgics as well as in his description of sexual love. More interestingly here, however, we might think of his allegory of the bee-keeper (which he takes from Varo) as an image of society in crisis: an image which fails because ultimately they represent 'the impossibility of projecting our world onto nature', Charles Martindale, *The Cambridge Companion to Virgil* (Cambridge: Cambridge University Press, 1997), 140. John Day's *The Parliament of Bees* (1641) title page declares the text to be 'an Allegoricall description of the actions *of good and bad men in these our daies*', whilst Samuel Hartlib's *The Reformed Common-Wealth of Bees* (1655) explores the relationship between a sustainable socio-economy and the bee. Drawing on the production of honey for the development of a national economy as well as the ideological image of the bee as it has been appropriated by both writers on husbandry as well as intellectuals since Virgil, Francis Bacon's *New Atlantis* (London, 1658), 29, for example, mentions the 'uses' of bees. See Raylor, 'Samuel Hartlib and the Commonwealth of Bees', 91–129.

upon, a continually changing, yet stable, unit of authority. Heresbach explains:

> For such is the nature of Bees, that with euery Prince, is bredde a common wealth, which as soone as they are able to trauaile, doo as it were disdayne yᵉ gouernment & fellowship of the old Bee, which most happeneth when the swarmes be great and lusty, and that the old stagers are disposed to send abroad their Colonies, and therefore you shall by two tokens specially know, when the newe Princes with their people will abroade. (181)

In Heresbach's description, we observe a system of order that is in continual motion; determined by work, youth, and a mutually cohesive commonwealth, the bees maintain their hive through the strong rising up to replace the weak. With every prince comes a new commonwealth and the old order is rejected and new boundaries explored. One of the first signs of the incoming prince bee is the establishing of new colonies. If Canterbury could have made his message more explicit he perhaps would have cited Heresbach. Strength of government and the consolidation of order lie in the acquisition of territory; or, as Canterbury concludes, 'Therefore to France, my liege' (1.1.213).

Canterbury's analogy defers to the natural world as an essential example of good government: structured, stratified, and industrious, the bee-hive configures power as a continual process of acquisition and authority. The disdain towards the 'government and fellowship of the old Bee' provides a lightly veiled threat that only the 'great and lusty' will survive. Canterbury subtly challenges his own thesis of providential design through the image of the bee colony in which monarchical power can only be retained by the 'lusty'. Observing a pervasive connection between sending 'abroad' and exercising authority, we can understand Canterbury's metaphor as indicative of the ways in which the natural world could endorse models of improvement. Canterbury, of course, wants it both ways: looking retrospectively at God's book of nature, he sees Henry as providentially destined to rule successfully; whilst looking forwards towards a potentially lucrative acquisition of France, he refers to a more secular model of industry. That is not to say, however, that these were necessarily exclusive positions. As recent historians of science have explained, seventeenth-century empiricism did not preclude theological interpretations of the natural world, and owed less to: 'some triumph of rationality—whether celebrated as enlightenment or decried as disenchantment—than ... [to] a profound mutation in the self-definition of intellectuals'.[69] Such mutation

---

[69] Datson and Park, *Wonders and the Order of Nature*, 18. Cf. Walsham, *The Reformation of the Landscape*, 374.

allowed for a degree of self-interest as well as self-definition and, for Canterbury, the natural world becomes a selective storehouse for the exposition of his imperialist values. Henry is similarly self-reflective in his attitude to the natural world, drawing his landscape around him as a mirror—not to God's work—but to his own authority. Telling the story of his great-grandfather's siege of England he declares:

> . . . the Scot on his unfurnished kingdom
> Came pouring like the tide into a breach
> With ample and brim fullness of his force
> Galling the gleaned land with hot assays
> Girding with grievous siege castles and towns. (1.2.148–53)

For Henry, power is a form of aggressive cultivation: 'galling' is a means of breaking up the ground, chafing, or furrowing.[70] Yet the land is already gleaned, gathered of its harvest, so that Henry reproduces a language of harassment, antithetical to cultivation, in honour of war. Here the landscape speaks Henry's language of conflict: the tide overwhelms the breach, pouring over its sides as his soldiers will cover French territory, and plucks up and takes down castles and towns, as reapers gather a harvest. The metaphors are powerful precisely because they affect the very images they contain. These images of obliteration represent the land as a force to be overcome, a passive marker of presence rather than a chorography of human life. When the King of France, understanding Henry's intentions, remembers the loss of the Battle of Crécy he articulates vanquish as an assault on the land:

> Of that black name, Edward, Black Prince of Wales,
> Whiles that his mountant sire, oh mountain standing,
> Up in the air, crowned with golden sun,
> Saw his heroical seed and smiled to see him
> Mangle the work of nature and deface
> The patterns that by God and by French fathers
> Had twenty years been made. This is a stem
> Of that victorious stock, and let us fear
> The native mightiness and fate of him. (2.4.53–64)

War is imaginatively reconstructed through the destruction of cultivated land. 'The patterns' of livelihood, ownership, habitation, and history that marked the French landscape are destroyed, defaced, in the acts of war. The emotive strength of France's argument is partly conveyed through this loss of history 'that by God and French father's | Had twenty years

---

[70] See particularly *OED* 3a.

been made'. 'The patterns' of agrarian destruction enter our imagination creating a hendiadys of God and French fathers, in which the King of France also evokes the German tradition of 'house-father literature' (*Hausväterliteratur*), which had entered England through European texts like those of Estienne, Olivier de Serres, and Heresbach.[71] His topography is precise, invoking 'patterns' which suggest some kind of mixed farming, either enclosures or strip-fields.[72] In the common field system, strip farming created a relationship between crops which Joan Thirsk calls 'a pattern of occupation'.[73] The king invokes the 'pattern' in recognition of France's status as economically stable and ethically secure.[74] The deface-ment of this pattern represents a destruction that penetrates the history of France, both its past and its immediate future. Anticipating a repetition of that history, 'a stem | Of that victorious stock', France reconstructs the destruction not just of a landscape but also of a network of national belonging. The past—collective, idealized, or imagined—comes to reside in the marks of the land, the footsteps and the furrows that have recorded and supported human life.[75] These are precisely the terms that Burgundy will return to in his plea for peace. Like Burgundy, the King of France perceives his land as a social discourse, marked by human habitation, God, industry, and investment. Paradoxically, then, France becomes the ethical centre of the play's world: for Henry, the land is a site of subjugation where power is recorded through destruction; for France, the land is social discourse, where life is manifest in material markers.

[71] As the title suggests, 'house-father' husbandry consolidated the social role of hus-bandry through its domestic counterpart. Celebrating management, control, productivity, and unity husbandry easily assimilated '[t]he dominant assumption of an ordered patri-archal structure', McRae, *God Speed the Plough*, 138.

[72] In reality sixteenth-century France was dominated by arable farming, produced on the basis of a simple two crop rotation. France's economy was largely sustained through the exportation of wine which enabled the country to move into a capitalist economy; see Frederick J. Baumgartner, *France in the Sixteenth Century* (New York: St Martin's Press, 1995), esp. 65–82. The seigniorial system remained in France longer than the feudal system in England, largely as a result of its absolutist system of monarchy and the fact that it had not negotiated private property rights, as the English had done through the Magna Carta, see Philip Pregill and Nancy Volkman, *Landscape in History: Design and Planning in the Western Tradition* (New York: John Waley and Sons, 1999), 226–30.

[73] Joan Thirsk, 'The Common Fields', *Past and Present*, 29 (December 1964), 9.

[74] The 'pattern' is used repeatedly in husbandry manuals, as a figure for a representation or model to imitate, but also as the thing itself. Richard Weston's text, for example, published in 1650, is titled: 'A discours of husbandrie used in Brabant and Flanders shewing the wonderfull improvement of land there; and serving as a pattern for our practice in this Common-wealth.' The pattern is identified as something ideal, a model of economic sustainability which should be replicated.

[75] See also Schwyzer, *Literature, Nationalism and Memory*.

Both Burgundy and the King of France refer to the devastation of their landscapes within a generalized context of national identification. This idea of 'nativity', or natural belonging, is under constant revision within the play, depending on the ethical values it imports. The 'native mightiness' that the King of France fears in Henry characterizes, in part, the sense of Englishness that the play develops (as well as satirizes), but it also imbues the land with a mythic status through the horticultural metaphors of grafting: 'This is a stem | Of that victorious stock, and let us fear | The native mightiness in him.' Henry approaches France not only with a history of supplanting but with the vigour of survival. Ironically revising the bad stock of Falstaff and company, France completes the images of Hal's transformation through a revision of his history. No longer defined by the nettles or waste of his youth, he is grafted onto the present through the retrospective power of history. The 'victorious stem' has grown into something that can lay waste to the history—and nature—of others. The figurative language of grafting, the stem, scion, or stock, is a conventional metaphor in this period, since it reflects the growing investment in improvement through the development of horticultural and agrarian methods both at home and abroad.[76] Intrinsic to the dynamic of grafting, however, is a sense of inequality, where one species or scion is stronger than the other. An aggressive strain is necessary for the successful grafting of stocks, but it also implies a certain irrepressibility. Taking such recourse in the language of strength, Thomas Hill celebrates the brassica Colewort in vigorous terms:

I purpose heere to intreate first of this Hearbe, that manye of the Latines also for the mightie stemme and armes like branches named the Colewort. Suche is the nature of this plant, that the same refuseth no condition of ayre, for whiche cause it may bee committed to the Earth in any time of the yeare.[77]

Such ideas of strength, robustness, and 'masculinity'—'mightie steeme and armes like branches'—are embedded in husbandry texts, partly as a result of their reiteration of a patriarchal order but also because of the ways in which they are constantly reasserting humanity's dominion over nature.[78] By interpreting horticulture in human terms, writers can rigorously defend processes of development and growth as positive.

---

[76] See especially Seed, *Ceremonies of Possession*, 16–40; and Bushnell, *Green Desire*, 84–107.

[77] Hill, *The gardeners labyrinthe*, 4.

[78] The moral censure embedded in these terms is perhaps nowhere more intensely expressed than in the Epilogue of Marlowe's *Doctor Faustus*, where the destruction of human potential is reiterated in the image of the felled tree: 'Cut is the branch that might have grown full straight.' In Shakespeare's *Titus Andronicus* we find the branch

When Henry rallies his troops before the Battle of Agincourt he speaks a language they understand, a language of shared values, of a unified vision and a collective landscape:

> And you, good yeomen,
> Whose limbs were made in England, show us here
> The mettle of your pasture; let us swear
> That you are worth your breeding—which I doubt not. (3.1.25–8)

Using the image of the horse, Henry yokes his soldiers to their earth through a highly determined sense of Englishness: as they were born in England so they are fighting to reclaim it—however far those boundaries may stretch. Henry appeals to the yeoman, who as a countryman and a soldier represented a central figure in the tenurial landscape. Crudely, the yeoman stands between the peasant and the landlord, working for one with a responsibility to the other. Henry appeals to this sense of duty and labour as he garners his men to the breach. Crucially, however, Henry speaks a language that these men understand: a language of belonging rooted in the land on which they work. The relationship between the husbandman and the soldier informs much of the dialogue between peace and good husbandry. An economically stable country is also a peaceful one, as the men in the cultivated fields are not on the battle field. Henry calls his men from the farms and into war; as they live from the land so they must also defend it. The relationship, however, between the soldier and the yeoman was deeply embedded in early modern literature—practical and belletristic. Heresbach's text, for example, begins with a justification of husbandry through its classical precedent:

M. Varro in his time saith there was great compliant made, that the Fathers forsaking the Plough and the Sicle, began to creep into Town, and busied them selves rather with Pageants and Midsommer games, then with the Vineyard or the Field, whereas the Governors of Rome so decided the year, as they assigned only the nineth day for business of the City, and the rest of t[h]e tune for the tillage of the Country, whereby being hardened with labour in peace, they might the better be able to abide the travails of war. (7ʳ)

The moral message is subtle but clear: cultivation strengthens a nation and controls idle pleasure. Despite James Siemon's claim that 'yeomanry's ... service as armed defender' was 'mythic', there is a great deal of contemporary

---

and body analogy in the pitiful image of Lavinia through Marcus's eyes: 'Speak, gentle niece, what stern ungentle hands | Have lopp'd and hew'd and made thy body bare | Of her two branches, those sweet ornaments, | Whose circling shadows kings have sought to sleep in' (2.3).

literature that supports the relationship between the two.[79] Joan Thirsk, citing Columella, writes that 'Farming . . . was a healthy invigorating life, which made men physically fit, ready to give great service in time of war.'[80] Francis Bacon observed that the 'husbandman is a strong and hardy man, the good footman' and Philip Sidney's *Arcadia* (1590) refers to husbandry as 'the child of peace', and of 'converting husbandrie to soldiery' with 'pitchforks and rakes'.[81]

The image of the yeoman as a standing soldier supported the representation of husbandry as beneficial to the commonwealth, on the grounds of economic and social stability. Moreover, the sense in which the farmer could fortify a country, as the Bishop of Durham makes clear, amplified anxieties about enclosures, depopulation, or migration. Despite Henry's rich rhetoric of brotherhood, the play exposes a hiatus in the two countries' ethical commitments. While France is shown to be attuned to the social implications of war, Henry's bravura flattens the landscape into a contested territory. The French commentaries allow us glimpses into this sense of difference and to the ways in which we are encouraged to make the connections between environment and ethics. In the Constable's conversation with the Dauphin, he attempts to mock the English with contempt for the climate:

> *Dieu de batailles!* Where have they this mettle?
> Is not their climate foggy, raw, and dull,
> On whom as in despite the sun looks pale,
> Killing their fruit with frowns? . . .
> O for honour of our land
> Let us not hang like roping icicles
> Upon our houses' thatch, whiles a more frosty people
> Sweat drops of gallant youth in our rich fields—
> 'Poor' may we call them, in their native lords. (3.5.15–18, 21–6)

The anxiety here seems to stem from an illogical relationship between body and environment. Reconstructing English bodies in the terms of crop, pasture, or flora, the constable contemplates how such a wet climate can enable strength and growth. Perceiving English weather as essentially inimical to cultivation, he marvels that 'a more frosty people' can 'sweat drops of gallant youth in our rich fields'. French superiority is constructed through an inherent strength of cultivation, while the English kill 'their

---

[79] 'Landlord not King', 26.
[80] 'Making a Fresh Start', 21.
[81] Bacon's comment is in response to parliament's attempts to repeal the enclosure statutes of 1601, see Thirsk, 'Making a Fresh Start', 21. Sidney's *Arcadia*, 7^v; 223^r.

fruit with frowns'.[82] Despite their apparent military weaknesses, the various ambassadors of France take refuge in their agrarian superiority. The strength of this country's position lies not in its ability to fight wars but in its ability to recognize the value of its losses way beyond that of territory. The Constable's comments draw our attention to the ways in which the English sit outside this value system—there is no objective correlative between their English bodies and their English soil.[83] Where Henry points to their mettle having been 'made in England', the Constable claims that's not possible. Given the strength of arguments that the French mediate through the land, the Constable appears to denude the soldiers of one of Henry's defining moments of kinship. For Henry the land is not conscientious, nor does it respond to a set of social codes through which political authority coheres; instead, it produces an obligation construed as production: 'let us swear | That you are worth your breeding—which I doubt not.' Until the battle is won, the landscape is a rhetorical tool; and after, it is a comprehensive commodity. The sense of difference, however, that the play relies upon in the construction of its victory is rather more unstable than it initially appears.

Burgundy remains the most lucid exponent of this ethical voice and yet the strength of his argument is supported by the pervasive relationship between the landscape and its destruction in war. The brutal reality is, of course, that the land will absorb the bodies of war, once again synthesizing the human and the landscape. When Mountjoy desires the freedom of the field to 'book' their dead we see how the land has become the ultimate

---

[82] The popular texts that came over from the continent were translated by Englishmen who prefaced their work with a sharp sense of difference, as well as similarity. Googe's translation of Heresbach, for example, makes a particular note of the vine. He explains: 'I have also been careful about the planting and ordering of the Vine, though some of my friends would have had it omitted, as altogether impertinent to our country' (4). This failure of the vine he puts down to 'slothfulness', civil discord, and unfamiliarity: 'There hath moreover good experience of late years been made, by two noble and honourable Bar[. . .] ons of this Realm, the Lord Cobham and the Lord Williams of Tame, who both had growing about their houses as good vines, as are in many places of France. And if they answered not in all points every man's expectation, the fault is rather to be imputed to the malice and disdain peradventure of the Frenchmen that kept them, then to any ill disposition or fault of the soil . . . or where have you in any place better, or pleasanter vines, then about Backrach, Andernach, and divers other places of Germany, that have in a manner the self same latitute [latitude]and disposition of the heavens that we have,' 4. On 'latitude', see Mary Floyd Wilson and Garrett Sullivan (ed.), *Environment and Embodiment in Early Modern England* (Basingstoke: Palgrave Macmillan, 2007).

[83] According to Wendy Wall, however, the husbandry manual supported an awareness of national difference through its construction of specific terms of identification: 'In short, readers prove their own national identity by fishing out true practices from foreign ones, identifying the "difference of our customs" from within this syncretic international work,' 'Renaissance National Husbandry', 775.

register of failure as well as triumph. Through the terms of the French, the play records one of the most important Acts of Elizabeth's parliament: 'Whereas the strength and flourishing estate of this kingdom is . . . greatly upheld and advanced by the maintenance of the plough.' Understanding Burgundy's speech within the context of socio-economic failure, Henry's imperialist victory seems more problematic than we might initially assume. Burgundy speaks a vital language within the play: a language of peace, of communality, sustainability, and futurity, Henry cannot accommodate this into his war; he sees a price where Burgundy needs a future. Yet at the close of the play, the Chorus intercedes, offering a glimpse of that future predicated on the terms of Burgundy's loss and gain:

> Small time, but in that small most greatly lived
> This star of England. Fortune made his sword,
> By which the world's best garden he achieved,
> And of it left his son imperial lord . . .
> Of France and England did this king succeed,
> Whose state so many had the managing
> That they lost France and made his England bleed. (6–8, 10–12)

Recovering Burgundy's best garden only to lose it again, bad management and blood return us to the cost of war.

4

Darkness Visible

Macbeth and the Poetics of the Unnatural

In contemporary environmental studies, the humanizing of nature, usually termed anthropocentrism, is understood as negative in its impact on our ecological world. The increasing pressure that human growth and development has put upon the natural world has led not only to a rapid depletion of natural resources but a whole-scale shift in the balance of the earth's bio-systems. Historically, however, recognizing that the natural world was in service to the human denotes a seminal discourse in the evolution of what we understand as empathy.[1] Through representing the non-human world in human terms we begin to invest nature with a set of emotions reconcilable to social needs. It is hardly surprising then, that, as humans, we need to invoke human emotions in order to make our non-human world intelligible. What marks the husbandry manuals of the seventeenth century as modern is the trace of this emerging discourse; of the shift away from a strictly allegorical or symbolic nature to a cultural or humanized nature.

Macbeth occupies a unique position within the discourses of husbandry that this book addresses. For in this play, we begin to witness an emerging distinction between nature and culture: a distinction that is central to the moral complexities that the play invokes. *Macbeth* represents a vital shift in the exploration of both the human and natural worlds. Here, in perhaps Shakespeare's bleakest tragedy, we find nature an altogether more human concept: perceptual, linguistic, and subjective, the natural world manifests as a border country through which the human must travel in order to

---

[1] See Höfele, *Stage, Stake and Scaffold*, for an exposition of the proximities of animal and violence and human entertainment in the social developments of empathy and imagination. Kate Soper's *What is Nature* outlines many of the most influential debates within historical and contemporary environmental criticism, as well as anthropocentrism. See also Boehrer, *Shakespeare Among the Animals*, Emily Brady, *Aesthetics of the Natural Environment* (Edinburgh: Edinburgh University Press, 2003), and Paul Taylor, *Respect for Nature: A Theory of Environmental Ethics* (Princeton: Princeton University Press, 1986).

assert his or her self-possession.[2] Nature is a limit that the human, at least according to the Macbeths, must exceed.[3] Crawling free from the social implications of a 'royalty of nature', human intervention begins to emerge as a powerful act of progressive individualism. Only by relentlessly rejecting the values embodied in organic nature can human culture identify itself as superior.

In this chapter, I locate nature as a site of cultivation as well as a set of apparently predetermined characteristics, in which the idea of nature emerges as a form of personal bondage. Central to this vision of a prohibitive nature are the terms of moral obligation that circulate through images of growth and harvest, social bonds and economic efficiency. As I have demonstrated in the preceding chapters, the social focus on cultivation in the sixteenth century supported its development in the public imagination as an ethically comprehensive endeavour, through which the domestic and regional economies could be rationalized for national stability. As the demands on the land became greater and expectations of production and surplus increased, the attitudes to the landscape also changed: overseas trade, balance of exports and imports, metal and mineral mining, and market experimentation gradually shifted the 'state' perceptions away from local areas of domestic production into urban areas of national industry.[4] Shakespeare's *Macbeth* partakes of this transition in the representation of a nature, not as a conservative force for moral obligation, but as a powerful, fragmentary, and enthralling image of human potential. The play's confrontation with competing concepts of human nature (mutable, individual,

---

[2] In *At the Borders of the Human* (London: Palgrave, 2002), Erica Fudge, Ruth Gilbert, and Susan Wiseman explore the question of the border in relation to the various liminal technologies that have both separated and endorsed human and non-human relationships.

[3] M. C. Bradbrook, however, perceives a more consistent and allegorical relationship between 'the King and the body politic. When the King is sick or disordered, the land is disordered too', 'The Sources of Macbeth', in Kenneth Muir and Philip Edwards (eds.), *Aspects of Macbeth: Articles Reprinted from Shakespeare Survey* (Cambridge: Cambridge University Press, 1977), 14.

[4] See particularly Thirsk, *Economic Policy and Projects*, and Appleby, *Economic Thought and Ideology*. Christopher Dyer, however, in his *Age of Transition* argues that the seeds of all these economic developments had been planted in the middle ages, and that far from representing a radical shift in England's economic and social development the sixteenth and seventeenth centuries developed and consolidated earlier practices. While I do not wholly disagree with Dyer, print made the circulation of information possible in such a way as to introduce new forms of agricultural practice and new perceptions of economic production in ways not possible before 1500. Despite James I's gesture towards the maintenance of tillage in his speech to the star-chamber in 1616, the majority of his policies reflect a fundamental investment in city-led commodities. Prioritizing artisan trades such as tanning, millinery, painting, plastering, and ship-building, James's socio-economics reflect a growing investment in the market values of commodities rather than the sustainability of the agrarian landscape, see *Full Statutes of the Realm*, 1. Jac. I. c. 22, 23, 24, 115–50.

and godless) are in many ways more complex precisely because they have no material manifestations in the form of landscape. The manifest realities of nature have been replaced by individual perceptions of it—delusional, partial, inconsistent, and emotional.

From the outset of the play the natural spaces are suggestive: largely oblique and often redundant they function as emotional weather rather than naturalistic space. Opening with some 'unnatural hags' on a heath reveals the play-world to be devoid of a sustainable nature in which growth governs images of value. Unlike *Lear* or *The Tempest*, however, the characters make no objections to their landscape, suggesting an indifference to their non-human world. Confronted by the blasted heath, the foul weather, and the prophecies of the withered and wild women, Banquo questions himself, rather than his surroundings:

> Were such things as we do speak about?
> Or have we eaten on the insane root
> That takes the reason prisoner? (1.3.83–5)

Subjecting himself to doubt, Banquo perceives his environment as a possible mutation of his own cognition. Human rationality comes into question as the physical body is shown to be unstable, susceptible, and vulnerable. As much as any other play by Shakespeare, *Macbeth* is fascinated by the status of humans—their definition, mutations, possibilities, and limits.[5]

As Macbeth tries to exceed his nature—'And to be more than what you were, you would | Be so much more than the man' (1.7.50–1)—so he will also unhinge himself from the non-human landscape that threatens to overcome him:

> That will never be.
> Who can impress the forest, bid the tree
> Unfix his earth-bound root? Sweet bodements! Good! (4.1.93–5)

The language of fixity corresponds to a nature that Macbeth depends on in order to exceed its limits. Nature takes a central role in the subjective equivocations of the play, and in this way records some of the major changes that were taking place in the period. Initially, however, images of

---

[5] In more strictly psychoanalytic terms than my work suggests, Robert N. Watson explores the nature of ambition in *Macbeth* in *Shakespeare and the Hazards of Ambition* (Philadelphia: University of Pennsylvania Press, 1985). Equally exemplary, but more concerned with the question of individualism, is Watson's *The Rest is Silence: Death as Annihilation in the English Renaissance* (Berkeley and Los Angeles: University of California Press, 1995).

fixity are central to Macbeth's experience of his own body. Responding to the witches' prophecies, he exclaims:

> If good, why do I yield to that suggestion
> Whose horrid image doth unfix my hair
> And make my seated heart knock at my ribs
> Against the use of nature? (1.3.135–7)

Macbeth identifies something unnatural in his bodily response to the witches' words: his hair creeps away from his skull and his heart beats an alternative rhythm. As Macbeth notices his body's divergence from its conventional functions so he also traces an equivocal image of profit in this unnatural course.

The term 'yield' has a 'remarkable sense-development' in the English language; its modern-day verb form has moved through a range of meanings all of which carry some trace of financial gain, profit, or recompense.[6] The specifically agrarian use of the noun develops in the fifteenth century, bearing the verb's sense of production or profit. Macbeth's expectations of his body are centred on a correlation between nature and morality—'if good, why do I yield to that suggestion'—or to paraphrase, 'why am I drawn to something that disrupts the normal functions of my body'. Giving in to, profiting by, or even harvesting the results of something that appears deviant forces Macbeth to disassociate himself from his own nature as a site of morality. As his physical response reflects something 'against the use of nature' he unhinges himself from the moral binaries that condition natural reflexes. Working against his own body, Macbeth must redefine the relationships between 'good' and 'nature'.

Within the play-world, however, such qualitative redefinitions of nature had already begun at the level of the landscape. In seventeenth-century England a 'blasted heath' was notoriously redundant and for the most part left for highland grazing (deer and cattle) or ploughed and re-planted. Markham's *Farewell to Husbandry* (1620) goes into some detail about this hostile landscape, describing it as barren and unfruitful:

But this earth of which I am now to intreat, beareth no grasse at all, but only a vilde, filthie, black-browne weede, which we call Lynge or Heath, the tender tops whereof Cattell and wilde Deere will sometimes crop, yet it is to them but little reliefe, and only maintaineth life and no more. (38)

---

[6] The *OED* explains the complex development of the word from Old English whilst being used as an equivalent of Latin *reddere* and French *render*. 'In some of the related languages the word has shown tendencies to develop in the same directions, but the only generally surviving senses on the Continent are "to be worth, to be valid, to concern, apply to", which are not represented at all in the English word.'

This landscape has almost no intrinsic value, only barely maintaining the life of some hardy bovine creatures. Later on in his manual, Markham will suggest ploughing it up and starting again in order to rescue some value from the land. The redundancy of such ground supported its frequent use as a metaphor for faithlessness and sin. Thomas Tuke's *Picture of a true protestant* (1609) makes eloquent use of such an image:

> For all their preferment, all their comlinesse is at the free disposement of their Architect [who] doth call & take vs to be a field vnto himselfe, out of the barren heath, and wide wildernesse of this sinfull world; & before he sowes the seeds of his graces, & sets the pleasant plants of true christia[n] vertues in our hearts, he prepares and fits vs ordinarily by the ministery of his word, ioyning therewith sometimes also crosses and aflictions, and some other things, which he hath prouidently prepared and wisely directeth for our good. (156)

Here the barren heath is the bare body in which the soul must plant its faith and erect its virtues. Reminding human nature of its nakedness before God, Tuke invokes the bare landscape as an image of our life's work and our spiritual duties. The body as the bare soil on which humans must sow, harvest, and reap the potential of life presents practices of cultivation as indicative of moral worth.[7] In *Macbeth*, however, the heath is neither cultivated nor habitable but a stark introduction to the absence of growth. This world has been violently severed from a sustainable nature long before we have arrived at it: only the 'temple-haunting martlet' will remain; a spectral vision of a lost landscape. This is not to suggest, however, that the play mourns its absent nature; to the contrary, it is a necessary casualty in the exploration of human limits.

The play's erasure of a sustainable organic world amplifies its emphasis on human action. Since there is very little in the play that we could construe as 'natural', these terms of value point less to comparisons and more to absence. The 'unnatural hags' on a blasted heath invite the audience into a world in which values of productivity, growth, and futurity are grotesquely parodied. While Macbeth and Lady Macbeth may find futurity in the prophecies of the witches, such incantations are

---

[7] In a translation of Grimaldus' *The Counsellor*, human potential is recognized through its aptitude for harvest: 'Notwithstanding, without the presence of God, no reason is good and perfect, for the diuine seedes beeing sowen in mens bodies, so much thereof as happeneth into the handes of good till-men, doth bring forth fruite according to him that did sowe them: but of the rest beeing handled by euill husbandry, doth (like vnto corne sowen in barren soyle) become br[a]mbles, and within short space decay and die,' Wawrzyniec Goslicki (trans.), *The counsellor Exactly pourtraited in two bookes. VVherein the offices of magistrates, the happie life of subiectes, and the felicitie of common-weales is pleasantly and pithilie discoursed* (London, 1598), 3.

stained by the context of sterility. Later in the play we return to the relationship between organic and human nature in Macbeth's subjective response to the witches' final prophecy in the movement of Birnam wood:

> Rebellious dead, rise never till the wood
> Of Birnam rise, and our high-placed Macbeth
> Shall live the lease of nature, pay his breath
> To time and mortal custom. Yet my heart
> Throbs to know one thing: tell me, if your art
> Can tell so much: shall Banquo's issue ever
> Reign in this kingdom? (4.1.112–18)

Macbeth finds reassurance in the implacability of nature—the powerful fixity of the 'earth-bound root' (compared, we imagine, to the uprooted King), the fixed term of Nature's lease, and the custom of mortality. Yet here again custom appears to assimilate nature as time; mortality and the lease of life represent a termination of a simultaneously social and natural contract.

The idea of a 'great bond' (3.2.52) between the human and non-human worlds is under scrutiny. Carefully exposing a changing moral economy, the play subjects the very terms of nature to doubt; the body, the landscape, the family, and the biological imperatives of eating and sleeping all become casualties of a war between the human and its nature. Fundamental to this conflict is an emerging sense of culture, in which the human selectively interprets his or her surroundings according to individual perceptions of agency.

In Christian theology, however, perception could be construed as a form of 'natural law' in which reason was identified as innate knowledge. One of the most sophisticated commentators on Anglican theology, Richard Hooker, in his *Lawes of Ecclesiastical Politie* (1594), discusses the relationship between human action and the natural world in his explanation of reason. For Hooker, this reason can be called natural law because it reflects Nature's unique pattern of beneficence:

And the law of reason or humaine nature is that, which men by discourse of naturall reason haue rightly found out themselues to be all for euer bound vnto in their actions. Lawes of reason haue these markes to be knowne by. Such as keepe them, resemble most liuely in their voluntarie actions, that very manner of working which nature her selfe doth necessarily obserue in the course of the whole world. The workes of nature are all behoouefull, beautifull, without super-fluitie or defect: euen so theirs, if they be framed according to that which the law of reason teacheth.

Here reason is a synthesis of experience, action, and knowledge based on a profound belief in God's presence in the creative order of the natural world. For Hooker, natural law governs human behaviour to the extent that it reveals a sympathetic world of beauty, decorum, and beneficence. To separate oneself from the 'workes of nature' is to ally oneself to a world of 'custome' in which there is little moral regulation:

> I deny not but lewd and wicked custome; beginning perhaps at the first amongst few, afterwards spreading into greater multitudes, and so continuing from time to time, may be of force euen in plaine things to smother the light of naturall vnderstanding, because men will not bend their wits to examine, whether things wherewith they haue bene accustomed, be good or euill.[8]

Natural understanding, or the effects of natural law, is pitched against 'custome', which is the unthinking acceptance of the multitude.[9] For Hooker, nature will always morally prevail over culture because it represents a reflective image of divine order. As Danby explains, 'the law it [Nature] observed was felt more as self-expression than as external restraint. It was a law, in any case, which the creature was most itself when it obeyed.'[10] The idea of integrity in nature is central to the development of culture, since the human, by way of reason, must redeploy this integrity not as a form of sympathy but as a mode of superiority. To be true to oneself, so *Macbeth* suggests, is to exceed the boundaries of nature not conform to them.

This is a play in which we observe, overtly for the first time in Shakespeare, the human at war with its own nature. This war—existential, psychological, biological, and martial—is individual, brutal, and incessant as it charts a search for the limits of a social consciousness construed as natural. The anxiety of human behaviour so often articulated as custom reflects an ambivalence towards the status of nature itself. Notoriously slippery, Nature could be invoked randomly to justify claims of damnation or approbation. Yet, as attitudes to the landscape entered into culture as expressions of human values, so the idea of an organic nature as separate from human industry became harder and harder to define. *Macbeth* occupies a crucial space in Shakespeare's works as it begins to explore a division between nature and culture at the level of human action. Unlike

---

[8] Richard Hooker, *The Lawes of Ecclesiasticall Politie, Eight Bookes* (London, 1604), 65; 66.

[9] Richard Brathwaite, in *The English Gentlewoman* (1631), fears such developments in women: 'There is nothing in its owne nature so absolutely good, but it may be corrupted; what was at first intended for some good *Vse*, if peruerted, declines into some apparant *Abuse*,' 5. Later in the text Brathwaite returns to this anxiety through custom: 'There is nothing on earth so pure, but abuse may *corrupt* it; nothing so good, but custome may depraue it,' 63.

[10] John F. Danby, *Shakespeare's Doctrine of Nature: A Study of King Lear* (London: Faber and Faber, 1962), 28.

King Lear, where the natural world appears to reflect the breakdown of social morality in the raging storms and blasted heath, *Macbeth* does not concede to a superior elemental nature; rather in an effort to unhinge human imperatives from a heritage of moral binaries the natural world recedes into something altogether more amorphous.[11]

As we observed in *Henry V,* the Christian polemics embedded in early husbandry manuals were dependent on an image of the earth's resources as flexible and empathetic. Nature's ability to produce and reproduce for human needs reflects a grand Christian narrative in which God rewards his people for labour whilst simultaneously providing them with a reflective model of hierarchical living. As the overtly Christian imperatives begin to slip away from agrarian discourses, however, nature becomes a more autonomous figure that is capable of sustaining and nurturing her community. In Gervase Markham's dedicatory epistle to his translation of Estienne's *Countrey Farme* he defines the natural world as:

this sacred goddesse, as she sheweth her beautie, in being clothed in her gaiest colours, and her perfection in her naturall kindnesse, by pressing out of her neuer drying brests (though euermore conceiued) euen millions of streames to feed (as with sweet milke) both the young and old fruit of her wombe. (A1ᵛ)

The representation of nature is striking for its human investment (as well as its relevance to Lady Macbeth): clothed, kind, and endlessly lactating, she becomes a powerful figure of maternity that is capable of looking after 'both the young and old fruit of her wombe'. Markham's extension of the maternal role beyond the infant to the 'old' presents this figure as fundamentally social in her ability to provide for everyone. As Nature presses 'out of her never drying breasts' a milk of 'natural kindness' she exposes a vital regard for regeneration which is valorized as human welfare. Sustenance and nurturing become the defining images of a 'kindness', or kinship, that is conceived as natural but meaningful as human. Where, in the sixteenth century, nature was a manifest reality of original sin, it is now a figurehead in the development of a socialized world. John Norden, in *The Surveyor's Dialogue* (1607), goes even further when he suggests that only 'the worst husbands' rely on nature as a model of her own potential:

Whereas if men were careful and industrious, they should find that the earth would yield in recompense for a good husband's travail and charge, *centum pro cento* without corrupt usury.[12]

---

[11] The nature of *King Lear* is notoriously provocative and has been increasingly addressed through ecocriticism. John F. Danby's study, however, remains the most persuasive within the context of early modern conceptions of nature.

[12] 226.

For Norden, and most of his contemporaries, human industry determined the translation of resources into riches. Good husbandry—careful and industrious—represents a process of full reward which is neither corrupt nor exploitative. The human figure is central to that process of translation from resource to product, or animal to industry. Estienne's advice, for example, on getting the ox to the plough includes subjecting the animal to human activity:

let them oftentimes see the Oxen that draw the plow, or which till the ground, or doe any other manner of worke: and to the end they may loose their naturall wildnesse, lead them to heare the noise of mills, of men, of forges, and other things which make great rumbling. (91)

The animal is literally humanized—or exposed to human experiences—in order to divest it of its own non-human nature, here construed as 'wildnesse'. Conversely, Markham in his *Cheape and Good Husbandrie* identifies equestrian dropsy through an alienation between beast and master:

The Dropsie is that euill habit of the body, which ingenderd by surfets and vnreasonable labour, altereth the colours and complexions of horses, and changeth the haires, in such an vnnaturall sort, that a man shall not know the Beast with which he hath beene most familiar.[13]

The human is the central point of understanding; whether through identification or assimilation, the master's recognition determines the criteria for naturalness. Even though the horse may have been subjected to 'unreasonable labour' the misrecognition of the animal renders the body as subject to 'evil habit'. The criterion through which nature becomes accessible, manageable, and useful comes to determine the ways in which the human subject may identify with it. Central to the Macbeths' mission is an increasingly violent need to denaturalize their world: part of this denaturalization will take place through their own bodies and part through their rendition of social codes; but central to both is a powerful belief in the debilitating effects of sympathy as they are understood to reside in conceptions of the natural.

Central to the play's erasure of the natural world is its comprehensive destruction of what we might term 'natural' impulses. Throughout the play the main protagonists draw attention to the ways in which they must fight their own bodies: Lady Macbeth's maternity, Macbeth's physical responses to fear, his delusions, and, ultimately, that most essential of natural impulses—sleep. The play exposes a radical confrontation with the

---

[13] Markham, *Cheape and Good Husbandrie* (London, 1614), 19.

body as a biologically determined entity: men, women, and witches are systematically shown to be denaturalized and therefore expelled from the cultural expectations of nature.

As the husbandry manuals of the seventeenth century move towards an agrarian technology that is less dependent on Christian models of reward and productivity and more focused on maximizing profit, a different semiotics of value begins to develop. In c. 1523? John Fitzherbert had written the 'natural man' into his text on husbandry as an example of the interrelationships between faith, labour and living. Writing of the Ten Commandments, he explains:

These be lyghte commaundementes, and nature byndeth a man to fulfyll, ob-serue, and kepe them, or els he is not a naturall man, remembryng what god hath doone for the[e]. (73ᵛ)

Fitzherbert supports his *Boke of Husbandry* through such recourses to Christian doctrine, its calendar, sermons, and prayer. To work the land and to be a 'natural man' are symbiotic elements of his grand narrative of preaching and profit. Yet for Markham, a hundred years later, expositions of the natural take place at the level of the animal but through the values of the human. Describing sows, for example, Markham focuses on their behaviour as mothers:

Many Sowes are so vnnaturall, that they will deuoure their Pigges when they haue farro'd them, which springeth from a most vnnaturall greedinesse in them: which to helpe, you must watch her when shee farroweth, and take away the Pigges as they fall, then take the wreckling, or worst Pigge, and annoint it all ouer with the iuyce of *Stonecrop*, and so giue it to the Sow againe: and if shee deuoure it, it will make her cast and vomite so extreamely, that the paine of the surfet will make her loathe to doe the like againe· But of all cures, the best for such an vnnaturall beast is to feede her and kill her. (94)

Without a hint of irony, Markham repudiates such unnaturalness with fattening and slaughter. The animal world that Markham represents is conditioned by ideas of good husbandry in which human values are simul-taneously reproduced and legitimized. Central to such legitimization is a value system in which financial gain and moral censure go hand in hand. Almost all the images of unnaturalness within these texts use social and economic relations as their vantage points.[14] In his section on goats, Mark-ham makes profit natural when he explains that, despite being rarely ill:

---

[14] Towards the middle of the seventeenth century, ideas of gain were specifically allied to the benefit of the commonwealth in which improvement could mean the translation of 'private profit' into general gain. In a record of petition for enclosures in Gloucestershire, one commentator writes that enclosing 'waste' ground is to 'the private benefit of them-selves and the general good of the commonwealth', Thirsk and Cooper (eds.), *Seventeenth Century Economic Documents*, 123.

onely the vnnaturall excesse of their lust maketh them grow soone olde, and so both past vse and profit. (83)

As excessive lust (Adam's uxuriousness leads him to follow Eve) compromises both the moral and natural order so it also threatens use and profit. For Markham such ethical reflections on the animal world also represent its efficiency and value. These models of naturalness become transparently cultural when they are mediated through human desires. *Macbeth* plots the triumph of humans over nature: in the protagonists we witness an overarching belief in the suppression of biological determinants—birth, sleep, sex, reason, and death.[15] Lady Macbeth's notorious speech in which she calls on nature to unsex her has long been the subject of critical anxiety. By virtue of a well-defined 'nature', the murderous or violent woman has always appeared more shocking than her male equivalent.[16] For a woman to be 'unsexed', that is, to deny her primary role as carer and nurturer, is an abrogation of a predetermined ethical character. A murdering female is inherently more evil because she has had to cross an encoded moral boundary associated with maternity.[17] Lady Macbeth appears to adhere to a notion of gender fixity when she invokes these specific terms of sex and maternity:[18]

> Come, you spirits
> That tend on mortal thoughts, unsex me here,
> And fill me from the crown to the toe, top-full

---

[15] In terms of modern psychology identifying conscience and sex as biologically determined may be rather provocative. I might qualify the former as a term of empathy: in other words an affective or cognitive ability to recognize and identify with another's feelings and the latter as reproductive organs.

[16] Whilst the status of murder as sin is unequivocal, recent feminist criticism has sought to re-evaluate the role of women in constructions of good and evil. Nel Noddings, in *Women and Evil*, explores these ethical and philosophical problems: 'Woman has been associated in a stereotypical way with both good and evil. As an "angel in the house," woman has been credited with natural goodness, an innate allegiance to a "law of kindness". But this same description extols her as infantile, weak, and mindless—a creature in constant need of male supervision and protection' (Berkeley and Los Angeles: University of California Press, 1981), 59. See also Mary Daly's *Pure Lust: Elemental Feminist Philosophy* (Boston: Beacon Press, 1984).

[17] Carol Chillington Rutter's 'Remind me How Many Children Had Lady Macbeth', *Shakespeare Survey: Macbeth and its Afterlife*, 57 (2004), 38–54, examines social anxieties about both mothers and children within the context of 'evil'. Lynn Enterline, however, in *Shakespeare's Schoolroom*, shows how gender pronouns were more fluid within the context of both pedagogy and parenting: 'The school that separated boys from their mothers physically and linguistically could also preserve the figure, and emotions, of precisely those its students were forced to leave behind,' 139.

[18] Ariosto, for example, refers to women who murder as 'without pitie', suggesting a depth of emotional betrayal, particularly in the condemned figure of Gabrina. See especially canto 22 of *Orlando Furioso*, trans. John Harington (London, 1607), 169[r].

> Of direst cruelty. Make thick my blood,
> Stop up th'access and passage to remorse,
> That no compunctious visitings of nature
> Shake my fell purpose, nor keep peace between
> Th'effect and it. Come to my woman's breasts
> And take my milk for gall, you murd'ring ministers,
> Wherever, in your sightless substances,
> You wait on nature's mischief. (1.5.39–49)

Focusing on her body, Lady Macbeth calls for the 'spirits' who 'tend on mortal thoughts' to separate her from her natural impulses. For the Jacobeans, the human body was made up of certain substances which included humours, solids, and spirits and reflected particular character 'types' as well as physical tendencies.[19] Whether the spirits that Lady Macbeth summons are those of her own 'mortal' body or those associated with the witches' power, they must serve to sever her from nature, rather than represent it.[20] Allying herself with something—or some spirit—outside of her own body, Lady Macbeth performs her first step towards the process of denaturalization.

Like Macbeth's human kindness, 'visitings of nature' bear traces of compunction or conscience and, to this end, like other 'natural' qualities must be denied. This extraordinary speech is not, I am suggesting, an exposition in evil but a recognition of the ways in which human 'nature' has been culturally bracketed. Lady Macbeth focuses on her female body as the engine of her nature and therefore the primary place of definition. Like Markham's goddess Nature, Lady Macbeth understands breast milk as the foundation of nurturing and production which cannot be reconciled with Duncan's murder. As part of her body's spirits or humours, Lady Macbeth's translation of physical substances reflects her bid for autonomy as she overrules her bodily secretions.[21] Infecting nature with

[19] The body, which, according to Estienne, is made up of spirits, humours, and solids (*The Countrey Farme*, 621), is dependent on the sustenance of all three. The idea of these spirits move between a physical and a metaphysical substance—an amorphous quality (something which can be cheered through hunting, for example, 690) and something more tangible (which is more akin to alcohol, 625). See Paster, *Humouring the Body*, and Korda, *Shakespeare's Domestic Economies*.

[20] In *Shakespearean Maternities: Crises of Conception in Early Modern England* (Edinburgh: Edinburgh University Press, 2008), Chris Laoutaris observes that 'The witches' ability to drain their victims of their vital and regenerative bodily essences seems to parallel Lady Macbeth's strange emasculating influence over her husband', 185.

[21] Despite the more general recognition that gall is a secretion of the liver it is usually associated with horses. It is characterized by an intense bitterness which appears to have facilitated its primary use as a metaphor. See also Jonathan Sawday, *The Body Emblazoned: Dissection and the Human Body in Renaissance Culture* (London: Routledge, 1995) and Lynn Enterline, *The Rhetoric of the Body from Ovid to Shakespeare* (Cambridge: Cambridge University Press, 2000).

the bitter gall registers the decline of the natural, transposing sustenance for poison, life for death.[22] The moral absolutes represented by the natural world become increasingly fragmented through an emerging idea of mutable human nature. The 'mischief' that Lady Macbeth refers to is altogether more human than the word 'nature' first suggests: emptying her body of any biological imperatives she invokes the conditions of social harm. The language of self-injury presents her body as the primary site of nature's destruction.

Perhaps the most powerful example of denaturalization, and certainly the most provocative, is Lady Macbeth's imagined assault on her child, an assault which radiates from the child's 'dashed brains' to her own maternal body:

> What beast was't then
> That made you break this enterprise to me?
> When you durst do it, then you were a man;
> And to be more than what you were, you would
> Be so much more than the man...
> I have given suck, and know
> How tender 'tis to love the babe that milks me;
> I would, while it was smiling in my face,
> Have plucked my nipple from his boneless gums
> And dashed the brains out, *had I so sworn*
> As you have done to this. (1.7.47–51; 54–9. My italics)

The primary subject of this speech is Macbeth's commitment—a commitment that she rationalizes as masculine. Although the power of her speech lies in the imagery of the infant, it is not the subject. Lady Macbeth invokes the image of a baby murdered at the moment of its governing impulse, to feed, as an exploration of her own human limits. The confrontation with her husband is centred on his apparently wavering commitment to Duncan's murder, a commitment, she claims, she would fulfil 'had I so sworn'. In order to impress upon Macbeth the significance of his oath she invokes the absolute limits of her endurance for compassion. The extraordinary collection of images that centre on nurturing and care become Lady Macbeth's final attempt at her own denaturalization. Far from revealing her as a monster, she discloses her own limits of kindness; limits that she is determined to exceed. Recognizing images of nurturing and care as 'natural' was a fundamental aspect of the Christianized world. More

---

[22] Janet Adelman rightly, I think, identifies the construction of this sentence as suggesting that the milk becomes gall, rather than is replaced by gall. The necessary infection must begin within Lady Macbeth's body and not external to it. See *Suffocating Mothers*, 133–5.

importantly, however, tracing those cultural qualities from the non-human to the human worlds made the landscape a resource as well as a model for social living.[23]

The landscape of the play, however, is not only bleak but shadowed by a seemingly perpetual fog, contagion, and night. Conventionally read as a symbol of diabolical agencies at work within the play, Shakespeare's creation of a 'transpicuous gloom' frequently leads to interpretations of the play centred on moral binaries.[24] Tracing these images of darkness through the husbandry manuals, however, reveals an environment that is less concerned with the representation of 'evil' than with the capacity of the human to alter nature. The most powerful rejection of the natural economy comes in the persistent invocations of and references to night. Night, where 'Nature seems dead' (2.1.26), represents the endless climate of slow decline—physical, moral, and social, nothing can survive the incessant dark that colludes with decay. Since light is predominantly associated with God, creation, and spirituality, night comes to develop complex affiliations with sin. William Jackson, in his polemical work *Celestial Husbandrie* (1616), understands the night as the province of turpitude:

> *Apollonius* reporteth one strange thing among the rest of his reports. That there was a people which could not see in the light, but in the darke: A strange report; yet it is here true by experience: The wicked cannot see any thing in the light of grace: they haue their light onely in the darkenesse of nature; for they here see and vnderstand through the darke cloudes of nature: No maruell then, if their heartes bee set vpon sinne, when they can see nothing but euill. (15)[25]

---

[23] In terms of jurisdiction, the land becomes an important mediator in establishing social values. Ideas of justice, legal definitions, and spaces represented, and re-invented, versions of natural law. Manwood's *Treatise on the Laws of the Forest* (1598) examines the forest space as an exercise in certain laws; some animals were subject to legal punishments in the same ways as humans and the law itself came to reflect a growing need for intervention in agrarian matters, notably the Elizabethan concern for poor relief and the protection of houses of husbandry.

[24] Caroline Spurgeon's *Shakespeare's Imagery and What it Tells Us* (Cambridge: Cambridge University Press, 1935) states: 'light stands for life, virtue, goodness; and darkness for evil and death'. More recently, William A. Armstrong explores the interrelations of dark and light in 'Torch, Cauldron, and Taper: Light and Dark in *Macbeth*', in Anthony Coleman and Anthony Hammond (eds.), *Poetry and Drama, 1570–1700* (London: Methuen, 1981), 47–59.

[25] Jackson frequently invokes the first-century Greek philosopher, thought to have been a contemporary of Christ's, in his explorations of righteousness. Nietzsche, however, in *The Birth of Tragedy* associates Apollo with an idea he terms Apollonian which represents a unity and order associated with absolute serenity, and, of course, light. Friedrich Nietzsche, *The Birth of Tragedy*, trans. Douglas Smith (Oxford: Oxford University Press, 2000), 16, 52.

Contrary to nature, this 'wicked' race of people can only see in the dark: darkness is their habitat and to that end 'they can see nothing but evil'. In Jackson's complex image, dark nature corresponds to a corrupt human nature: here, darkness is self-inflicted to avoid the 'light of grace'. The implication is that 'dark nature' is a manifestation of evil in terms that correspond to the material world. As the faithful walk in the light of God, so the wicked survive in the shadows of their individualized, separated selves. Darkness here is a condition, not a reality. Like the 'light of grace', the 'dark clouds of nature' represent the human's response to faith, but where the light may be external, affecting the human subject, the dark clouds are internal, revealing the subject's perversion. In this way the night becomes powerfully associated with states of being and yet in *Macbeth* it must act upon the characters as well as reveal their moral blindness.

The idea of night as the death of nature, however, was certainly available in the temporal cycles of growth and decay. Within the terms of husbandry darkness could be simulated in order to manipulate the life cycle of the animal or plant. Conrad Heresbach's advice on fattening a goose to its full value potential is to:

hang her vp in a darke place, stopping her eares with Peason, or some other thing, that by neyther hearing, nor seeing of any thing, shee be not forced to stroggel, or crye: after, they geue her pellets of ground Malt, or Barly steeped in water thryse a day, setting by them water and grauell, by which maner of feeding, they make them so fatte. (165ʳ)

Denuded of sensation and movement, night does indeed seem to be the death of nature when it can simulate the loss of both sight and sound. The night's capacity to disorientate or deny the animal its full faculties meant that it became a dubious place of training, and in the case of horses, breaking:

But if you find that the...vncomelinesse of his trot commeth out of a naturall carelesnesse, or in of his way, and that by reason of a dull and heauie disposition wherewith he is [in]fected, he is not by anie of the former wayes to be reclaimed, then you shall when the nights are most darke and clouded, euen so thicke, that you can see your hand (for euer the darker the better:) then you shall take out your and ride him into some new-plowed field, where the lands lye most high and [un] euen, or into the like vncertaine and much worne wayes, and there trot him roundly and swiftly, rushing him now ouer-thwart, then end-wise, sometimes another, not suffering him to take leisure, or regard to his way, [h]ow dangerous or false of foot-hold soeuer it be: And although at first (as it is most [l]ikely) he will stumble, or be readie to fall, yet doe not you make anie care thereof, but bearing a good stiffe hand vpon him, strike your spurres hard into his [si]des, and the more he stumbles, the more encrease you the swiftnesse of his pace, [o]nely by no meanes whatsoeuer suffer him to gallop. (133)

Working against something like temperament, here construed as 'natural carelesnese' or 'disposition', the dark night disempowers the horse, making him stumble and fall against the ploughed furrows and the rider's spurs. Night—enforced or natural—is used as a method of disorientation through which the husbandman can control his animals, for either profit or use. In this way, night becomes a force against nature, a structure of oppression in which nature itself can be corrected or affected.

As 'instruments of darkness', the witches represent an extension of this perversion of nature through which the human subject may be altered under false conditions. These 'unnatural hags' have the capacity to work upon human natures as Heresbach's husbandmen might work on animals, controlling, confusing, and manipulating their physical realities. Metaphorically, however, such an unnatural night—or absence of light—facilitates doctrines of sin through constructions of 'seeing': as the dark hides the heavens, so moral blindness denies God.[26] As the Macbeths wade through the 'night's great business' towards their irrevocable bloody depths, they increasingly demand the night, or the closed eye, to obscure their visions:

> Come, thick night,
> And pall thee in the dunnest smoke of Hell,
> That my keen knife see not the wound it makes,
> Nor heaven peep through the blanket of the dark
> To cry, 'Hold, hold'. (1.5.49–53)

The play's imagery constantly draws our attention to the significance of night, perversely guiding us to the moral eclipse of Duncan's murder.[27] Although much of the action will be consumed by darkness despite the daylight hours, our first introduction to night is in its appropriate context. After Macbeth and his wife have determined on their course of killing the king, we move to Banquo who asks Fleance, 'How goes the night, boy?' (2.1.1). Observing the intense blackness, 'the moon is down', Banquo declares:

> There's husbandry in heaven:
> Their candles are all out . . .

---

[26] Robert Pogue Harrison explores an interpretation of the myth of giants in which the forest space became an image of anxiety as its canopy of trees obscured the skies, *Forests: The Shadow of Civilization* (Chicago: University of Chicago Press, 1993).

[27] Kenneth Muir in 'Image and Symbol in *Macbeth*' identifies many of the play's images, including night, *Shakespeare Survey*, 19 (1966), 45–54.

> Merciful powers,
> Restrain in me the cursed thoughts that nature
> Gives way to in repose. (2.1.4–5; 8–10)

The tension that Banquo observes between the unnaturally dark night and the nature of cursed thoughts identifies a conflict between the human and inhuman world that is central to the play as a whole. Banquo's human nature responds to an anxiety that he cannot fully articulate, and night's husbandry—her moral prudence—is a further example of the withdrawal of the manifest world. Like the receding images of maternity and growth, nature's sparks of light begin to fade. Although the play's representations of the natural world are almost entirely subjective, they are paradoxically comprehensive. As Banquo observes the absence of the moon and stars, so Lady Macbeth tells the night, 'stars hide your fire'. Alongside the Christian symbolism of darkness and the practical applications of night for sensory manipulation, in philosophical terms night represents a space without meaning. If our manifest world is given meaning by observation then without the conditions of observation meaning is lost.[28] The increasingly pervasive gloom that settles over the play comes to reflect an acute loss of value—moral, social, epistemological.

The erosion of these values, however, takes place through a complex contamination of what nature has come to mean. Almost every instance of the word in the play refers to a human rather than non-human nature, and yet the strange climates of Inverness, Forres, or Dunsinane confuses our perceptions of nature. The nauseating ambiguity of the play-world is always in evidence. The presence of the 'temple-haunting martlet', the 'guest of summer', suggests clemency, but the witches are associated with a perpetual rain.[29] The pervasive 'foul' and 'fair', or rain and sun, points to a climate that is wholly unpredictable—capricious and apparently unnatural in its ability to contain, simultaneously, growth and mutation. Relegating the witches to the supra-natural Banquo understands that they 'look not like the inhabitants of the earth' so that when they disappear, he observes, the 'earth has bubbles as the water has' (1.3.78). Banquo suggests that the

---

[28] Whilst Betrand Russell understands epistemological reality as experience, rational, and perceived, the Czech philosopher Jan Patoča examines the ways in which our discernible realities present us with a relationship of things which, once removed in darkness, deny our existence meaning. See particularly *Plato and Europe*, trans. Petr Lom (Stanford, Calif.: Stanford University Press, 2002), 38–50.

[29] Although, in this context, 'haunting' means to visit regularly or habitually, the supernatural suggestions are significant. According to the *OED* Shakespeare is among the first writers to use this term in relation to ghosts or spectres (here it cites *Dream* and *Richard II*) so that we might imagine the martlet to appear as an ambivalent link between the play's natural and unnatural worlds: a vestige of nature in transition to a spectral world.

witches disappear into some kind of cosmic vortex, and yet this image of bubbles is usually associated with rain. According to Estienne:

he shall foretell great aboundance of Raine, if the Clouds be darke, deepe, and thicke: if the drops of water falling from the Skies be somewhat whitish, and make great bubbles and great falls here below. (26)

Reading Banquo's formulation of the witches as earthy rain registers a further perversion of nature in the representation of weather. As the possibility of a natural world recedes from the play's vision, we are taunted with ideas of growth and cultivation. Given the sterility of the play's environment, Duncan's choice of metaphor takes on further significance when he tells Macbeth:

> I have begun to plant thee, and will labour
> To make thee full of growing. (1.4.29–30)

Extending the sentiment to Banquo, he replies:

> There if I grow,
> The harvest is your own. (1.4.34–5)

These brief images of organic growth jar against the wider fabric of contamination, amplifying their irony. Duncan positions himself as the husbandman to Macbeth's career, promising him both development and futurity. Banquo, however, takes the metaphor to its completion by returning the profit back to the king. The power of these images lies in their redundancy: since we know that neither Duncan nor Banquo will survive Macbeth's aspirations the signs of cultivation hang in the air as vestiges of a lost world. More sinister, however, is how the language of cultivation is translated into destruction. As Macbeth's 'ambition' will turn from 'vaulting' to 'thriftless', so the semantics of profit will reveal devastation rather than reward. Similarly, part of Macbeth's instructions to the murderers is 'where to plant yourselves' (3.1.129), reflecting with macabre irony the absence of growth.

Perhaps unsurprisingly, given the witches' prophecies, Banquo is most particularly associated with ideas of cultivation. Having supported the metaphor of growth in his interaction with the witches, 'If you can look into the seeds of time | And say which grain will grow and which will not' (1.3.57–8), Banquo returns to the image after Duncan's death:[30]

---

[30] In '*Macbeth*: Speculations and Source', Jonathan Goldberg identifies the play's prevailing concerns with genealogy: 'the king lives to bestow, to give gifts which are contracted within him and which are extended without', in Howard and O'Connor (eds.), *Shakespeare Reproduced*, 256. In *Hamlet without Hamlet*, de Grazia pursues the idea of genealogy through the land and the existential implications of human life and death.

> yet it was said
> It should not stand in thy posterity
> But that myself should be the root and father
> Of many kings. (3.1.3–6)

It is in this 'root' that Macbeth fears Banquo's 'royalty of nature' (3.1.49). Macbeth will have such a nature killed in his friend but in himself he has a tougher war to win, if, as Lady Macbeth tells us:

> yet I do fear thy nature:
> It is too full of the milk of human kindness
> To catch the nearest way. (1.5.14–16)

Such human kindness is usually understood as representative of the social bonds of kinship which prevent humans from wilfully inflicting pain on each other. But milk—figurative or substantive—in this play is always more suggestive that it initially appears. Shortly after Lady Macbeth reveals her anxiety about her husband, she will turn to the image of milk in herself:

> Come to my woman's breasts
> And take my milk for gall, you murd'ring ministers,
> Wherever, in your sightless substances,
> You wait on nature's mischief. (1.5.46–9)

Lady Macbeth's contamination of her milk alienates her from motherhood, so it also reflects the play's larger interest in the rejection of nature. The images of nurturing associated with the lactating Mother Nature are central to Lady Macbeth's models of rejection. As she fears nature's bonds in her husband so she also rejects any vestiges in herself. In this way the gender associations become predominantly cultural, representing a feminized nature that is more ideological than biological.[31] Human bonds are rejected through their images in nature, whereby forms of nourishment are denied and the cycles of growth and procreation come to an end.

Despite the marked absence of a recognizable landscape, the death of nature creeps invidiously in through the destruction of biological needs. As the Macbeths deny each other the milk of human kindness so they will be denied 'great nature's second course, | Chief nourisher in life's feast'. The move from milk to sleep is not unexpected since both represent a primary human need. Yet central to the apparent success of the protagonists is their

---

See also William C. Carroll's introduction to *Macbeth: Texts and Contexts* (Boston: Bedford, St Martins, 1999), in which he discusses 'the crisis of sovereignty', 3–10.

[31] As Kate Soper identifies, Jonathan Dollimore observes the necessity of this distinction in our understandings of the politics of gender and sex, *The Idea of Nature*, 119–21.

persistent denial of natural impulses. Lady Macbeth articulates this imperative to rise above nature through her gendered assaults on her husband. Asking Macbeth to be 'so much more than a man' is asking him to exceed the human boundaries determined by nature: to become, as it were, more than a human. Her value system recognizes human impulses as constrained by biological needs and social bonds: as she pushes the limits of those conditions she perceives herself to be invulnerable. So long as human needs are embedded in a coherent fabric of natural relations they remain vulnerable to rejection. As the relations between nature and culture, or the human and non-human, become more divisive the characters move into a dramatic confrontation with their own biological determinants. Despite the apparently endless night of the play, the protagonists cannot sleep. In a powerful perversion of nature, Shakespeare exposes the 'natural' conditions of sleep and yet denies the body its instinct. As the dark determines an absence of moral codes associated with nature, so sleep takes over from night in its representation of a further distortion of what natural has come to mean:

> Methought I heard a voice cry 'sleep no more;
> Macbeth doth murder sleep, the innocent sleep,
> Sleep that knits up the ravelled sleeve of care,
> The death of each day's life, sore labour's bath,
> Balm of hurt minds, great nature's second course,
> Chief nourisher in life's feast.' (2.2.34–9)[32]

As sleep becomes the boundary of the body's day so it determines a cycle of labour and rest, distress and care: 'the season of all natures' (3.4.142). To interrupt or deny this cycle is to expose a 'great perturbation in nature' (5.1.21). Both references to nature here, however, are to the biological natures which depend on sleep. Lady Macbeth's strange, delirious torpor is amplified by the constant light she carries at her side: having pushed herself to the absolute limit of her human nature she roams inhumanly in perpetual candlelight. Interrupting, perturbing, or corrupting nature is necessary to Lady Macbeth's project and her insomnia performs the bodily disruption that she had worked so hard to solicit. A further, and dramatic, extension of this disruption is her candle companion—as though she carries her dehumanization around with her as a Promethean marker of

---

[32] The proliferation of cloth imagery has been identified within the play and forms a fascinating nexus to the subject of domesticity within the play. See Korda, *Shakespeare's Domestic Economies*, Peter Stallybrass, 'Worn Worlds: Clothes and Identity on the Renaissance Stage', in Margreta de Grazia et al. (eds.), *Subject and Object in Renaissance Culture* (Cambridge: Cambridge University Press, 1996), Cleanth Brooks, *The Well Wrought Urn: Studies in the Structure of Poetry* (New York: Harcourt, Brace, 1947).

human triumph over nature.[33] Sleep functions in the play as a further expression of the kind of biological nature that the Macbeths worked so perniciously to destroy. In Estienne's *The Countrey Farme*, one of the remedies for sleeplessness is human breast milk:

> To cause them to sleepe which cannot well slumber, it is good to make a Frontlet with the seed of Poppie, Henbane, Lettuce, and the iuice of Nightshade: or the milke of a woman giuing a girle sucke. (42)

Estienne's specificity in identifying the nursing of a baby girl strikes a chord in a play in which the most shocking—and the most touching— nature is female. Here, the milk of human kindness—that of nursing, nurturing, and maternity—is also the milk of sleep: 'chief nourisher in life's feast'.[34] As the biological and the organic become powerfully synthesized in the husbandry manuals, so the play works hard to separate them. Rendering his main characters chronically sleepless, Shakespeare severs them from the bodily needs that define them as social.

Milk, both symbolically and materially, is central to the interrelations between the moral and social economy, the human and the non-human. The powerful way in which images of milk are deployed in *Macbeth* makes it a distinctly human(e), and in this way female, substance.[35] Women are predominantly associated with milk, from the figure of Mother Nature, nursing, to the domestic product. However, as an animal by-product milk was central to every aspect of the household economy and almost all husbandry manuals include a section on dairy. In *The English Housewife* (1616), one of the most comprehensive manuals to specifically address women, Markham explains:

> A cow must be gentle to her milker, so she must be kindly in her own nature; that is, apt to conceive and bring forth, fruitful to nourish, and loving to that which springs from her; for so she bringeth forth a 'double profit'.[36]

---

[33] Fire is fascinating within the context of the human and natural worlds, since it operates as both human advance and human destruction. In *Prometheus: Archetypal Image of Human Existence*, Karl Kerényi examines the paradox of the theft of fire within elemental nature: 'this sacred nature of fire, which it shares with all the living things that grow in man's environment and provide him with sustenance, explains why the acquisition of fire was experienced as theft, desecration', trans. Ralph Manheim (Princeton: Princeton University Press, 1991), 53.

[34] In *Staging Domesticity*, Wall explores milk as a 'national foodstuff fully attuned to some "original body"; as such, it is made to bear the weight of a critique of foreign and aristocratic habits', 131.

[35] In almost every other play by Shakespeare, milk is used as an adjective, describing the colour white, or figuratively. The exceptions to this are single instances in *The Winter's Tale* and *King Lear*.

[36] *Countrey Contentments, or The English Hus-wife* (1616), 177.

The cow is identified as simultaneously social ('gentle') and natural ('kindly') in the right performance of her duties. The worth of the animal is represented in terms of a 'double profit', by which she can both reproduce and nourish. The qualities which Markham attributes to his animal are distinctly human: understanding her as 'loving' and 'gentle' exposes the gradual socialization of agrarian semantics. Nature is no longer justified as God's gift but as the reproduction of socially acceptable values.[37]

When Duncan is murdered under the guise of hospitality, Macbeth breaks a fundamental code of nature. Leading up to the murder of both Duncan and Banquo, the protagonists are consistently referred to as hosts, culminating in the dumb shows of food and service that preface the king's death and Banquo's ghostly return.[38] The terms which anticipate Duncan's reception at Inverness are apparently sympathetic: the architecture of Macbeth's castle, the 'delicate air' of summer, and the tender way in which the martlet and its 'procreant cradle' are described culminate to suggest a place of sanctuary.[39] Similarly, Lady Macbeth's attention to her own 'service | In every point twice done and then done double' (1.6.15–16) indicates the extent of her preparations for the king, which are then amplified through the performance of 'servants with dishes and service over the stage' (SD 1.7).[40] The theatrical focus on images of hospitality makes way for the anxiety of sanctuary that the 'host' represents:

> First, as I am kinsman, and his subject,
> Strong both against the deed; then, as his host
> Who should against his murderer shut the door,
> Not bear the knife myself. (1.7.13–16)

In Macbeth's articulation of his self-betrayal, he recognizes his first breach of nature: he should not only provide but he should protect; not only serve

---

[37] Fitzherbert, for example, does not include a section on dairy; Thomas Tusser refers to dairy constantly within the context of store, maintaining the necessity of dairy products for the household as well as its economy: 'Good huswife in dayry, that nedes not be tolde, | deserueth her fee, to be payde her in golde' (fo. 71ᵛ).

[38] Macbeth refers to his dream of kingship as 'home', meaning thoroughly, in this context. Richard of Gloucester, however, uses the word home in a similarly homicidal context in *3 Henry VI*.

[39] Such a description, however, is not unequivocally benign since the martlet, or swift, was often represented in heraldry as footless: 'to symbolize the son's position as having no footing in the ancestral lands'. Figuratively, 'The Martlet . . . [is] also giuen for a difference of younger brethren, to put them in minde to trust to their wings of vertue and merit, to raise themselues, and not to their legges, hauing little land to put their foot on.' J. Guillim, *Display of Heraldrie* (1610), as cited by the *OED*. See also definitions to both *n¹* and *n²*.

[40] Lady Macbeth conflates cloth imagery with that of the harvest: 'single', 'double', 'deep', and 'broad' could all refer to depths of cloth; equally, however, 'loads' is a distinctly agrarian measure.

but defend. Making his transition from the host to the murderer, Macbeth is forced to confront the limits of nature within the context of his own home. Despite Markham's suppression of the female body in his text, the kitchen remains predominantly associated with women, and Lady Macbeth assumes this responsibility when she tells her husband to 'leave all the rest to me' (1.5.72).[41] The literal performance of food and hospitality that signifies the Macbeths' home, however, is profoundly unsettling since it pre-empts a further destruction of value associated with nature—charity.

The nature that the protagonists of *Macbeth* consistently contend with is the socialized nature of culture: the nature that assumes empathy, discloses bonds, and determines needs. In order to separate nature and culture—or the natural and customary—the play subjects biological and ideological spaces to scrutiny. While the idea of a mother nature is emptied out of images of nurturing and productivity, the home, as a space of hospitality and domestic cohesion, is similarly destroyed.[42] As Felicity Heal argues in her study of hospitality:

While Scripture provided the most powerful spur to hospitable behaviour it was acknowledged that natural law also enjoined it. It was not only [Sir Henry] Wotton who believed English hospitality to be natural: when Strafford's deputy in Ireland, Christopher Wandesford, wrote his book of instructions for his children in 1636 he assumed that good entertainment was an obligation binding in the natural ethical code. 'The common Rule of Hospitality', he wrote, 'will enforce you to bounty, and all kind of fair treatment to Strangers, the Law of Nature requires it'.[43]

The construction of hospitality as natural is similarly expressed in images of the land, as well as discussions of them. The survey maps that accompanied

---

[41] In *Staging Domesticity*, Wendy Wall explores the quotidian way in which butchery and bloodshed were a part of the housewife's life. Exploring the space of the kitchen she exposes the proximity between violence and sustenance in realm of domestic cooking. See particularly her discussion of 'domestic drama', 189–220.

[42] Geraldo U. de Sousa, in *At Home in Shakespeare's Tragedies* (Aldershot: Ashgate, 2010), explores the idea of habitat, domestic space, and dwelling. De Sousa is particularly interested in the structures of indoor and outdoor spaces in *Macbeth*, which he sees as central to the play's collapsing of moral binaries. In the husbandry manuals, such a division of space is always gendered. In this context, the witches' occupation of an outdoor space is not only threatening but destructive. Laura Gowing, in her important book *Domestic Dangers*, focuses on the early modern history of structures of female domesticity, whilst Wendy Wall's *Staging Domesticity* examines the relationship between butchery and service through the space of the kitchen; and Natasha Korda's *Shakespeare's Domestic Economies: Gender and Property in Early Modern England* (Philadelphia: University of Pennsylvania Press, 2002) explores the increasingly important role of women in the development of the domestic economy.

[43] Felicity Heal, 'The Idea of Hospitality in Early Modern England', *Past and Present* (1984), 73.

the developing imperatives of agrarian improvement were often justified
by moral marginalia. Cyprian Lucar, whose *Treatise Named Lucarsolace*
(1590) propounded the statute measure of the acre, included in his
margins a description of the 'disposition, industrie, studies, manners,
trades, occupations, honestie, humanitie, hospitalitie, apparel, and other
moral vertues of the inhabitants' (50–2).[44] These virtues are written into
images of the land as though they are essential qualities of habitation: to
live here is to take part in a recognizable network of social, economic, and
ethical relations. Deriving from Christian models of charity, hospitality
represents the recognition of fundamental human needs—food, warmth,
safety.[45] Like Lucar, William Camden, in his *Annals*, conflates ideas of
humanity and hospitality when he describes Elizabeth I's anxiety at
repatriating the Dutch rebels in 1572 as knowing she would 'commit a
great inhumanity, and violate the lawes of Hospitality, if shee shoulde
deliver them into the hands of a Cut-Throat' (351). The 'duties of
humanity and hospitality' are, according to Camden, to one's country,
'a second Diuinity' (182). Through the idea of the land, as well as its
representations, hospitality became a national virtue associated with strict
ethical codes of provision and protection.[46] As a cultural interpretation of
nature hospitality appeared to reflect essential images of 'bounty' and
sustenance: deriving from the term 'host', however, it was a distinctly
human act of reception and entertainment.[47]

The sense of partnership that these manuals reveal briefly elides
sexual difference in the construction of a home.[48] Shakespeare's redef-

---

[44] As cited by McRae, *God Speed the Plough*, see also 185–90.

[45] The Eastern models of hospitality from which Graeco-Roman and Christian ones
developed.

[46] Heal extends this to the Scots, who were also known for their hospitality, unlike the
Europeans, 71, and P. Hume Brown (ed.), *Early Travellers in Scotland* (Edinburgh:
Edinburgh University Press, 1978), xix–xxi.

[47] Derrida, in his discussion of the ambivalence of hospitality, elides its Christian
heritage and focuses on the Latin form of 'host', which means enemy (*Of Hospitality:
Anne Dufourmantelle Invites Jacques Derrida to Respond*, trans. Rachel Bowlby (Stanford,
Calif.: Stanford University Press, 2000), 45). Working from a post-structuralist idea of
difference, Derrida deconstructs common assumptions of amity in hospitality and exposes
the violence—linguistic and individual—that takes place in asking someone into one's
home. For Derrida, such an act forces the 'guest', or stranger, to adopt the 'host's' hearth,
idioms, and desires thereby erasing, or fragmenting, themselves.

[48] Markham's attitude to the sexes is unusual. In a translation of Aristotle's *Discourses of
Government* (1598), Loys le Roy writes: 'Considering also that the husbandry and *[h]*
uswifery of man and woman are not all one, for it is his office to get and bring in, and hers to
keepe and lay vp. So also wisdome is a vertue proper to the commander, all other vertues are
common both to commaunders and obeyers: but wisdome belongeth not to an obeyer, but
only a true opinion: for he that is in subiectio[n], is like vnto a maker of pipes, and he that is
in authority, like vnto him that playeth on the pipes' (145).

inition of the home as a place of violence rather than safety is played out in the couple's extraordinary speeches. As Lady Macbeth forces her husband to exceed the limits of his human nature, so she explodes her own. Severing her imaginary body from an idea of nature, she fantasizes about dashing the brains of a smiling infant. Killing in the act of nourishment—'plucked my nipple from its boneless gums'—Lady Macbeth forces her husband to imaginatively reconstruct an image of betrayal beyond that of either a kinsman or a host. Breaking a bond understood as natural—'loue of parents cannot be concealed, tis natur-all, and they that are inhumane in this kinde, are vnworthy of that aire they breathe'—Lady Macbeth begins their semantic journey away from the values of social nature towards those of personal individualism.[49] The home becomes a place of transition for the couple, where they change their 'single state' into something boundless, denaturalized, and unpredictable.

The porter is central to the redefinition of this space as he occupies the hinterland between inside and outside. The endless knocking that follows the death of Duncan sounds Macbeth's advance into his reign of horror. The gates to his castle stand as the entrance to both home and hell, as the porter plays out his sinister reception:

Who's there in the name of Belzebub? Here's a farmer that hanged himself on the expectation of plenty. Come in time! Have napkins enow about you; here you'll sweat for't. (2.3.3–6)

Invoking the image of a destitute farmer the porter recalls the similar 'expectation of plenty' which Duncan expressed in Macbeth. Presumably on his way to hell through suicide, the sin of self-destruction is the first to enter Macbeth's castle. The brutal irony of the porter's image, in which the farmer will sweat his labours in hell, sustains the tragedy of this figure.[50] The porter's taunting of his imaginary guests performs the entrance of sin through corrupted codes of hospitality, just as Lady Macbeth's spurious horror at the death of Duncan resonates through the space in which it took place: 'What, in our house!' (2.3.85). The porter's delusional drama redefines this space as one of hostility: those who

---

[49] Robert Burton, *The Anatomie of Melancholy* (London, 1621), 513. Lady Macbeth does, of course, perceive the murder as an act of solidarity with her husband rather than one of unique personal reward. A similar destruction occurs, of course, in the murder of Duncan, who is asleep. Like the sucking infant, the king was murdered during the course of his fulfilment of an essential physiological need.

[50] All three of the spectral figures that the porter welcomes suggest failure—the impover-ished farmer, the scrimping French tailor, and the Jesuit Garnet.

come inside the castle are no longer guests but enemies.[51] This radical revision of values began with the human body in order to make way for a new human will. Yet the body as an emblem of nature stubbornly persists throughout the play: as Duncan's wounds are like 'a breach in nature' (2.3.115), Banquo's body will return to Macbeth's home, haunting his hospitality with spectres of the 'seeds of . . . kings'.

The play violently severs the human from the natural world in order to expose the ways in which human limits have been constructed as predetermined—natural, even. The landscape, the physical body (including its gendering), biological imperatives, physiological needs, and the socialized space of the home are imagined to inhere in an essentialized human nature. The brutalization of nature is necessary to the disentanglement of individual human will from a set of predetermined characteristics understood as natural. These characteristics are both represented and translated by a landscape in which all value (moral and economic) is defined according to human relations: those 'strong knots of love' (4.3.27). The relationships between the human and non-human spaces become markedly more complex through the printed husbandry manuals as the agrarian landscape now becomes visible through the written form. Mediated through the written text, terms of value, appreciation, and anxiety become specifically represented by human identifications with its non-human world.

According to Andreas Höfele, Macbeth is a figure in whom 'the boundary between human and in-human becomes obsessively intense'; this boundary, I would suggest, is determined by a nature that the protagonists seek to destroy.[52] Where, however, for Höfele, Macbeth allies himself with the brutal world of nature through the figure of the tortured animal, I would suggest precisely the opposite: that Macbeth separates himself from a non-human world in which nature is valorized through social values. Only by destroying that world can Macbeth relieve himself of the endless spectres of sociable living—and of mortality itself.

Yet despite the couple's destruction of naturalized spaces, ideas of nurturing and growth continue to haunt the play. The play's attention to the ways in which concepts of nature construct social expectations exposes the instrumental ways in which the central characters try to liberate themselves from a set of predetermined characteristics. Their eventual destruction suggests that human nature is bound to necessarily

---

[51] Anne Dufourmantelle, in her dialogue with Derrida, explains: 'If we can say that murder and hate designate everything that excludes closeness, it is insofar as they ravage from within an original relationship to alterity,' 4.

[52] *Stage, Stake, and Scaffold.*

limiting force of essential determinants which should remain consistent with, say, Hooker's natural law. But the play's equivocations go deeper than this: nature and culture are not so readily distinguished, nor are the 'natural' limits of human behaviour. In spite of Lady Macbeth's putative alchemy, milk remains a dominant image, albeit an increasingly ambivalent one. The play returns to the image of milk in Malcolm when, declaring himself unfit for kingship, he admits:

> Nay, had I power, I should
> Pour the sweet milk of concord into Hell,
> Uproar the universal peace, confound
> All unity on earth. (4.3.97–100)

Declaring his own recipe for universal chaos, Malcolm reminds us that milk stands in opposition to hell. By pitching these images against each other, Malcolm recalls nature as social, harmonious, and generous: the milk of nature is inherently that of human nature representing concord, kindness, and familial care. Malcolm relies on images of nature in order to impress upon Macduff that he is an unsuitable king: mutilating the value of terms such as 'graft' and 'grow', Malcolm explains that:

> Our country sinks beneath the yoke,
> It weeps, it bleeds, and each new day a gash
> Is added to her wounds. (4.3.39–41)

Malcolm's yoke is not that of the plough drawing the ox but the tyrant violating the human landscape of social bodies. Synthesizing the body and the earth, harvest is replaced by homicide, growth by destruction. The constant rejection of this nature—the humanized nature of the organic world—casts a profound shadow over Macbeth's world. The very insistence of natural images, both biological and ecological—milk, bodies, trees, harvest, night, sleep—haunts the play-world with a social economy that it cannot support. The Macbeths' brutal resistance to this world of humanized nature reveals the power that such nature had in the moral minds of the audience.

Occasionally the play allows a glimpse of those natural relations to re-emerge: Lady Macbeth's confession that she could not kill Duncan because he resembled her father or Macduff's response to the murder of his family: 'What, all my pretty chickens and their dam | At one fell swoop?' (4.3.218–19). Yet the representation of human bonds as natural is consistently unresolved within the play. Despite Lady Macduff's insistence that her husband's absence reveals that he 'loves us not, | He wants the natural touch' (4.2.8–9), she is never enlightened as to why Macduff has left nor is he allowed to grieve: 'O I could play the woman with mine eyes' (4.3.230). The feminization of nature renders the woman natural and so the female body becomes a vestige of those 'true knots of love' that the Macbeths work so hard to destroy. It is hardly surprising then that any reflections on this world should come from a woman. Lady Macduff's role is brief and tragic but it is she who most acutely articulates the perversions of the play-world:

> But I remember now
> I am in this earthly world, where to do harm
> Is often laudable, to do good sometime
> Accounted dangerous folly. (4.2.76–9)

Although dramatically conscious of the power of nature to inform social codes of ethical living, the play does not try to reinstate them:

> Alas poor country,
> Almost afraid to know itself. It cannot
> Be called our mother, but our grave. (4.3.165–7)

Ross's indictment of his landscape is profound: denuding nature of her maternity he observes death rather then life. The images of growth and nurturing through which the play explored its landscape of values are now totally redundant. Ross follows this vision of the country through a series of human emotions that contaminate the air:

> where nothing
> But who knows nothing, is once seen to smile;
> Where sighs, and groans, and shrieks that rend the air
> Are made, not marked; where violent sorrow seems
> A modern ecstasy. (4.3.167–70)

This is now an entirely human landscape where all that is produced is human misery but without human responsibility: 'made, not marked'. As was clear through the speeches of Burgundy in *Henry V*, social relations, which presuppose moral accountability, are given definition in nature through an overarching narrative of growth and sustenance: once these images are erased so too is the moral fabric they represent. Ravished by sorrow rather than faith, the 'modern' landscape that Ross describes is echoed in a treatise on the state of France in the 1590s:

See here a Country in an extacie, distracted in her selfe, and transported out of herselfe, ready to fall into a falling sicknesse, like the soule of a distempred man.

Writing of the Wars of Religion, Robert Dallington goes on to explain the moral climate of a country ravaged by conflict:

O people voyde of iudgement: O blinded people: O Nation without Counsell, and without wisedome! See here a people, among whom it was a slander to doe well, and glorie to excell others in cruelty:[53]

In terms that are remarkably similar to Lady Macduff's indictment of her 'earthly world', these renditions of conflict strike at the heart of a country that has been emptied of its moral registers—distracted, sick, distempered. Such an ecstasy invokes the triumph of human individualism over national need. At the beginning of the seventeenth century, Shakespeare's *Macbeth* appears to respond to a growing secularization of nature, through which the human can seek to redefine the values of its social ambitions: but as Watson observes: 'The neat patterns of action and imagery in *Macbeth* prove only that nature has powerful reflexes, not that it has a sympathetic consciousness.'[54] The distinction between reflex and sympathetic consciousness is fundamental to the development of an agrarian economy in which nature as a resource must be separated from nature as a representation. The persistent explosion of boundaries construed as natural (gender, biological, social, physical) traces the emergence of culture in which human interference becomes the defining marker of value. But in a brilliant twist of irony, culture comes to the rescue in the form of nature:

> Though Birnam be come to Dunsinan,
> And thou opposed, being of no woman born,
> Yet I will try the last. (5.7.60–2)

As the Macbeths triumphed over their natures, so human intercession will triumph over them: and Macduff, a caesarean witness to the power of human intervention, presides over a moral victory in which culture wins. The play's exploration of the language of nature as it has developed through an imaginative reconstruction of social values begins to reveal the ways in which nature has become unhinged from a history of fixed signs. The interfaces between human and organic nature in the forms of sex, sleep, birth, milk, or blood come to express the limits and potential of human intervention. Military ingenuity and medical intrusion restore Scotland's future. But this is not a testimony to the conservative values of Elizabethan cosmology. Instead it is a powerful exploration of the developing distinctions—ingenious and destructive—between nature and culture.

---

[53] *The View of France* (London, 1604), 20[r], 20[v].   [54] *The Rest is Silence*, 135.

5

Even Better than the Real Thing?

Art and Nature in *The Winter's Tale*

There are surely no more explicit gestures towards the politics of human intervention than those in *The Winter's Tale*. Famed for its discussion of 'nature and art', this play explores, albeit ironically, the relative values of essential and modified nature. At the centre of this debate is an argument about human interference and the moral implications of scientific experimentation in the development of the civilized world. The ethics of this debate reside in conceptions of the relative values of nature and culture, and the extent to which humans may improve—literally and figuratively—on the world around them. While Sidney may offer the poets a brazen nature for their Midas imaginations, the physical nature of the early modern landscape offered cultivators the potential for transformations beyond their imaginations. As an agent of change, the husbandman, improver, or projector supported the potential profits of human intervention in the natural world. From a basic food product to a fine trinket, a medicinal remedy to a vast increase in production, cultivating the natural world was a potentially lucrative business.

The debate in the second half of the play in which Perdita and Polixenes briefly focus on the ethics of intervention depends, dramatically, on the ironic layers of meaning attached to questions of hybridization. The real pleasure of this moment belongs not to Perdita's knowledge of horticulture but to the audience's knowledge of human ambition and the inherent complexities of transformation upon which both humanism and husbandry depended. As part of the long sheep-shearing scene this, and much of the action in Bohemia, takes place in a putatively rural setting which has often led critics to identify the play with a pastoral tradition.[1]

---

[1] Within the context of the pastoral, however, *As You Like It* has probably received the most critical attention as it is more explicit about the court/country antithesis. Extending the role of the pastoral beyond that of leisure and pleasure into something more polemical, the rural space has often been associated with versions of misrule—or unfettered imagination. In this context, criticism of *A Midsummer Night's Dream* and *The Merry Wives of*

Within this tradition the rural space can function as a refuge from the court, a hinterland in which the subject is not bound to city laws, or an exile in which the subject may transform, redefine, or even discover itself.[2] To that end, the pleasure and trepidation that such rural spaces incited made them infinitely suitable for the theatre, offering a microcosmic image of the stage itself—dramatic, conflicted, and perceptual.[3] The pastoral, however, provides a set of different expectations from the 'wild' forest: while the forest may allow the anarchic to erupt and threaten the boundaries of the civilized world, the pastoral belongs to an ideological tradition in which the life of the shepherd represents simplicity, ease, and innocence. In both cases the rural space supports a fantasy—where the self can escape the shackles of the social world and even identity itself.

It is within this tradition that I want to re-examine *The Winter's Tale*. The pastoral, I suggest, is no longer the province of rural escapism but is in the process of being replaced by a new fantasy: consumerism. In a play putatively invested in the rural for both resolution and disruption, the pastoral is no longer an adequate ideological model for the Jacobean imagination: instead a new dream begins to emerge; the dream of trans-formation offered by the purchasing potential of the rural class. As many critics have observed, the play is replete with 'business': economic, emo-tional, and practical. The language of investment modulates the move-ment of the drama through its various processes of loss and profit, ownership and remuneration. Stanley Cavell has written of the play's preoccupation with telling and (re)counting and the complex dynamic between fact and fiction inherent in the language of telling and tallying.[4] More recently Valerie Forman has examined the play within the context of

---

Windsor has proved the most penetrating. See particularly Roberts, *The Shakespearean Wild*; Barber's classic study of subversion, *Shakespeare's Festive Comedy*; and Watson's metaphys-ical study of nature, which includes a chapter on *As You Like It, Back to Nature*.

[2] For a discussion of the role of law and the question of testimony within the play, see particularly Lorna Hutson, *The Invention of Suspicion: Law and Mimesis in Shakespeare and Renaissance Drama* (Oxford: Oxford University Press, 2007), Subha Mukherji, *Law and Representation in Early Modern Drama* (Cambridge: Cambridge University Press, 2006), Luke Wilson, *Theaters of Intention: Drama and the Law in Early Modern England* (Stanford, Calif.: Stanford University Press, 2000).

[3] See also Marienstras, *New Perspectives on the Shakespearean World*, esp. 11–47. Char-lotte Scott, 'Dark Matter: Shakespeare's Foul Dens and Forests', *Shakespeare Survey*, 61 (2011).

[4] Cavell observes, for example, that 'In *The Winter's Tale*—beyond the terms of tell and count themselves, and beyond account and loss and loss and gain and pay and owe and debt and repay—we have money, coin, treasure, purchase, cheat, custom, commodity, exchange, dole, wages, recompense, labour, affairs, traffic, tradesman, borrow, save, credit, redeem, and—perhaps the most frequently repeated economic term in the play—business,' *Disowning Knowledge in Seven Plays of Shakespeare* (Cambridge: Cambridge University Press, 1987), 200. See also Michael Bristol, 'In Search of the Bear: Spatiotemporal Form

what she calls a 'global economics', where the theatre itself records processes of exchange, in which we observe the movement from loss to profit, and vice versa, as fundamental to drama itself. For Forman the theatre is profitable precisely because it represents transformations which require investment and analysis, risk and recuperation.[5] As new economic criticism has shown, understanding the terms of exchange through which money, credit, and obligation moved in this period frequently points to the multiple ways in which social relationships were both coordinated and made meaningful.[6] Extending this argument through the early modern husbandry manuals, I show that cultivation offers a further model of transformation which is increasingly defined by consumerism. The husbandman's ability to transform the land from potential to product supports an emerging fantasy, where the rural space is no longer defined by its organic nature but by production. As the values of production become increasingly complicated by questions of 'art', the idea of nature re-emerges in the play's wider conflicts between truth and illusion. In *The Winter's Tale*, Bohemia offers a new space for the exploration of nature where human interference triumphs in the form of illusion, and where art offers the ultimate fantasy—that of change itself.[7]

Central to the play's concepts of change is the dramatic role of illusion; of transforming death into life, recovering the past, paying for fantasy, and translating the peasant into the princess. Such transformations are partly embedded in an emerging consumer economy where processes of transformation are commodified and repackaged as saleable goods. Clothes, ballads, trinkets, linen, and comestibles offer potential social mobility as well as articles of faith, love, or truth. To take part in the brave new world of commodities is also to recognize the power of art and the triumph of human intervention.

The late plays' recourse to illusion as the governing source of resolution has deepened our critical awareness of meta-theatre and the power that art offers for the restitution of order, but the quest for truth that underpins these plays presents spectators with an increasingly complex ontological

and the Heterogeneity of Economies in *The Winter's Tale*', *Shakespeare Quarterly*, 42 (1991), 145–67.

[5] *Tragicomic Redemptions: Global Economics and the Early Modern English Stage* (Philadelphia: University of Pennsylvania Press, 2008).

[6] Linda Woodbridge (ed.), *Money and the Age of Shakespeare: Essays in New Economic Criticism* (New York: Palgrave Macmillan, 2003). Craig Muldrew, *The Economy of Obligation: The Culture of Credit and Social Relations in Early Modern England* (Basingstoke: Palgrave Macmillan, 1998).

[7] Forman observes that Bohemia is a place 'that is marked by the sale and purchase of foreign commodities necessary to create the wealth necessary for those purchases', *Tragicomic Redemptions*, 94.

struggle, as 'art' becomes the defining logic of theatrical pleasure. In *The Winter's Tale* art emerges as a structure of belief in which fantasy resides for the absolute fulfilment of desire. It is to these structures of wish-fulfilment that the natural world belongs. Almost exclusively determined by human intervention, however, 'great creating nature' gives way to an altogether more powerful substance—art. By focusing on the second half of the play, I trace how the drama's rewarding structures of resolution are tied to forms of art and exchange, in which dreams are bought and sold. Buying and selling are no longer rooted in a rural economy of subsistence living but a vibrant market of aspiration in which the human capacity to intervene in their surroundings has developed beyond the landscape and into the lives of others. In what follows, I will examine this putatively pastoral place, not as the province of an ideological literary tradition but as the lively exploration of emergent capitalism.[8]

Critical tradition has often situated *The Winter's Tale* within the context of the pastoral, in which rural life is presented as an idealist alternative to the court or the city. Such idealism, of course, occludes a fundamental relationship between the country and the agrarian economy. As Stuart policies began to develop through more analytic models of economic interest and looked less to the socially driven imperatives of the previous century, questions of value became more complex.[9] The requirements of a developing 'consumer society' demand that pasture grounds be understood for their role in the evolution of a market economy which depends upon the producers like the Shepherd, the traffickers like Autolycus, and the consumers like Mopsa and Dorcas. The refrain that characterizes the sheep-shearing festival is not that of merry laughter but the dogged

---

[8] I use the term capitalism to refer to a structure of waged labour, but not, as yet, to Marx's definition of the proletariat as the major class of wage earners. Admittedly, there has been a tendency in recent scholarship to lean on the rather fuzzy interpretations of this period as one from 'feudalism to capitalism' and the inherent problems that such observations produce. Ian Archer's essay, 'Economy', in Kinney (ed.), *The Oxford Handbook of Shakespeare*, 165–81, makes this point very well. There is, however, no denying that the development of the printing press, navigation, overseas trade, and the destabilization of serfdom enabled the economic and social fabric of England to change during this period. The extent to which we can oversimplify those changes and collapse long-term developments into short-term changes remains in contention.

[9] Dyer maintains the existence of consumerism well before the period in question. However, according to his analysis it remains provincial and sporadic. With the development of print, as well as merchant trading and joint stock companies, the possibilities and potential for consumption radically widened. Inevitably, ideas of value began to change, too. The rise of wage labour and the increased choice and availability of goods meant that traditional conceptions of essential value had to give way to new definitions of use value. See particularly Dyer, *An Age of Transition?*, Appleby, *Economic Thought and Ideology*, Thirsk, *Economic Policy and Projects*, Jonathan Gil Harris, *Sick Economies* (Philadelphia: University of Pennsylvania Press, 2004).

insistence from Autolycus that we 'buy, buy, buy'. In shifting my focus to the dramatization of the countryside and the characters that both inhabit and define the rural economy I will attend to the ways in which the action of Bohemia extends the play's wider interrogation of both art and nature. Tracing the tensions between a suggestive pastoral structure and a nascent capitalist discourse, *The Winter's Tale* begins to question the nature of value—moral, financial, material, and ethical—and the value of nature, human and non-human. Far from representing a rural idyll, Bohemia extends the play's larger concern with the cost of truth through a focus on both the fantasy and potential of consumption.

The introduction to Bohemia is notoriously dramatic: conditioned by shipwreck, exile, stormy skies, a ravenous bear, hallucinations and death, it does little to anticipate a chorography of leisure or the 'irrepressible bent for song' associated with the pastoral.[10] Rather than representing an opportunity to escape the toxicity of Leontes' court, Bohemia begins as a threatening and destabilizing experience: the mariner, focusing our attention on the climate, declares: 'the skies look grimly | And threaten present blusters' (3.3.3–4) only to confirm any sense of developing anxiety through his apparent knowledge of this landscape: 'Besides, this place is famous for the creatures | Of prey that keep upon't' (3.3.11–12). The mariner's fears are instantly justified through the 'savage clamour' of the bear that will devour Antigonus. The hostility of this place is dramatically played out through the spectacular vision of a bear—albeit briefly— embodying the theatre of both entertainment and cruelty as he crosses the stage in front of an audience who delight in both his hunger and his destructiveness.[11] Despite the fraught description of this countryside, beset with birds of prey, bears, and wolves, the Old Shepherd's entrance registers a figure that is predominantly associated with an idea of rustic simplicity, apparently unaffected by the potential threats to his life. While the representation of the shepherd in English Renaissance poetry has been explored for its defining characteristics of blithe simplicity, the early modern theatre had yet to commit to a comprehensive image of pastoral life. From Marlowe's Scythian shepherd in *Tamburlaine*, through *Mucedorus'* hero

[10] Jerry Bryant, '*The Winter's Tale* and the Pastoral Tradition', *Shakespeare Quarterly*, 14/4 (1963), 391. Bryant, however, identifies many of these elements with both romance and pastoral but he sees Shakespeare's treatment of them as largely satirical: 'it seems likely that Shakespeare was spoofing the accounts of storms and wild animals', 393.

[11] Hoëfle's *Stage, Stake and Scaffold* carefully examines the proximities of these spaces and the ways in which the bear-baiting developed a culture of entertainment and torture to which the public theatre was profoundly indebted. See also Jason Scott-Warren, 'When Theatres were Bear-Gardens: or, What's at Stake in the Comedy of Humours', *Shakespeare Quarterly*, 54 (2003), 63–82.

in disguise, to Fletcher's *Faithful Shepherdess*, the representation of these rural figures was variously inflected by Greek romance, in which innate nobility revealed a superiority beyond that of vocation.[12] Fundamental to almost all representations of the shepherd, however, was a belief in the value of rural life; of its status as a sanctuary from the corruption of court and its ability to afford a kind of isolation that could be interpreted as either a refuge or an escape. In *The Winter's Tale*, however, Shakespeare does not ally the Old Shepherd with any of these concepts: on the contrary, the Shepherd's life is one of insecurity and strain; one, it would seem, he is only too happy to leave behind.

In 1963 Jerry Bryant claimed that 'It is curious that no appraiser or appreciator seems to have puzzled over the kinship of *The Winter's Tale* with the pastoral tradition.'[13] In the twenty-first century, however, 'the pastoral tradition' appears as a critical commonplace in almost all introductions to the play as well as a great deal of the scholarship dedicated to it.[14] But whether it is 'puzzled over' or simply assumed is debatable. Bryant, largely in response to Greg's claim that Shakespeare's play, and its source *Pandosto*, 'owe nothing of their treatment to pastoral tradition, nothing to convention, nothing to aught save life', examines the Renaissance interest in the pastoral through its classical precedents, notably the Sicilian eclogues of Theocritus and the Greek romance of Heliodorus.[15] Despite the relatively idealized view of Theocritus' shepherds, singing to

---

[12] Although *Tamburlaine* makes little concession to the pastoral tradition, the characterization of the hero's heritage suggests his capacities as both a wanderer and a survivor. *Mucedorus*, on the other hand, supports a hugely ambivalent image of the pastoral: fraught by the bestiality of Bremo, the role of the shepherd is taken up by the hero as a disguise rather than a vocation.

[13] '*The Winter's Tale* and the Pastoral Tradition', 387.

[14] Whilst all the major modern editions (Oxford, Cambridge, and Arden) of the play devote a section to the 'pastoral', Robert Henke describes Shakespeare as having a 'persistent interest in the pastoral', which he makes 'explicit' use of in both *The Winter's Tale* and *As You Like It*, see 'Ruzante and Shakespeare: A Comparative Case-Study', in Michele Marrapodi (ed.), *Shakespeare and Renaissance Literary Theories: Anglo-Italian Transactions* (Farnham: Ashgate, 2011), 159; 160. Paul Yachnin understands 'the Christian metaphor of the virtuous human community as a flock of sheep', 'Sheepishness in *The Winter's Tale*', in Laurie Maguire (ed.), *How to do Things with Shakespeare* (Oxford: Blackwell, 2008), 216–17, while Bruce Boehrer perceives the sheep as 'less an animal than a textual effect', *Animal Characters*, 166. Stephen Greenblatt, on the other hand, interprets the sheep-shearing festival as 'an urban fantasy of rural life', *Will in the World: How Shakespeare Became Shakespeare* (New York: W. W. Norton, 1943), 40. Louis Montrose provides one of the most articulate explorations of the pastoral in his essay 'Of Gentlemen and Shepherds: The Politics of Elizabethan Pastoral Form', *ELH* 50 (1983), 415–59. For further examinations of the genre see Sukanta Chaudhuri, *Renaissance Pastoral and its English Developments* (Oxford: Clarendon Press, 1998).

[15] W. W. Greg, *Pastoral Poetry and Pastoral Drama* (London: A. H. Bullen, 1906), 411. As cited by Bryant, 'The Winter's Tale and the Pastoral Tradition', 387–8.

wood nymphs and complaining of their loves, these images are, according to Bryant, rooted in a realism that is almost entirely lost when the mode becomes mediated through the political and ideological agendas of Virgil: 'since the aim of these writers was not to recreate an accurate picture of a shepherd's life, the scene became idealized and stereotyped, a quality which we always associate today with the pastoral as a form, ignoring the realistic beginnings of the tradition'.[16] The pastoral filtered into English writings as a synthesis of satire and idealism, fantasy and reality providing a specific form of imaginative construction that enabled the existence, and sometimes exploration, of antithesis. In *The Winter's Tale* the structural and temporal space of Bohemia supports the recognition of antithesis, as Time self-consciously stands between the two countries in dramatic division. Presenting this kind of structural logic allows Bohemia to occupy structurally the space of the country, focusing our attention on the shepherd-nymph-princess Perdita as well as the putative realities of country life. Such pastoral traditions as existed, however, were predominantly poetic rather than dramatic, since they had developed from the humanist focus on Virgil's *Georgics* and *Eclogues*.[17] Although neither of these seminal works was translated into English until the beginning of the seventeenth century, they were staple texts of a grammar school education and therefore, according to Annabel Patterson, 'a public short-hand'.[18] For Patterson, the process of translation and retranslation fixes these works in the minds of their students whilst simultaneously unhingeing them from the acute political context in which they were originally conceived. As a result:

the Virgilian code and the ideological possibilities it represented passed out of the cabinet of the lone intellectual, isolated and besieged, into the terrain of politics proper and became widely disseminated as a public language.[19]

---

[16] Bryant, 'The Winter's Tale and the Pastoral Tradition', 387–8.

[17] Michelle O'Callaghan argues that under James the pastoral became a distinctly royalist mode, which resulted in a reorientation away from these earlier forms of Spenserian satire, 'Pastoral', in Michael Hattaway (ed.), *A New Companion to Renaissance Literature*, vol. i (Oxford: Blackwell, 2010), 232. Callaghan suggests, as do others, that the genre is male, homosocial in its celebration of male relationships in a hostile environment. For her, though, Mary Wroth's *Urania* is 'part of a wider feminisation of pastoral romance in both its narrative and dramatic forms', 234.

[18] Fletcher is an exception here. Patterson, *Pastoral and Ideology*, 140. Although the *Aeneid* appears to have been translated into English in the mid-sixteenth century, the *Eclogues* and *Georgics* do not appear in English until James Harrington's 8-volume edition in 1658. See William Thomas Lowndes and Henry George Bohn (eds.), *The Bibliographer's Manual of English Literature*, vol. iv (London: Bell and Daldy, 1871), 2784.

[19] O'Callaghan, 'Pastoral', 134.

Part of this dissemination encouraged a 'contract' between the georgic and pastoral modes, which, under the Stuarts, developed into a fully articulated dialogue between ethics and politics.[20] The contract of genres brought together the conventionally polarized visions of labour and pleasure so that labour, or cultivation, could be valued as part of the processes of learning and the responsibilities to the commonwealth. In the interpretations of pastoral and georgic models in poetry husbandry is usually understood to belong to a negative image of labour, anxieties of poverty, and the fragility of subsistence living.[21] While there are certainly examples of this kind of bipartite structure in the lyrical poetry, the husbandry manuals support a rewriting of this tradition in humanist discourse since they import ideologies of profit, reward, and economic development through strategies of work that tend to valorize a kind of auto-didacticism for the rising gentry.[22] In the work of the humanists, for example, Keith Thomas observes 'the high value of work in a secular vocation' since it 'urged the importance of leading an active life for the good of the commonweal'.[23] The humanist traditions through which these manuals develop make the necessity for labour transparent in such a way as to cleanse it of its socially disreputable implications and resurrect a Christian tradition of recuperation through work (the sweat of Adam's brow becomes increasingly less punitive and more inspirational).[24]

Yet the idea of the pastoral still persists as an expression of rural pleasure, sequestered from the anxieties of real physical labour and dedicated to the leisure and enjoyment of a life apparently free from urban

[20] Patterson attributes this development to Francis Bacon, who, she says, in *The Advancement of Learning* in 1605 'recognized a new century and a new English monarch by proposing a programme of intellectual husbandry, whose fruits would be great advancements in the proximate fields of ethics and politics' (135). See also Michelle O'Callaghan, *The Shepherd's Nation: Jacobean Spenserians and Early Stuart Political Culture* (Oxford: Oxford University Press, 2000), 26–62.

[21] Cain and Abel are often interpreted according to two different ways of life, the pastoral and the agricultural, which provide an emblematic extension of the curse of Adam after the fall. The qualitative logic, however, seems slightly strained, although according to Paul Freedman: 'After the murder of Abel, God promised that the earth would not yield its produce bountifully for Cain (Genesis 4: 12), who could therefore be regarded as an emblem of fruitless agricultural labour,' *Images of the Medieval Peasant* (Stanford, Calif.: Stanford University Press, 1999), 93.

[22] In *The Ends of Life*, Keith Thomas explores what he terms 'a highly negative view of work' in the early modern period. Identifying that idleness was the 'badge of a gentleman', to paraphrase Robert Burton, Thomas examines the cultural attitudes to labour over the seventeenth and eighteenth centuries, 83.

[23] *The Ends of Life*, 85–6.

[24] Bushnell, in *Green Desire*, suggests that images of work are suppressed or confused in the gardening manuals as precisely who is doing the work (a hired hand or the gentleman reader) is not clear; however, the work itself is valorized by the very passage it creates to productivity and pleasure, 84–107.

demands.[25] The realities of pastoral farming were, of course, very different. John Aubrey records a stark picture of sheep and arable farming in the south of England:

> On the downes, sc. the south part where 'tis all upon tillage, and where the shepherds labour hard, their flesh is hard, their bodies strong: being weary after hard labour, they have not leisure to read and contemplate of religion, but goe to bed to their rest, to rise betime the next morning to their labour.[26]

Pasture lands tended to fall into two categories: wood pasture (which was a relatively recently cleared area of woodland, enclosed and therefore only lightly populated); and pastoral vale lands (which were 'associated with subdivided fields and common field farming').[27] Although in *The Winter's Tale* the Shepherd and his son do not represent the kind of images of hard labour that Aubrey describes, they certainly suggest some of the anxieties of subsistence living. While literary representations of the pastoral tend to recreate the rural space as one of refuge, constructions of refuge are always being shaped by the specific pressures from which they provide an escape. In *The Winter's Tale*, Bohemia can act as a pastoral space because it provides temporal, and geographical, relief from the infection of Leontes' court. Etymologically, the term pastoral develops from St Gregory's *Cura Pastoralis* to mean someone or something concerned with spiritual care; logically evolving through Christ the shepherd and the lamb, the term acquires its ovine associations in the sixteenth century.[28] In this way rural

---

[25] The most powerful exponent of this tradition in modern scholarship is, of course, Raymond Williams, whose *The Country and the City* reveals the ways in which labour, poverty, and strain are erased in many literary representations of rural life in order to reaffirm the multiple beneficences of nature and the aristocracy. James Turner's important book *The Politics of Landscape* develops Williams's thesis through some of the major seventeenth-century poets. The representation of antithesis continues to inform the understanding of Shakespeare's 'pastoral'; in *As You Like It*, such an antithesis is continually reinforced by the Duke Senior who, in exile in the forest of Arden, finds 'sermons in stones, books in the running brooks and good in everything'. In *The Country and the City Revisited: England and the Politics of Culture, 1550–1850* (Cambridge: Cambridge University Press, 1999), Gerald MacLean, Donna Landry, and Joseph P. Ward explore the critical legacy of Williams's book and the ways in which interdisciplinary studies have pushed the boundaries of Williams's thesis into wider negotiations with the fields of geography, art history, and history: see particularly 1–23.

[26] As cited by Overton, *Agricultural Revolution in England*, 50. Overton gives no further bibliographical details.

[27] Overton identifies the ways in which areas of land created particular demographic networks, in which the absence of manorial control in wood pasture regions created more unorthodox inhabitants and the legacy or presence of manorial structures in sheep-corn areas effected a more conventional population, see *Agricultural Revolution in England*, 41–55.

[28] The *OED's* first example of the word within the context of 'a literary work portraying rural life' is 1584.

life becomes synthesized with spiritual care apparently divesting it of labour, poverty, and dearth. In the sixteenth century, however, the figure of the shepherd began to absorb much of the anxiety about enclosures. The enemy to tillage, the shepherd could represent self-interest, laziness, and the decay of husbandry. In *The First Book of Cattell* (1587), Leonard Mascall writes about the 'chief commodities' of both beasts; declaring that 'sheepe [are] one of the chiefest & fruitfullest for the vse of man' to that end, he explains:

The shepheard ought to bee of a good nature, wise, skilfull, countablo, and right in all his doings, wherein few is to bée found at this present. Specially in villages and towns: that by their idlenes & long rest, they grow new to wax stubborn and are giuen (for the most part) to frowardnes and euill, more then to good profit to their maisters, and euil manered, whereof bréedeth many théeuish conditions, being pickers, lyers, and stealers, and runners about from place to place, with many other infinite euils. (190)[29]

Drawing on a Christian interpretation of idleness as sin, Mascall identifies the anxiety of depopulation that accompanied enclosures and the partitioning of common ground. Although Mascall recognizes, indeed endorses, the importance of wool in the life of an English man or woman, he gestures at the moral responsibility of the shepherd to uphold conventional values of labour. The moral implications of enclosures ran deep in anti-enclosure material but even at the level of practicalities they also signalled a fundamental breakdown in the cohesion of village life, as Joyce Appleby explains:

Unlike so many other features of the market economy that were unobtrusively innovative, enclosures were visible departures from customary ways. The social consequences of turning open fields to private farms were starkly apparent.[30]

Despite the classical and biblical heritage of the pastor/shepherd, the realities of the early modern figure were more fraught. Mascall's suggestion that the logical progression of idleness is crime gestures at a highly contentious moment in the history of agrarian development where the landless poor were often forced into the status of a vagabond through depopulation or loss of labour. Whilst Mascall's tone is censorious, an early seventeenth-

---

[29] Bruce Boehrer draws on this passage in his reading of *The Winter's Tale*, in which he develops his analysis of what he calls the 'textual effect' of the sheep in early modern literature. Boehrer goes so far as to accuse Shakespeare, and others of 'a literary temperament', who 'seemed unable to distinguish the flesh-and-blood-beasts from their figurative counterparts', *Animal Characters*, 164.

[30] Appleby, *Economic Thought and Ideology*, 59.

century account of the vale of Tewkesbury suggests a far greater awareness of social responsibility:

> There being no kind of trade to employ men, and very small tillage, necessity compelled poor men to... stealing of sheep and other cattle, breaking of hedges, robbing of orchards, and what not; insomuch that the place became famous for rogues... and Bridewell was erected there to be a terror to idle persons.[31]

'Compelled' into crime, the poor living in pasture zones become idle rogues who are controlled through intimidation, rather than relief. The reality of the decay of tillage through increased animal grazing appears to leave little room for singing or festivals.[32] Since the demands of animal husbandry were less than those of agricultural labour the 'domestic system' responded through developing a dual industry of both food and cloth production. Eventually, mercantile pressures on greater labour, longer hours, and increased production 'doomed the domestic worker to extinction', but it was precisely the landless and vagrant who 'produced the first and most convinced advocates of projects in provincial communities'.[33] The seventeenth-century investment in projects which facilitated the growth of a consumer market made way for the cottage industry of the 'idle poor'. In 1628 the surveyor Matthew Bedell described the economic relationships between the worker, the commodity, and the seller in Rothwell, West Yorkshire:

> In this town the inhabitants make great store of bone lace, whereby their poor are employed and themselves much enriched. They make a quick return of this commodity for it is fetched and carried away from their doors by chapmen continually resorting thither.[34]

---

[31] As quoted by Thirsk, *Economic Policy and Projects*, 164. Thirsk identifies a 'major crisis' at the beginning of the seventeenth century, as 'the natural increase of population, experienced by the kingdom as a whole, was combined with the migration of landless people into these districts from arable areas', *Economic Policy and Projects*, 164.

[32] William C. Carroll explores some of the complexities of the debates that surrounded enclosure in ' "The Nursery of Beggary": Enclosure, Vagrancy, and Sedition in the Tudor-Stuart Period', in Burt and Archer (eds.), *Enclosure Acts*, 34–47. As Carroll observes, 'Whether one argued for or against enclosures as state policy, however, the common spectre of social discord was the nightmarish vision of a new-created race of masterless men, of beggars and vagabonds wandering the roads, homesteading on dwindling common wastes, poaching and fence breaking at will; ironically, vagabonds had even been hired to participate in local enclosure riots by the disputants,' 38–9.

[33] Thirsk, *Economic Policy and Projects*, 156; 157.

[34] Corporation of London Record Office, GCE Estates, Rentals, 6.16. As cited by Thirsk, *Economic Policy and Projects*, 157.

The chapmen here represent a vital character in the traffic of local trade and exchange. The vivid image of the ever-present trader moving goods between the poor and the rich discloses one of the ways in which rural communities responded to the economic crises of enclosures.[35] Equally powerful, however, is the creation of a market in which luxury goods could be distributed among the lower classes.[36] In the seventeenth century, pastoral areas, far from representing the shepherd lazily tending to his sheep, became predominantly associated with the conflicted conditions of depopulation, market potential, and cottage industry.

Bearing in mind that England's major industry at this point was wool, we begin to see the significance of the shepherd in the early modern imagination. A complex image of competing values, the shepherd, and the rural community he inhabited, could simultaneously represent exploitation and investment, disenfranchisement and market potential.

As Shakespeare's most famous shepherd initiates the audience into a new time frame, we observe these values in motion. Having discovered the baby and her belongings, the Old Shepherd instantly decides to dispense with his flock on the sight of the gold:

We are lucky, boy, and to be so still requires nothing but secrecy. Let my sheep go; come, good boy, the next way home. (3.3.119–22)

The Shepherd's response to Perdita's gold is to 'let my sheep go', suggesting that this is not a vocation but a means of living. The comment instantly identifies the Shepherd with an attitude to the countryside that is far from idealized: indeed, his insistence on secrecy amplifies the anxieties of individualistic gain. Moreover, the Shepherd had entered the stage enumerating his worries: he has lost two sheep, fears the wolf, and is troubled by the follies of his youthful son. The Shepherd does not speak on behalf of a merry band who takes pleasure in the putative simplicity of their livelihoods; he speaks with the voice of someone who understands financial gain as a release and a reprieve. The money that the Old Shepherd finds with Perdita allows him to give up sheep-farming: this is

---

[35] Gregory King's records of the seventeenth-century economy reveals, however, that towards the middle and end of this period, due to the ongoing development of consumer industries, 'more agricultural wealth was being created in pastoral than in arable country, though it might not be equitably distributed between the classes', Thirsk, *Economic Policy and Projects*, 174.

[36] Thirsk writes: 'Some of the cash for these items, particularly the ribbons and lace, would have been drawn from the pockets of yeoman and craftsmen, but only a small fraction could have been spent by husbandmen and artisans,' *Economic Policy and Projects*, 176. Christopher Dyer, however, suggests that consumption, beyond subsistence, was in evidence in the fourteenth century, *An Age of Transition*, esp. 126–61.

not a life of contentment but one of poverty and anxiety. It is never entirely clear whether the Shepherd keeps hold of or spends Perdita's fairy gold but it is clear that he is not a shepherd for the love of a pastoral lifestyle.[37] The dramatic focus on money both begins and dominates this half of the play.

Autolycus' entrance into the landscape of the play-world marks a decisive moment in the direction of the comedy. For Forman, he is 'an agent of the play's profit and a sign of it as well'.[38] As a self-confessed fallen courtier he represents the synthesis of these two worlds rather than the antithesis. It is never explained why he fell from grace, but as a failed attendant to Florizel, who later resumes this role in his exchange of clothes with Camillo, the implication is that he has fallen on hard times and therefore been reduced to begging, cozening, and exploiting—exposing the court/country antithesis as less fixed and more insidious than is traditionally presented. The rural space enables the politics of self-interest to emerge as versions of liberty. Subjecting perceptions of liberty to doubt, however, we perceive a competitive struggle for acquisition and mobility, in which truth and consumption become the defining models of aspiration.

Autolycus presents himself as a tinker: 'My traffic is sheets—when the kite builds, look to lesser linen' (4.3.23). Playing on the semantics of cloth, Autolycus declares himself to be a pedlar or a chapman predominantly trading in ballads and cloth. Drawing on the material relationships between printed texts, linen and cultivation, Autolycus allies himself with a relatively new trade: that of the licensed vagabond.[39] Whilst most editors gloss this phrase as a reference to bed linen, suggesting that Autolycus identifies with the bird of prey as a 'stealer of sheets', the word sheet tended to be used within the context of printed texts.[40] The implication is that when the kite builds her nest with scraps of linen we must look to buy a lesser linen which is simultaneously the text as well as the cloth, since cloth sheets are traditionally made from hemp, which is, of course, a 'lesser

---

[37] The Clown later alludes to the money when he attempts to bribe the disguised Autolycus to secure his release from Bohemia (4.4.795). Forman understands Perdita's objects as 'expenditures necessary to an economy of overseas trade and investment', *Tragicomic Redemptions*, 94.

[38] *Tragicomic Redemptions*, 100.

[39] In May 1606 there was a petition to license chapmen which, under article 39 of Elizabeth's statute, rendered them vagrants and therefore subject to 'corporal punishment' (*Calendar of State Papers, James I*, vol. xlv (1609), 6 May, p. 509).

[40] Orgel, for example, paraphrases this line: 'Just as the kite steals small pieces of linen to build its nest, my business is the theft of sheets.' For sheets as texts see James Donaldson's *Husbandry Anatomized* (1697), Elias Cole's *The Young Scholars Best Companion* (1690).

linen'. Conflating the material production of cloths Autolycus registers the extent of his trade as well as the nature of production itself.[41]

Autolycus defines his 'revenue' as twofold: one as 'a snapper up of unconsidered trifles' and the other, as 'the silly cheat' (4.3.25–7). Autolycus' commitment to 'traffic' and exploitation exposes one of the most powerful ways in which Shakespeare draws on his contemporary economy. The image of consumption is introduced by the servant even before the pedlar arrives: 'He sings tunes faster than you'll tell money; he utters them as he had eaten ballads, and all men's ears grew to his tunes' (4.4.185–7). The figurative consumption of the product he has come to sell establishes the appetite for such goods. In this powerful image of the cheating pedlar, Shakespeare synthesizes the rapaciousness of a material culture in which profit can be translated into acquisition. Julia Reinhard Lupton, however, identifies the metaphors of consumption as particularly relevant to the theatre, since they draw on an image of expiration relevant to both:

His fardel is 'fasting' because all of his goods have been eaten up by buyers, an image that taps the digestive metaphor resident in consumption. These are the things of theatre, not in its status as the art of action, but in its penchant for display and its frank and garrulous celebration of its own disappearance 'within two hours' (*Hamlet*, 3.2.125).[42]

Yet such images of consumption become increasingly associated with the kind of self-delusion with which the play is so concerned. These are not the theatrics of communal delight or even invention but the disaggregating power of individual fantasy. Announcing Autolycus' arrival the servant describes the cornucopia of delights that the pedlar can offer:

He hath ribbons of all the colours i'th'rainbow; points, more than all the lawyers on Bohemia can learnedly handle, though they come to him by th' gross; inkles, caddises, cambrics, lawns—why, he sings 'em over as they were gods or goddesses. You would think a smock were a she-angel, he so chants to the sleeve-hand and the work abut the square on't. (4.4.206–12)

The comic reflection that Autolycus 'sings 'em over as they were gods or goddesses' draws on the developing status of luxury goods. The mock iconography not only gestures at the anxiety of idolatry that the statue scene will later expose, but it also reveals the play's fascination with forms

---

[41] Fitzherbert's section on 'spring duties' for the housewife reveals the product potential for hemp or flax: 'they make shetes, bordclothes towels, shertes, smockes, and suche other necessaryes' (61ᵛ).

[42] *Thinking with Shakespeare*, 183. Forman, however, observes that 'the fardel serves as the sign of the rematerialisation of loss as a profit', *Tragiccomic Redemptions*, 94.

of fantasy and self-delusion. Part of the comedy of Autolycus' project is his exploitation of ignorance and self-delusion: he sells goods, we later discover, to a delighted audience who cannot tell the difference between genuine and counterfeit; such delusion, of course, runs deep within the play. Forms of fantasy are reconfigured by certain characters as individual realities: while in the first half of the play, fantasy is the arachnid imaginings of Leontes' mind; in the second half, fantasy materializes in the form of consumer goods, vividly playing out tokens of self-delusion, the quantification of love, and the dangers of idolatry.

Although lost to a modern audience, most of the goods that the servant identifies had a particular resonance in the early seventeenth century. Cambric, caddise, and lawn were all types of cloth and were largely imported from France and Holland. Cambric was a relatively new import and was only established in the domestic market in the late seventeenth century.[43] Inkle, however, was a cheap tape, so cheap, in fact that 'the term was replete with cultural overtones':

Because the inkle frame was both cheap and simple to construct and easy to use, the weaving of inkle became a stand-by occupation for the poor and intermittently employed in a similar way to nail making. As a result 'inkle weaver' became a pejorative term and some of the opprobrium became attached to inkles themselves.[44]

Given the social implications of inkles, the list of commodities reveals the developing purchasing power of the lower classes. From fine cloth to cheap tape, imported goods and peasant labour, Autolycus' bag exposes a growing economy of both aspiration and acquisition. His entrance hijacks one of the major conventions of pastoralism for the propagation of consumerism; he comes in singing, not of unrequited love as the Sicilian tradition of shepherds would have it, but of the possibilities of purchase:[45]

> Lawn as white as driven snow,
> Cypress black as e'er were crow,
> Gloves as sweet as damask roses,
> Masks for faces and for noses,
> Bugle-bracelet, necklace-amber,

---

[43] See Nancy Cox and Karin Dannehl (eds.), *The Dictionary of Traded Goods and Commodities 1550–1820* (Wolverhampton: University of Wolverhampton, 2007).

[44] Cox and Dannehl (eds.), *The Dictionary of Traded Goods*.

[45] Autolycus is not, of course, a strictly pastoral figure but one who hovers on the margins of the pastoral life. Indeed he occupies the hinterland between the country and the court, banished and itinerant he appears to represent a certain initiative in surviving on the opportunities of the domestic market.

> Perfume for a lady's chamber,
> Golden coifs and stomachers
> For my lads to give their dears,
> Pins and poking sticks of steel;
> What maids lack from head to heel—
> Come buy of me, come, come buy, come buy;
> Buy lads, or else your lasses cry; come buy. (4.4.219–30)

Moving swiftly up the social scale from inkles to far more expensive and aesthetic goods, Autolycus sets his commodities to the merry song of the festival. The refrain—'come buy of me, come, come buy, come buy'— isolates the imperatives of the occasion. From this point the success of the feast is not in the drunken laughter which the Shepherd remembers, but in the acquisition of goods. As the Clown says: 'Come, bring away thy pack after me; wenches, I'll buy for you both' (4.4.309–10). Like much of the play, Autloycus' list represents the coexistence of fantasy and reality. While many of these goods may have struck a chord with a Whitehall audience, for those at Blackfriars and the Globe only a small proportion would have been affordable. The fine lawn cloth—black or white—was traditionally the province of the nobility, as was an amber necklace or a 'bugle bracelet'.[46] An imported resin, amber could not frequently be found in the inventories of London retailers until the end of the seventeenth century. Similarly, although gloves perfumed with Jessamy oil were made in England, the best quality were imported from Spain and Italy. The golden coifs that Autoylcus refers to were almost exclusively the province of the monarchy and conventionally associated with ceremonial occasions: it may be that such an article refers to the wedding celebrations of Princess Elizabeth or it may be a further example of the fantasy that Autolycus sells.[47] The dream of change that the play inspires is deeply rooted in the mobility of the social and moral self: Perdita may always be a princess, but ultimately she takes the Shepherd and the Clown with her.

---

[46] In a record of a highway robbery in 1678, Middlesex County Records lists the value of a stolen amber necklace at 20 shillings (vol. iv: 1667–8, 81–113). Another inventory of a robbery in 1624 lists the value of a 'purse of glasse bugle' as 'worth five shillings' (vol. ii: 1603–25, 103–18).

[47] In an inventory of Henry VII expenses for the year of 1519 there is listed 'Coifs of silk and gold, set with pearls', J. S. Brewer (ed.), 'Henry VIII: October 1519', *Letters and Papers, Foreign and Domestic, Henry VIII*, vol. iii: *1519–1523* (1867), 162–72. Equally magisterial is the description of the obsequies of the King of Sweden who buried his two wives: 'the Queens being in gowns of black velvet, with guards of gold upon them, and each had a crown upon her head and a sceptre in her hand of silver and gilt. Underneath the crown were coifs of gold,' *Calendar of State Papers, Elizabeth I, Foreign and Domestic*, vol. iii: 1560–1.

While dramatically diverting and amusing, the figure of Autolycus also provides a unique window onto the social economy of the seventeenth century. As the focus of the agrarian economy shifted from domestic to national, the Crown's investment in projects and monopolies led to an increasing interest in consumer choice and the production of goods, both for the internal and external market. A developing awareness of the need to balance import and export led to a more analytical attitude to the market and one which began to see the economic significance of both 'free trade' and a flexible monetary value. Although analytical economic models were only in their infancy in the seventeenth century the idea of an independent monetary system was beginning to be explored through the works of Thomas Mun, Gerard Malynes, and Edward Misselden.[48] Despite their differences—crucially between Malynes's Aristotelian belief in essential value and Misselden's commitment to the market setting its value rather than the monarchy—they made way for the development of a fiscal economy.

Autolycus' vibrant list imports objects of contemporary interest into the traditional mode of pastoral song. Beginning with such luxury goods as his customers could only dream of, he ends with the far more realistic, relevant, and useful commodity of the pin. Joan Thirsk devotes a good deal of space to the role of pins—one of 'life's necessities'—in the seventeenth-century economy, of their ubiquity and role in changing perceptions of the import/export market as well as the domestic project.[49] Autolycus, disguised, bearing goods, and attesting to their value and validity, brings the articles of social mobility into a fantasy space of role-playing. His presence and his 'pack' promise, albeit briefly, transition: from unloved to loved, plain to beautiful, ignorant to informed. The play's mock insistence on the iconic value of these goods reveals the power that trade could occupy in the cultural imagination. Although only in its infancy, justifications of consumption and exchange were still allied to a

---

[48] See particularly Joyce Oldham Appleby's *Economic Thought and Ideology*, 24–51.

[49] Thirsk, *Economic Policy and Projects*, examines the changing pin industry and its representation of the changing economic attitudes of the sixteenth and seventeenth centuries. Thomas Smith in *Discourse of the Commonweal* (1549) observes that the great quantity of pins being imported from Holland into the country was draining resources and occluding a valuable source of domestic industry, see 78–87. As it became more and more clear than certain imports were a negative drain on the home economy, more and more domestic manufacturing—where possible—took place. Pins started to be made in England from imported brass wire in the 1560s and 1570s. For an indication of the scale of import see Brian Dietz (ed.), *The London Port Book 1567–8* (London: London Record Society, 1972), which records tens of thousands of pins being imported to the capital, 154–6.

Tudor ideology of the commonwealth in which the body was the dominant image of cohesion and health.[50]

Gerard Malynes, who was 'in 1600 appointed to the Royal commission for establishing the true par of exchange', propounded an essentially Aristotelian conviction that money's value must be defined by the quality of its internal substance, gold or silver.[51] In this treatise of 1622, *The Maintenance of Free Trade*, he identifies the significance of trade in the following terms:

the preseruation and augmentation of the wealth of your Highnesse Realmes and Dominions, to bee effected by the Rule of iustice grounded vpon *Aequality* and *Aequity* according to *Ius gentium,* which is chiefly maintained by the *Lawe Merchant.* The knowledge whereof, is of such moment, that all other Temporall Lawes (without it) are not compleate, but imperfect . . . (Dedicatory Epistle)

Malynes's rhetoric assumes an emotive relationship between equity and equality in which trade, with its implicit financial benefits, determines an ideological structure of gain, security, justice, and morality. Invoking the spiritual and physical development of the human body, he goes on to explore the ethical implications of a flourishing market:

The First as the *Body,* vpheld the world by *Commutation* [exchanging] and *Bartring* of commodities, vntill money was deuised to bee coyned.

The Second, as the *Soule in the Body,* did infuse life to Traffique by the meanes of *Equality* and *Equity,* preuenting aduantage between Buyers and Sellers.

The Third, as *the Spirit and faculty of the soule* (beeing seated euery where) corroborateth the *Vitall spirit* of *Traffique,* directing and controlling (by iust proportions) the prices and values of commodities and monyes. (2–3)

Through terms like 'infuse', 'life', and 'soul', the monetary market is given an internal energy that is represented as inherently good, creative, and self-regulating. The processes of exchange, profit, and acquisition became translated into something akin to spiritual development.[52] Through the image of the body as the primal agent of exchange, Malynes gives a real presence to money, whereby it takes on the role of the body and the soul

---

[50] Christopher Dyer observes that a version of consumerism was available to peasants in the preceding centuries, *An Age of Transition*, 33–5.

[51] Gil Harris's *Sick Economies* explores the seminal work of Malynes within the context of the bodily metaphors of health and decay, see esp. 89, 94.

[52] See Jonathan Gil Harris's *Foreign Bodies* (Cambridge: Cambridge University Press, 1998) which explores Thomas Starkey's *A Dialogue Between Reginald Pole and Thomas Lupset* through the conceptualization of the body as a politic state and how 'This endogenous understanding of the body politics' pathologies lends rhetorical weight to Starkey's insistence that England's social, political, and economic systems of organization must be restructured to ensure the nations health,' 35. See also Harris's *Sick Economies*, 138–54.

becomes an image of justice or equality in the rates of exchange between buyers and sellers. Supporting an image of money as governed by its own material composition creates an idea of economic exchange which is self-governing and stable, driven entirely by the value—in both senses of the word—of its presence.[53] Similarly, the perception of an inherently valuable system of exchange allows figures like Autolycus to believe they are selling an ideology as well as an article. Autolycus' genuflection to his market goods anticipates the ways in which Malynes understood the English economy.[54] The later revelation, however, that Autolycus' bag was full of 'counterfeit' gloriously severs the link between its assumed and essential value, attesting to the play's commitment to disclosing the architecture of fantasy, as well as endorsing it.

Yet, as the sheep-shearing scene becomes somewhat divided in its dramatic impetus—the empiricist exchanges between Perdita and Polixenes, the high-flown idealism of Florizel, and the avid consumerism of the shepherdesses—the pastoral tradition almost disappears from view. The rustic characters are simplified not through their labours or responsibilities but through their attitudes to acquisition:

Clown: If I were not in love with Mopsa, thou shouldst take no more of me; but being enthralled as I am, it will also be the bondage of certain ribbons and gloves. (4.4.231–3)

As money assumes the value of its composition, so certain ribbons and gloves assume the value of the love they represent. The Clown's suggestions of bondage are more than metaphorical, since they imply his own enslavement to the labours of surplus and financial gain. The term bondage was only just beginning to accrue its meaning of literal (or metaphorical) enslavement (*OED*, 1611), since it was primarily defined as a feudal position of tenure in villeinage, in which the lord held supreme rights over the peasant's land and living.[55] The Clown's language speaks—to humorous effect—of his economy in transition: love may be the master as he develops rights to his own land and lady, but he transfers his bondage to a surplus economy in which purchase determines status.

---

[53] David Landreth's *The Face of Mammon* (Oxford: Oxford University Press, 2012) explores the complex terms of value embedded in conceptions of money, from the content of precious metal through devaluation of its composition to the creation of symbolic value.

[54] Thomas Mun and Edward Misselden, would, however, develop an economic model of analysis on the basis of a more flexible and independent market driven economy. See, particularly, Joyce Oldham Appleby on this subject, *Economic Thought and Ideology*, 41–72.

[55] The idea of bondage is of course implicit within the terms of feudalism as we notice that Shakespeare uses it within the context of enslavement in *1 Henry VI* 5.3.

The sheep-shearing scene's focus on Autolycus and the ways in which the various characters respond to his 'trumpery' supports a theatrical emphasis on the newly developing trade. The pleasure and leisure associated with the pastoral tradition is absorbed into the character of the pedlar, who translates communal mirth into individual gain. The multiple facets of Autolycus' role—court reject, cozener, pedlar, comic, plot device—playfully represent this new kind of consumerism within the context of the play's wider interrogation of the role of fantasy in the resurrection and destruction of human life. Perhaps one of the most articulate expressions of the relationship between the two halves of the play is Mopsa's invocation of the quality of truth. Despite the wonderful goods that Autolycus claims to have in his pack he is probably most clearly identified with the ballad.[56] Having already declared himself to 'traffick in sheets' the conversation that takes place about ballads is one of the most comic and ironic within the play:

Mopsa: Pray now, buy some. I love a ballad in print, a-life, for then we are sure they are true. (4.4.257–8)

Like Jonson in *The Staple of News*, Shakespeare is satirizing the book trade as well as the early forms of newspaper, which, like the ballad, owed its heritage to the oral tradition of story telling.[57] But there is more than the print trade at stake in Mopsa's comment: the nature of truth haunts the play, like the old man in the churchyard in Mamillius' story. As a seller of ballads, Autolycus himself represents the veracity of their narratives: his real presence, as it were, was part of the ballad's context of truth and the speaker attests to these claims in the distribution of the material. Such a concern with the status of the ballad's narrative is, according to Natascha Würzbach and Gaynor Wallis, a peculiarly early modern development:

Although the street ballad adopts elements from the traditional topos, it expands it through its claim to topicality and through direct conversion into didactic literature. The public is to be offered not so much truths propagated by scholarly tradition, but instruction into ways of the world, to be gleaned from events which are contemporary, either because of their actual core of reality or because of the fiction adopted . . . The arousing of emotion and fear, however, which is also part and parcel of the presenter's projection of his persona reinforces the topicality of what is reported in the same way as the fictions

---

[56] We can also assume that given the range of stage properties available to The King's Men, the ballad would be a much more visually accessible prop than, say, pins or ribbon.

[57] See Ian Donaldson's *Ben Jonson: A Life*, in which he refers to the play as revealing Jonson's 'satirical eye on early developments in the field of journalism', 306.

proving authenticity. In all the forms of the claim to authenticity the presenter sets himself up as the guarantor of the truth and therefore the importance of his message.[58]

Mopsa's credulity is therefore entirely appropriate within the context of the ballad tradition and Autolycus perfectly performs his role as the 'guarantor of truth' in supplying civic witnesses: 'Five justices' hands at it, and witnesses more than my pack will hold' (4.4.281–2). Yet the rustic characters are buying more than 'truth'; they are buying information, novelty, and modernity:

MOPSA: Is it true, think you?
AUTOLYCUS: Very true, and but a month old. (4.4.264–5)
MOPSA: Pray you now, buy it.
CLOWN: come on, lay it by, and let's see more ballads. We'll buy the
             other things anon. (4.4.270–2)

The dizzy delight of these characters is supported through the presentation of choice. The rural characters are theatrically defined by the exchanges that take place over Autolycus' bag: the wonder of new ballads, and the glorious range of trumpery. The sheer sparkle and newness of these goods provides a spectacular arrangement for the representation of transformation.[59]

Autolycus offers a brave new world of choice, social mobility, information, and acquisition, such as would have been unthinkable, even in Shakespeare's memory.[60] The vibrant interruption of contemporary consumerism into the putatively festive environment of the sheep-shearing scene complicates any strictly pastoral interpretations of Bohemia. Autolycus' insistence that the guests of the sheep-shearing feast 'buy, buy, buy' shifts the feast from its historic emphasis on consuming food to a more urgent focus on buying trinkets.[61]

---

[58] Natascha Würzbach and Gaynor Wallis, *The Rise of the English Street Ballad 1550–1650* (Cambridge: Cambridge University Press, 1990), 52. See also 49.

[59] Within this context Forman writes: 'The profitability in *The Winter's Tale* might be modelled on the earlier form of profitable art: the commodified ballads rematerialised in the spectacle of the theatre from which they are and are not elided', *Tragicomic Redemptions*, 107.

[60] Joyce Oldham Appleby offers a general statistic for the sixteenth century in which she estimates that 'husbandmen and labourers—two thirds of village populations at the least—had produced no more than the staple necessities of life: corn, meat, butter, cheese, cloth and fuel, and then only in quantities sufficient to meet their own needs'. By the seventeenth century, however, there was 'cash and something to spend the cash on' even for 'humble peasants, labourers, and servants', *Economic Thought and Ideology*, 7; 8.

[61] The First Folio seems to almost recollect these terms when Heminge and Condell instruct their readers: 'whatever you do, Buy', A3.

Despite the superficial structure of communal pleasure, the feast itself provides a space in which the characters reveal their considerable differences both in how they perceive as well as how they are perceived. Although the intentions and attitudes of the characters suggest an investment in this rural festival, there is an overarching strain placed on this festivity from the outset. Against the suggestive backdrop of rural camaraderie emerges a rapacious delight in the opportunities of consumption; such delight, however, is ethically ambiguous. To what extent is Autolycus' exploitation of these simple figures endorsed as comical? Selling a fiction to those happy enough to buy it is something the play returns to in the statue scene. Here, however, the various characters are somewhat divided by their competing fantasies. While the rustic characters are diverted from the scene's wider tensions by Autolycus, Perdita pursues her own delusions with the prince. Perdita is always at some remove from this festival—her reluctance to play the hostess is reiterated in various keys by the Clown and the Old Shepherd who observe her inability to reproduce the traditions of the past:[62]

> Fie, daughter, when my old wife lived, upon
> This day she was both pantler, butler, cook;
> Both dame and servant; welcomed all, served all;
> Would sing her song, and dance her turn; now here
> At upper end o'th'table, now I'th'middle;
> On his shoulder, and his; her face o'fire
> With labour, and the thing she took to quench it
> She would to each one sip. You are retired,
> As if you were a feasted one and not
> The hostess of the meeting. (4.4.55–64)

The Shepherd's memories present a feast that cannot be recuperated: his animated representations of laughter, drunkenness, social liberty, and satiation expose Perdita as an inadequate hostess. She cannot accommodate herself to this role despite her family's expectations. Her rather restrained attitude to the disguised Camillo and Polixenes continues to expose her as inflexible—she cannot, it seems, perform the role of hospitality which

---

[62] The Clown asks: 'what will this sister of mine do with rice?' (4.3.38). Perplexed by the culinary uses of this grain, this comment suggests Perdita's deviation from tradition as well as her inexperience. Rice was occasionally used in sweet tarts and could be grown in England but Estienne is circumspect about the crop: 'If you will sow rice you may doe it: but it is like to proue rather a worke of curiositie than of profit; for rice is a commoditie properly belonging and growing amongst the Indians, from whence also it is brought hither vnto vs in France,' *The Countrey Farme*, 566. Thomas Dawson lists rice as an ingredient in *The Good Housewife's Jewel* (1577).

requires the host to please her guests above herself.[63] The now-famous conversation which develops between Perdita and Polixenes about the values of intervention and essentialism amplifies the ways in which this scene functions within the play. Whilst Perdita reveals herself to be completely ignorant of the lifestyle in which she has been raised, Polixenes discloses himself as a hypocrite and Florizel the lone supporter of pastoral idealism that the play cannot, as a whole, uphold. Alongside the conflict of interest that this scene supports, the feast is maintained by the persistent refrain of Autolycus' 'buy, buy, buy'. The Shepherd's nostalgia for an experience that cannot be replicated forces us to engage with this rural space not as a province of idealized power relations but as a new space of individual conflict. As each character takes up a different position it becomes an increasingly incongruous place.

If there is any remnant of the pastoral in this play then it is almost entirely at the behest of Florizel, who doggedly maintains an aesthetic fantasy of idealized relations, even in the face of resistance. Focusing on the prince's curiously hyperbolic response to Perdita, Philip Weinstein observes that this is not only 'an insufficient frame of reference for the son of a king' but that Florizel 'confuses the lusty and many-faceted sheep-shearing feast with an unreal Arcadian paradise'.[64] As Perdita stands, a model of resistance, with her rice, withholding of pied flowers, inhospitable coyness, and insistence on the reality of their situation, Florizel responds with the frivolous call to jollity that the feast seems to lack:

> Apprehend
> Nothing but jollity. The gods themselves,
> Humbling their deities to love, have taken
> The shapes of beasts upon them. . . .
> Their transformations
> Were never for a piece of beauty rarer,
> Nor in a way so chaste, since my desires
> Run not before mine honour, nor my lusts
> Burn hotter than my faith. (4.4.24–7; 31–5)[65]

In stark contrast, however, is Perdita's insistence on the power relations that such an event is meant to suppress:

---

[63] Julia Reinhard Lutpon explores the question of hospitality and its relationship to entertainment in *The Winter's Tale* in *Thinking with Shakespeare*, 161–85.

[64] 'An Interpretation of the Pastoral in *The Winter's Tale*', *Shakespeare Quarterly*, 22/2 (Spring 1971), 103, 105. However, he goes on to suggest that Florizel's idealism exposes him as being as flawed as his structural opposite, Leontes, and that part of the play's logic is to educate the prince in the realities of good governance that Leontes so grossly abused.

[65] Weinstein, 'An Interpretation of the Pastoral', 98–100.

O, but sir,
Your resolution cannot hold when 'tis
Opposed, as it must be, by th'power of the King. (4.4.35–6)[66]

Perdita, however, remains somewhat aloof from the whole event. From the outset, she shows herself to be reluctant—unable even—to perform the roles conventionally attributed to the hostess. Such a critical distance becomes most fully articulated in the conversation between her and Polixenes about the relative values of nature and art.

Much of the interest in this debate has been focused on the apparently conventional attitudes it presents to human intervention as a mode of either fulfilment or degradation.[67] These debates take multiple forms and are always informed by their various agendas, be they Christian, Platonic, empiricist, or humanist. By the seventeenth century, however, there were very few proponents of a purist nature, since the entire economy depended upon human intervention—and exploitation.

As we have seen, the development of the husbandry manuals through the sixteenth century follows an increasingly secular trend as the biblical injunction 'In the sweat of thy face shalt thou eat bread, till thou return unto the ground' (Gen. 3: 19) becomes absorbed into a more commercial attitude to profit and improvement. This shift, however, was largely supported by an image of the earth as self-generating rather than divinely fixed. In *The New Found World* (1568) the French cosmographer André Thevet invokes the human body to explain the difference between Art and Nature:

Let vs first take example by the humayne body. Al the art and excellencie of nature is hidden within: also of al other naturall bodies, the exterior or outwarde parte is nothing in comparison if that of the interior part it taketh not his perfection. The earth sheweth outwardly a sorowful and heauy face, being for the most parte couered with stones, thornes and thistles, or such lyke: but if the husbandman minde to open it with the plough, he shall finde this vertue so excellent, redy to bring him forth abundance, and to recompence him a thousand folde. (1ᵛ)[68]

---

[66] Stephen Orgel's work on the masque specifically identifies pastoralism with Stuart codes of power in which the genre performs an illusion of prosperity and harmony. See also Low's *The Georgic Revolution* and Patterson, *Pastoral and Ideology*.

[67] See John Pitcher's edition for the most recent anthology of contributors to this debate (London: Methuen, 2010). See also Jennifer Munroe, 'It's all about the gillyvors: Engendering Art and Nature in The Winter's Tale', in Bruckner and Brayton (eds.), *Ecocritical Shakespeare*, 139–54. Munroe cites Raphael Lyne's comment that the debate here is 'a curiously empty argument', 140; Lyne, *Shakespeare's Late Work* (Oxford: Oxford University Press, 2007), 102. See also Rebecca Laroche's essay 'Ophelia's Plants and the Death of Violets', in Bruckner and Brayton (eds.), *Ecocritical Shakespeare*, 211–21.

[68] See Franck Lestringant for a discussion of Thevet's work, and, interestingly, within the context of the debate between art and nature, his apparent atheism, *Mapping the*

Nature, here, like the human body, is raw potential capable of improvement and excellence but not without labour. Art is human intervention to the point of transformation: alchemical, even, taking a raw material and making it 'recompence him a thousand folde'. Similarly, in his book *The Morall and Natural Historie of the* East Indies (1604), Jose de Acosta sets out an explanation for his title:

> So as although this new *World* be not new, but old, in respect of the much which hath beene written thereof; yet this historie may in some sort be held for new; for it is partly historicall, and partly philosophicall, as well for that they are the workes of nature, as of free-will; which are the deedes and customes of men, the which hath caused mee to name it the Naturall and Morall Historie of the *Indies*. (sig. 3)

Here, human intervention is revealed as 'free-will; which are the deeds and customes of men'. In this way, Acosta represents the social economy as a moral interpretation of the elemental and material world of God's nature. While texts invested in the development and exploitation of natural resources focused on the superiority of human intervention, biblical metaphors relied on an emotive relationship between purity and restraint:

> Againe, Christ seeking to draw the harts and affections of men from carefull seeking after the vaine trash, and transitorie pelfe of this wretched world, (which most men with anxietie and griefe of mind so greedily hunt after) willeth vs to consider and behold the Lillies, not those that by art and labour are planted and sowne in gardens, but those that of their owne accord without the helpe of man, grow in the open field.[69]

Even within the context of the Tudor history of this debate, however, Perdita's response to Polixenes is decidedly old-fashioned: she presents herself as obstructive and resistant in such a way as to not only compromise her own future but repudiate the scene's spirit of commercialism:

> Sir, the year growing ancient,
> Not yet on summer's death nor on the birth
> Of trembling winter, the fairest flowers o'th'season
> Are our carnations and streaked gillyvors,
> Which some call nature's bastards; of that kind
> Our rustic garden's barren, and I care not
> To get slips of them. (4.4.79–85)

Renaissance World: The Geographical Imagination in the Age of Discovery (Cambridge: Polity Press, 1984).

[69] Levinus Lemnius, *An Herbal for the Bible* (1587), 174.

There is some confusion here as to what time of year Perdita actually thinks it is: a sheep-shearing feast would rarely take place in autumn—'the year growing ancient'—but early summer, and probably well before the flowering of gillyvors in July. Perdita's rather pompous response provides an opportunity for her to further separate herself from the crowd: the natural nobility that Polixenes observes in her is defined by a purist attitude to the landscape. Yet what constitutes purity is increasingly ambiguous, both within the terms of the play and those of the husbandry and gardening manuals.

Within the first half of the play, the question of purity or innocence is powerfully dramatized through the narratives of both Hermione and Mamillius. Leontes' gross misrepresentation of his wife forced the image of innocence into the domain of spectacle: putting innocence on trial confronts the audience with a question as to what purity looks like. Notoriously circumstantial, the image of innocence veered from the monotone white face to the blush of modesty or shame.[70] Perdita rejects the streaked gillyvors because their synthesis of colour suggests human intervention to the point of manipulation. Alongside the perennial greens of the plants she accepts, the carnation might well look rather exotic, but it was precisely this kind of exoticism that was being celebrated and valorized through Dutch still lifes and horticultural experimentation.[71] Art, or

---

[70] In *Much Ado About Nothing*, Hero's response to Claudio's accusations of infidelity produces a complex reaction from her lover who interprets her body as a double deception:

> Behold how like a maid she blushes here!
> O, what authority and show of truth
> Can cunning sin cover itself withal!
> Comes not that blood as modest evidence
> To witness simple virtue? Would you not swear,
> All you that see her, that she were a maid,
> By these exterior shows? But she is none:
> She knows the heat of a luxurious bed;
> Her blush is guiltiness, not modesty (4.1.32–40).

Similarly, in *Twelfth Night*, Viola's description of Olivia's beauty rests on the harmony of these colours: ''Tis beauty truly blent, whose red and white | Nature's own sweet and cunning hand laid on' (1.5). Mukherji, in *Law and Representation in Early Modern Drama*, explores the tangled relationship between the artifice of law and the artifice of what should be the natural body in chapter 4, 135–73.

[71] See Robert Watson's *Back to Nature* for an analysis of the allegorical and material relationships between the natural world and still life painting, 166–255. See also Fred Meijer's introductory essay on the relationship between allegory and composition, reality and illusion, in *Dutch and Flemish Still Life Paintings* (Oxford: Ashmolean Museum, 2005), 22–34. Norbet Schneider explores the carnation as an allegorical image, which, 'from the late Middle Ages onwards' became associated with the crucified Christ 'because of the nail shaped from of petals and fruit', *Still Life* (London: Taschen, 2003), 90. The tulip was, of course, another example of the ways in which human intervention created a nature so aesthetic that it came to occupy an almost iconic space within Europe, Harold Cook,

human skill, was a necessary step on the journey towards both enlightenment and improvement and it was precisely these kinds of arguments that supported the interventionist attitudes of English colonizers.[72] Polixenes' response to Perdita takes part in the discourse between intervention and essentialism and reflects a shift in the understanding of nature: from the Aristotelian concepts of a self-fulfilling organism to the more contemporary images of a machine governed by external (godly) laws:[73]

> For I have heard it said
> There is an art which in their piedness shares
> With great creating nature. (4.4.86–8)

In Polixenes' terms, great creating nature is not distinct from the human body but analogous to it: sharing a mechanistic framework in which God structures the material world according to certain patterns and movements. In sharing 'an art' with nature, the human body is understood as capable of reproducing certain patterns which are intrinsic to the universe, not separate from it.[74] The implication of a material world which can be imitated and reproduced by human intervention is suggestive of—although not yet full articulated by—Galileo's representation of the natural world as quantitative and produced by efficient causes which can be observed and interpreted through the human mind.[75] Francis Bacon, who was especially interested in the prolonging of human life through the strategic application of knowledge and experience, observes nature as a

---

Matters of Exchange: Commerce, Medicine and Science in the Dutch Golden Age (New Haven: Yale, 2007).

[72] See Patricia Seed on the peculiarly English interpretations of the landscape and images of ownership, *Ceremonies of Possession*, esp. 28–34.

[73] In *The Idea of Nature*, R. G. Collingwood traces the profound changes that took place in Renaissance cosmography. Through the seventeenth century, the idea of natural law as external to the mechanistic world would become increasingly secular as the structure of material elements was increasingly understood to be governed not by God, but by magnetism and gravity. See particularly 95–105.

[74] There is a certain sophistication to this argument which develops from an Aristotelian model of nature through the work of Copernicus and Bruno: 'The material world is conceived as infinite space, not empty but full of yielding and plastic matter which recalls to our minds the ether of more modern physic; in this ether are innumerable worlds like ours, forming in their totality a universe not itself changing or moving but containing all change and movement within itself,' *The Idea of Nature*, 99.

[75] Although he doesn't elaborate, John Pitcher observes in his introduction to the play that 'Just around the date of *The Winter's Tale*, the art and nature debates had come alive again, and it seemed possible that art might give back to nature some of its former fecundity,' 55. Polixenes' view of nature seems to occupy a hinterland between the classical Greek view of nature as self-creative and the emerging, empirical view of nature as mechanical.

model from which the human can learn, but ultimately exceed. For Bacon, art is an extension of nature; and therefore an expression of human superiority. In his natural history *Sylva Sylvarum* (1627) he isolates such an experimental attitude to the natural world:

> Some *Experiment* would be made, how by *Art* to make *Plants* more *Lasting*, than their ordinary Period; As to make a *Stalke* of *Wheat*, &c. last a whole yeare. You must euer presuppose, that you handle it so, as the *Winter* killeth it not; For we speake onely of *Prolonging* the *Naturall Period*. I conceiue, that the *Rule* will hold; That whatsoeuer maketh the *Herbe* come later, than at his time, will make it last longer time.[76]

Within this context Art 'prolongs' nature rather than compromises it: indeed, we are never encouraged to see them in conflict with each other but as a dynamic that can lead only to improvement.[77] In *The New Atlantis*, Bacon revisits this relationship through the language of cultivation:

> In these wee practise likewise all Conclusions of *Grafting*, and *Inoculating*, as well of *VVilde-Trees*, as *Fruit-Trees*, which produceth many Effects. And we make (by Art) in the same *Orchards*, and *Gardens, Trees* and *Flowers*, to come earlier, or later, then their *Seasons;* And to come vp and beare more speedily then by their *Naturall Course* they doe. We make them also by *Art* greater much then their *Nature;* And their *Fruit* greater, and sweeter, and of differing *Tast, Smell, Colour,* and *Figure*, from their *Nature*. And many of them we so Order as they become of *Medicinall Vse*. (35)

Bacon understands the value that the natural world can offer mankind— both as a model of growth and reward and as a vital resource in the development of human science. The kind of monotone purity that Perdita celebrates is rarely valued above species development: indeed, in contemporary terms, it would be perverse to do so. Thomas Dawson, for example, in *The Good Housewife's Jewel* (1597) lists carnations as one of the ingredients for the water of life, whilst Simon Kellwaye identifies carnations and gillyflowers as one of the 'wholesome herbes' for the defence against the plague.[78] The value of plants for human health supported an interpret-

---

[76] 147. Cf. Bacon's attitude to the lengthening of human life in his preface to 'The History of Life and Death', in *Sylva Sylvarum*.

[77] Similarly, Bacon suggests that art can extract potentials in nature that would have otherwise remained dormant, or in a state of haphazard statis. See Francis Bacon, *Abecederium Nouum Naturae*, in *The Oxford Francis Bacon*, ed. Brian Vickers and Graham Rees, 15 vols. (Oxford: Oxford University Press, 1996–), xiii: *The Instauratio Magna: Last Writings*, ed. Graham Rees (2000), 291; 218. See also Subha Mukherji's essay in *Fictions of Knowledge: Fact, Evidence, Doubt* (Basingstoke: Palgrave, 2011).

[78] Dawson, *The Good Housewife's Jewel*, 47ᵛ. Kellwaye, *A defensatiue against the plague contayning two partes or treatises* (1593), 3ʳ.

ative link between flora and God, since it evinced a causal logic in the materiality of the natural world. John Northbrooke, in *The Poor Mans Garden* (1571), makes this logic transparent in his rhetorical moves between bodily health and heavenly spirituality:

But God, whose wisdome surpasseth mans foolishenes, hath prouided a sufficient salue for euerie sore, and a remedie for mans vntowardnes, and knowyng the nature of the disease, hath also planted simples of his grace, whereof he maketh medicines to heale the greate sore of mans corruption. For as a good phisition is well grounded in the nature of Hearbes and Plantes, whereof are made salues and remedies for the diseases of the bodie, and is neuer destitute either of a good Garden, well replenished with al maner holsome hearbes, or else of a trustie learned Apothecarie to prouide the same: So God doth neuer leaue his ordinarie meanes vnoccupied and vnprouided. (Epistle to the Reader)

The 'good Garden' is a storehouse of salvation: it provides medicines for the body and an image of God's bounty for the soul. Northbrooke's image is determined by a material logic in which that which surrounds us is also our salvation: transferring this logic to faith, he suggests that God's mercy will always heal us if we know how to ask for it.[79] The power of such analogies shows some of the ways in which the garden is being reconstructed in the early modern imagination. Previously confined to monasteries or subsistence living the garden did not become a source of income or recreation until the late sixteenth century.[80] The medicinal properties of these plants supported their place in the kitchen garden where they could facilitate the use of the space for both aesthetic pleasure and domestic utility. Perdita's restrictive attitude to her garden betrays her ignorance as well as her imprudence. In *Five Hundred Points of Good Husbandry*, Tusser makes little distinction between attitudes to husbandry or horticulture:

If fild to bearne corne, a good tillage doth craue
what think ye of garden, what garden wold haue.
In filde without cost, be assured of weedes:
in garden be suer, thow loesist thy seedes . . .

---

[79] Like Thomas Tuke's *Celestial Husbandrie*, Richard Robinson's *The Vineyard of Virtue* uses metaphors of cultivation to examine the social and religious lives of human beings. Robinson's book presents a 'plant' of virtue which is elaborated on through lengthy descriptions, apothegms, and proverbial wisdoms. The plant 'Amitie', for example, 'is a virtue, which rendreth due beneuolence for mutuall good wil reciued betweene man and man, and bringeth forth the communicating of humane soceitie, after such sorte that in nature it sociateth man with God . . .', 28ᵛ.

[80] John Dixon Hunt, *Gardens and the Picturesque: Studies in the History of Landscape Architecture* (Cambridge, Mass.: MIT Press, 1994); John Dixon Hunt and Peter Willis (eds.), *The Genius of the Place: The English Landscape Garden, 1620–1820* (Cambridge, Mass.: MIT Press, 1975).

At spring (for yᵉ sommer) sowe garden ye shall,
at haruest (for winter,) or sowe not at all.
Oft digging, remouing, or weding (I se)
makes herbe the more holesome, & greater to be...
Newe set do ask watring, with pot or with dish
newe sowne do not so, if ye do as I wish.
Through cunning wᵗ dybble, rake, mattock & spade:
by line & be leauel, trim garden is made. (fos. 43ᵛ–44ʳ)

Applying a similar logic to Northbrooke's, Tusser suggests that the pursuit of profit is a form of good management, equally relevant to the garden, body, or the field. The 'cunning' use of the 'dybble' that Perdita refuses exposes her reluctance to intervene in an industry dependent on management. Tusser's specific use of the terms of health and success (wholesome and great) indicates the importance of intervention. Perdita's representation of intervention as supporting 'nature's bastards' attempts to impeach human interference in specifically moral terms.[81]

Within the play the term 'bastard' is violent and destructive yet in horticulture it was predominantly neutral, meaning hybrid or imitation (for example, marjoram or saffron).[82] Perdita's rejection of grafting and the use of scions exposes her interpretation of the natural world as overwhelmingly social. She imposes her own status anxiety onto the landscape as a means of articulating a bodily innocence or even difference from the 'rustic' garden in which she has grown up. The garden as a figurative space for the identification of social values is not uncommon, yet what makes this space particularly fraught for the characters is their competing investments in it.[83] While Perdita tries to fashion her innocence in unified images of purity, Polixenes sexualizes the biological imperatives of natural reproduction:

Yet nature is made better by no mean
But nature makes that mean; so over that art
Which you say adds to nature, is an art
That nature makes. You see, sweet maid, we marry
A gentler scion to the wildest stock,
And make conceive a bark of baser kind
By bud of nobler race. This is an art

---

[81] Dabhoiwala's *The Origins of Sex* explores the early modern policing of sexual relationships outside of marriage and the extent to which illegitimate children were condemned by their parent's actions, see particularly 27–31.

[82] The word *pied*, however, is much less ambivalent and was often associated with the coats of fools (pied jerkin) or, in the case of horses, a sturdy rather than elegant breed.

[83] See my Introduction for a discussion of this image in *Richard II* and *Hamlet*.

Which does mend nature—change it rather—but
The art itself is nature. (4.4.89–97)

The noun 'mean' in Middle English can refer to sexual intercourse or coupling, which, in Polixenes' terms, exposes reproduction as a biological imperative determined by nature's impulse to recreate or reproduce.[84] The strangely sexualized terms through which Polixenes views grafting amplify the differences in this debate: while Perdita's resistance to intervention reveals her as antagonistic to progression; Polixenes' language discloses a peculiar prurience. The terms 'marry' and conceive never appear as substitutes for grafting in garden or husbandry manuals; they are predominantly social terms which refer to human rather than non-human intercourse. Polixenes' language valorizes sex as a form of nature—a natural impulse, perhaps—and speaks for a justification of desire—'the art itself is nature'—rather than in support of social mobility. Polixenes' preference for 'change' as a qualification of the word 'mend' reveals that he is not quite as committed to the social politics of grafting as he initially appeared. Rather than transform nature, he suggests, hybridization substitutes one thing for another. In these terms of change, the bud of nobler race is no longer compromised by the process of grafting since it is not transformed but replaced. The subtle distinctions that Polixenes makes retain the powerful differences between 'gentle' and 'wild': they can never offer transformation only substitution. In Aristotelian terms, this is an important distinction, since transformation requires that the seed of one become the seed of another, thereby taking part in a process of metamorphosis in which the *anima* remains intact.

In horticultural terms, however, grafting is a specialized process which requires an affinity between the two forms. Charles Estienne explains the necessary 'agreement':[85]

And to speake the truth, the mingling of kinds and differing rootes of Trees, (if it be not according to, and jumping with the naturall vertues of them both, and according to an agreement in some good measure of perfection, and yet furthermore well and throughly allowed and approued by reason:) becommeth rather a monstrous birth, and an inforcement of nature, than any profitable impe either for the health of man, or for the sauing and sparing of it selfe. Hereof are sufficient vvitnesses, I know not how many sorts of Apples, Peares, and Cherries, this

---

[84] Now obsolete, *OED*, n¹. Richard, as Duke of Gloucester, on the other hand, is derisory about the process, expressing the low state to which the kingdom has sunk: 'graft with ignoble plants' (*Richard III*, 3.7.127).

[85] *New Orchard and Garden*, 120. See Rebecca Bushnell's *Green Desire* for a wide-ranging discussion of early modern gardening manuals and their role in creating a new bourgeois ethic of labour and pleasure.

iumbled together by offering force vnto nature without judgement or reason: and but that they become somewhat admirable vnto the eye, they yeeld no profit vnto the bodie of any man, more than to draine his purse drie. (388–9)

Estienne's emotive use of such terms as 'monstrous', 'perfection', 'health', and 'profitable' presents the hybridization of trees as peculiarly social. The 'natural vertues' that he stipulates in support of grafting require reason and approval to endorse a set of relations which can produce both profit and admiration, whilst Tusser, on the other hand, expresses an entirely efficient view: 'Graffe good fruite all, or graffe not at all.' Like Polixenes, however, Estienne retains a qualitative difference between his wild and 'reclaimed' stock:

To graft vpon the wild stocke, hath more hold, and is more durable than that which is vpon the reclaimed tree: but the fruit of the reclaimed tree is of a better taste, as likewise the fruit of the graft will be which is grafted vpon a tree which blossometh and flowreth at the same time, and hath a liuing and moist barke, and the reason thereof is verie apparent. (346)

Taste and profit remain on the side of nobility and grafting emerges as an ambivalent project in the development of fruit trees. For Estienne, at least, the art is not nature: for nature 'jumbles together' where art observes affinity. The nature of Polixenes' grafting is simply reproduction; it makes no great claims to the science of selective breeding. The significance of this discussion lies in its dramatic irony as both characters disclose an ideology that is profoundly at odds with their desires.

POLIXENES: Then make your garden rich in gillyvors,
             And do not call them bastards.
PERDITA: I'll not put
             The dibble in earth to set one slip of them;
             No more than, were I painted, I would wish
             This youth should say 'twere well, and only therefore
             Desire to breed by me. Here's flowers for you,
             Hot lavender, mints, savoury, marjoram,
             The marigold that goes to bed wi'th'sun,
             And with him rises weeping. (4.4.98–106)

The scene's focus on exchange is parodied in Perdita's plants: she cannot give her guests the flowers that they want or those which most become them. Her antagonism towards cultivation stems from a mistrust of aestheticism: the streaked carnation or the painted face are, for Perdita, manipulations of a natural product that encourage superficial or unstable responses. Whereas Polixenes appears to confine his theories to the garden, Perdita takes her anxieties into the realm of human relations.

As her fellow guests at the sheep-shearing scene adorn themselves with Autolycus' 'trumpery', Perdita's response seems curiously pious and mean-spirited. Whilst Perdita rejects this kind of aesthetic idolatry, Autolycus happily trafficks fakery:

Ha, ha, what a fool honesty is! And trust, his sworn brother, a very simple gentleman. I have sold all my trumpery; not a counterfeit stone, not a ribbon, glass, pomander, brooch, table-book, ballad, knife, tape, glove, shoe-tie, bracelet, horn-ring, to keep my pack from fasting. They throng who should buy first, as if my trinkets had been hallowed and brought a benediction to the buyer; by which means I saw whose purse was best in picture, and what I saw to my good use I remembered... So that in this time of lethargy I picked and cut most of their festival purses. (4.4.592–601; 609–11)

Autolycus' triumph in having cozened most of the guests exposes the play's larger interest in forms of delusion, truth, and knowledge. Listing a more modest selection of goods than those he began with, Autolycus shares his delight in having duped those foolish enough to believe in 'hallowed' trinkets and to defer to the commodity as though it 'brought benediction to the buyer'. Within the consumer market the language of idolatry developed an ambiguous status: while on the one hand, the word 'trinkets' could simultaneously be applied to Catholic artefacts and small material objects; on the other, some of the objects themselves possessed iconic status. Autolycus has one such object in his bag—the 'tawdry lace' that the Clown has promised Mopsa (4.4.248–9) was an article of much admiration in the seventeenth century:

Tawdry lace or 'St Audrey's lace', a neck-tie commonly made from silk, was in great demand by the fashionable women of the 16th and 17th century. 'St. Audrey's ribbons', held in veneration even in the 16th century as having touched the shrine of St. Etheldreda, were in wide demand.[86]

Articles such as this fed into contemporary consumer culture translating their iconic status into one of social aspiration.[87] Mopsa's excitement reveals the extent to which the developing consumer markets enabled goods to reach the rural classes. The life of 'St Audrey's ribbon' from

---

[86] R. B. Pugh et al. (eds.), 'City of Ely: Fairs', *A History of the County of Cambridge and the Isle of Ely*, iv: *City of Ely; Ely, N. and S. Witchford and Wisbech Hundreds* (Victoria County History, 2002), 50.

[87] Peter N. Stearns defines 'consumerism' in the following terms: 'Consumerism refers to an attachment to purchasing goods not necessary for personal or familial survival, and a value system that makes this attachment an important part of personal and social evaluation,' *Handbook of Economics and Ethics*, ed. Jan Peil (Cheltenham: Edward Elgar Publishing Ltd, 2009), 62.

shrine to shepherd girl exposes the wonderful potential of purchasing.[88] The status of these objects—as indeed the status of art within the play— remains in contention. As St Audrey's ribbon is totemic so Autolycus' goods are merely copies. He is of course selling his companions a dream: of love, social mobility, or even holy protection. The counterfeit object collapses the distinctions between art and nature, fact and fiction. The 'real' status of these goods is irrelevant, it is what they represent that matters. At the moment of its apotheosis, when nature becomes art, we are inclined to believe that the only necessary contingent is belief—as Paulina tells us: 'It is required | You do awake your faith.' Faith, as the ability to trust in what you want to believe in, becomes the defining logic of the play and it is human intervention that makes faith possible. From the counterfeit commodities, the streaked gillyvour, to the statue of Hermione, art is the new nature.

Autolycus' intentions and exploitations may be radically less profound than Paulina's but both scenes require a certain consumption—a 'magic...as lawful as eating'. The images of consumption through which the play redefines its pastoral status come to a climax in the statue scene. Perdita's rather bathetic response to the discovery of her relationship with Florizel—that she will 'But milk my ewes and weep' (4.4.447)—comically dispatches with any idealized notions of the rural space. Rather than return to the life of a shepherd's daughter, she escapes with her lover to Sicilia (the province of the pastoral tradition), to be confronted by the extraordinary power of art and nature. Paulina's elaborate choreography of the actors in this performance has long been in development. As she—the purveyor of both faith and magic—leads the characters to an altar of art, Leontes' reaction returns us to the wonders of consumption:

> If this be magic, let it be an art
> Lawful as eating. (5.3.110–11)

Despite Paulina's insistence on the 'carver's excellence', and Leontes' observation of the 'fine chisel', Hermione's statue is, of course, not art but nature. The spectacular illusion that Paulina creates depends on an absolute faith that art can replicate nature. Investing this moment with a kind of terrified awe, Paulina invites her audience to imagine the art that could prolong, outdo, and rescue life, only to reveal that there is no such thing. The idea that art can improve on nature through human intervention is radically undermined by the revelations of this scene. Only

---

[88] Arjun Appadurai, 'Introduction and the Commodities of Value', in Appadurai (ed.), *The Social Life of Things* (Cambridge: Cambridge University Press, 1986).

nature can give life, move, kiss, 'hang about his neck', and speak. The play leads us to the point of acceptance—of a hungry desire to believe in that art, to accept the conditions of Hermione's return, and to devour the totemic replica of a past we can never redeem. Greedy as the audience are for the gift of nature they accept art in its stead. Insubstantial yet affective it reminds us of what there once was: 'Blindingly undiminished, just as though/By acting differently we could have kept it so.'[89] Yet the playwright's final trick is to resurrect nature at the point at which we had accepted art. Carried along by the play's debates over the ethical status of fantasy and ready to accept the necessary implications of human intervention, the drama resurrects nature as the ultimate source of pleasure. The living, aged Hermione fulfils her audience's dreams beyond any artistic perfection or carver's hand. Yet the debate is not redundant. For intellectual theorists like Francis Bacon, nature must remain under scrutiny as the potential province of art. Observing nature's capacity for self-renewal, Bacon declares:

And then (that which is the Mystery of that Obseruation) young *Boughes*, and *Leaues*, calling the Sap vp to them; the same Nourisheth the *Body*, in the Passage. And this we see notably proued also, in that the oft Cutting, or Polling of *Hedges, Trees*, and *Herbs*, doth conduce much to their Lasting. Transferre therefore this Obseruation to the Helping of Nourishment in *Liuing Creatures:* The Noblest and Principall Vse whereof is, for the *Prolongation* of *Life; Restauration* of some Degree of *Youth;* and *Inteneration* of the *Parts:* For certaine it is, that there are in *Liuing Creatures* Parts that Nourish, and Repaire easily. (*Sylvan Sylvarum*, 19)

For Bacon, the art of lengthening human life is, indeed, nature but what makes it art is the human capacity to observe, reason, and implement:

Life is short, and *Art* long. Therefore our labours intending to perfect *Arts,* should by the assistance of the Author of Truth and Life, consider by what meanes the Life of man may be prolonged.[90]

Paulina presents an illusion that brutally and majestically confronts the audience with the competing powers of nature and art, of the magic of human intervention and the ultimate superiority of the real over the counterfeit. While the majority of the play leads the audience into a willing agreement with art, fiction and the potential for change that such fantasies allow, the spectacular dénouement rests all its theatrical power in the triumph of nature. The play closes belonging to three women

---

[89] Philip Larkin, 'Reference Back', in *The Complete Poems*, ed. Archie Burnett (New York: Farrar, Straus, Giroux, 2013).
[90] *The Historie of Life and Death* (London, 1638), 2.

who all believe in nature—Perdita's purism, Paulina's mock statue, and Hermione's ageing face testify to a belief in the nobility of the real thing, when the 'art itself is nature'.[91]

[91] Jennifer Munroe reaches a similar conclusion, in her essay 'It's all about the gillyvors', but for Munroe the representation of nature is gendered throughout and belongs to a understanding of nature which 'ultimately values women's connection to Nature making them nearer to the source of creation itself', 152.

6

Prospero's Husbandry and the Cultivation of Anxiety

The masque of *The Tempest* has often puzzled critics of the play: theatrically engaging, it represents one of the play's most self-conscious examples of magic in action. Yet, as Francis Barker and Peter Hulme observed, 'the interrupted masque' introduces 'a jarring note into the harmony of this supposedly most highly structured of Shakespeare's late plays'.[1] The significance of the masque is unclear, dispensed as it is by Prospero amidst his mortal charter of ephemera. For the audience, like Ferdinand, the masque is our only point of access into Prospero's magic. It is a glorious performance of the great powers to which the magus refers. Unlike the other manipulations in the play, the action of the masque manifests and disappears directly before our eyes. But what is the fabric of this vision? In an apparently sterile landscape somewhere in the Mediterranean, Prospero introduces a distinctly English countryside, marked by nibbling sheep, agrarian husbandry, and enclosed fields.[2] The images to which the goddesses refer celebrate the beauty and fertility of a rural landscape, from which the human participants are ultimately excluded. Prospero summons this masque as a ceremonial structure for the union of Ferdinand and Miranda: bereft of any such structures on this 'bare island', Prospero apparently imports the goddesses to ratify desire as marriage, and marriage as production. The burgeoning landscape of his magical vision is, of course, illusory; inculcated from books and utensils, Prospero's magic appears at moments of crisis.

---

[1] 'Nymphs and reapers heavily vanish', John Drakakis (ed.), *Alternative Shakespeares* (London: Routledge, 1988), 202.

[2] There is a vast amount of criticism on the subject of the location and significance of the island in *The Tempest*, the most salient of which is Roland Greene, 'Island Logic', in William Sherman and Peter Hulme (eds.), *The Tempest and its Travels* (London: Reaktion, 2000), and Barbara Fuchs, 'Conquering Islands: Contextualising *The Tempest*', *Shakespeare Quarterly*, 48/1 (Spring 1997), 45–62, and Jerry Brotton's 'Carthage and Tunis: *The Tempest* and its Tapestries', in Sherman and Hulme (eds.), *The Tempest and its Travels*, 132–7.

Through the masque, cultivation appears magical, transformative, and capable of generating produce and plenty where none exists. Occupying a space somewhere between art and nature, this late play seems to suggest a relationship between magic and husbandry, where art, at least for Prospero's vision, can reproduce nature. But, unlike in *The Winter's Tale*, the existence of that nature is ambiguous: why in such an apparently hostile environment does Prospero turn to the cultivated English landscape for a fantasy of socialization? The masque exposes the audience to a set of well-defined images in which cultivation endorses certain cultural expectations. Readily absorbed into the play's nuptials, the masque offers a glimpse into the ceremonial structures of both landscape and husbandry. Supporting a creative context of production and prosperity, the goddesses recreate a fantasy of belonging from which the characters have been hitherto excluded. Offering a glimpse of something beyond the island, the masque celebrates a discernible relationship between nature and art. This relationship is defined by husbandry itself: social, productive, ceremonial, and transformative, the cultivated landscape occupies the only space of cultural authority to which the play defers.[3] Equally brief, illusory, and insubstantial, this apparently authorized space 'leave[s] not a rack behind'. In what follows, I will explore the relationship between nature and fantasy, cultivation and art. Setting key ideological fantasies in context, I will examine the interrelationships between Prospero's masque, Gonzalo's commonwealth, and the 'bare island' itself.

Having subjected Ferdinand to a form of hard labour, manipulated his daughter's feelings, and orchestrated the young couple's meeting, Prospero celebrates the initial success of his 'project' with a magical masque. Arriving first, Iris, the rainbow goddess, calls on her fellow spirit of the land:

> Ceres, most bounteous lady, thy rich leas
> Of wheat, rye, barley, vetches, oats, and peas;
> Thy turfy mountains, where live nibbling sheep,
> And flat meads thatched with stover them to keep;
> Thy banks with pionèd and twillèd brims,
> Which spongy April at thy hest betrims
> To make cold nymphs chaste crowns. (4.1.59–65)[4]

---

[3] In this way, of course, husbandry anticipates colonial practice. A number of recent studies explore the play in relation to the New World: these include Sherman and Hulme (eds.), *The Tempest and its Travels*, Shahzad Z. Najmuddin, *Shakespeare's 'The Tempest': Its Political Implications and the First Colonists of Virginia* (Crewe: Trafford, 2005), Andrew Fitzmaurice, *Humanism and America: An Intellectual History of Colonisation, 1500–1625* (Cambridge: Cambridge University Press, 2003).

[4] William Shakespeare, *The Tempest*, ed. Stephen Orgel (Oxford: Oxford University Press, 1987). All references, unless otherwise stated, are to this edition. John Considine, in

Into a radically bleak environment, Prospero introduces, by virtue of his magic, an extraordinary picture of cultivated land. Here Iris addresses Ceres, the goddess of husbandry and, more generally, agrarian land, within the context of the landscape she represents. Invoking a well-defined image of mixed farming, Iris summons a picture of cultivated land, containing both arable crops and livestock. Ceres' landscape, marked at every point by human intervention, exposes one of the ways in which this goddess could represent the role of cultural achievement in the natural world. As an emblem of agrarian production Ceres alerts us to the idea of prosperity as it is mediated through rural images. Frequently appearing in dedications, Ceres is a vision of the earth as a deliverance from want. George Wither's *The Shepherd's Hunting* observes: '*Ceres* to vs grants | Our fields and flockes shall helpe our outward wants';[5] Thomas Tusser includes the muse as a vision of both prosperity and pedagogy:

Yet Ceres, so did bolde me,
with her good lessons tolde me,
that rudenes cannot holde me,
from doing [the] countrye good.[6]

Tusser applies to the goddess as a force of social good—a force that extends to the unsophisticated and emboldens the individual to 'doing [the] countrye good'. For Tusser, Ceres can broker the gap between the uneducated and the commonwealth as a 'natural' image of industry and investment. Within this iconic role, Ceres was often folded into husbandry manuals as an image of successful husbandry but also as a brief reminder of the humanist history through which these manuals had developed. Charles Estienne also invokes her, first in a rather throw-away reminder to the reader of the appropriate use of soil: 'Dame Ceres ioyes in heauy ground, and Bacchus in the light'; and secondly as a sympathetic symbol of human industry, in which the ox is 'the cheefe companion of man in his labours, and the trusty seruant of the Goddesse Ceres'.[7] Man and goddess are joined in their occupation through the 'trusty servant' of the animal. Heresbach also includes such sentiments through the use of

his article ' "Thy bankes with, pioned and twilled brims": A Solution to the Double Crux', *Shakespeare Quarterly*, 54/2 (2003), locates one other use of the word 'pioned' in John Bulwer's *Anthropometamorphosis*, which is applied to the description of a woman's shoulders, denoting their 'downward' or 'sloping' appearance.

[5] London, 1615, dedication.
[6] *Five Hundred Points of Good Husbandry*, 2.
[7] *Five Hundred Points of Good Husbandry*, 128.

adage and aphorism.[8] Ceres occupied a vivid role in the English cultural imagination precisely because of the ways she could represent, in heavenly form, agrarian industry as a shared human and non-human goal. Standing somewhere between the heaven and the earth, Ceres endorsed a vision of husbandry in terms that were directly applicable to the human world. She is not exceptional or arcane, but relies, so Heresbach tell us, on the same methods of production as the human—the ox and the plough. Prospero summons these goddesses to his barren island through their context of agrarian production and their figurative language of 'foison and plenty'.

Iris introduces 'rich Ceres' with a set of very specific images; Iris's paean incorporates flat and hilly land, open champion or open pasture and enclosed pastures. Within her 'rich leas' there are six arable crops which will serve for human food and animal fodder ('peas'); there are turfy mountains on which sheep graze, and flat meadows with shelters for lambing made from straw ('thatched with stover'). Enclosing these fields are hedges—pioned and twilled brims[9]—which have been laid through the traditional method of intertwining wood, usually blackthorn, across poles to form a weave which then grows into itself to create a sturdy boundary.[10] The blackthorn, or sometimes whitethorn (otherwise known as hawthorn), is used because it is pliable and thorny, and therefore a natural deterrent to wandering sheep. It grows quickly and thickly and

---

[8] *Foure Bookes of Husbandry*, 84.

[9] Howard Furness's Variorum edition (1892) fully outlines the editorial history of this phrase, in which he sets out the two schools of thought that surround the controversy: those who emend the phrase to include peonies and those who 'suspect some agricultural operation'. The latter he first attributes to W. E. Henley, whom he describes as 'the first vindicator of the folio'. See also Frank Kermode's treatment of the phrase in his edition (Cambridge, Mass.: Methuen & Co. Ltd, University of Harvard Press, 1954), 97 n. 64.

[10] The process of hedge-laying is often referred to as hedging and ditching, since it requires the digging of a ditch to provide both drainage and support. Thomas Hill, in *The gardeners labyrinthe* (1577), discusses this process in his section on the various types of enclosures recommended by eminent Roman agriculturalists, including Columella and Varro: 'The Auncient husband men did besides these inuent the cating vp of banckes & countermres of earth, round aboute the Garden plotte, much lyke to the trenches in tyme of warre aboute Bulwarkes and Tentes: and these they especially made neere to high wayes, or by Riuers, and in Marrishes or Fennes lying open, or other Fieldes, that the Garden plot might on such wise be defended, from the damages and harmes, both of Theeues, Cattell, and Landfloudes,' *The gardeners labyrinthe*, 13. Hill's allusion to the trench is central to our understanding of Ceres's landscape, since 'pioned' is often taken to be a corruption of 'pioning' which comes from the French word 'peon' meaning foot soldier or trencher/ digger. Spenser's similar use of 'pryoning' in *The Faerie Queene* often corroborates this reading, and Shakespeare uses 'pioneer' in this context in *Hamlet, Henry V, Othello*, and *The Rape of Lucrece*: 'with painfull pryoinings | from sea to sea he heapt a mighty mound', Edmund Spenser, *The Faerie Queene* (1590), II.X.63.7–8. Although this seems an appropriate glossing of Spenser's phrase, 'pryoning' is often used in husbandry manuals to mean pruning.

flowers in the spring, bearing a white or pale cream flower, which the winds of April might well blow off (betrims) for the crowns of chaste nymphs. This landscape is marked at every point by the human hand. The fodder and food crops, enclosures, and 'pole-clipped vineyards' define a space of production and sustainability. Why then does Prospero use these images as portals to a social contract of marriage rather than cultivation? Relying on a cultural cohesion between the land and the human, Prospero imports a cultivated landscape for the value of its social codes. Blessing their union, the goddesses support images of fertility and abundance that Prospero hopes to impose on the young couple; the significance of which will go well beyond the boundaries of the masque. Despite the ethereal natures of these 'messengers', their role is peculiarly social in the context of Prospero's dynastic aspirations.

Ceres brings with her detailed images of 'foison and plenty' and of a cyclical nature in which profit and produce define the successful agricultural year. Against 'this desolate isle' we are forced to imagine 'sunburn'd sickle-men', 'barns and garners never empty', 'plants with goodly burden bowing', and 'bosky acres' covered by the 'rich scarf' of Iris's rainbow. Central to these images of abundance is a scriptural resonance which identifies the moral and social scope of Prospero's plan. Writing of seventeenth-century colonial practice, Patricia Seed refers us to 'the most popular biblical quotation in the English occupation of the New World— Gen. 1: 28, "multiply and replenish the earth, and subdue it"—[which] was often described as the grand charter given to Adam and his posterity and Paradise'.[11] Yet the 'grand charter' of English colonial activity abroad is translated by Prospero into something affecting human behaviour rather than economic activity.[12] The site of produce is Miranda, not the 'green plot' of the masque, and the future in contention is that of Milan, not the island. Nature becomes a cultural shorthand for the expression of social values, and bereft of any institutional frameworks Prospero imports a cohesive cultural logic through the language of cultivation. The masque, with its images of fertility, productivity, and possession, provides a visual incantation over Miranda and Ferdinand, treating their bodies as the

---

[11] Seed, *Ceremonies of Possession*, 32.

[12] There is a vast body of work on *The Tempest* and colonialism, and the most convincing of these studies include Jennifer Richards and James Knowles (eds.), *Shakespeare's Late Plays: New Readings* (Edinburgh: Edinburgh University Press, 1999) and Crystal Bartolovich and Neil Lazarus, *Marxism, Modernity and Post-Colonial Studies* (Cambridge: Cambridge University Press, 2002). See also Russ McDonald's essay 'Reading *The Tempest*', *Shakespeare Survey*, 43 (1990), which argues that the politicization of *The Tempest* has flattened out the 'poetic complexity' of the play, 15–28. Meredith Anne Skura, 'Discourse and the Individual: The Case of Colonialism in *The Tempest*', *Shakespeare Quarterly*, 40 (1989).

landscape to be blessed for futurity. Adam's 'charter' and the assimilation of Genesis into the human's relationship to the land supported an emotive relationship between fertility and futurity. While husbandry manuals and discourses on colonial activity registered this productivity through agricultural improvement, in Christian polemics the figurative implications of husbandry were centred on spiritual growth. 'God's House of Husbandry' or 'Celestial Husbandry' proved popular subtitles for Protestant sermons as the body and the soul became fertile corollaries to the land. Thomas Tuke's *The Picture of a True Protestant, or God's House and Husbandry* (1607) provides an extremely dense conflation of these images as the Church (the field) is sustained by its followers (the husbandmen):

Moreouer, fields are not in their perfect glory so soone as they be taken in: and the plantes and seedes that are set and sowne in them, come not presently, but by degrees to their full perfection, and growth. So the Church is pefited [perfected] by degrees: her plantes grow vp by little and little: and the seedes of Gods graces, which are sowen in our hearts spring vp, grow, and wickednesse are not at one instant, but by degrees remoued and taken away. And as no field is inclosed and taken out of the heath or common in one moment of time, but one part after another.[13]

Tuke's laboured attention to time and the 'degrees' though which both perfection and wickedness are sown or removed presents the faithful husbandman as assiduously labouring for his own course of righteousness. Tuke's choices of images, sowing, cultivating, and inclosing, are presented as positive by virtue of his analogies with the Church. The value system is clear: the land, like the faithful body and soul, must be nurtured and tended to, but only when it carries some intrinsic value:

Euen so the Church of God (as a spacious and fruitfull field is full of variety of plants, (as it were) and hearbs. Many and diuers are her fruits. And some part of her, some persons that belong vnto her, are more fruitfull and excellent then other, according to the difference of their mowle, or of the cost & labour which is spent vpon them. There is not the same influence of heauenly graces descending from aboue, vpon them all alike. The Sunne of righteousnes doth not send downe the beams of his effectuall operation equally vpon them.[14]

---

[13] Thomas Tuke, *The picture of a true protestant: or, Gods house and husbandry wherein is declared the duty and dignitie of all Gods children, both minister and people* (London, 1609), 158.

[14] Tuke, *The picture of a true protestant*, 154. 'Mowle', now spelled 'mool', is an early modern variation on the word 'mole', meaning earth or soil. There are multiple variations (19, in fact) on the spelling of the word, which seems to be in use, mostly in the north, between the fifteenth and twentieth centuries (*OED*). In the context of Hamlet's speech to Horatio on the drunkards and customs of Denmark—'So, oft it chances in particular men, | That for some vicious mole of nature in them, | As in their birth—wherein they are not

Despite the putative universality of the images of land management, here we are told that 'the Sunne of righteousnes' does not shine on everyone. As in Shakespeare's Sonnets, images of reproduction centre on a sense of intrinsic worth by which only the valuable can be reproduced. The sense in which God ethically cleanses the human world, condemning the wicked and sustaining the good, is evinced through the language of cultivation as it seeks to encourage the profitability of our socio-economic worlds. Prospero reproduces this ethical attitude in presiding over the couple: setting them amid the masque's ceremony marks them out as worth investing in and as images of futurity beyond the boundaries of 'this desolate isle'. The power of Tuke's metaphor lies in its readability: we know what it means to see the sun shining, to labour on the earth, and to reap a healthy harvest; and yet we do not know how to make it shine. Paradoxically, the inscrutability of God can be made visible through the caprice of nature, and, in this way, the earth's abundance performs both righteousness and profit, playing out a kind of divine approval at the point of its greatest obscurity. Absorbing the Christian into the mythological, Prospero secularizes this marriage as a ceremony of possession and reproduction marked by the landscape through which human endeavour has survived.[15] Allying himself with both the reapers and the goddesses, Prospero performs his magical power as a figure of creativity— summoning production, plenty, and a social world in which abundance secures prosperity. The play's masque is a recognition of the power of the land to inform social behaviour as well as to consolidate individual values, but, perhaps more subversively, it is also an image of control, cultivating allegiances under the auspice of profit.

The complex semantic relationship between faith and cultivation meant that metaphors of husbandry were at their most mobile in the context of Christianity. Devolving their authority from Genesis, images of husbandry became extremely powerful ways of representing civility as the human development of the earth. Yet blessing the landscape was a peculiarly English custom, which had roots in both Scripture and folklore: 'Gen. 1: 28 was ritually repeated as an incantation to cure infertile soil and animals. Together with the Lord's prayer, the generic prayer for healing rites, it was invoked in rituals to render soil fertile for grazing and

---

guilty, | Since nature cannot choose his origin'—the implications are fascinating. Always taken to mean mark or physical blemish, 'mole' could, of course, mean soil out of which nature is incapable of growing anything decent, condemning the body to corruption.

[15] Russ McDonald observes the play's interest in reproduction through the repetition of both image and diction: 'The tendency of words and phrases to repeat themselves may be linked to the play's profound concern with reproduction, in various senses from the biological to the political,' 'Reading *The Tempest*', 17.

harvesting.'[16] This compelling synthesis of Christianity and folklore rendered the human subject powerful through the ability to apparently intervene in the productivity of the earth. Such a socially cohesive event put the needs of the community at the forefront of their physical landscape and registered the necessity of both fertility and harvest in their socio-economic lives. Prospero's reproduction of these rituals through the figures of the goddesses focuses the economic attention on his daughter and Ferdinand rather than the landscape they inhabit. Prospero's project, of course, is to cultivate people rather than land, and fundamental to this cultivation is the decentring of the island's chorography.

The detailed vision that the goddesses create supports, albeit briefly, a context for the couple that the island cannot reproduce. The landscape is invoked to determine a set of social expectations, which are elaborately orchestrated through the fertility rituals of the land. According to Alexandra Walsham's exploration of the interrelationships between religious worship and landscape, Psalms 103 and 104 were often recited at Rogationtide 'to give thanks to God for the increase and abundance of the fruits of the earth'.[17] Rogationtide was a medieval ritual which took place during Ascension week in which members of parishes would beat the bounds, as a 'yearly perambulation of the community's uttermost limits and landmarks'.[18] Also a time for 'feasting and drinking', this ritual not only celebrated agrarian production as a communal need but it also imaginatively reinvented the parish boundary. But according to some of the most celebrated reformers, the ritual incantation of blessings on the earth approximated to magic and, perhaps worse, superstition.[19] In *The Tempest*, however, the masque of the goddesses willingly invokes this synthesis of magic, medievalism, and rural tradition in order to introduce the couple to a set of social expectations that the island profoundly lacks. Prospero's magic invites the characters into a long-held tradition in the church calendar in which the land—and its boundaries—mediates between the past and the future, gratitude and expectation.

The destabilization of the Church as the single place of worship that took place after the Reformation allowed the natural world to emerge as a more individualized space of ritual and spiritualism.[20] Within this con-

---

[16] Seed, *Ceremonies of Possession*, 34.   [17] *The Reformation of the Landscape*, 254.
[18] *The Reformation of the Landscape*, 252.
[19] Walsham cites William Tyndale in this context who 'complained of the superstitious assumptions that underpinned these "gang day" practices and condemned the reciting of scripture to "the corn in the field . . . that it should better grow"', *The Reformation of the Landscape*, 253.
[20] Walsham discusses the various ways in which sectarian faiths inhabited the landscape as a ritualistic space of worship. *The Reformation of the Landscape: Religion, Identity and*

text, nature remained a persistent force in the interpretation and manifestations of God, but it was not determined as an unimpeachable force of damnation or approval. Through a discourse of husbandry, however, culture could emerge as the art of nature: the productive rationalization of a hitherto unintelligible world. In these terms, culture emerges as the intelligent, developed, and rational interpretation of nature for human benefit: 'For the question of cultural recognition—of what counts as culture—is intimately connected to the question of what counts as belonging.'[21] Cultivation reproduces images of belonging precisely because it records the practices by which whole communities interact with their environment. Turning the natural into the supernatural we are encouraged from the outset to understand the play's environment as the supreme metamorphosis of nature into art. But this art points to the absence of landscape rather than an extension of it. This is not the art of Polixenes' nature which could change and mend organic forms of flora: Prospero's art is an altogether different form of human intervention in which the nature in question is that of human perception. Husbandry is the art of making nature culture.

The importance of 'beating the bounds' in Rogationtide stemmed from the necessities of neighbouring communities to determine their boundaries and therefore avoid any 'legal or tithe disputes'. The tradition through which these rituals grew up recognized the role of borders in both containing and protecting divided communities. In Iris's speech she invokes a boundary that has long been a thorn in *The Tempest* editor's side: the 'pioned and twilled brims' of Ceres' landscape refer to a man-made boundary, the hedge, which was used to enclose sheep, determine ownership, and protect grazed pasture from elemental assaults.

The act of enclosing is central to the image of the border, whether it takes place through a hedge or a fence. Thomas Thomas, in his Latin/English dictionary of 1587, defines an enclosure in the following terms:

A hedge . . . a mound, an inclosure. A hedge or fence of thorns, bushes, brambles. A hedge or fense of stakes and long poles lying overthwart, or of poles. A soldier or warlike fense: a rampier, a trench, a fense made with a ditch and a bank of earth.[22]

Iris's pioned and twilled brims refer to a process by which a ditch is dug (pioned) and then poles are laid (twilled) to form a hedge, but Thomas's definition alerts us to the multiple ways in which such borders performed:

Memory in Early Modern Britain and Ireland (Oxford: Oxford University Press, 2011), esp. 233–96.

[21] *The Reformation of the Landscape*, 164.
[22] *Dictionarium linguae Latinae et Anglicanae*.

a warlike fence, a trench, or a hedge, the boundary kept the human (and animal) both in and out. For the English, however, the hedge also had a uniquely symbolic role in the formation of the cultural landscape. Discussing the practices of English colonists abroad, Patricia Seed explains that 'From the fourteenth century onward, the fence or hedge acquired another significance as well: the principal symbol of not only ownership, but specifically private ownership of land.'[23] Because of the ways in which hedges were understood to both legitimize and represent possession they were employed extensively by English colonists to signify ownership.[24] The brims in Ceres's landscape symbolize both enclosure and possession, and in these ways they support an imaginative reconstruction of human intervention, 'agrarian logic', and contemporary history of possession and dispute. Within the 'desolate isle' of *The Tempest* they record a set of images that define social and economic communities.

Enclosures are a powerful example of the ways in which we can trace social history through the configurations of borders, their vestiges, and destructions. Despite their profound role in the history of economic change, enclosures generated a far more multifaceted debate than is often suggested.[25] They are divided into two grand phases; early enclosures, which cover the medieval and early modern periods; and parliamentary enclosures which cover the eighteenth and nineteenth centuries and culminate in, indeed precipitate, the agricultural and industrial revolutions.[26] The early enclosures of the sixteenth and seventeenth centuries were advanced by a number of factors; partly they were a continuation of the enclosures that took place after the dissolution of the monasteries and the dividing up of land owned by the Church, and partly they took place as a part of the growing initiatives towards improvement, the rise of the

[23] Seed, *Ceremonies of Possession*, 20, see also 20–5.

[24] *The Tempest* has been central to the development of post-colonial criticism over the last century, which I do not have the space to develop here. We might notice, however, that in the context of colonial practices abroad there were two fundamental actions in the establishing of both rights and ownership. One was to erect a dwelling and the other was to erect or establish a fence or hedge: the island on *The Tempest* is without either and is strikingly devoid of any intervention.

[25] McRae, in *God Speed the Plough*, 80–96, traces the various ways in which contemporary texts responded to enclosure measures in the early seventeenth century. James Seimon gives a strong sense of some of the prevailing attitudes of the period, 'Landlord not King', 21. Carroll, ' "The Nursery of Beggary" ', 34–47.

[26] Joan Thirsk's work on enclosures is formidable and provides the most consistent and thorough records that we have, beginning as she did by dividing England into farming regions, which provided a unique picture of the regional farming methods and communities of late medieval and early modern England. See 'Seventeenth-Century Agriculture and Social Change', *Agricultural History Review*, 18 (1970). See also Francis Pryor's very neat summation of a great body of history in *The Making of the British Landscape: How We Have Transformed the Land, from Prehistory to Today* (London: Allen Lane, 2010), esp. 380–98.

yeoman, and the breakdown of feudalism.[27] Enclosures came with a great deal of opportunity in the form of independent ownership, freedom from feudal ties and obligations, and having the right to control the management and farming of your land. They also came, however, with many problems; depopulation in the decay of houses of husbandry, eviction from farm dwellings, and the loss of work in the shift from arable to pasture, as well as the separation of the land from the yeoman's home. The competing claims for liberty and destruction that the enclosure signifies are constantly at work in the very language of its representation. The particular forms of enclosure, the hedge or fence, for example, alerts us to a form that attests to both a conflict and a resolution. In *Henry V*, decay was writ large in the image of prisoners like hedges, wild and mismanaged: as a symptom of 'unnaturalness', the unruly border presented Burgundy's France as vulnerable and disordered. Here in Iris's speech, however, these borders suggest an organic harmony, stability, and a system of production that is both efficient and beneficent.[28]

In these visual images the border serves as a representation of control and possession; above all suggesting a human logic to the organization of the land. Alongside the rituals of fertility and harvest, the demarcations of the land expose Prospero's masque as importing a specific set of social codes, which the young couple must observe. A testimony to the role of

[27] Edwin Gay is suspicious of any kind of generality in the discussion of enclosures, which he suggests gained steady momentum throughout the sixteenth century rather than in the peaks usually associated with changing religious and economic climate. He does, however, draw our attention to the various Acts of Husbandry and Tillage that took place (crucially under both Henry VII and Elizabeth I) in which to enclose without legal agreement was an offence and the rights of these acts lay markedly with the husbandman rather than the landowner. 'Inclosures in England', *Quarterly Journal of Economics*, 17/4 (August 1903), 576–97.

[28] Discussing Shakespeare's acquisition of land, Park Honan pieces this event from 'scraps of Shakespeare's talk' in Thomas Greene, 'a solicitor for the Stratford Corporation', *Diary*. Park Honan, *Shakespeare: A Life* (Oxford: Oxford University Press, 1998), 384. In 1602 Shakespeare had bought 107 acres of land in what was then known as Old Stratford. In the autumn of 1614 William Combe, the nephew of the newly deceased and 'richest soul' in Stratford John Combe, drew up plans to enclose the open fields in Old Stratford, Bishopton, and Welcombe. The council unanimously resisted the proposal and, in an effort to prevent any resulting violence, offered compensation to landowners, including Shakespeare, who would then stand to lose nothing if the land was enclosed. According to Thomas Greene, Shakespeare appeared comparatively sanguine about such measures; Greene coolly noted that 'they mean in April to survey the land, and then to give satisfaction and not before'. However, enclosure of the land in fact began in December: 'Out near Welcombe, to prepare for hedge-planting, Combe's men dug a trench which soon extended for "at least fifty perches", 275 yards.' At least 2 acres of Shakespeare's land (a representation 'of what Shakespeare had earned from a life's work') in 'leas or grassy strips' were 'lying in the Dyngyllis and about Welcome hilles' and 4 acres stretched 'between Welcome Church way and Bryneclose way' (Màiri Macdonald, 'A New Discovery about Shakespeare's Estate in Old Stratford', *Shakespeare Quarterly*, 45 (1994), 87–9).

human intervention in the landscape, Ceres' images define cultivation as a process of mediation between order and abundance, creation and control. Allying himself to such images Prospero defines his own mastery by association. Presiding over the dance of the seven reapers, we see Prospero as a creative force who can control the earth's retinue. Such images of mastery are, of course, fundamental to the human's dominion over nature. Although not necessarily oppressive, this relationship between the human and the natural world is central to the ways in which the husbandry manuals express the role of agricultural improvement in the economic sustainability of the commonwealth. Gervase Markham's *The Good Husbandman* (1613) declares from the outset that:

A husbandman is the Master of the earth, turning sterility and bareness, into fruitfulness and increase...whereby all commonwealths are maintained and upheld.[29]

Overseeing the dancing reapers and goddesses of 'foison and plenty', Prospero performs the role of the husbandman 'turning sterility and bareness into fruitfulness and increase'. Except, of course, he doesn't for he cannot make the transition from magus to master: for he is not 'Master of the earth' but 'master of a full poor cell' and it is not the earth he cultivates but his daughter. The gross failure in Prospero's system of control is highlighted by the frail 'fabric' of his illusion. Bereft of any systematic abilities to impose order or propagate development on the island, Prospero turns to magic to fabricate a set of social conditions through which we can identify success. Incapable of management—either here or in Milan—Prospero uses his art to simulate the social conditions of a sustainable world. His 'brave utensils' provide our only possible glimpse into his modes of operation. Defined by John Worlidge's *Systema Agriculturae* (1669) as 'Instruments used in any art, especially husbandry', the term utensil equivocally moves between the instruments of art and those of husbandry.[30] Whatever Prospero's books contain—and whatever his utensils may be—the only power they afford him is brief; unsustainable, and in this way he appears as a radically flawed husbandman and projector, incapable of building a commonwealth, only an illusion.

The questions of rule, government, or commonwealth that the play explores are persistently mediated through illusion. Where Prospero's magic manifests in the form of cultivation, Gonzalo's culture is devoid of intervention, depending on a self-creating nature that denies any relationship between the human and non-human world.

---

[29] Gervase Markham, *The Good Husbandman* (London, 1613), A3^{r-v}.

[30] John Wolridge, *Systema Agriculturae* (London, 1669), 13.

Like Prospero's goddesses, Gonzalo's vision appears at a dramatic moment of social crisis. As Prospero reaches for the occult, bereft of any social mechanisms with which to make the union between Miranda and Ferdinand meaningful, so Gonzalo, surrounded by competing ambitions of personal gain, reaches towards his own fantasy of social autonomy. Gonzalo's foray into the question of commonwealth appears to come from nowhere. In the middle of a somewhat fractious exchange between the shipwrecked men, Gonzalo is diverted into a reverie: 'Had I plantation of this isle, my lord' (2.1.141). Using the language of cultivation, Gonzalo imagines himself in a position of strategic development, which he identifies as one of agrarian improvement in the form, literally, of planting.[31] Gonzalo's attitude to development is strikingly at odds with Prospero's, who appears never to have 'planted' anything. Yet Antonio and Sebastian, perpetuating the barbed atmosphere, respond in such a way as to characterize Gonzalo as incapable of good husbandry. Suggesting a critical level of incompetence, the two men accuse him of sowing nettle seed, docks, or mallows. Casting Gonzalo's 'plantation' in the light of weeds renders him as apparently incapable of management or agrarian improvement. Touching on a 'public shorthand' for failure, the men invoke cultivation as an image of improvement. Suggesting a profound ignorance of the landscape, Sebastian and Antonio attempt to indict Gonzalo's character through his associations with bad husbandry. Although most husbandry manuals refer to these plants as weeds, Gervase Markham's *Farewell to Husbandry* identifies their presence as a marker of rich ground, ripe for plantation:

for that ground which though it beare not any extraordinary abundance of grasse, yet will loade it selfe with strong and lusty weedes, as Hemblocke, Docks, Mallowes, Nettles, Ketlocks, and such like, is vndoubtedly a most rich and fruitfull ground for any graine whatsoeuer. (7)

Significantly, rather than condemn this type of landscape as 'inimical to cultivation', Markham identifies its richness and fertility.[32] Gonzalo's failure is one of judgement: rather than identify these weeds as an indicator of fertile ground he 'sows' rather than ploughs them. Gonzalo's self-promotion to 'king' is set against Sebastian and Antonio's accusations of

---

[31] Cf. Edward Phillips's *New World of Words* (London, 1658), 273. It doesn't come into meaning as a noun until Kersey's dictionary of 1702, although Orgel notes that Gonzalo means 'to colonize' whereas Antonio and Sebastian take it in the sense of 'planting' (134 n. 141). It is very likely, however, that this is the meaning Gonzalo intended since this is how the word is glossed until the early eighteenth century. Cf. Speed, *Ceremonies of Possession*, who explains that the word 'plantation' comes from 'planting', which means to take possession, 29–32.

[32] See *The Tempest*, ed. Orgel, 134 n. 142.

bad management. Their amusement at Gonzalo's attitude to the island is reiterated through their vastly differing perspectives; where Gonzalo sees 'lush and lusty' grass, Antonio sees 'tawny' ground. Antonio thinks the island stinks, 'as 'twere perfumed by a fen', and Gonzalo perceives that 'Here is everything advantageous to life' (2.1.49–50). The competing perceptions of the place not only allow for the comedy to emerge in this scene but they also register the landscape as a perception: a construction of thought. Fundamental to this thought act is the subjective associations of hostility or empathy.

When Sebastian tells us that Gonzalo 'doth but mistake the truth totally' (2.1.57) we are encouraged to recognize the ways in which perceptual 'truths' operate within the play. The landscape will always be a construction of thought, a subjective truth, or an imposed illusion: any objectivity that we can wrest from these visions lies in their consensual implications for our social worlds. For most of the shipwrecked party, the island is a profoundly threatening environment, but for Gonzalo it promotes the possibility of autonomy through which he can fashion himself a king.[33] Despite Adrian's announcement that the island is a 'desert', 'uninhabitable, and almost inaccessible', Gonzalo persists in his construction of a socialized space through terms of apparent human liberty. Banning trade and institutionalized law, he goes on:

> Letters should not be known; riches, poverty,
> And use of service, none; contract, succession,
> Bourn, bound of land, tilth, vineyard, none;
> No use of metal, corn, or wine, or oil;
> No occupation, all men idle, all,
> And women too, but innocent and pure;
> No sovereignty—(2.1.148–54)

Gonzalo's commonwealth specifically erases the foundations upon which all such ideas of civilization have been built: letters, service, and cultivation. For Gonzalo they are socially divisive forms of individualism and oppression. His attention to commodities and labour rejects both work and acquisition as unhappy imperatives of a stratified society, in which the single goal is 'No occupation, all men idle, all.'[34] Such perceptions of

---

[33] Adrian is perhaps an equivocal exception, as someone who apprehends the place as 'uninhabitable, and almost inaccessible' but also capable of producing 'sweet' air (2.1.39, 47).

[34] In *The Ends of Life*, Keith Thomas explores seventeenth- and eighteenth-century attitudes to work, in which idleness and labour occupy equivocal moral positions. While idleness was a dangerous state of moral laxity, it was also a desired objective representing then, as now, a form of ease associated with wealth and status, see particularly 78–109.

labour are not utopian: More's Hythloday had declared nearly a century earlier that 'a carter, a smith, or a ploughman, [are] employed in labours so necessary, that no commonwealth could hold a year without them'. Equally perplexing is Gonzalo's self-promotion: presiding over a community of idle people would not sustain his monarchy; in fact, according to Xenophon, persuading people to 'take pleasure in their labour' is fundamental to a successful commonwealth:

The man who could stir up his labourers when they saw him had something of the disposition belonging to a king.[35]

In rejecting the models of authority and labour which most classical, agrarian, and humanist texts promoted, Gonzalo reveals himself to have no serious interest in either plantation or government. Foremostly he rejects the service and servitude upon which he believes social economic structures to have been built. Invoking idleness as the ideal state in which his community would live, however, was not without contention.[36] Frequently associated with the devil, idleness was condemned by all writings on husbandry, not only as an immoral state of being but antithetical to the production upon which life depended. Writing the first comprehensive text of husbandry in 1523 Fitzherbert warns the female:

That is to say | alway be doynge of some good warkes | that [the] deuyll may fynde the alway occupied for as in a standynge water are engendred wormes | ryght so in an ydle body are engendred ydle thoughtes. Here mayst thou se that of ydelnes cometh dampnaryon [damnation] | and of good warkes & labour cometh saluacion . . . Now thou wyfe | I trust to shewe to the dyuers occupacyons | warkes and labours that thou shalte not nede to be ydle no tyme of the yere. &c. (fo. clviii[r–v])

Labour and salvation are synthesized as similar exercises of spiritual and physical profit.[37] Fitzherbert speaks through a long tradition of Christian

---

[35] Thirsk, 'Making a Fresh Start', 20.

[36] Thomas Elyot, for example, in *The Blanket of Sapience* (1564) declares: 'Idleness without learning is death, & the grave of the quicke man', 31[v].

[37] Gervase Markham's *The English Housewife* (London, 1631), addresses the female as 'the mother and mistress of the family, . . . [who] hath her most general employments Within the house; where from the general example of her virtues, and the most approved skill of her knowledges, those of her family may both learn to serve God, and sustain man in that godly and profitable sort which is required of every Christian', 2. These attitudes to women are, of course, relative, and the fact that Markham even writes to a female within the domestic sphere marks him out from his predecessors, notably Fitzherbert who has one section, in his *Book of Husbandry*, on treating a woman like a horse: 'The fyrst is to be mery of chere | y[e] second to be well paced | the thyrde to haue a brode forehede | the fourth to haue brode buttocke| y^ fyfte to be harde of warde | the syxte to be asy to lepe vpon | the. vii. to be good at longe iourney | the. viii. to be wel sturrynge vnder a man | the. ix. to be alway

representations of labour, and these traditions were readily absorbed into the more secular writings of the seventeenth century in which it was widely accepted that without production you cannot create profit. Gonzalo's commonwealth is a febrile fantasy of status and economic freedom. Gonzalo does not address the moral issues he raises; instead he simply removes any incitements to anarchy—education and money—and relies on a common vision to produce a common wealth. But of course there is no common wealth; without riches, traffic, or poverty money becomes a redundant marker of success:

> All things in common nature should produce
> Without sweat or endeavour. Treason, felony,
> Sword, pike, knife, gun, or need of any engine
> Would I not have, but nature should bring forth
> Of it own kind all foison, all abundance
> To feed my innocent people. (2.1.157–62)

This 'foison' will later be reiterated by Iris in her equally illusory landscape of plenty reminding us of its moral endorsement of a thriving society. Yet in doing away with cultivation as well as weapons and tools, Gonzalo reveals a radically unstable environment which denies any form of individual improvement. Such a position was grossly at odds with prevailing attitudes to economic endeavour, in which labour and production defined moral and social worth. Gonzalo's 'common nature' recognizes the natural world as capable of sustaining human life without human intervention.[38] Such an idea would have been ludicrous and regressive in seventeenth-century politics, as well as blasphemous. As Elizabeth's Acts against the decaying of houses of husbandry reveal, cultivation is fundamental to 'the strength and flourishing estate of this kingdom'.[39] Human cultivation of the natural world defined and described a long history of both superiority and atonement: to denude the human of that was to deny him or her a place in the world; as Francis Bacon observed in a House of Commons debate about the repeal of enclosure statutes in 1601, 'the husbandman is

---

besy with the mouthe | the. x. euer to be chowynge on the brydell' (fo. xxxiiv). I explore the question of women and husbandry in my chapter on *Macbeth*.

[38] 'All things in common' echoes Cade's rebellion—'all the realm shall be in common' (*2 Henry VI*, 4.2.66)—and is, within these terms, a dubious call to edenic living since, as William C. Carroll observes: 'Ironically, the same Tudor authorities who passed laws restricting enclosures in an attempt to preserve common fields and wastes and reduce the numbers of displaced poor were at the same time frightened of the idea that *all* things should be in common,' '"The Nursery of Beggary"', 42.

[39] 39 & 40 Elizabeth Cap. II.

a strong and hardy man, the good footman'.[40] Throughout the husbandry manual, labour emerges as a form of 'correction' or 'amendment' by which the gentleman intervenes in an imperfect world: 'the diligence of the Farmer may by his industrie ouercome the weaknesse of a ground, euen as well as all sorts of wild Beasts may be tamed by the painefulnesse of man.'[41] To work is to 'overcome', to 'tame', and to display 'industry'.

Gonzalo's imaginary 'plantation' is a source of comedy within the play: it defines him as self-aggrandizing and delusional and we are never required by the drama to take it seriously. As he himself admits, 'who in this kind of merry fooling am nothing to you. So you may continue, and laugh at nothing still' (2.1.175–6). Yet the long-standing critical attention to this speech is almost wholly sustained by the parallels with Montaigne's essay 'On Cannibals'. Re-telling the story of the Tupinamba Indians of Brazil, he explains:

They are even savage, as we call those fruites wilde, which nature of hir selfe, and of hir ordinarie progresse hath produced: where as indeede, they are those which our selves have altered by our artificiall divises, and diverted from their common order, we should rather terme savage. In those are the true and most profitable vertues, and naturall properties most lively and vigorous, which in these we have bastardized, applying them to the pleasure of our corrupted taste. And if notwithstanding, in divers fruites of those countries that were never tilled, we shall finde, that in respect of ours they are most excellent, and as delicate vnto our taste; there is no reason, arte should gaine the point of honour of our great and puissant mother Nature. We have so much by our inventions, surcharged the beauties and riches of her workes, that we have altogether over-choaked her: yet where ever her puritie shineth, she makes our vaine, and frivolous enterprises woonderfully ashamed. (p. 103)[42]

Montaigne focuses on a vision of 'our great and puissant mother Nature', which is uninterrupted by human 'invention'. For Montaigne, nature reflects a set of essential, uncorrupted, qualities which are by their freedom from human intervention inherently superior. Indicting human 'frivolity', greed, and senseless industry, Montaigne calls for a re-evaluation of the ethical superiority of art: 'there is no reason, arte should gaine the point of honour.' For Montaigne, nature prompts an ethical interrogation into the

---

[40] A. E. Bland, P. A. Brown, and R. H. Tawney, *English Economic History: Select Documents* (London, 1914), 274. Cf. Thirsk, 'Making a Fresh Start', 21.

[41] Estienne, *The Countrey Farme*, 10. See also 5.

[42] Michel de Montaigne, *Essays vvritten in French by Michael Lord of Montaigne, Knight of the Order of S. Michael, gentleman of the French Kings chamber: done into English, according to the last French edition, by Iohn Florio reader of the Italian tongue vnto the Soueraigne Maiestie of Anna, Queene of England, Scotland, France and Ireland, &c. And one of the gentlemen of hir royall priuie chamber* (London, 1613).

values of human enterprise. Unlike Gonzalo, however, Montaigne's interest is not in producing a society of perpetual ease but in identifying the ethical imperatives of human intervention. Industry promotes acquisition and acquisition promotes greed. Montaigne's warnings are not idealistic but point to a very real—and contemporary focus—on the ethical limits of human intervention.[43]

The complex ethical networks that inform such debates are constantly at work in the language of the husbandry manual. Reynolde Scot, for example, in his *Perfite platforme of a Hoppe Garden* (1574), condemns the man who 'placeth his private profite before common humanitie, to erect unto himselfe and his posteritie, a kingdom of vanitie and ydlenesse'.[44] Scot's comment exposes the moral ambiguity of 'ydlenesse'; where for Gonzalo it is freedom, for Scot it is anti-social individualism. Yet almost all texts promoting the development of the commonwealth, pursue public labour as the marker of moral worth:

that a noble and worthy personage adourned in dede with heroical vertues, brenneth with a certaine wonderfull desyre and luste, to further yᵉ comon weale, with whiche desyre beyng pricked and inwardly, tickeled he valiautly ventureth vpon most hyghe and ieoperdous maters, nought regardyng his owne priuate weale, but his countreys vtilitie and benefite.[45]

The history of emphasis on public gain, rather than 'private weale', is largely what informed anxieties about the rise of projectors in the seventeenth century. Increasingly viewed as self-interested, these figures evinced an attitude to agrarian development that paid less regard to the economic lives of wage earners and more to their personal pockets. In this way, the ethics of human intervention became less allied to Christian models of charity and labour and increasingly defined by market prices.

The play's invocation of two alternative social landscapes in Prospero's masque and Gonzalo's kingdom look to nature as the source of culture.

---

[43] The projector was one of the central figures in ethical debates between intervention and exploitation. A frequent subject of discussion, the rise of the projector coincided with the opportunities for overseas development, trade monopolies, and the expansion of the agricultural market as well as urban centres of exchange. Whilst projects were encouraged to boost the economy they were also derided as examples of opportunism and exploitation. Questioning the prevailing assumption that early modern entrepreneurialism was associated with greed and individualism, Craig Muldrew's *The Economy of Obligation: The Culture of Credit and Social Relations in Early Modern England* (Basingstoke: Palgrave, 1998) explores a more civic understanding of credit and exchange. Jennifer Richards, however, in *Rhetoric and Courtliness* builds on Muldrew's work through her nuanced readings of the language of commerce, and the multiple ways in which *utilitas* (profit) and *honestas* (truth) can be used in the market place; see, particularly, chapter 4.

[44] As quoted by McRae, *God Speed the Plough*, 151.

[45] Richard Tavener, *The second Book of the Garden of Wisdom* (London, 1542), fo. 3ʳ.

For Prospero, the cultivated landscape supports an institutional framework of production and order; for Gonzalo, freedom from industry 'promotes a deregulation of state intervention in the promotion of leisure and idleness'. Both visions supply the play with an imaginative reconstruction of value through which profit and sociability can be defined. As David Norbrook suggests, 'every figure on the island has some kind of vision of a society that would transcend existing codes and signs'.[46] Cultivation is central to the reconstruction of these social visions precisely because it depends upon the imaginative rehabilitation of socio-economic codes. Increasingly, art or cultivation was construed through an empirical attitude which supported agrarian development as a form of human reason so that Gonzalo's utopian vision represents him as not only unethical but delusional. The status of the human becomes intricately bound to their attitudes to cultivation. William Lawson's preface to his *New Orchard and Garden* makes a compelling statement on the value of 'art':

Art reformeth, being taught by experience and therefore must we count that Art the surest, that stands vpon experimentall rules, gathered by the rule of reason (not conceit) of all other rules the surest.

No longer supported by an allegorical context of Christian duty, cultivation emerges as a progressive rationale in support of human development. Explaining that gardens and orchards make us 'happy', Lawson goes on to justify his subject in grand terms:

Husbandry maintaines the world; how ancient, how, profitable, how pleasant it is, how many secrets of nature it doth containe, how loued, how much practised in the best places, and of the best.[47]

The 'best places' of *The Tempest* are mediated through Prospero's magic, referring us to a recognizable space of human value. Within the terms of the husbandry manual and England's rapidly increasing investment in improvement, Gonzalo's plantation appears as anything but ideal. Yet central to the foregrounding of these imaginative reconstructions of culture is the nature of the island itself. When Alonso, returning to his full consciousness after Prospero's spell, remarks, 'These are not natural events, they strengthen, | From strange to stranger' (5.1.227–8), we might assume that the natural emerges as an antithesis to the supernatural, or the

---

[46] '"What care these roarers for the name of king?" Language and Utopia in *The Tempest*', in J. Hope and G. McMullan (eds.), *The Politics of Tragicomedy: Shakespeare and After* (London: Routledge, 1992), 159.
[47] Lawson, *A New Orchard and Garden* (London, 1618), A3ʳ, A3ᵛ.

irrational. Attempting to orientate himself within this experience, however, Alonso goes on to observe:

> This is as strange a maze as e'er men trod,
> And there is in this business more than nature
> Was ever conduct of. (5.1.242–4)

For Alonso, nature is a commander of rational knowledge in which the material world provides ontological orientation through its apparent structures of familiarity.[48] In this way, nature joins the human to the non-human world, supporting a feeling of belonging; but it is from this sense of belonging that Alonso feels excluded: it is strange. This sense of estrangement is part of the island experience where the absence of a familiar nature severs the characters from their rational, and social, selves. From the outset Alonso expresses his sense of anxiety through an alienation from nature, and from the ways in which nature represents a familiar human experience. Focusing on one of the few topographical details of the island, Alonso conflates his subjective experience with the physically confusing 'maze'. It is not clear whether Alonso's maze is figurative or organic, whether he refers to the labyrinthine structure that Gonzalo appeared to notice earlier (3.3.2) or whether he speaks of his own delirium. The instability of the image, however, is revealing since it evokes the play's wider commitment to nature as a structure of either belonging or alienation. In its literal sense a maze is a carefully arranged structure, comprising conflicting paths, of which only one provides the 'correct' route out. Both ornamental and entertaining, the maze appears to have been a feature of the English landscape since the fourteenth century.[49] The value of the image, however, in whatever form it appears within the play, lies in its representation of disenfranchisement. The play's interest in conditions of bondage is partly evinced in the fabric of the island itself, as its apparently hostile environment subjects the shipwrecked party to feelings of confusion, loss, and anxiety. The maze represents this synthesis of physical and emotional environment: a perfect example of natural artifice, the maze imposes sensory disruption through its physical inter-

---

[48] The relationship between the subject and object is a fundamental concern of early modern literary criticism and has been widely influenced by the philosophy of science as well as anthropology. See particularly Ann Rosalind Jones and Peter Stallybrass, 'Fetishizing the Glove in Renaissance Europe', in Bill Brown (ed.), *Things* (Chicago: University of Chicago Press, 2004); Margreta de Grazia, Maureen Quilligan, and Peter Stallybrass (eds.), *Subject and Object in Renaissance Culture* (Cambridge: Cambridge University Press, 1996); Henry S. Turner (ed.), *The Culture of Capital: Property, Cities and Knowledge in Early Modern England* (New York: Routledge, 2002).

[49] The *OED* cites the first use in this context in Chaucer's *Legend of Good Women c.*1430 (1386).

ruption of space. Using nature as a method of orientation, the play-world both fragments and restructures its physical environment in order to alienate or include the individual.

The storm that begins the play is, we later discover, part of Prospero's grand 'project', and like every successful projector he has to know when to make a fortuitous moment his own:

> I find my zenith doth depend upon
> A most auspicious star, whose influence
> If now I court not, but omit, my fortunes
> Will ever after droop (1.2.181–4).[50]

Prospero's application to the arcane workings of the celestial spheres sets the context of his project in motion. Invoking the workings of a nature beyond the capabilities of the stage, Prospero represents himself as instrumental in the play's transformation of nature into art. The power of this art, however, lies in its ability to exploit nature as a socially affective tool. In the midst of the storm, Gonzalo exclaims:

Now would I give a thousand furlongs of sea for an acre of barren ground – long heath, brown furze, anything. (1.1.66–8)

As they approach such an acre of barren ground the irony of Gonzalo's wish becomes clear: this barren ground will offer him little relief, only bare life. Identifying the land as the province of the human, however, Gonzalo reaches for an environment of survival. Apparently facing a death by drowning, Gonzalo asks for little more than dry land in his plea, but the specificity of this landscape anticipates the hostility of the island. The juxtaposition here between an unruly elemental nature and a secure form of human habitation is thrown into relief by Gonzalo's comment. Primitive and basic, nature records the difference between life and death; as the play develops, however, those differences become complicated by fantasies of living. Inflicting nature upon the humans as a form of art elucidates the role that human intervention will play in the construction of their various realities.

The chorography of the island is notoriously imprecise. We are never given a comprehensive picture of the landscape, only brief references to certain features: there are 'toothed briars, sharp furzes, pricking gorse, and thorns', a 'filthy-mantled pool', some 'brine-pits' as well as 'fresh springs', and a 'maze trod indeed | Through forth-rights and meanders'. Until the

---

[50] Peter Hulme reads this storm as a hurricane within the context of the Bermuda pamphlets. See 'Hurricanes in the Caribbees: The Constitution of the Discourse of English Colonialism', in Frances Barker et al. (eds.), *Literature and Power in the Seventeenth Century* (Colchester: University of Essex, 1981), 55–83.

shipwrecked party arrive there are only three people and a spirit on the island, so we can assume that it is small if these paths have been so well trodden by so few. Apart from these spare details we are told that the island is 'barren' and 'almost uninhabitable'. Prospero is without a house, according to Caliban, and despite the odd references to fertility, there seems little to eat except 'pignuts' and 'marmosets'. Despite the occasional diverting detail, the island remains generally free from human intervention.[51] Ariel refers to 'this most desolate isle' (3.3.80), Trinculo observes an unenclosed landscape—'Here's neither bush nor shrub to bear off any weather at all' (2.2.18–19)—and Caliban registers some capacity for cultivation as the only character who refers to its fertility, claiming that he showed Prospero both 'barren place and fertile' (1.2.338). Later, attempting to ingratiate himself to Stephano and Trinculo, he will again refer to 'every fertile inch of the island' (2.2.141). Locating this potential fertility seems to be one of Caliban's major assets and yet in both instances we are informed of it fails to produce anything beyond subsistence. Against this apparently hostile landscape, however, the language of production emerges as a discourse of both potential and improvement. Suggesting that 'hereditary sloth' prevents him from usurping Alonso, Sebastian observes his future—and his self—as impoverished without intervention. Antonio, however, spurring his friend, declares:

> O!,
> But if you but knew how you the purpose cherish
> Whiles thus you mock it, how in stripping it
> You more invest it—(2.1.221–4)

Employing the language of cultivation, Antonio refers his companion to a process of pruning which encourages growth. Stripping a plant or tree of its leaves or branches not only supports new growth but in a striking parallel with Antonio's import, it also reflects an act of regeneration or 'transplanting'. Charles Estienne, on the subject of transplanting fruit trees, writes:

> breake off the points of their roots, and strip them of all their branches, before you set them downe againe in their new appointed standing: and know, that a double remoue doth make the wild to become free conditioned and better, bringing vnto them great aduantage. (338)

As Estienne suggests, 'stripping' conditions the 'wild' and proves advantageous to growth. Stephano picks up on Antonio's language of cultivation

---

[51] See Marienstras, *New Perspectives of the Shakespearean World*, for a discussion of 'ideology' and fertility in *The Tempest*.

in his observation of the Duke's own ability to 'yield'. But where for these men terms of cultivation reflect acts of personal growth and private advantage, Prospero's rendition of such ambition is distinctly at odds with good husbandry. Describing to Miranda the history of their exile, Prospero recognizes himself as the tree to his brother's destruction:

> . . . he was
> The ivy which had hid my princely trunk,
> And sucked my verdure out on't. (1.2.85–6)

The image of usurpation associated with the power of ivy to grow parasitically supports Prospero's representation of the competing values of these natural images. Prospero, the 'princely trunk', and Antonio, the sucking ivy, represent this deposition as a violation of nature in which the noble species is depleted by the ignoble. Good husbandry would, of course, prevent such an event from taking place since human intervention would remove the ivy. Prospero presents himself as a passive victim of contamination through an image which is both allegorical and practical. Although Tusser warns of the dangers of ivy, it was also a useful plant, if well managed, in the preparation of medicinal remedies.[52] In religious texts, however, ivy had entered the moral imagination in precisely the ways that Prospero invokes. Thomas Tuke, in *The picture of a true protestant, or God's house of husbandry*, uses the image of the ivy to describe the necessity of righteousness in preachers of the Protestant faith:

If Ministers be profane themselues, who like *rootes* should conuey piet[y] to the people, what can bee exspected at their hands besides profanenesse and Atheisme, vnlesse God in mercy do restraine, and guide them? For the wickednesse of Ministers (is *serpens malum*) doth creepe like *Iuy,* and spread like a *leprosie,* and is as pestilent and infectious as the *Plague*.[53]

The moral implications of Tuke's ivy are clearly present in Prospero's image of his brother's behaviour. Tuke's minister represents righteousness at both a social and personal level; contaminate him and the whole community suffers. Despite Prospero's own failings as a duke, he looks to his brother for the language of bad management, and makes quite clear the wider implications of his usurpation. Against the sterile landscape of the island, such images of management and growth are thrown into relief, providing subjective commentaries on the relative successes of their social

---

[52] Of the most popular husbandry manuals, it is only Tusser's *Five Hundred Points of Good Husbandry* that mentions ivy as a threat to the health of trees. In May, he advises 'Let ivy be killed | Or tree will be spilled.'

[53] Tuke, *The picture of a true protestant*, 38.

worlds.[54] Good or bad husbandry provides a collective discourse through which individual ambitions can be measured. Set against the terms of his usurpation, Prospero inhabits the island as a temporary space, redefining the terms of human intervention, deploying his investment in the island as a site of moral, rather than agrarian, production. Ultimately, however, in order to fix the terms of social justice through which the play moves, it must invoke the kind of agrarian nature of which the island is bare. Only by importing a recognizable landscape of social relations— labour, profit, production—can the play test the solidity of its moral world.

The practices and effects of human intervention are central to the ways in which the natural world can be reconstructed as cultural. The sense of bondage imposed by the hostility of the island is amplified by the play's investment in systems of both labour and freedom. Yet central to the ideology of the husbandry manual was emancipation and the development of skills that could lead from subsistence to sustainability. Having summarized the key moments in the agricultural year, Estienne writes:

> Thus our Husbandman, according to the opinion of *Oliver de Serres,* hauing enriched his memorie with these knowledges, shall liue a Free man, and no Bondslaue, a Master, and no Prentice, to his Farmer or Baylie.

To be a 'free man' is to be 'master'. Estienne cites the authority of de Serres, a highly respected French agriculturalist, to reinforce his point that knowledge of the land is also its control: the 'Royaltie and Chiefetie of the whole'.[55] Yet for the islanders of *The Tempest,* such control will always elude them. Despite Caliban's claim for 'every fertile inch o' the' island', it is never described again as such. For Ariel it is a 'most desolate isle' (3.3.80), to Adrian it is a 'desert' and 'almost inaccessible' (2.1.36, 39), and to Antonio it is without 'means to live' (2.1.51). Freedom is impossible, according to Estienne and de Serres, without cultivation. Within these terms, Gonzalo's fantasy of having the 'Royaltie and Chiefetie of the whole world' is radically flawed: bereft of the human structures of cultivation he will never be free or masterful. For Caliban, on the other hand, freedom is a social contract in which service fosters a collective ambition. Having shown Prospero 'every fertile inch o th'isle', and laboured in the collecting of wood, Caliban appears to represent the values of husbandry,

---

[54] Employing potent terms within the context of my argument here, Stephen Greenblatt's essay 'The Cultivation of Anxiety' explores the way in which, for example, Edgar can cultivate fear in the Dover Cliff scene, in order to also alleviate it, 92–124. In Greenblatt's terms cultivation becomes a powerful metaphor for the exploration of power relations.

[55] Estienne, *The Countrey Farme,* 20, 21.

but without the attendant rewards. In this way, labour becomes the single most powerful expression of Prospero's transformation of nature into art. When Caliban sings his song of celebration, he reproduces a relationship between liberty and labour that is dependent on service:

> 'Ban, 'Ban Ca-Caliban,
> Has a new master—get a new man!
> Freedom, high-day! High-day, freedom! Freedom, high-day! (2.2.179–80)

Just how Caliban construes his new freedom is unclear, as is the state of freedom itself.[56] Only Ariel comes close to the fantasy of complete freedom, as we imagine the spirit's journey from the cloven pine, through Prospero's service, to the boundless passage of the air. But for the mortal bodies on this island, labour is a requisite for the movement between the natural and human worlds. In the absence of any kind of formal structure of government, Prospero uses his art to impose labour as a condition of bondage.

Ideas of labour are largely produced through the performance of wood or stick bearing. Dramatized for the display of physical endurance, overseeing the collecting of wood is an apparently fundamental part of Prospero's authority. When Caliban imagines the possibility of defying the magus, he reveals his relief in these terms:

> A plague upon the tyrant that I serve!
> I'll bear him no more sticks, but follow thee,
> Thou wondrous man. (2.2.156–8)

Caliban repeatedly returns to this issue of fetching wood as a mark of his servitude. When such an image, however, is reproduced by Ferdinand it is as a test of both his commitment and suitability. Although labour acquired a social value through the terms of production associated with both profit and reward, authority was dependent upon the delegation of duties, as Heresbach states:

> To euery man his taske I doo assigne,
> VVhen this is doone I get me to my booke.[57]

Heresbach's instructions afford the husbandman the power of both delegation and knowledge. The forms of nature upon which Prospero depends demand a physical articulation of labour in servitude. Like Heresbach's husbandman, Prospero too assigns his task and retires to his books. But the power of his role emerges in the way he oversees or supervises his

---

[56] See also Bate, 'The Humanist Tempest'.   [57] *Foure Bookes of Husbandrie*, 3ʳ.

labourers. Immediately after Caliban has rejected this office we see Ferdinand '*Enter . . . bearing a log*':

> There be some sports are painful, and their labour
> Delight in them set off; some kinds of baseness
> Are nobly undergone; and most poor matters
> Point to rich ends. (3.1.1–4)

In anticipation of profit, Ferdinand appropriates his labour as a form of pleasure. Defining service according to the ethical attitudes with which it is performed, Ferdinand introduces certain criteria through which actions can be both performed and judged. The 'rich ends' to which he looks identify Miranda as the profit of his labour and return us once again to the human as the object of cultivation. In taking pleasure in his task, Ferdinand invokes one of the fundamental precepts of humanism and husbandry. The relationship between *utilitas* and *voluptas* was central to almost all forms of education (spiritual, practical, and ethical) since it assumed a moral relationship between labour and reward. Ferdinand spiritualizes the relationship between poverty and richness in his labours of love.[58] Yet as we see him 'work'—'My sweet mistress | Weeps when she sees me work, and says such baseness | Had never like executor' (3.1.11–13)—we are reminded of the competing moral discourses that labour produces. Through Miranda's tears and his unique position— 'never the like executor'—Ferdinand separates himself from the implications of this service. Caliban's labour, on the other hand, is akin to punishment (where Ferdinand's is to profit) so that forms of human cultivation re-emerge as moral exercises:

> But as 'tis,
> We cannot miss him. He does make our fire,
> Fetch in our wood, and serves in offices
> That profit us. What, ho, slave! Caliban!
> Thou earth, thou, speak! (1.2.310–14)

The 'profit' that Prospero refers to supports his fantasy of authority, in which service reproduces a form of moral control.[59] Prospero once again fulfils his role as the human cultivator, discriminating between his labourers and keeping an eye on his own ends:

[58] See William Rockett, 'Labour and Virtue in *The Tempest*', *Shakespeare Quarterly*, 24/ 1 (Winter 1973), 77–84.

[59] See Thirsk, *Economic Policy and Projects*, esp. 133–57, Appleby, *Economic Thought and Ideology*, and also Barbara Anne Sebeck's essay 'People, Profiting and Pleasure in *The Tempest*', in Patrick Murphy (ed.), *The Tempest: Critical Essays* (London: Routledge, 2001), 473.

For there are but few, either Hindes [farm-hands], day-Labourers, or Labourers by great, which doe not loue their Masters profit a great deale lese than their owne, and euery day are behind hand in one dutie, or piece of worke or other, which ought to haue beene done.[60]

The image of the lagging labourer who cares less for his master's profit than his own supports the role of the master as one of vigilance and surveillance. Prospero's command over the action that takes place on the island presents him within this context of authority: watching, noting, and ever ready to admonish.

Prospero's project relies on importing forms of cultivation associated with the terms of social contract: marriage, service, and profit require him to invest the imaginative space of the island with a comprehensive vision of human order. Without the requisite landscape upon which to build such an order, Prospero fabricates the images through which we recognize social and economic value. The thwarted husbandman, Prospero invests in the islanders as a form of cultivation 'turning sterility and bareness into fruitfulness and increase'. Having failed to develop Caliban—'A devil, a born devil on whose nature | Nurture can never stick'—Prospero turns his project to Antonio and his companions:

> The rarer action is
> In virtue than in vengeance. They being penitent,
> The sole drift of my purpose doth extend
> Not a frown further. (5.1.27–30)

Transforming sin into penitence, isolation into marriage, and resentment to grace, Prospero's project is complete. Under the play-world's conditions of morality, Prospero appears as the successful projector; or good husbandman. Cultivating nature through art, Prospero invokes an illusory social fabric for the pursuit of his vision. Since the island is barren, bare, and sterile Prospero manifests nature as art. Within this context, husbandry provides a powerful discourse for the interpretation and explication of these ideas. Transformative in itself, the art of husbandry celebrates the role of intervention in the social and economic framework of human life. As Markham suggested, to turn barrenness into fertility is mastery indeed. Prospero disports himself according to conditions of cultivation and the ways in which these conditions not only represent forms of authority but also correspond to a set of moral codes deeply embedded in the development of the husbandry manuals. While Markham speaks through a slow secularization of the relationship between profit and social

---

[60] Estienne, *The Countrey Farme*, 15.

worth, John Fitzherbert's *Boke of Husbandrie* folds great tracts of spiritual admonition into his agrarian advice:

And therfore it is conuenyent that a manne shulde be penytent, contryte, and aske god mercye and forgyuenesse of his synnes and offences that he hath done, wherof speketh Chrysostme, *Nemo ad deum aliquando flens accessit quod non postulauerit accepst.*[61]

These lines mark the end of Fitzherbert's text and follow on from a section on charity and the giving of alms. Written for a 'yong gentyll man that intendeth to thrive' so it ends as a moral reminder of the relationship between penitence, contrition, and mercy.[62] Thriving, cultivating, and husbandry move well beyond the landscape and into the spiritual hearts of the Christian man or woman. The penitence that Prospero seeks from the travellers is intricately tied to his moral husbandry, as are the transformative powers of cultivation itself. William Jackson's sermon *Celestial Husbandrie* elucidates the semantic relationships between tillage and grace:

Plow vp your fallow ground. The difference betweene the English and the Originall is this: For our *fallow ground* in the English, the Originall hath *it new fallow:* For so the word *niru* doth import: And likewise the vulgar Latine hath it, *innouate, renew yee:* for the minde is to be altered and changed: And this doth fitly agree with the word...which importeth properly *a change of the minde,* or *vnderstanding.*[63]

Exploring the word 'fallow' and 'plow' through ideas of renewal in both Greek and Latin, Jackson draws together the senses in which these terms suggest 'a change of the mind, or understanding'. For Prospero, cultivation supports such a change of mind: a change that he construes as penitence. In this way, cultivation becomes a profound discourse for social emotion: cohesive, directive, and judgemental, it supports a set of human relations upon which both success and deliverance depend.

Pursuing a set of socially acceptable goals—grace, repentance, unity— Prospero turns to his art as a reactionary form of human intervention. The logic of this intervention is predicated on an ability to use nature as a cultural tool: imposing order, enforcing labour, constructing ceremony, and manipulating morality, forms of cultivation emerge as socially coherent impulses. Gonzalo's commonwealth, on the other hand, which disposes of all government and office, appears as a comic failure, in which

---

[61] *The Boke of Husbandrie* (2nd edn. 1540), 89ᵛ.
[62] This is included in the 2nd edition of 1540, 57ʳ.   [63] London, 1616, 58.

nature stands in service to idle men and women. Prospero's instructions to labour, his intervention in the elemental world as a form of punishment, and his sacralization of marriage through conditions of order and profit enable him to expose the islanders to forms of moral control.[64] One of the persistent problems, however, with any critical analysis of this play, is the profound suspension of the magic upon which it depends. Necessarily dramatic, Prospero reveals his art, like the theatre itself, to be subjective, consensual, and formative. Ceremonially abjuring his rough magic or drowning his books, Prospero shows such stuff to be the brief symbols of an ontological fantasy.

After the masque has performed its sacramental role in the unification of the young couple, Prospero disposes of the goddesses, telling a puzzled Ferdinand:

> The cloud-capped towers, the gorgeous palaces,
> The solemn temples...
>   ...shall dissolve,
> And, like this insubstantial pageant faded,
> Leave not a rack behind. (4.1.152–6)

The architecture that Prospero conjures through this simile is nothing that we have seen on stage: rather, distinct from the masque, it takes root in our imaginations as a collective—and always subjective—visualization of past, as well as possible, realities. Such towers and palaces are the buildings of their pasts, their imaginations, and not the images they have just witnessed. Recalling the cities of their minds, Prospero makes an analogy between illusion and reality in which one form is no more stable than the other. Mortality takes the place of magic, exposing the extent to which death and delusion affect all human life. But the vivid demolition of the human landscape is an attempt to reassure the young prince of the inexorable pace of life and death, pleasure and destruction. We should, he suggests, be no more afraid of our dreams dissolving than the substantial structures of the human world. The interface between human creation and human destruction is not, perhaps, as arcane as it might seem. Referring to the riots that took place in London after certain areas, including Shoreditch, were enclosed by hedges, John Stow writes:

---

[64] The critical relationship between God and Prospero is, as yet, under-developed though often observed, but is especially fascinating for Shakespeare scholars who perceive the author as essentially secular. See Charles Downing, *The Messiahship of Shakespeare* (London: Greening, 1901), 51. Robert Grainger's eschatological text *Prospero's Island: Navigating Pastoral Care* (Victoria, BC: Trafford, 2010) reads the play, alongside islands more generally, as a journey to self-knowledge and the value of community.

all the hedges about the City were cast downe, and the ditches filled up, and every thing made plaine; such was the diligence of those worke-men.

Destroying the newly created partitions of common-land, the rioters diligently 'make plaine' the human markers that oppress them. Although the success of their rioting meant that 'those fields were never hedged':

> But afterward wee saw the thing in worse case than ever, by meanes of inclosure for Gardens, wherein are builded many faire Summer houses, and as in other places of the suburbes, some of them like Midsummer Pageants, with Towers, Turrets, and Chimney tops, not so much for use or profit, as for shew and pleasure, and bewraying the vanity of mens mindes, much unlike to the disposition of the ancient Citizens, who delighted in the building of Hospitals, and Almes-houses for the poore, and therein both imployed their wits, and spent their wealths in preferment of the common commoditie of this our City.[65]

'Worse' than enclosures, the fields were bought up for gardens and filled with summer houses. Unprofitable constructions, devised exclusively for 'shew and pleasure', these erections resembled the stuff of vanity, 'like Midsummer pageants, with Towers, Turrets and Chimney tops'. Stow's moral indictment emerges through a critical comparison between architecture and cultivation: the social conscience has dropped from the city's view as hospitals and almshouses are replaced by private extravagance. Here, however, Stow is echoing Heresbach who similarly claimed that, according to Varro, 'there was great complaint made, that the Fathers forsaking the Plough and the Sicle, began to creepe into the Towne, and busied them selues rather with Pageantes and Midsommer games, then with the Uineyard or the Feeld'.[66] Varro, Heresbach, and Stow record the moral decay of their social lives through the discourse of the pageant and the field. Stow's description of London is remarkably similar to Prospero's discourse on the ephemeral nature of life. Human intervention, whether through agrarian cultivation or architecture, records the moral value of our social lives. For Prospero these values are always in transition—evocative, discursive, sacramental, or punitive—the inhabited landscape records the socially powerful relations of human lives. Gonzalo's commonwealth, bereft of such intervention, labour, or habitation, registers the absence of any moral fabric. Invested in 'innocence' but sustained by idleness, his plantation is a testimony to his own delusions.

---

[65] John Stow, *The Survey of London* (London, 1633), 476.
[66] Heresbach, *Foure Bookes of Husbandrie* (1577), 7 ʳ⁻ᵛ.

7

Conclusion

Man comes and tills the field and lies beneath. (Tennyson, *Timothus*)

Shakespeare wasn't a farmer: he was a landlord. In 1602 he purchased 107 acres of open fields in Old Stratford. Lying in nineteen scattered strips of land, these furlongs lay in and around the north and east of the town. The purchase of his land—for the substantial sum of £320—has fascinated Shakespeare's biographers, since it seems to mark the playwright's 'return' to the country, or at least record some investment in it.[1] According to a document in 1625, Shakespeare bequeathed 'the said land with his daughter in marriage to Mr Hall of Stratford', in 1607. In 1605 Shakespeare bought half-shares in the town's Corporation tithes which included both arable and pasture land, and amounted, according to Park Honan, to about one fifth of the whole. Shakespeare left the husbandry to Anthony Nashe, whose father had farmed the land previously.[2] Various elements of this purchase, and subsequent settlement on Susanna, have troubled scholars: did Shakespeare, as was usual, retain a life interest in this land; and why did he invest his money in Stratford, rather than London? For Graham Holderness: 'Shakespeare's property dealings all partake of the rather sour mundanity of this grudging return to the provinces.'[3] The 'sour mundanity' that Holderness observes manifests in relation to a specific moment in Shakespeare's later years. In 1614 William Combe, from whom Shakespeare had bought land in 1602, attempted to enclose large areas of arable land around Stratford, including some of Shakespeare's. The town council, which included Shakespeare's 'cousin',

---

[1] Wells describes the late years of Shakespeare's life within these terms: 'Shakespeare was a rich man, a householder and a landowner, possessed of a grand mansion with barns and extensive gardens . . . a large area of land which he leased for farming, and a major investment in tithes. All this centred on Stratford, the accumulated product of years of careful husbandry of income earned in the theatre,' *Shakespeare For All Time*, 36.

[2] Honan, *Shakespeare: A Life*, 291–3. See also Macdonald, 'A New Discovery about Shakespeare's Estate in Old Stratford'.

[3] *Nine Lives*, 85.

Thomas Greene, opposed the measures and sought the playwright's support. According to Schoenbaum's documentation, however, Greene reported Shakespeare's reluctance to intervene since 'he and Mr Hall say they think there will be nothing done at all'.[4] This apparent reluctance to intercede in a measure that would drastically affect the lives of his own community reveals a man 'clearly behaving in ways not worthy of his genius and penetrating moral insight'.[5] The accusation that Shakespeare's indifference to enclosures represents a lack of moral insight reveals the extent to which attitudes to the land provide an interpretative apparatus through which we can discover ethical, as well as personal, objectives. For those biographers who cannot reconcile the imperatives of a businessman with those of a creative intellectual, the Welcombe enclosures have always been a problem.[6] Stephen Greenblatt is perhaps more resigned than most scholars when he writes:

Perhaps, as some have said, Shakespeare believed in modernizing agriculture and thought that in the long run everyone would prosper; more likely, he simply did not care. It is not a terrible story, but it is not uplifting either. It is merely disagreeably ordinary.[7]

But Shakespeare *did* care. No other playwright of his cohort appears more aware of the nature of good husbandry, the politics of cultivation, and the price of improvement. Shakespeare, as his plays suggest, was profoundly conscious of the economics of cultivation; of its impacts on social welfare, and the moral legacy of a Christianized landscape. But Shakespeare was also aware of the irrepressible pace of improvement and the ways in which enclosures focused landowners on the economic value of their land and the potential it offered for private investment. As I explored in the previous chapter, enclosures were a notoriously divided issue.[8]

---

[4] This is also recorded by Honan, *Shakespeare: A Life*, 387; S. Schoenbaum, *William Shakespeare: Records and Images* (Oxford: Oxford University Press, 1981), 64–91. See also C. M. Ingleby (ed.), *Shakespeare and the Enclosure of Common Fields at Welcombe* (1885).

[5] Holderness, *Nine Lives*, 85.

[6] On this conflict see Bate, 'The Humanist Tempest', 173; Peter Ackroyd, *Shakespeare the Biography* (London: Chatto & Windus, 2005), 386; Greenblatt, *Will in the World*, 383; Wells, *Shakespeare For All Time*, 39–40.

[7] Greenblatt, *Will in the World*, 383.

[8] Following Joan Thirsk, McRae discusses the ways in which the term 'improvement' radically developed during this period. From a negative term of exploitation, which sought to destabilize the moral economy of land use, it developed 'from cultivating for profit to a "sense of moral duty to exploit more efficiently the riches of the natural world"', *God Speed the Plough*, 136. See also Thirsk, 'Plough and Pen', 300. For a further discussion of the divided representations of enclosures, see Joan Thirsk, *The Rural Economy of England* (London: The Hambledon Press, 1984), 65–84; 183–216. Richard Henry Tawney, *The Agrarian Problem in the Sixteenth Century* (London: Harper and Row, 1967). Overton, *Agricultural Revolution in England*.

Shakespeare's reluctance to intervene in the Welcombe enclosures tells us more about his rise from son of a husbandman to private landowner and the ways in which socio-economic mobility alters ethical perspectives on farming. As Gerard Malynes suggests, good husbandry is about equity as well as ethics, and perhaps for Shakespeare there was no longer a contest between them.

In one of Shakespeare's most explicitly moral plays, however, the relationship between ethics and equity comes sharply into focus. In act 2.3 of *Timon of Athens*, discussing the debt into which he has sunk, Timon instructs his steward, Flavius, to sell his lands:[9]

> FLAVIUS: 'Tis all engaged, some forfeited and gone;
> And what remains will hardly stop the mouth
> Of present dues: the future comes apace:
> What shall defend the interim? and at length
> How goes our reckoning?
> TIMON: To Lacedaemon did my land extend.
> FLAVIUS: O my good lord, the world is but a word:
> Were it all yours to give it in a breath,
> How quickly were it gone!
> TIMON: You tell me true.
> FLAVIUS: If you suspect my husbandry or falsehood,
> Call me before the exactest auditors
> And set me on the proof. So the gods bless me,
> When all our offices have been oppress'd
> With riotous feeders, when our vaults have wept
> With drunken spilth of wine, when every room
> Hath blazed with lights and bray'd with minstrelsy,
> I have retired me to a wasteful cock,
> And set mine eyes at flow. (2.2.141–57)

Mocking Timon's reckless generosity, Flavius exposes the true cost of his expenditure. The land—lost in a word—goes only some way to paying off a debt which has been accrued by 'riotous feeders' at drunken parties. Setting himself in direct contrast to these people and these occasions, Flavius invokes his husbandry as a mark of integrity. Flavius' invective emerges through a set of juxtapositions designed to expose the value of prudence: the drunken excess of Timon's rich guests is amplified by Flavius' husbandry;

---

[9] *Timon of Athens*, famously, is the only Shakespeare play to which Marx refers. In *The Power of Money* (1844), Marx understands Timon's speech on money as exposing the transformative power of the currency, which is simultaneously liberating and distorting: 'Money is the alienated ability of mankind.'

retiring to bed early, he cries tears as the vaults weep wine. Flavius' response is one of moral superiority played out through the contrasting fluids that represent sorrow (tears) and excess (wine). Timon's land stands as a failed image of futurity—'the future comes apace: | What shall defend the interim?'—exposing Timon's gross lack of judgement in gambling his assets on fleeting pleasures. In order to highlight the profundity of Timon's faults, Flavius draws on a Christian language of immorality in which he accuses his master of an imprudence that extends beyond the boundaries of material excess and into the very ethical fabric upon which successful rule depends.

William Jackson's sermon *The Celestial Husbandrie* (1616) describes the sin of drunkenness in terms that support Flavius's good husbandry:

These gallant Epicures, and christened Athests, sit knocking on their benches, calling for more, and more: and yet more drinke; crowning this day with ryots, and blessing the morrow with promised sursets.[10]

The deluded drunks who bless 'the morrow with promised sursets' have no future: crowning their day with riots rather than honest labour they apparently invert the very foundations upon which the future depends. Jackson's tone, like Flavius', is mocking, exposing these 'gallant Epicures' as braying fools. The 'wastful cock' to which Flavius 'retires' is unlikely to be the 'wine spout, left wastefully flowing' that the Norton editors suggest, but the cockerel—wastefully crowing to announce a morning and a day for which these drunkards bear no responsibility.[11] Flavius' moral invective is predicated on a set of images, outlined throughout the preceding chapters, which centre on good husbandry—prudence, thrift, and provision. Within these terms, waste is more than foolish; it is unethical because it fractures the order upon which righteous living depends. Rejecting Flavius' 'sermon', Timon cries 'no more'. The 'husbandry' to which Flavius refers is more than household management; as the chapters on the Sonnets and *Henry V* make clear, it is an ethical language of social relations.

Such anxieties of waste and a lack of futurity are reminiscent of Shakespeare's early sonnets and the ways in which the speaker could lay siege to the young man's conscience through accusations of solipsism. The language of account here is moral as well as financial. The implication is that the steward can stand before God with a clear conscience, unlike his lord, whose estate has 'ebb[ed]'. Finally confronting Timon with the extent of his debts, Flavius exposes his lord to charges of character as well as account:

---

[10] Jackson, *The Celestial Husbandrie*, C2ʳ.

[11] The Norton gloss is surprising since there is no precedent for this interpretation in the *OED*. In fact, up until the eighteenth century, the noun is used predominantly to mean bird or haycock.

> O my good lord,
> At many times I brought you my accounts,
> Laid them before you; you would throw them off
> And say you summed them in my honesty.
> When for some trifling present you have bid me
> Return so much, I have shook my head and wept,
> Yea, 'gainst th'authority of manners prayed you
> To hold your hand more close. I did endure
> Not seldom nor no slight checks when I have
> Prompted you in ebb of your estate
> And your great flow of debts. (2.2.127–37)

Timon is not only imprudent, wasteful, and misguided; he is ungentlemanly. Within this exchange, husbandry emerges as a moral marker—supporting a socio-economic discourse that situates the self within an ethical context of civic responsibility.

This book has charted the extent to which attitudes to husbandry could reveal a discourse of social relations, which became more complex as ideas of improvement restructured the relationship between the individual and the commonwealth. From the beginning of the history of the printed husbandry manual, Scripture, prayer, sacraments, and ritual supported the organization of the agricultural year. As the emphasis on charity and communal living dropped from these texts, questions of social welfare were suppressed by a greater emphasis on individual economic investment and national equity. Peasants, women, and children could be absorbed into new models of wage labour which would improve household incomes and support national industries. Those at the top would—so the theory goes—invest in those at the bottom. Despite the long legacy of Christianity in the development of husbandry manuals in the sixteenth century, the growing emphasis on individual improvement allowed husbandry itself to emerge not as an inherently righteous practice but as a marker of individual endeavour. 'Good' and 'bad' persist as qualitative distinctions in the ethical representations of husbandry for both the self and the state. As Markham explains, the aim of his book is 'to behold whatsoeuer shall bring a publique good to your Country'.[12] Such conceptions of 'public good', however, are always in transition. Investment, enclosure, expenditure, export, improvement, and projects follow an economic curve in which the present, more often than the future, commands attention.

The Welcombe land was not, ultimately, enclosed. Like Stow's description of the London suburbs, the ditches were dug and refilled by industrious men and women who maintained the value of their landscape beyond

---

[12] *Cheape and Good Husbandrie*, 3ᵛ.

'the vanity of mens mindes'. Shakespeare's lack of moral and practical intervention tells us less about his personal character than it does about the role of cultivation in the socio-economic history of early seventeenth-century England. The people who dug the ditches and the people who 'endeavoured to hinder the malefactors from their unlawful digging' record the ways in which cultivation represented competing visions in the structure of economic development.

Elizabeth I's late sixteenth-century Acts, which sought to prevent the dispossession of the rural poor through a restitution of tillage, gave way, under James I, to a greater focus on domestic industry and artisan trades. Later, during the 1650s, Walter Blith's *The English Improver Improved* (1653) propounds the development of agriculture through enclosures and the various benefits they bring:

> But for satisfaction to the first extreme maintayned by that generation of strange men that oppose Enclosure, yet see every day the Rents of those Lands Improved, some doubled, some more, some less, and the Land certainly advanced by it, one Acre made worth three or four, and after a while will bear more Corn without soyl for three or four year, than divers Acres as it was before in Common, that onely say Enclosure may as easily be made without depopulation as with it; and to the other Extreme [sic].[13]

For Blith, and those writing in the mid-seventeenth century, practices construed as improvement, including enclosures, are represented as common sense—as though to refrain from forms of private investment would retard the course of human development. Although writing after Shakespeare's death, Blith's text records a growing investment in the economic viability of the landscape; a viability that can now be expressed, not through the terms of social welfare, but through a rational application to profit, in which the new moral duty is, in the words of Joan Thirsk, to 'exploit more efficiently the riches of the natural world'.[14]

As I have shown, traces of such exploitation run throughout Shakespeare's plays and poems, supporting a ceaseless discourse of futurity upon which human life depends. As Parolles tells Helena in *All's Well that Ends Well*: 'It is not politic in the commonwealth of nature to preserve virginity. Loss of virginity is rational increase' (1.1.119–20). Playing on the paradox of loss for increase, Parolles wittily observes the ways in which the human has rationalized the driving imperative to production. From the body to the tilled landscape, images of cultivation show how 'reason' has supported a long discourse of human intervention. Human 'reason', as Iago

---

[13] Blith, *The English Improver Improved* (London, 1653), 75.
[14] Thirsk, 'Plough and Pen', 300.

observed, is the 'balance of our lives', but how we understand—and implement—reason is always under discussion.

In 1668, in a treatise on the advancement of learning, the theologian Joseph Glanvill wrote in defence of the Royal Society, attempting to reconcile Christian providence with the 'increase of science'. For Glanvill, and many other intellectuals of his day, there was no conflict between a providential universe and one which can be interrogated for the benefit of 'human life'. Deferring to the '*ingenious Moderns*', Glanvill identifies the Royal Society as dedicated to finding 'out those *Aids* that *Providence* hath laid up in nature to help us against the *inconveniences* of *this* State, and to make such *applications* of things as may tend to *universal benefit*'.[15] Within this developing tradition of scientific rationalism, the natural world is a repository for 'universal benefit', whereby human observation and intervention may 'help us against the inconveniences of this state'. Mid-seventeenth century and speaking to an intellectual elite, Glanvill uses the terms of mastery, management, and use to support a vision of nature which develops—and even prolongs—human life. The 'state' that Glanvill refers to is more than the commonwealth; it is the human condition.

Glanvill's comment understands nature as a resource through which the human subject may advance and ultimately exceed. Within these terms God's providential landscape is a prompt to human ambition: providing the apparatus for development and the materials for mastery. The terms through which we receive Glanvill's nature are codified in order to present the human as the fundamental mediator between the divine and the earthly, the existing and the possible. Here human art—like Markham's husbandman or Shakespeare's Prospero—is responsible for the translation of 'aid' to 'benefit'; 'nature' to 'state'. Glanvill's voice is of the future and the extraordinary potential of human intercession in nature. Unlike modern science, however, there is no ethical dilemma for Glanvill and the Royal Society: characterized in providential terms, so long as the human observes nature in this way he or she continues on God's path to spiritual enlightenment and physical development.

Nobody writing or thinking about the natural world in the early modern period can separate it from the 'scriptural lens' through which early moderns perceived their landscape. Through forms of cultivation, however, and the texts through which practices of cultivation were both valorized and developed, intervention in the natural world has become increasingly associated with human development. Written deep into the legibility of the natural world is the apprehension of time: of sustainability,

---

[15] *Plus Ultra*, 88.

futurity, productivity, and our own human mortality. While scientific development may prolong human life—and the quality of that life—it also threatens to erode the moral foundations through which cultivation developed.

In 1611, appealing to the king on the depletion of forests, Arthur Standish wrote a pamphlet entitled *The Commons Complaint*. Focusing on the effects of deforestation through the country's reliance on timber as its major resource for both building and fuel, Standish sought to draw the king's attention to the urgent need for renewable resources:[16] 'All are given to take the profit present, but few or none at all regard the posteritie or future times.'[17]

Standish's pamphlet addresses both economic and ethical concerns. Calling for greater 'industry' in the domestic market, he encourages the growing of fruit trees, rather than relying on imported fruit, urges a more sustainable attitude to timber, and suggests a number of measures through which to reduce crop threats and vermin. Finally, he addresses dearth and the causes of rural poverty. The language in which Standish addresses the king is remarkably modern—accusing the public of a lack of 'respect' for resources, Standish urges the planting of trees in headlands and hedges to expand timber resources; otherwise 'no wood no kingdom'.[18] Establishing the necessity for sustainability, Standish writes that by 'observing these small directions thou mayest performe some part of the cause of thy creation'. Repositioning the human within the context of life, Standish foregrounds the role of cultivation in 'giving glorie to thy Creator, honour, pleasure and profite to thy King, Countrey and thy Self, also by feeling and relieving thy Christian brothers wants'.[19] The future, so Standish proclaims, is dependent on pleasure, profit, feeling, and the recognition of the self within the context of king, country, and brotherhood. The mantra 'no wood no kingdom' resonates throughout Standish's text and supports a representation of the kingdom as everyone's responsibility.

In February 2011, the Conservative Prime Minister made a U-turn on one of the recently elected government's most controversial policies—to privatize England's woodland. Admitting 'It's a cock-up. We just did not think', the environment secretary announced that the government had responded to intense public feeling: 'We have heard, we have listened. The

---

[16] See Paul Warde's *Energy Consumption in England* for a discussion of Standish. Cf. Paul Warde and Sverker Sörlin (eds.), *Nature's End: History and the Environment* (Basingstoke: Palgrave Macmillan, 2011).

[17] *The Commons Complaint* (London, 1611), A2ᵛ–A3ʳ.

[18] *The Commons Complaint*, 2.　　[19] *The Commons Complaint*, Bʳ.

consultation will be canned.'[20] More extraordinary, however, is who they listened to:

The U-turn represents a victory for an unlikely coalition of disparate groups launched in October...One poll suggested that 84% of the country opposed the sale.

It would seem that Standish's 'no wood no kingdom' still resonates and continues to record the ways in which human intervention records and represents the values of our social lives: 'What is important...is that we increase access to our forests [and] we increase biodiversity.'

Central to the profound public response to the government's proposals was a belief in public access rather than private investment. The National Trust's motto 'For Ever, For Everyone' encapsulates the necessity to preserve historic sites for universal benefit. Yet, as this book has hoped to demonstrate, the contingents of universal benefit are governed by human intervention. As preservation and cultivation develop alongside each other as forces for human good, the ways in which we respond to human intervention are always in contention.

In the sixteenth century, the language of cultivation rapidly developed: fuelled by the printing industry, humanistic models of pedagogy, providential teachings, the development of overseas trade, and the rationalization of provincial farming books on husbandry came to dominate the secular market. These manuals developed through a comprehensive tradition of estate management in which the text could form the locus of domestic farming. Including daily prayers, feast days, and sacramental festivals, the husbandry manual of the early sixteenth century was written to be read aloud as a form of moral instruction as well as a practical guide. Printed husbandry manuals offered an insight into the relationships between the land and its cultivators. Predicated upon a language of mastery, these texts offer the idea of success, development, growth, and improvement through a socialization of the natural world: 'I hope the Lord will so bless and succeed these labours, that many of you will be called from holding the *Plow* on earth, to wear the *Crown* of glory in heaven; which is the sincere desire.' The husbandman carries forth the image of both his beginning and his end: 'Whose memory is written on the earth' (*2 Henry VI*):

and thy body to the grounde, earth to earth, asshes to asshes, dust to dust.[21]

---

[20] *The Guardian*, 16 February 2011.
[21] The Book of Common Prayer (1549), fo. 126ᵛ.

Bibliography

PRIMARY SOURCES

A. T., Practitioner in Physike, *A Riche store house or Treasury for the Diseased* (1596).

Abbot, George, A Sermon Preached at Westminster, 26 May 1608.

Adams, Thomas, *A divine herball together with a forrest of thornes* (London, 1616).

Ariosto, Ludovico, *Orlando Furioso*, trans. John Harington (London, 1607).

Aristotle, *Discourses of Government*, trans. Loys le Roy (1598).

Bacon, Francis, *Sylva Sylvarum* (London: William Lee, 1627).

Bacon, Francis, *Abecederium Nouum Naturae*, in *The Oxford Francis Bacon*, ed. Brian Vickers and Graham Rees, 15 vols. (Oxford: Oxford University Press, 1996–), xiii: *The Instauratio Magna: Last Writings*, ed. Graham Rees (2000).

Bacon, Francis, *New Atlantis* (London, 1658).

Bacon, Francis, *The Historie of Life and Death* (London, 1638).

Bacon, Francis, *The Two Books of Francis Bacon, Of the proficience and aduancement of learning, diuine and humane To the King* (London, 1605).

Blackstone, William, *Commentaries on the Laws of England: A Facsimile of the First Edition 1765–1769* (Chicago: University of Chicago Press, 1979).

Blith, Walter, *The English Improver Improved* (London, 1653).

Brathwaite, Richard, *The English Gentlewoman* (1631).

Bulwer, John, *Anthropometamorphosis* (London: J. Hardesty, 1650).

Buoni, Thommaso, *Problems of Beautie and all Humane Affections*, trans. S.L. (London, 1606).

Burton, Robert, *The Anatomie of Melancholy* (London, 1621).

Cole, Elias, *The Young Scholars Best Companion* (London, 1690).

Coote, Edmund, *The English Schoolmaster* (London, 1596).

Dallington, Robert, *The View of France* (London, 1604).

Dawson, Thomas, *The Good Housewife's Jewel* (London, 1577).

Day, John, *The Parliament of Bees* (London, 1641).

Donaldson, James, *Husbandry Anatomized* (London, 1697).

Elyot, Thomas, *The Blanket of Sapience* (London, 1564).

Elyot, Thomas, *The Boke named The Governor* (London, 1537).

Erasmus, Desiderius, *The comparation of a vyrgin and a martyr* (London, 1537).

Erasmus, Desiderius, *Novum Testamentum* (1516).

Estienne, Charles, *Maison rustique, or the Countrey Farme* (London, 1616).

Estienne, Charles, *The Countrey Farme*, trans. Gervase Markham (London, 1616).

Fitzherbert, John, *Boke of Husbandry* (London, 1525).

Gerard, John, *The Herball* (London, 1597).

Glanvill, Joseph, *Plus Ultra* (London, 1668).

Green, Mary Anne Everett (ed.), 'Addenda, Queen Elizabeth—Volume 31: June 1589.' *Calendar of State Papers Domestic: Elizabeth, Addenda 1580–1625* (1872).

Green, Mary Anne Everett (ed.), 'Queen Elizabeth—Volume 262: January 1597.' *Calendar of State Papers Domestic: Elizabeth, 1595–97* (1869), 342–55.

Grimaldus, *The Counsellor*, trans. Wawrzyniec Goslicki as *The counsellor Exactly pourtraited in two bookes. VVherein the offices of magistrates, the happie life of subiectes, and the felicitie of common-weales is pleasantly and pithilie discoursed* (London, 1598).

Guillim, J., *Display of Heraldrie* (1610).

Hartlib, Samuel, *The Reformed Common-Wealth of Bees* (1655).

Henley, Walter de, *Boke of Husbandry* (Wynken de Worde, 1508).

Heresbach, Conrad, *Foure Bookes of Husbandrie*, trans. Barnabe Googe (London, 1577).

Hill, Thomas *The gardeners labyrinthe, containing a discourse of the gardeners life* (London, 1577).

Hooker, Richard, *The Lawes of Ecclesiastical Politie, Eight Bookes* (London, 1604).

Jackson, William, *The Celestial Husbandrie, or the tillage of the Soul* (London, 1616).

Kellwaye, Simon, *A defensatiue against the plague contayning two partes or treatises* (1593).

Lawson, William, *A New Orchard and Garden* (London, 1631).

Lemnius, Levinus, *An Herbal for the Bible* (1587).

Manwood, John, *Treatise on the Laws of the Forest* (1598).

Markham, Gervase, *The English Housewife*, ed. Michael Best (London: McGill-Queen's University Press, 1986).

Markham, Gervase, *Cheape and Good Husbandrie* (London, 1614).

Markham, Gervase, *Farewell to Husbandry* (London, 1620).

Markham, Gervase, *The English Husbandman* (London 1613).

Markham, Gervase, *The Good Husbandman* (London, 1613).

Montaigne, Michel de, *Essays vvritten in French by Michael Lord of Montaigne, Knight of the Order of S. Michael, gentleman of the French Kings chamber: done into English, according to the last French edition, by Iohn Florio reader of the Italian tongue vnto the Soueraigne Maiestie of Anna, Queene of England, Scotland, France and Ireland, &c. And one of the gentlemen of hir royall priuie chamber* (London, 1613).

Nashe, Thomas, *The Unfortunate Traveller and Other Works*, ed. J. B. Steane (Harmondsworth: Penguin, 1972).

Phillips, Edward, *New World of Words* (London, 1658).

Rastell, John, *An exposition of certaine difficult and obscure words, and termes of the lawes of this realme* (London, 1579).

Robinson, Richard, *The Vineyard of Virtue* (1579).

Shakespeare, William, *Henry V*, ed. Gary Taylor (Oxford: Oxford University Press, 2008).

Shakespeare, William, *The Tempest*, ed. Frank Kermode (Cambridge, Mass.: Methuen & Co. Ltd, 1954).

Shakespeare, William, *The Tempest*, ed. Howard Furness (Philadelphia: J. B. Lippincott Company, 1892).

Shakespeare, William, *The Tempest*, ed. Stephen Orgel (Oxford: Oxford University Press, 1987).

Shakespeare, William, *The Winter's Tale*, ed. John Pitcher (London: Methuen, 2010).

Smith, Thomas, *Discourse of the Commonweal* (London, 1549).

Standish, Arthur, *The Commons Complaint* (London, 1611).

Starkey, Thomas, *A Dialogue Between Reginald Pole and Thomas Lupset* (London, 1536).

Stow, John, *The Survey of London* (London, 1633).

Tavener, Richard, *The second Book of the Garden of Wisdom* (London, 1542).

Thomas, Thomas, *Dictionarium linguae Latinae et Anglicanae* (London, 1587).

Townsend, H. T., *Historical Collections* (1680).

Trigge, Frances, *A Humble Petition of the Church and Commonwealth* (London, 1604).

Tuke, Thomas, *The picture of a true protestant: or, Gods house and husbandry wherein is declared the duty and dignitie of all Gods children, both minister and people* (London, 1609).

Tuke, Thomas, *The True Trial and turning of a sinner* (London, 1607).

Tusser, Thomas, *Five Hundreth Pointes of Good Husbandrie* (London, 1573).

Tusser, Thomas, *Five Hundred Points of Good Husbandry* (1573), ed. Geoffrey Grigson (Oxford: Oxford University Press, 1984).

Wilson, Thomas, *The Arte of Rhetorique* (London, 1553).

Wither, George, *The Shepherd's Hunting* (London, 1615).

Wolridge, John, *Systema Agriculturae* (London, 1669).

SECONDARY SOURCES

Ackroyd, Peter, *Shakespeare the Biography* (London: Chatto & Windus, 2005).

Adelman, Janet, *Suffocating Mothers: Fantasies of Maternal Origins in Shakespeare's Plays* (London: Routledge, 1992).

Albright, Evelyn M., 'The Folio Version of Henry V in Relation to Shakespeare's Times', *PMLA* 43 (1928), 722–56.

Alpers, Paul, *What is Pastoral?* (Chicago: University of Chicago Press, 1996).

Altman, Joel, ' "Vile Participation": The Amplification of Violence in the Theater of Henry V', *Shakespeare Quarterly*, 42/1 (1991), 32.

Anderson, Benedict, *Imagined Communities: Reflections on the Origins and Spread of Nationalism* (London: Verso, 1983).

Appadurai, Arjun, 'Introduction and the Commodities of Value', in Arjun Appadurai (ed.), *The Social Life of Things* (Cambridge: Cambridge University Press, 1986).

Appleby, Joyce Oldham, *Economic Thought and Ideology in Seventeenth-Century England* (Princeton: Princeton University Press, 1978).

Archer, Ian, 'Economy', in Arthur Kinney (ed.), *The Oxford Handbook of Shakespeare* (Oxford: Oxford University Press, 2012), 165–81.

Armstrong, William A., 'Torch, Cauldron, and Taper: Light and Dark in Macbeth', in Anthony Coleman and Anthony Hammond (eds.), *Poetry and Drama, 1570–1700* (London: Methuen, 1981).

Ault, Warren O., 'Open-Field Husbandry and the Village Community: A Study of Agrarian By-Laws in Medieval England', *Transactions of the American Philosophical Society*, NS 55/7 (1965), 1–102.

Barber, C. L., *Shakespeare's Festive Comedy: A Study of Dramatic Form and its Relation to Social Custom* (Princeton: Princeton University Press, 1959).

Bartolovich, Crystal, and Neil Lazarus, *Marxism, Modernity and Post-Colonial Studies* (Cambridge: Cambridge University Press, 2002).

Barton, Anne, 'The King Disguised: The Two Bodies of Henry V', in Joseph G. Price (ed.), *The Triple Bond: Plays, Mainly Shakespearean, in Performance* (University Park, Pa.: Pennsylvania State University Press, 1975).

Baumgartner, Frederick J., *France in the Sixteenth Century* (New York: St Martin's Press, 1995).

Bennett, Judith M., 'Conviviality and Charity in Medieval and Early Modern England', *Past and Present*, 134 (February 1992), 19–41.

Beresford, Maurice, *Essays in the Economic and Social History of Tudor and Stuart England*, ed. F. J. Fisher (Cambridge: Cambridge University Press, 1961).

Bland, A. E., P. A. Brown, and R. H. Tawney, *English Economic History: Select Documents* (London, G. Bell and Sons, Ltd, 1914).

Boehrer, Bruce, *Shakespeare Among the Animals: Nature and Society in the Drama of Early Modern England* (Basingstoke: Palgrave, 2002).

Boehrer, Bruce, *Animal Characters: Nonhuman Beings in Early Modern Literature* (University Park, Pa.: University of Pennsylvania Press, 2010).

Booth, Stephen, *Shakespeare's Sonnets* (New Haven: Yale University Press, 2000).

Bradbrook, M. C., 'The Sources of *Macbeth*', in Kenneth Muir and Philip Edwards (eds.), *Aspects of Macbeth: Articles Reprinted from Shakespeare Survey* (Cambridge: Cambridge University Press, 1977).

Brady, Emily, *Aesthetics of the Natural Environment* (Edinburgh: Edinburgh University Press, 2003).

Brenner, Robert, 'The Social Basis of English Commercial Expansion, 1550–1650', *Journal of Economic History*, 32/1 (March 1972).

Brenner, Robert, 'The Agrarian Roots of European Capitalism', *Past and Present*, 97 (November 1982).

Brewer, J. S. (ed.), 'Henry VIII: October 1519', *Letters and Papers, Foreign and Domestic, Henry VIII*, vol. iii: *1519–1523* (1867).

Bristol, Michael, 'In Search of the Bear: Spatiotemporal Form and the Heterogeneity of Economies in *The Winter's Tale*', *Shakespeare Quarterly*, 42 (1991), 145–67.

Bromley, James M., *Intimacy and Sexuality in the Age of Shakespeare* (Cambridge: Cambridge University Press, 2012).

Brooks, Cleanth, *The Well Wrought Urn: Studies in the Structure of Poetry* (New York: Harcourt, Brace, 1947).

Brotton, Jerry, 'Carthage and Tunis: *The Tempest* and its Tapestries', in William Sherman and Peter Hulme (eds.), *The Tempest and its Travels* (London: Reaktion, 2000), 132–7.

Brotton, Jerry, and Lisa Jardine, *Global Interests: Renaissance Art between East and West* (London: Reaktion Books, 2000).

Brown, P. Hume (ed.), *Early Travellers in Scotland* (Edinburgh: Edinburgh University Press, 1978).

Bruckner, Lynne, and Dan Brayton (eds.), *Ecocritical Shakespeare* (Farnham: Ashgate, 2011).

Brükner, Martin, and Kirstin Poole, 'The Plot Thickens: Surveying Manuals, Drama and the Materiality of Narrative Form in Early Modern England', *English Literary History* (2002), 617–48.

Bruster, Douglas, *Drama and the Market in the Age of Shakespeare* (Cambridge: Cambridge University Press, 1992).

Bryant, Jerry, '*The Winter's Tale* and the Pastoral Tradition', *Shakespeare Quarterly*, 14/4 (1963).

Burrow, Colin, *The Complete Poems and Sonnets of Shakespeare* (Oxford: Oxford University Press, 2004).

Bushnell, Rebecca, *A Culture of Teaching: Early Modern Humanism in Theory and Practice* (New York: Cornell University Press, 1996).

Bushnell, Rebecca, *Green Desire: Imagining Early Modern English Gardens* (Ithaca, NY: Cornell University Press, 2003).

Callaghan, Dympna, 'Looking Well to Linens', in Jean Howard and Scott Cutler Shershow (eds.), *Marxist Shakespeare* (London: Routlege, 2001), 53–81.

Callaghan, Dympna, *Shakespeare's Sonnets* (Oxford: Blackwell, 2007).

Carroll, William C., '"The Nursery of Beggary": Enclosure, Vagrancy, and Sedition in the Tudor-Stuart Period', in Richard Burt and John Michael Archer (eds.), *Enclosure Acts* (Ithaca, NY: Cornell University Press, 1994), 34–47.

Carroll, William C., *Macbeth: Texts and Contexts* (Boston: Bedford, St Martins, 1999).

Cartelli, Thomas, 'Jack Cade in the Garden: Class Consciousness and Class Conflict in *2 Henry VI*', in Richard Burt and John Michael Archer (eds.), *Enclosure Acts: Sexuality, Property and Culture in Early Modern England* (Ithaca, NY: Cornell University Press, 1994), 48–67.

Cavell, Stanley, *Disowning Knowledge in Seven Plays of Shakespeare* (Cambridge: Cambridge University Press, 1987).

Chaudhuri, Sukanta, *Renaissance Pastoral and its English Developments* (Oxford: Clarendon Press, 1998).

Cheney, Patrick, *Shakespeare, National Poet-Playwright* (Cambridge: Cambridge University Press, 2004).

Cheney, Patrick, *The Cambridge Companion to Shakespeare's Poetry* (Cambridge: Cambridge University Press, 2007).

Cheney, Patrick, *Reading Sixteenth Century Poetry* (Oxford: Wiley-Blackwell, 2011).

Cohen, Walter, 'The Undiscovered Country Shakespeare', in Jean Howard and Scott Cutler Shershow (eds.), *Marxist Shakespeare* (London: Routlege, 2001), 128–58.

Colie, Rosalie, *The Oaten Flute: Essays on Pastoral Poetry and the Pastoral Tradition* (Cambridge, Mass.: Harvard University Press, 1975).

Collingwood, R. G., *The Idea of Nature* (Oxford: Clarendon Press, 1945).

Considine, John, ' "Thy bankes with, pioned and twilled brims": A Solution to the Double Crux', *Shakespeare Quarterly*, 54/2 (2003).

Cook, Harold, *Matters of Exchange: Commerce, Medicine and Science in the Dutch Golden Age* (New Haven: Yale, 2007).

Cosgrove, Denis, *Social Formation and Symbolic Landscape* (London: Croom Helm, 1984).

Cosgrove, Denis, and Stephen Daniels (eds.), *The Iconography of Landscape* (Cambridge: Cambridge University Press, 1988).

Cox, Nancy, and Karin Dannehl (eds.), *The Dictionary of Traded Goods and Commodities 1550–1820* (Wolverhampton: University of Wolverhampton, 2007).

Crawford, Julie, 'Women's Secretaries', in Vin Nardizzi and Will Stockton (eds.), *Queer Renaissance Historiography* (Farnham: Ashgate, 2009).

Dabhoiwala, Faramerez, *The Origins of Sex* (London: Allen Lane, 2011).

Daly, Mary, *Pure Lust: Elemental Feminist Philosophy* (Boston: Beacon Press, 1984).

Danby, John F., *Shakespeare's Doctrine of Nature: A Study of King Lear* (London: Faber and Faber, 1949, 1962).

Darby, H. C., 'The Changing English Landscape', *Geographical Journal*, 117 (1951).

Datson, Lorraine, and Katherine Park, *Wonders and the Order of Nature, 1150–1750* (New York: Zone, 2001).

Dietz, Brian (ed.), *The London Port Book 1567–8* (London: London Record Society, 1972).

Dillon, Janette, *Shakespeare and the Staging of English History* (Oxford: Oxford University Press, 2012).

Doloff, Steven, 'Polonius's Precepts and Thomas Tusser's Five Hundred Points of Good Husbandrie', *Review of English Studies*, 42/146 (May 1991).

Donaldson, Ian, *Ben Jonson: A Life* (Oxford: Oxford University Press, 2011).

Downing, Charles, *The Messiahship of Shakespeare* (London: Greening, 1901).

Drakakis, John (ed.), *Alternative Shakespeares* (London: Routledge, 1988).

Dubrow, Heather, *English Petrarchanism and its Counterdiscourses* (Ithaca, NY: Cornell University Press, 1995).

Duncan-Jones, Katherine, *Shakespeare's Sonnets* (London: Thomas Nelson, 1997).

Dutton, Richard, 'The Dating and Contexts of *Henry V*', in Paulina Kewes (ed.), *The Uses of History in Early Modern England* (San Marino, Calif.: Henry Huntingdon, 2006).

Dyer, Christopher, *An Age of Transition? Economy and Society in England in the Later Middle Ages* (Oxford: Clarendon Press, 2005).

Edwards, Philip, *Threshold of a Nation: A Study in English and Irish Drama* (Cambridge: Cambridge University Press, 1979).

Egan, Gabriel, *Shakespeare and Marx* (Oxford: Oxford University Press, 2004).

Egan, Gabriel, *Green Shakespeare: From Ecopolitics to Ecocriticism* (London: Routledge, 2006).

Empson, William, *Some Versions of Pastoral* (New York: New Directions, 1974).

Enterline, Lynn, *The Rhetoric of the Body from Ovid to Shakespeare* (Cambridge: Cambridge University Press, 2000).

Enterline, Lynn, *Shakespeare's Schoolroom: Rhetoric, Discipline and Emotion* (Philadelphia: University of Pennsylvania Press, 2012).

Erne, Lukas, *Shakespeare as Literary Dramatist* (Cambridge: Cambridge University Press, 2003).

Evans, George Ewart, *The Farm and the Village* (London: Faber and Faber, 1969).

Falls, Cyril, *Elizabeth's Irish Wars* (London: Methuen, 1950).

Fineman, Joel, *Shakespeare's Perjured Eye: The Invention of Poetic Subjectivity in the Sonnets* (Berkeley and Los Angeles: University of California Press, 1986).

Fitz, L. T., 'The Vocabulary of the Environment in *The Tempest*', *Shakespeare Quarterly*, 26/1 (Winter 1975), 42–7.

Fitzmaurice, Andrew, *Humanism and America: An Intellectual History of Colonisation, 1500–1625* (Cambridge: Cambridge University Press, 2003).

Fletcher, Anthony, *Growing Up in England: The Experience of Childhood 1600–1914* (New Haven: Yale University Press, 2008).

Forman, Valerie, *Tragicomic Redemptions: Global Economics and the Early Modern English Stage* (Philadelphia: University of Pennsylvania Press, 2008).

Fowler, Elizabeth, *Literary Character: The Human Figure in Early English Writing* (Ithaca, NY: Cornell University Press, 2003).

Fox Genovese, Elizabeth, 'The Many Faces of Moral Economy: A Contribution to the Debate', *Past and Present*, 58 (February 1973), 161–8.

Freedman, Paul, *Images of the Medieval Peasant* (Stanford, Calif.: Stanford University Press, 1999).

Fuchs, Barbara, 'Conquering Islands: Contextualising *The Tempest*', *Shakespeare Quarterly*, 48/1 (Spring 1997), 45–62.

Fudge, Erica, *Perceiving Animals: Humans and Beasts in Early Modern English Culture* (New York: St Martin's Press, 1999).

Fudge, Erica, Ruth Gilbert, and Susan Wiseman, *At the Borders of the Human* (London: Palgrave, 2002).

Fumerton, Patricia, *Unsettled: The Culture of Mobility and the Working Poor in Early Modern England* (Chicago: University of Chicago Press, 2006).

Fussell, G. E., *The Old English Farming Books from Fitzherbert to Tull 1523 to 1730* (Aberdeen: Aberdeen Rare, 1978).

Gasper, Des, *The Ethics of Development* (Edinburgh: Edinburgh University Press, 2005).

Gay, Edwin, 'Inclosures in England', *Quarterly Journal of Economics*, 17/4 (August 1903), 576–97.

Goldberg, Jonathan, 'Macbeth: Speculations and Source', in Jean E. Howard and Marion O'Connor (eds.), *Shakespeare Reproduced: The Text in History and Ideology* (London: Methuen, 2005).

Goldstone, Jack A., 'Capitalist Origins of the English Revolution: Chastity and Chimera', *Theory and Society*, 12/2 (March 1983), 143–80.

Gonner, E. C. K., 'The Progress of Inclosure during the Seventeenth Century', *English Historical Review*, 23/91 (July 1908), 477–501.

Gowing, Laura, *Domestic Dangers* (Oxford: Oxford University Press, 1996).

Grainger, Robert, *Prospero's Island: Navigating Pastoral Care* (Victoria, BC: Trafford, 2010).

Grazia, Margreta de, 'The Scandal of Shakespeare's Sonnets', *Shakespeare Survey*, 46 (1994), 35–49.

Grazia, Margreta de, *Hamlet without Hamlet* (Cambridge: Cambridge University Press, 2007).

Greenblatt, Stephen, *Will in the World: How Shakespeare Became Shakespeare* (New York: W. W. Norton, 1943).

Greenblatt, Stephen, 'The Cultivation of Anxiety: King Lear and his Heirs', *Raritan*, 2 (1982)

Greenblatt, Stephen, *Shakespearean Negotiations: The Circulation of Social Energy in Renaissance England* (Berkeley and Los Angeles: University of California Press, 1988).

Greenblatt, Stephen, *Learning to Curse: Essays in Early Modern Culture* (London: Routledge, 1990).

Greene, Roland, 'Island Logic', in William Sherman and Peter Hulme (eds.), *The Tempest and its Travels* (London: Reaktion, 2000).

Greene, Thomas, ' "Pitiful Thrivers": Failed Husbandry in the Sonnets', in Patricia Parker and Geoffrey Hartman (eds.), *Shakespeare and the Question of Theory* (New York: Methuen, 1985).

Greene, Thomas, ' "The expense of Spirit" and Social Class', in Harold Bloom (ed.), *Shakespeare's Poems and Sonnets* (Broomall: Chelsea House, 1999).

Greg, W. W., *Pastoral Poetry and Pastoral Drama* (London: A. H. Bullen, 1906).

Hadfield, Andrew, 'Henry V', in Richard Dutton and Jean E. Howard (eds.), *A Companion to Shakespeare's Works: The Histories* (London: Blackwell, 2003).

Halpern, Richard, *The Poetics of Primitive Accumulation: English Renaissance Culture and the Genealogy of Capital* (Ithaca, NY: Cornell University Press, 1991).

Harris, Jonathan Gil, *Foreign Bodies* (Cambridge: Cambridge University Press, 1998).

Harris, Jonathan Gil, *Sick Economies* (Philadelphia: University of Pennsylvania Press, 2004).

Harrison, Robert Pogue, *Forests: The Shadow of Civilization* (Chicago: University of Chicago Press, 1993).

Harrison, Robert Pogue, *Gardens: An Essay on the Human Condition* (Chicago: University of Chicago Press, 2008).

Harrison, Thomas Perrin, 'A Note on *The Tempest*', *Modern Language Notes*, 25/1 (January 1910), 8–9.

Hartley, Dorothy, *Lost Country Life: How English Country Folk Lived, Worked, Threshed, Thatched, Rolled Fleece, Milled Corn, Brewed Mead* (New York: Pantheon, 1979).

Heal, Felicity, 'The Idea of Hospitality in Early Modern England', *Past and Present* (1984).

Helgerson, Richard, *Forms of Nationhood: The Elizabethan Writing of England* (Chicago: University of Chicago Press, 1992, 1994).

Henke, Robert, 'Ruzante and Shakespeare: A Comparative Case-Study', in Michele Marrapodi (ed.), *Shakespeare and Renaissance Literary Theories: Anglo-Italian Transactions* (Farnham: Ashgate, 2011).

Herman, Peter C., 'O 'tis a gallant king: Shakespeare's *Henry V* and the Crisis of the 1590s', in Dale Hoak (ed.), *Tudor Political Culture* (Cambridge: Cambridge University Press, 1995).

Herman, Peter C., 'What's the Use? Or, The Problematic of Economy in Shakespeare's Procreation Sonnets', in James Schiffer (ed.), *Shakespeare's Sonnets: Critical Essays* (London: Routledge, 1999).

Hill, Christopher, 'The Norman Yoke', in *Puritanism and Revolution: Studies in the Interpretation of the English Revolution and the Seventeenth Century* (London: Secker & Warburg, 1958).

Höfele, Andreas, *Stage, Stake and Scaffold* (Oxford: Oxford University Press, 2011).

Holderness, Graham, *Shakespeare: The Histories* (New York: St Martin's Press, 2000).

Holderness, Graham, *Nine Lives of William Shakespeare* (London: Continuum Publishing Corporation, 2011).

Holland, Peter, *English Shakespeares: Shakespeare on the English Stage in the 1990s* (Cambridge: Cambridge University Press, 1997).

Honan, Park, *Shakespeare: A Life* (Oxford: Oxford University Press, 1998).

Hopcroft, Rosemary L., 'The Social Origins of Agrarian Change in Late Mediaeval England', *American Journal of Sociology*, 99/6 (May 1994), 1559–95.

Horigan, Stephen, *Nature and Culture in Western Discourses* (London: Routledge, 1988).

Howard, Jean E., and Marion F. O'Connor (eds.), *Shakespeare Reproduced* (London: Methuen, 1987).

Howard, Jean, and Scott Cutler Shershow (eds.), *Marxist Shakespeare* (London: Routledge, 2001).

Hulme, Peter, 'Hurricanes in the Caribees: The Constitution of the Discourse of English Colonialism', in Frances Barker et al. (eds.), *Literature and Power in the Seventeenth Century* (Colchester: University of Essex, 1981), 55–83.

Hulme, William H., 'A Probable Source for Some of the Lore of Fitzherbert's *Book of Husbandry*', *Modern Philology*, 6/1 (July 1908), 129–32.

Hunt, John Dixon, *Gardens and the Picturesque: Studies in the History of Landscape Architecture* (Cambridge, Mass.: MIT Press, 1994).

Hunt, John Dixon, *Greater Perfections: The Practice of Garden Theory* (Philadelphia: University of Pennsylvania Press, 2000).

Hunt, John Dixon, and Peter Willis (eds.), *The Genius of the Place: The English Landscape Garden, 1620–1820* (Cambridge, Mass.: MIT Press, 1975).

Hutson, Lorna, *The Usurer's Daughter: Male Friendship and the Fictions of Women in Sixteenth Century England* (London: Routledge, 1994).

Hutson, Lorna, *The Invention of Suspicion: Law and Mimesis in Shakespeare and Renaissance Drama* (Oxford: Oxford University Press, 2007).

Ingleby, C. M. (ed.), *Shakespeare and the Enclosure of Common Fields at Welcombe* (1885).

Jones, Ann Rosalind, and Peter Stallybrass, 'Fetishizing the Glove in Renaissance Europe', in Bill Brown (ed.), *Things* (Chicago: University of Chicago Press, 2004).

Jones, Mike Rodman, *Radical Pastoral, 1381–1594* (Farnham: Ashgate, 2010).

Kerényi, Karl, *Prometheus: Archetypal Image of Human Existence*, trans. Ralph Manheim (Princeton: Princeton University Press, 1991).

Kerrigan, John, *The Sonnets and A Lover's Complaint* (Harmondsworth: Penguin, 1986).

Khan, Coppélia, *Roman Shakespeare: Warriors, Wounds and Women* (London: Routledge, 1997).

Kinney, Arthur (ed.), *The Oxford Handbook of Shakespeare* (Oxford: Oxford University Press, 2012).

Kitch, Aaron, *Political Economy and the States of Literature in Early Modern England* (Farnham: Ashgate, 2009).

Korda, Natasha, *Shakespeare's Domestic Economies* (Philadelphia: University of Pennsylvania Press, 2002).

Landreth, David, *The Face of Mammon* (Oxford: Oxford University Press, 2012).

Landry, Donna, *Noble Brutes: How Eastern Horses Transformed English Culture* (Baltimore: The Johns Hopkins University Press, 2008).

Laoutaris, Chris, *Shakespearean Maternities: Crises of Conception in Early Modern England* (Edinburgh: Edinburgh University Press, 2008).

Larkin, Philip, *The Complete Poems*, ed. Archie Burnett (New York: Farrar, Straus, Giroux, 2013).

Laroche, Rebecca, 'Ophelia's Plants and the Death of Violets', in Lynne Bruckner and Dan Brayton (eds.), *Ecocritical Shakespeare* (Farnham: Ashgate, 2011), 211–21.

Leonard, E. M., 'The Inclosure of Common-Fields in the Seventeenth Century', *Transactions of the Royal Historical Society*, NS 19 (1905), 101–46.

Leslie, Michael, 'The Spiritual Husbandry of John Beale', in Michael Leslie and Timothy Raylor (eds.), *Culture and Cultivation in Early Modern England: Writing and the Land* (Leicester: University of Leicester Press, 1992), 151–72.

Leslie, Michael, and Timothy Raylor (eds.), *Culture and Cultivation in Early Modern England: Writing and the Land* (Leicester: University of Leicester Press, 1992).

Lestringant, Franck, *Mapping the Renaissance World: The Geographical Imagination in the Age of Discovery* (Cambridge: Polity Press, 1984).

Low, Anthony, *The Georgic Revolution* (Princeton: Princeton University Press, 1985).

Low, Anthony, 'Agricultural Reform and the Love Poems of Thomas Carew; with an Instance from Lovelace', in Michael Leslie and Timothy Raylor (eds.), *Culture and Cultivation in Early Modern England: Writing and the Land* (Leicester: University of Leicester Press, 1992).

Lowndes, William Thomas, and Henry George Bohn (eds.), *The Bibliographer's Manual of English Literature*, vol. iv (London: Bell and Daldy, 1871).

Lupton, Julia Reinhard, *Thinking with Shakespeare: Essays on Politics and Life* (Chicago: University of Chicago Press, 2011).

Lyne, Raphael, *Shakespeare's Late Work* (Oxford: Oxford University Press, 2007).

Lyne, Raphael, *Shakespeare, Rhetoric and Cognition* (Cambridge: Cambridge University Press, 2011).

Macdonald, Màiri, 'A New Discovery about Shakespeare's Estate in Old Stratford', *Shakespeare Quarterly*, 45 (1994), 87–9.

McDonald, Russ, 'Reading *The Tempest*', *Shakespeare Survey*, 43 (1990).

MacLean, Gerald, Donna Landry, and Joseph P. Ward (eds.), *The Country and the City Revisited: England and the Politics of Culture, 1550–1850* (Cambridge: Cambridge University Press, 1999).

McRae, Andrew, 'Husbandry Manuals and the Language of Agrarian Improvement', in Michael Leslie and Timothy Raylor (eds.), *Culture and Cultivation in Early Modern England: Writing and the Land* (Leicester: University of Leicester Press, 1992).

McRae, Andrew, *God Speed the Plough: The Representation of Agrarian England, 1500–1660* (Cambridge: Cambridge University Press, 1996).

McRae, Andrew, 'To Know One's Own Estate: Surveying and the Representation of the Land in Early Modern England', *Huntington Library Quarterly*, 56/4 (Autumn 1993), 333–57.

Manley, Lawrence, *Literature and Culture in Early Modern England* (Cambridge: Cambridge University Press, 1995).

Mann, Jenny C., *Outlaw Rhetoric: Figuring Vernacular Eloquence in Shakespeare's England* (Ithaca, NY: Cornell University Press, 2012).

Marienstras, Richard, *New Perspectives on the Shakespearean World* (Cambridge: Cambridge University Press, 1985).

Martindale, Charles, *The Cambridge Companion to Virgil* (Cambridge: Cambridge University Press, 1997).

Meijer, Fred, *Dutch and Flemish Still Life Paintings* (Oxford: Ashmolean Museum, 2005).

Miller, Naomi J., 'Playing "the Mother's Part": Shakespeare's Sonnets and Early Modern Codes of Maternity', in James Schiffer (ed.), *Shakespeare's Sonnets: Critical Essays* (Oxford: Routledge, 1999).

Moisà, Maria, 'Conviviality and Charity in Medieval and Early Modern England', *Past and Present*, 154 (February 1997), 19–41.

Montrose, Louis, 'Of Gentlemen and Shepherds: The Politics of Elizabethan Pastoral Form', *ELH* 50 (1983), 415–59.

Muir, Kenneth, 'Image and Symbol in Macbeth', *Shakespeare Survey*, 19 (1966), 45–54.

Mukerji, Chandra, 'Material Practices of Domination: Christian Humanism, the Built Environment, and Techniques of Western Power', *Theory and Society*, 31 (February 2002), 1–34.

Mukherji, Subha, *Law and Representation in Early Modern Drama* (Cambridge: Cambridge University Press, 2006).

Mukherji, Subha, 'Trying, Knowing and Believing: Epistemic Plots and the Poetics of Doubt', in Subha Mukherji, Jan-Melissa Schramm, and Yota Batsaki (eds.), *Fictions of Knowledge: Fact, Evidence, Doubt* (Basingstoke: Palgrave, 2011).

Muldrew, Craig, *The Economy of Obligation: The Culture of Credit and Social Relations in Early Modern England* (Basingstoke: Palgrave Macmillan, 1998).

Muldrew, Craig, 'The Culture of Reconcilliation: Community and the Settlement of Economic Disputes in Early Modern England', *Historical Journal*, 39/4 (December 1996), 915–42.

Muldrew, Craig, 'Interpreting the Market: The Ethics of Credit and Community Relations in Early Modern England', *Social History*, 18/2 (May 1993), 163–83.

Munroe, Jennifer, 'It's all about the gillyvors: Engendering Art and Nature in *The Winter's Tale*', in Lynne Bruckner and Dan Brayton (eds.), *Ecocritical Shakespeare* (Farnham: Ashgate, 2011), 139–54.

Najmuddin, Shahzad Z., *Shakespeare's 'The Tempest', its Political Implications and the First Colonists of Virginia* (Crewe: Trafford, 2005).

Nelson, Eric, 'Shakespeare and the Best State of the Commonwealth', in David Armitage, Conal Condren, and Andrew Fitzmaurice (eds.), *Shakespeare and Early Modern Political Thought* (Cambridge: Cambridge University Press, 2009).

Nixon, Rob, *Slow Violence and the Environmentalism of the Poor* (Cambridge, Mass.: Harvard University Press, 2011).

Noddings, Nel, *Women and Evil* (Berkeley and Los Angeles: University of California Press, 1981).

Norbrook, David, ' "What care these roarers for the name of king?" Language and Utopia in *The Tempest*', in J. Hope and G. McMullan (eds.), *The Politics of Tragicomedy: Shakespeare and After* (London: Routledge, 1992).

O'Callaghan, Michelle, *The Shepherd's Nation: Jacobean Spenserians and Early Stuart Political Culture* (Oxford: Oxford University Press, 2000).

O'Callaghan, Michelle, 'Pastoral', in Michael Hattaway (ed.), *A New Companion to Renaissance Literature*, vol. i (Oxford: Blackwell, 2010).

Overton, Mark, *The Agricultural Revolution in England: The Transformation of the Agrarian Economy 1500–1850* (Cambridge: Cambridge University Press, 2011).

Parker, Patricia, *Shakespeare from the Margins: Language, Culture and Context* (Chicago: University of Chicago Press, 1996).

Paster, Gail Kern, *Humouring the Body: Emotions and the Shakespearean Stage* (Chicago: University of Chicago Press, 2004).

Patoča, Jan, *Plato and Europe*, trans. Petr Lom (Stanford, Calif.: Stanford University Press, 2002).

Patterson, Annabel, *Pastoral and Ideology: From Virgil to Valéry* (Berkeley and Los Angeles: University of California Press, 1987).

Patterson, Annabel, *Shakespeare and the Popular Voice* (Oxford: Basil Blackwell, 1989).

Payne, Susan, '(Re)fracted Art and Ordered Nature: Italian Renaissance Aesthetics in Shakespeare's *Richard II*', in Michael Marrapodi (ed.), *Shakespeare and Renaissance Literary Theories: Anglo-Italian Transactions* (Farnham: Ashgate, 2001).

Pequigney, Joseph, *Such is my Love: A Study of Shakespeare's Sonnets* (Chicago: University of Chicago Press, 1985).

Potter, Lois, *The Life of William Shakespeare: A Critical Biography* (Oxford: Wiley-Blackwell, 2012).

Poynter, F. N. L., *A Bibliography of Gervase Markham, 1568?–1637* (Oxford: Bibliographical Society, NS XI, 1962).

Pregill, Philip, and Nancy Volkman, *Landscape in History: Design and Planning in the Western Tradition* (New York: John Waley and Sons, 1999).

Pryor, Francis, *The Making of the British Landscape: How We Have Transformed the Land, from Prehistory to Today* (London: Allen Lane, 2010).

Pugh, R. B., et al. (eds.), *A History of the County of Cambridge and the Isle of Ely*, iv: *City of Ely; Ely, N. and S. Witchford and Wisbech Hundreds* (Victoria County History, 2002).

Raber, Karen, 'Recent Ecocritical Studies of English Renaissance Literature', *English Literary Renaissance*, 37/1 (2007).

Rabkin, Norman, 'Either/Or: Responding to *Henry V*', in *Shakespeare and the Problem of Meaning* (Chicago: University of Chicago Press, 1981).

Ransom, John Crowe, 'Shakespeare at Sonnets', *Southern Review*, 3 (1937–8), 531–53.

Raylor, Timothy, 'Samuel Hartlib and the Commonwealth of Bees', in Michael Leslie and Timothy Raylor (eds.), *Culture and Cultivation in Early Modern England: Writing and the Land* (Leicester: University of Leicester Press, 1992), 91–129.

Reynolds, G. F., 'Trees on the Stage of Shakespeare', *Modern Philology*, 5/2 (October 1901), 153–68.

Reynolds, Philip, *To Have and to Hold: Marriage and its Documentation in Western Christendom* (Cambridge: Cambridge University Press, 2007).

Richards, Jennifer, *Rhetoric and Courtliness in Early Modern Literature* (Cambridge: Cambridge University Press, 2003).

Richards, Jennifer, and James Knowles (eds.), *Shakespeare's Late Plays: New Readings* (Edinburgh: Edinburgh University Press, 1999).

Robert, Jeanne Addison, *The Shakespearean Wild: Geography, Genus, and Gender* (London: University of Nebraska Press, 1991).

Roberts, Jeanne Addison, 'Falstaff in Windsor Forest: Villain or Victim?', *Shakespeare Quarterly*, 26/1 (Winter 1975), 8–15.

Robertson, M., *The Problems of the Shakespeare Sonnets* (London: George Routledge, 1926).

Rockett, William, 'Labour and Virtue in *The Tempest*', *Shakespeare Quarterly*, 24/1 (Winter 1973), 77–84.

Rosmarin, Adena, 'Hermeneutics versus Erotics: Shakespeare Sonnets and Interpretive History', *PMLA* 100 (1985), 20–37.

Rossiter, A. P., *Angel with Horns: And Other Shakespeare Lectures* (London: Longmans, 1961).

Rothenberg, David, *Survival of the Beautiful: Art, Science and Evolution* (London: Bloomsbury, 2012).

Rutter, Carol Chillington, 'Remind me How Many Children Had Lady Macbeth', *Shakespeare Survey: Macbeth and its Afterlife*, 57 (2004), 38–54.

Rutter, Tom, *Work and Play on the Shakespearean Stage* (Cambridge: Cambridge University Press, 2008).

Sawday, Jonathan, *The Body Emblazoned: Dissection and the Human Body in Renaissance Culture* (London: Routledge, 1995).

Schalkywk, David, 'Is Love an Emotion: Shakespeare's Twelfth Night and Antony and Cleopatra', *Symplokē*, 18 (2010), 99–130.

Schalkwyk, David, *Shakespear, Love and Service* (Cambridge: Cambridge University Press, 2008).

Schama, Simon, *Landscape and Memory* (London: Harper Perennial, 2004).

Schiffer, James, *Shakespeare's Sonnets: Critical Essays* (London: Routledge, 1999).

Schneider, Norbert, *Still Life* (London: Taschen, 2003).

Schoenbaum, S., *William Shakespeare: Records and Images* (New York: Oxford University Press, 1981).

Schoenfeldt, Michael, *A Companion to Shakespeare's Sonnets* (Oxford: Blackwell, 2007, 2010).

Schoenfeldt, Michael, *The Cambridge Introduction to Shakespeare's Poetry* (Cambridge: Cambridge University Press, 2010).

Schoenfeldt, Michael, *Bodies and Selves in Early Modern England: Physiology and Inwardness in Spenser, Shakespeare, Herbert, and Milton* (Cambridge: Cambridge University Press, 1999).

Schwyzer, Philip, *Literature, Nationalism and Memory* (Cambridge: Cambridge University Press, 2004).

Scott, Charlotte, 'Dark Matter: Shakespeare's Foul Dens and Forests', *Shakespeare Survey*, 61 (2011).

Scott-Warren, Jason, 'When Theatres were Bear-Gardens: or, What's at Stake in the Comedy of Humours', *Shakespeare Quarterly*, 54 (2003), 63–82.

Sebeck, Barbara Anne, 'People, Profiting and Pleasure in *The Tempest*', in Patrick Murphy (ed.), *The Tempest: Critical Essays* (London: Routledge, 2001).

Sedgwick, Eve Kosofsky, *Between Men: English Literature and Male Homosocial Desire* (New York: Columbia University Press, 1985).

Seed, Patricia, *Ceremonies of Possession in Europe's Conquest of the New World, 1492–1640* (Cambridge: Cambridge University Press, 1995).

Shammas, Carole, 'The Domestic Environment in Early Modern England and America', *Journal of Social History*, 14/1 (Autumn 1980), 3–24.

Sherman, William, and Peter Hulme (eds.), *The Tempest and its Travels* (London: Reaktion, 2000).

Siemon, James R., 'Landlord not King: Agrarian Change and Interarticulation', in Richard Burt and John Michael Archer (eds.), *Enclosure Acts* (Ithaca, NY: Cornell University Press, 1994).

Simkhovitch, Vladimir G., 'Hay and History', *Political Science Quarterly*, 28/3 (September 1913), 385–403.

Skinner, Quentin, et al. (eds.), *The Cambridge History of Renaissance Philosophy* (Cambridge: Cambridge University Press, 1988).

Skura, Meredith Anne, 'Discourse and the Individual: The Case of Colonialism in *The Tempest*', *Shakespeare Quarterly*, 40 (1989).

Slack, Paul, *From Reformation to Improvement: Public Welfare in Early Modern England* (Oxford: Clarendon Press, 1997).

Smith, Bruce, *Homosexual Desire in Shakespeare's England: A Cultural Poetics* (Chicago: University of Chicago Press, 1991).

Smith, Dennis, Norbert Elias, and Michel Foucault, ' "The Civilizing Process" and "The History of Sexuality": Comparing Norbert Elias and Michel Foucault', *Theory and Society*, 28/1 (February 1999), 79–100.

Soper, Kate, *What is Nature? Culture, Politics and the Non-human* (Oxford: Blackwell, 1995).

Sousa, Geraldo U. de, *At Home in Shakespeare's Tragedies* (Aldershot: Ashgate, 2010).

Spier, Robert F. G., and Donald K. Anderson, Jr, 'Shakespeare and Farming: The Bard and Tusser', *Agricultural History*, 59/3 (July 1985).

Spurgeon, Caroline, *Shakespeare's Imagery and What it Tells Us* (Cambridge: Cambridge University Press, 1935).

Stallybrass, Peter, 'Worn Worlds: Clothes and Identity on the Renaissance Stage', in Margreta de Grazia et al. (eds.), *Subject and Object in Renaissance Culture* (Cambridge: Cambridge University Press, 1996).

Stearns, Peter N., *Handbook of Economics and Ethics*, ed. Jan Peil (Cheltenham: Edward Elgar Publishing Ltd, 2009).

Sullivan, Garrett A., Jr., *The Drama of Landscape: Land, Property and Social Relations on the Early Modern Stage* (Stanford, Calif.: Stanford University Press, 1998).

Sullivan, Garrett A., Jr., 'Voicing the Young Man: Memory, Forgetting and Subjectivity', in Michael Schoenfeldt (ed.), *A Companion to Shakespeare's Sonnets* (Oxford: Blackwell, 2007), 331–42.

Tarboroff, June, ' "Wife, unto thy garden": The First Gardening Books for Women', *Garden History*, 11/1 (Spring 1983), 1–5.

Tawney, Richard Henry, *The Agrarian Problem in the Sixteenth Century* (London: Harper and Row, 1967).

Taylor, Charles, *Sources of the Self: The Making of Modern Identity* (Cambridge: Cambridge University Press, 1989).

Taylor, Paul, *Respect for Nature: A Theory of Environmental Ethics* (Princeton: Princeton University Press, 1986).

Thirsk, Joan, 'The Common Fields', *Past and Present*, 29 (December 1964), 9.

Thirsk, Joan, 'Seventeenth-Century Agriculture and Social Change', *Agricultural History Review*, 18 (1970).

Thirsk, Joan, 'The Origin of the Common Fields', *Past and Present*, 33 (April 1966), 142–7.

Thirsk, Joan, *Economic Policy and Projects: The Development of a Consumer Society in Early Modern England* (Oxford: Clarendon Press, 1978).

Thirsk, Joan, 'Plough and Pen: Agricultural Writers in the Seventeenth Century', in T. H. Aston et al. (eds.), *Social Relations and Ideas: Essays in Honour of R. H. Hilton* (Cambridge: Cambridge University Press, 1983).

Thirsk, Joan, *The Rural Economy of England* (London: The Hambledon Press, 1984).

Thirsk, Joan, 'Making a Fresh Start', in Michael Leslie and Timothy Raylor (eds.), *Culture and Cultivation in Early Modern England: Writing and the Land* (Leicester: University of Leicester Press, 1992).

Thirsk, Joan, 'Nature versus Nurture', *History Workshop Journal*, 47 (Spring 1999), 273–7.

Thirsk, Joan, and J. P. Cooper (eds.), *Seventeenth Century Economic Documents* (Oxford: Clarendon Press, 1972).

Thomas, Keith, *Man and the Natural World* (London: Allen Lane, 1983).

Thomas, Keith, *The Ends of Life: Roads to Fulfilment in Early Modern England* (Oxford: Oxford University Press, 2009).

Tilley, Morris Palmer, *A Dictionary of the Proverbs in England in the Sixteenth and Seventeenth Centuries* (Ann Arbor: University of Michigan Press, 1950).

Tillyard, E. M., *The Elizabethan World Picture* (New York: Vintage, 1959).

Tudeau-Clayton, Margaret, *Jonson, Shakespeare and Early Modern Virgil* (Cambridge: Cambridge University Press, 1998).

Turner, Henry S. (ed.), *The Culture of Capital: Property, Cities and Knowledge in Early Modern England* (New York: Routledge, 2002).

Turner, James, *The Politics of Landscape* (Cambridge, Mass.: Harvard University Press, 1979).

Vendler, Helen, *The Art of Shakespeare's Sonnets* (Cambridge, Mass.: Harvard University Press, 1997).

Walker, Penelope, and Eva Crane, 'The History of Bee-Keeping in English Gardens', *Garden History*, 28/2 (Winter 2000), 231–61.

Wall, Wendy, 'Renaissance National Husbandry: Gervase Markham and the Publication of England', *Sixteenth Century Journal*, 27/3 (Autumn 1996).

Wall, Wendy, *Staging Domesticity* (Cambridge: Cambridge University Press, 2002).

Wall, Wendy, 'Unhusbanding Desires in Windsor', in Richard Dutton and Jean E. Howard (eds.), *A Companion to Shakespeare's Works: The Comedies* (Oxford: Blackwell, 2003, 2008).

Walsham, Alexandra, *The Reformation of the Landscape* (Oxford: Oxford University Press, 2011).

Warde, Paul, 'The Idea of Improvement, c.1520–1700', in Richard W. Hoyle (ed.), *Custom, Improvement and the Landscape in Early Modern Britain* (Farnham: Ashgate, 2011).

Warde, Paul, and Sverker Sörlin (eds.), *Nature's End: History and the Environment* (Basingstoke: Palgrave Macmillan, 2011).

Warde, Paul, *Energy Consumption in England and Wales, 1560–2000* (Rome: Instituto di Studio sulle Società del Mediterraneo, 2007).

Watson, Robert N., 'Horsemanship in Shakespeare's Second Tetralogy', *English Literary Renaissance*, 13/3 (Autumn 1983), 274–300.

Watson, Robert N., *Shakespeare and the Hazards of Ambition* (Philadelphia: University of Pennsylvania Press, 1985).

Watson, Robert N., *The Rest is Silence: Death as Annihilation in the English Renaissance* (Berkeley and Los Angeles: University of California Press, 1995).

Watson, Robert N., *Back to Nature: The Green and the Real in the Late Renaissance* (Philadelphia: University of Pennsylvania Press, 2006, 2008).

Wayne, Valerie, *The Flower of Friendship: A Renaissance Dialogue Contesting Marriage* (Ithaca, NY: Cornell University, 1992).

Weinstein, Philip, 'An Interpretation of the Pastoral in *The Winter's Tale*', *Shakespeare Quarterly*, 22/2 (Spring 1971).

Wells, Stanley, *Shakespeare for All Time* (London: Macmillan, 2002).

Wells, Stanley, and Paul Edmonson, *Shakespeare's Sonnets* (Oxford: Oxford University Press, 2004).

Whiting, Bartlett Jere, *Early American Proverbs and Proverbial Phrases* (Stanford, Calif.: Harvard University Press, 1977).

Whyte, Nicola, *Inhabiting the Landscape: Place, Custom and Memory, 1500–1700* (New York: Windgather Press, 2009).

Wilcox, Helen, 'Lanyer and the Poetry of Land and Devotion', in Patrick Cheney (ed.), *Early Modern English Poetry* (Oxford: Oxford University Press, 2007).

Williams, Raymond, *The Country and the City* (Oxford: Oxford University Press, 1973, 1975).

Wilson, Luke, *Theaters of Intention: Drama and the Law in Early Modern England* (Stanford, Calif.: Stanford University Press, 2000).

Wilson, Mary Floyd, and Garrett Sullivan (eds.), *Environment and Embodiment in Early Modern England* (Basingstoke: Palgrave Macmillan, 2007).

Wojciehowski, Hannah Chapelle, *Group Identity in the Renaissance World* (Cambridge: Cambridge University Press, 2011).

Womack, Peter, 'Imagining Communities: Theatres and the English Nation in the Sixteenth Century', in David Aers (ed.), *Culture and History, 1350–1600* (Detroit: Wayne State University Press, 1992).

Woodbridge, Linda (ed.), *Money and the Age of Shakespeare: Essays in New Economic Criticism* (New York: Palgrave Macmillan, 2003).

Wootton, David, *Galileo: Watcher of the Skies* (New Haven: Yale University Press, 2010).

Wright, George T., *Shakespeare's Metrical Art* (Berkeley and Los Angeles: University of California Press, 1988).

Wright, George T., 'Troubles of a Professional Meter Reader', in Russ McDonald (ed.), *Shakespeare Reread: The Texts in New Contexts* (Ithaca, NY: Cornell University Press, 1994).

Würzbach, Natascha, and Gaynor Wallis, *The Rise of the English Street Ballad 1550–1650* (Cambridge: Cambridge University Press, 1990).

Yachnin, Paul, 'Sheepishness in *The Winter's Tale*', in Laurie Maguire (ed.), *How to do Things with Shakespeare* (Oxford: Blackwell, 2008).

Index